YARDARM
and
COCKPIT

YARDARM
and
COCKPIT

David D. Allyn

© 2013 by David D. Allyn
All Rights Reserved.

No part of this book may be reproduced in any form or by any electronic or mechanical means including information storage and retrieval systems without permission in writing from the publisher, except by a reviewer who may quote brief passages in a review.

Sunstone books may be purchased for educational, business, or sales promotional use. For information please write: Special Markets Department, Sunstone Press, P.O. Box 2321, Santa Fe, New Mexico 87504-2321.

Book and Cover design › Vicki Ahl
Body typeface › ITC Benguiat Standard
Printed on acid-free paper
∞

Library of Congress Cataloging-in-Publication Data

Allyn, David D.
 Yardarm and cockpit / David D. Allyn.
    pages cm
 Includes bibliographical references and index.
 ISBN 978-0-86534-923-0 (softcover : alk. paper) -- ISBN 978-0-86534-924-7 (hardcover : alk. paper)
 1. Allyn, David D. 2. Adventure and adventurers--United States--Biography. 3. Airpilots--United States--Biography. 4. Sailors--United States--Biography. 5. Skydivers--United States--Biography. I. Title.
 CT9971.A55A3 2012
 629.13092--dc23
 [B]
                    2012041437

WWW.SUNSTONEPRESS.COM
SUNSTONE PRESS / POST OFFICE BOX 2321 / SANTA FE, NM 87504-2321 /USA
(505) 988-4418 / ORDERS ONLY (800) 243-5644 / FAX (505) 988-1025

To my grandchildren~
Victoria Allyn
Bailee Allyn
Charlee June Allyn
and those yet to be born
and
in memory of James Lee Frey
my son-in-law~
a sad loss to the preservation of US World War I and World War II history

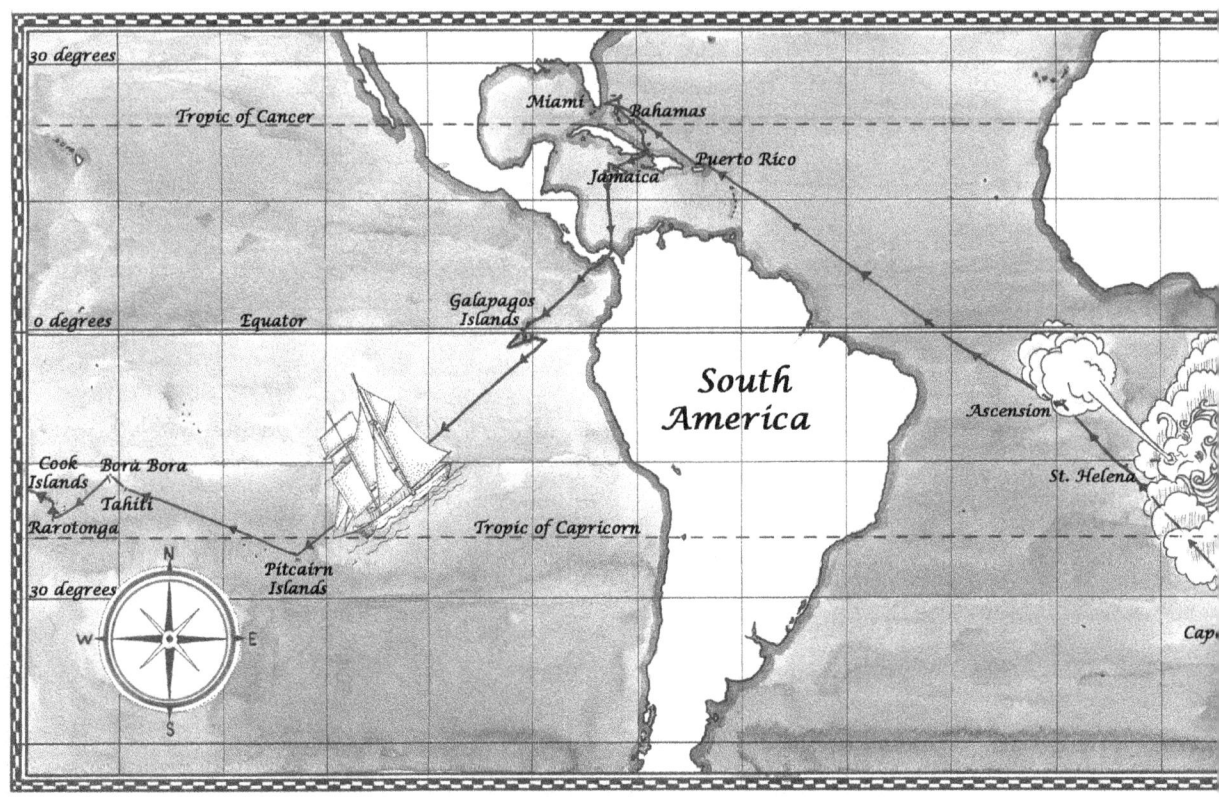

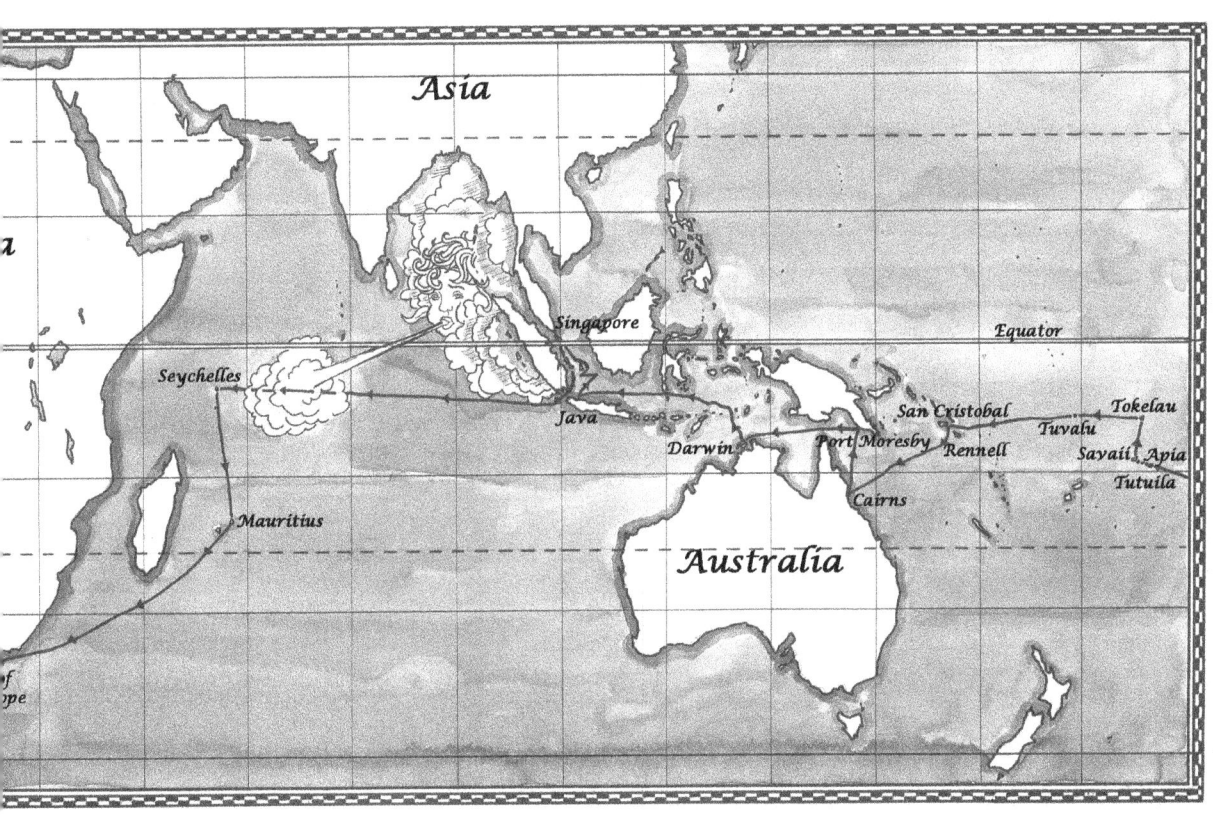

CONTENTS

YARDARM
The Last Complete Around-the-World Voyage of the Brigantine Yankee

1 The Great Adventure Begins ≈ 13
2 Good Times at Cap Haitien and Panama Canal Transit ≈ 25
3 Panama to Galapagos and Insanity at Sea ≈ 39
4 Shellback Ceremony and The Galapagos Adventure ≈ 44
5 A Grand Downwind Slide—19 Days, 2,500 Miles ≈ 55
6 Living With the Ancestors of *The Mutiny on the Bounty*, Pitcairn Island ≈ 60
7 O' Tahiti, Paradise Found ≈ 72
8 Samoa and the Polynesian Atolls of the South Pacific ≈ 98
9 "You Him Big Fella No Smart" and An Operation on the Dinner Table ≈ 116
10 Becalmed in the Coral Sea ≈ 132
Glossary of Sailing Terms ≈ 139
Glossary of Diving Terms ≈ 141

COCKPIT
Sixty-Five Years Flying Vintage Aircraft

Preface ≈ 145

1 The Beginning: The End of the Golden Age, 1946 to 1954 ≈ 147
2 High School Kid With a Brand New Set of Wings, 1955 to 1959 ≈ 159
3 Flight School in Ardmore, Oklahoma and The Little Yellow House, 1960 to 1963 ≈ 181
4 Four-Engine Flying Boat in Tahiti—A Trip Back in Time and North Atlantic in January with One Caged C-46, 1963 to 1964 ≈ 207
5 Chicago White Sox, DC-7B and Air Caicos DC-4M Northstar, 1964 to 1966 ≈ 237
6 Northstar, Central, South America and Dolphin Aviation, 1966 to 1972 ≈ 265
7 Ferrying Bipes, Bombers, and Fighters and Jumping Out of Perfectly Good Airplanes, 1968 to 1972 ≈ 290
8 Wings of Yesterday and Airshows, Barnstorming, 1973 to 1982 ≈ 332
9 Ferrying Old Airplanes and Our Good Friends, 1982 to present ≈ 371
10 ILS to LAX 25 Left ≈ 397

Appendix A: Aircraft I Have Flown ≈ 400
Appendix B: Characters and Friends ≈ 402
Glossary ≈ 405

YARDARM

**The Last Complete
Around-the-World Voyage
of the
Brigantine Yankee**

1

The Great Adventure Begins

Dear Grandchildren,

    I made my first dive in Bermuda in April 1954. I was thirteen and my father, your great-grandfather, was a kind and thoughtful gentleman with a big heart and an intense interest in helping other people and enjoying and supporting us kids in our learning years and our early interests. I expressed an interest in making a dive with this commercial dive company in Bermuda. We made arrangements and shoved off early one morning. The dive equipment consisted of a weighted helmet that fit over my shoulders, with my head in this square glass chamber, topped off with a lead top and a pressure hose going into the base of the helmet and an air release valve also at the base. When you breathed in, the water level inside the helmet would rise to your chin and when you breathed out, the level would decrease to about the middle of your neck. The rig was designed to go no deeper than thirty feet. It came my turn to dive and the divemaster asked if I was nervous. I told him I can't wait, let's go. That is the way I have always been: afraid of nothing. I have shown no fear at hundreds of shipwreck dives, sailing through bad storms, jumping out of airplanes, or flying 139 different types of aircraft—sometimes powerful and dangerous types of aircraft. But I digress.

    Slowly we descended the ladder until I was completely submerged. My first look around absolutely blew me away. I was surrounded by this beautiful blue haze of the ocean itself. The reefs were totally fascinating, as were the thousands of busy fish of all sizes who were constantly on the move.

    I was on a planet unimaginable to the topside dweller. My heart beat with a joy I had never felt before, as it still does today every time I dive. Even after the many thousand dives I have done, the feeling remains the same. All too quickly our dive was over and we surfaced and climbed the ladder and I was a changed boy. I knew then that I acquired on that dive a deep interest in that marvelous underwater world that would last me the rest of my life. And it has. What a wonderful thing for me as a young boy to have a father who was receptive to my young desires and dreams and helped me achieve them. I didn't know that at the time, but I do now. Thanks, Dad, you were the greatest.

    I checked out on SCUBA the next year in Hawaii. My instructor went by the name of "Panama" and was a short Hawaiian guy who I believe to this day really liked me and took me under his wing. The first dive was forty-five feet, with no BC (buoyancy compensator), no pressure gauge, and no depth gauge. Just fins, tanks, weights, and muscle. How little we knew in those days.

    I continued diving in Jamaica and slowly built experience through high school. I soloed an airplane on Dec. 21, 1956, my sixteenth birthday. Again, encouragement from Dad. My life of adventure had begun.

After school I worked as a roustabout in the oil fields of Great Bend, Kansas, and three months later went to Bakersfield, California, where I met my heavy-drinking, lifelong friend Leo Devit. We were a natural to be friends. He was as intensely passionate about diving as I was. We also both had an interest in sailing a small boat around the world. This last interest became an addiction so strong that we spent every spare moment going from harbor to harbor, just looking for the right boat. We had no money, but who the hell cared about that. Leo and I went to U.S. Divers where we each bought a double tank rig, fins, mask, weights and belt, a 3-stage regulator, and a ½-inch wet suit—all for the humongous sum of $125.00 each. I also bought a book written in French—that for twelve dollars could be translated to English—on how to dive safely. Wow, was it nice in those days. We proceeded to teach ourselves how to dive at Morrow Bay, California. Visibility was five to six feet on a clear day. With the water temperature up and down the California coast and the Pacific Coast of Mexico ranging from 50°F to a balmy high of 61°F, we certainly appreciated the wetsuits. We both cut our teeth, so to say, on those coastlines and became more experienced and better, safer divers with each dive. How we survived the novice period, God only knows. Some divers in those days did not. During our forays to the different dive sites, we were constantly looking for heavy-duty sailing vessels to continue our dreams of sailing and diving around the world.

"Hey, Leo! This is it!" says I. Leo agreed. We had found a beautiful thirty-foot Friendship sloop and were convinced this was the vessel we would sail around the world. For weeks we talked, slept, and dreamed about our adventure and that boat.

Dad got wind of it and, being much smarter than the both of us, flew out to Bakersfield to diplomatically inform us that we were both suicidal. I was crushed. But Dad always had a better way (Man, why was he always right? Damn.) Well, he had been doing some research because I think he really wanted us to be successful at something very few people had ever done. Thanks, Dad.

Mom on *Yankee*

Dad on *Yankee*

To make a long story short, Dad had found a 110-foot school ship called *The Albatross*, which was currently transiting the Panama Canal and heading for Lunenberg, Nova Scotia. Leo and I flew to Darian, Connecticut, where we interviewed and were accepted as crewmembers for a one-year cruise by square rig sailing ship around the South Pacific. We were both totally psyched and excited beyond reason.

So back to California to pack, then we were on our way to Miami, where we would sail her to Lunenberg for refit, and then off to the islands of the South Pacific. Wow! Passing through Joplin, Missouri, we got the news that the training sailing ship *Albatross* had been knocked down in the Gulf of Mexico by a white squall and had sunk, taking thirteen hands with her. Crash—devastation beyond imagination. Dad to the rescue again: "Boys, turn south and head for Miami and MacArthur Causeway because you are both signed onto the 110-foot square rigged sailing ship *Yankee*, bound around the world." Dad, you are the greatest.

At Biscayne Bay, Leo and I stood alongside this magnificent white, round-sterned, clipper-bowed sailing ship—two masts sticking up what appeared all the way to the moon, three square yards and miles of rigging lines and stays, lines all a symmetrically perfect mass of confusion that Leo and I would learn to understand intimately—every function and reason for every single stay, halyard, buntline, sheet, vang line, course sheets, and brace lines. How to sail her in every kind of weather and point of wind, and we got damn good at it. Standing there I marveled at the symmetry of her wooden decks, the beauty of her deckhouses and portholes. Damn, she is a real ship of the sea. We were both in heaven and were really going to begin an adventure of a lifetime. There was a dive compressor on board and because Leo and I were experienced divers, we were put in charge of diving operations, which in short meant that we were going to dive in every port, every rock, every island we went to. It don't get any better.

The actual voyage was to start two months hence, so Leo and I shipped out on *Yankee* as ordinary seamen. In that two months, we both worked our watches and got to know every nook and cranny of *Yankee* and got good at helm work and sail changing so that when the around the world crew came on board, Skipper had two experienced seamen to help train the new greenhorns.

Harvey talking to Mom

On our way

Coming to Bimini

On July 14, 1961, we were anchored off of Bimini awaiting the arrival of fifteen around the world crewmembers. When work was through, aboard ship Leo and I donned our scuba tanks, weights, and fins and went over the side for a 45-foot dive. We were anchored on a sand bottom. Being in the bosom of the sea and in her warm and blue womb was—and still is—a wonderful feeling for me. We were towards the end of our dive when four porpoises showed up and began to play with us, even allowing us to stroke their bodies with our hands. What a wonderful contact between sea dwellers and land dwellers. I remember to this day that enlightening experience as though I were with them again every time I think about it.

The next day we made two more dives but saw no porpoises. That afternoon we motored the ship's launch to shore to meet and party with our new shipmates, and party we did. Lots of cold beer and food under the stars and waving fronds of the palm trees on the tropical island of Bimini, a small, low, sandy atoll covered with coconut palms and surrounded by the blue Atlantic ocean. The main town is situated on the southwest side of the island.

We had twenty-two new crewmembers show up. In the group were five women— Big Gloria was to eventually marry the skipper; Little Gloria was lots of fun and funny, but no sailor and ended up leaving *Yankee* in Australia; Eileen Dickey, also no sailor but invaluable in the galley, was the only crewmember to make it all the way around the world. There were two other female members, but they didn't last long enough for me to get to know them.

Leo, Doc, Gypsy, Mirve the Rigger, Iggy, Jim2, Guy Gunsberg, CB "Bulldog" Pace, Harvey Segal, Art the Cook, Dave the Helper, and John the Engineer were all my friends and great sailors.

Sam is a fictitious name for one of the guys who led a group of misfits on board who basically did not belong. Most of them had an arrogant attitude toward the group I hung out with, and they did not last long on the journey.

There was also a 78-year-old man, Mr. Chaulker, who joined us. ol' Chaulker lived in his own world but we all respected the guy for having the guts to make his last adventure a reality.

Then there was Jim1, a mentally ill young man whose parents pawned him off on us. His name will come up again later in the book.

On July 16th, with all crewmembers assembled on the stern deck for pre-briefing, we prepared to hoist anchor and set sail, bound around the world and the beginning of an adventure of a lifetime.

On every ship's crew there are different groups of people who enjoy each other's company better than others. It was no different on *Yankee*. Unfortunately, Sam's group were not only arrogant but seemed to think of themselves as better than the rest of us. It actually became a game with us and produced a few moments in time that were hilariously funny. As it turned out, most of Sam's group were real slackers when it came to real sailing and, with the exception of three, all left the ship by the time we got to Panama, and one in Tahiti. One of them became a good friend and a great sailor later in the trip. I will refer to them only as Sam's group just for reasons of diplomacy.

Yankee crew

My bunk

July 17. Let's set the record straight. Yes, we upped anchor by hand and set sail, but to hear Sam's version you would think it was all done by his group alone. This did not sit well with the crew. Leo and I were the most experienced besides Skipper and Mate John. Sam seemed to have forgotten the instructions he received from us both on the handling of the sails. He was very right about the lack of enthusiasm and seasickness in some of the crew. This was to plague us until we reached Panama and those who were having problems left the ship. They were all very nice people but were admittedly a menace to the rest of the competent crew and did not belong on a sailing ship. I hope they all fared well in their lives. One exception was "Doc" Dick Cardines. He suffered from terrible seasickness but stuck it out. Then one day, three months later in the South Pacific, Doc happily exclaimed, "Whoopie! My seasickness is gone!" and it never came back. I gained tremendous respect for Doc and we became good friends.

July 18. I had just been relieved from the 4 to 8 (a.m.) watch and could see that we were in for a squally day. After breakfast, Sam was bragging that he had personally ungimballed the meal table for the first time. Gimballed means that the table is locked to the deck and does not move. Ungimballed means the table will stay stationary by gravity while the ship rolls around it so the dishes won't fall from the table. My point is the table is and was ungimballed at every meal. Sam must not have noticed. Oh well. Anyway, I came on deck just in time to help shorten sail as there was a black-looking squall coming right at the port beam. After shortening sail, I ran below and grabbed a bar of soap just as the squall hit. Alright. Fresh water galore, we all thought. I lathered myself up along with Leo, Harvey, and some others. We no sooner got all lathered than the squall passed and there we stood in the sunshine with unmentionable language flowing from everybody's mouths. We had to rinse off with salt water. Thanks, Mother Nature. Later that day we tacked across the stern of the 150-foot *Polynesia*, a beautiful staysail schooner. Just imagine in 1961 a gorgeous brigantine with her majestic sails sailing in close company with another sailing ship. The grey skies, deep blue ocean, and two bright white sailing ships on the very seas that were called the Spanish Main, noted for the 17th century pirates. We were close to our next port: Nassau.

Polynesia

Yankee

July 18. A lazy day. We motored most of the day at 1,500 rpm, our two 6-71 diesels would only move *Yankee* through the ocean at 3 knots. I hated those engines. When *Yankee* was only under sail, she would creak, groan, and squeal like a sailing ship should do and I would go to sleep at night listening to our sailing ship's music. Skipper had us cleaning most of the day. He was a hell of a sailor and could be a tyrant at times, but mostly we didn't mind. Little did we know that this would play a big role in causing insurmountable problems that culminated in breaking up our voyage twelve months later in the Coral Sea, bound for Australia.

When the trip started, or I should say before the trip started, Skipper assigned me to clean the bilge—that portion of a ship where both hulls come together and form the bilge, a nasty place where everything drips down from above, including some very unappetizing materials and all mix with the seawater, oil, and other things that collect in the bilge of all ships. It is a dark, dank, foreboding place that smells bad and is as close to hell as you can imagine. The pumps that pump excess water that seeps into all ships are located, all four of them, in line down the center of the bilge. All have screens and all have to be cleaned after pumping the bilges dry. This is where you find the rotted carcasses of the vermin and whatever else is trapped on the screens. After I cleaned each pump and had the bilges dried out, I proceeded to scrub each section of the bilges and it took me nearly a week to do this displeasing job. I would come up on deck after a day in the bilges and look like an African native, totally black from head to toe. Skipper began calling me 'Bilge' and the name stuck. Guy complimented me on my job. Thanks, Guy, for your kind words. It was a valiant effort and a tough job.

July 19. We arrived at our homeport, Nassau, around noon. Leo and I found a good restaurant and feasted on salad and ice cold milk, satisfying a craving developed by days at sea with neither of these available. Guy, Harvey, and Keith were setting up a party for us all and Leo and I enjoyed the day hiking around town, culminating in a cold beer-drinking bout at the Purple Onion.

July 20. The next day, Leo and I had a great time renting a couple of scooters and cruising around the island. That night we had our party: good food, good limboing, and a chance to see our fellow crewmates. I still didn't know who the "deadheads" were in Sam's group. I intended to make friends with our new shipmates and we had a great evening.

Deck scene

Going aloft

July 22. Left Nassau harbor under full sail. All sails set with a following wind, *Yankee* plowing a white wake through the inner harbor and out to sea. All along the harbor front were throngs of people waving and cheering. What a magnificent sight we must have been. I felt very proud to be a part of this adventure—an adventure that would change my life forever and give me wonderful memories that have lasted to this day. Once out of harbor, we doused the squares and bent her up into the wind to clear the windward channel and bear off several hours later for the island of San Salvador. At midnight we tacked south off the island of Abaco. We had 150 miles to go. When *Yankee* was hard on the wind, she was very slow but a steady ship. It would take us three days to go 150 miles.

July 23. We tacked all day down the coast of the low island of Eluthera, all day spent tacking back and forth, with our progress being very slow. I wondered who the slobs were Sam was bitching about. Probably Leo and me and some others who were having too much fun on Nassau and didn't conduct ourselves the way Sam thought we should. No wonder we felt uneasy around Sam's group. We had one member of that group that was on a real power trip. He thought he was in charge of the deck and did things that were a definite menace and disregarded the unity of the rest of the crew. He would throw belayed ropes off and with no concern for the Captain's orders say we needed to tack ship, as if he knew better than Skipper. It was apparent that we needed to watch him like a hawk. It seemed to all of us that he was unbalanced, to say the least. We were very relieved when he left us in Panama.

One day while en route to San Salvador, we had a nice beam reach. About 3.5 on the scale and *Yankee* showed her heels at 7 knots and riding the rather large swells with ease, lifting gently and just as gently rolling to starboard. It was an exhilarating and glorious ride and was one point I love about sailing.

July 24. According to our wayward friend, he was responsible for everything good that happened and he was personally responsible for all work done on board. I guess the crew just sat around doing nothing. Turns out Guy Gunzberg is about the best sailor on board, a very good and reliable hand. Working with tarred marlin and as hot as it was Guy certainly lived up to the sailors' name "A Real Tar." He was repairing just about everything that needed marlin wrapping. Soon the whole ship had this wonderful smell of marlin tar. I was on the privileged 4 to 8 watch where we got the sunrise and sunset, the two best times of day as far as I am concerned. Since work didn't start until after breakfast, we never got the heavy work and all day off unless there was sail handling to do. Then it was "all hands on deck" anytime, day or night. But I would rather handle sails any day than chipping, tarring, and serving ratlines and shrouds. Then we would go on watch at 4 p.m. after work hours. I would always work my wheel trick (sailor's terminology for steering) to coincide with first dinner call. For one hour I was the only person on deck. Just me and that big square rigged sailing ship. It was the best hour of the day. If you ever go to sea, take the 4 to 8. It is the best watch of all. 8 p.m. you are off until 4 a.m.

July 25. Guy and his crew basically finished the servings and did a hell of a job. I didn't envy him as it was hot, backbreaking work. He did a grand job of it. We dropped the hook off of Cockburn Town on San Salvador and went ashore about sundown. Most Bahamian islands are low, sandy and unexciting. San Salvador was no exception. The houses were spread along each side of Main Street and all were lighted with kerosene lanterns. Very quaint, giving us the feeling that we had stepped back in time 100 years. The people were very polite and kind and a pleasure to talk to. All of this and under a canopy of palm trees, we were really living our adventure. We passed a couple of grubby-looking bars and were about to go into one of them when some American Navy and Air Force guys showed up and invited us to their PX for some beers in air-conditioned comfort. Back to the 20th century. They showed us a really good time. Go Navy. Go Air Force. They told us to look up two Americans in an air-conditioned bar just outside of town. We stopped in and were introduced to an outstanding married couple from the U.S.A. who made us feel welcomed and at home. We made their establishment our base of operations.

July 26. Leo and I made an early morning dive and encountered many barracuda—a fierce-looking fish who has a reputation he doesn't really deserve, being generally benign. They stayed with us throughout the dive. I thought they were magnificent fish and added a sense of excitement to the dive.

July 27. Set sail for Cap Haitien, Haiti, 400 miles south. *Yankee* was pitching and rolling most of the night, making it difficult to move around. Doc was really seasick.

July 28. Very rough. So far a normal day at sea. On watch again at 4 p.m.

July 29. Looking forward to making landfall this morning. The tyrant in Skipper showed up in force just before our watch ended. One of the ladies who really should not have been aboard a sailing ship had slept on deck that night and hung her sleeping bag up in the rigging to air out. The rigging on a sailing ship is used for sailing a ship and anything in the rigging that is not supposed to be there can and will endanger the ship in an emergency. We told her not to do that, at which she threw her head back and went below. The skipper came on deck and when he saw her sleeping bag, he exploded. Shouting swear words, he took her sleeping bag and her clothes, which were also hanging there, and threw them over the side. There ensued a terrible row between her and Skipper. We tried not to smile, remembering that we had told her not to hang her things in the rigging. She left the ship soon after. Bye bye. Soon after that, we were buzzed by a four-engine Neptune as we spotted the high peaks of Haiti. Just before dark we entered the harbor at Cap Haitien. As we entered, we were all looking at the bow of a big freighter sticking straight up out of the water. Hope that does not happen to us.

Clowning aloft

Helm and binnacle

2

Good Times at Cap Haitien and Panama Canal Transit

Wham, bang. We had arrived at the dock in Cap Haitien on the island of Haiti. As I remember it, Skipper was at the helm and misjudged. Wow, you should have heard the cursing going on, oh my aching ears. Anyway, I don't remember the pilot doing the docking as Sam said but I sure could be wrong.

Yankee in Haiti

Police and Tonton Macoute

Haiti is on one side of the line drawn directly down the middle of the island and on the other side is the Dominican Republic. At the time of our visit, the controlling dictator of Haiti was "Papa Doc" Duvalier, a murderer who enforced his will with a paid army of special police called the "Tonton Macoute," an evil force that could come into your home at will, take what they want, kill you or drag you off to a dungeon somewhere and do what they want with you. Consequently, the people of Haiti lived in fear and were generally an unhappy population. There have been no less than 140 attempts to assassinate this lucky devil, none of which succeeded. Old Papa Doc succumbed to natural causes and the power was inherited by his son "Baby Doc," a blithering idiot who was run off the island. As of this writing, Baby Doc is back in Haiti, the reasons for which are the subject of much speculation.

In my later life I was to be very involved in the control of this evil Papa Doc, even though I was only a pilot at the time. As I said before, the other side of the island was the island nation of the Dominican Republic. Its dictator was another evil devil by the name of Juan Trujillo, who ruled by terror just as Papa Doc did on the other side of the island. On his way home (home being a palace) he was machine-gunned to death by his own army in an ambush along the side of a road. Free elections were set up based on the same freedoms we have here. When I became involved, the president's name was El Presidente Baligar. He was a good man who set aside three hours every morning to talk with the average person on the street, in his office, and in person. To maintain a stronger balance of power for the Dominicans, the U.S. contracted Cavalier Aircraft to build up a force of P-51D fighters and for Air Caicos (who I flew for at the time) to fly all the support parts to the capitol city of San Juan. Papa Doc had inferior T-6 aircraft in his force. So as a pilot, I played a small part in subduing this evil monster, Papa Doc.

Back to our time in Haiti. The island is very mountainous, with lush jungles in the highlands and cool rushing rivers in abundance. You don't have to go far out of town these days to find the once lush and beautiful tropical paradise that Cap Haitien used to be. As soon as we cleared customs, where they confiscated all of our guns, Leo, Keith, Henry (Mirv the rigger), and I left the ship and checked into the Tres Jolie Hotel, a first-class resort hotel set atop a hill just outside of town. The beautiful rooms and access to a big swimming pool cost $6.50 a day and it truly was luxurious. The actual harbor at Cap Haitien was filthy so we made no dives while we were there. We walked around Cap Haitien, a total slum but at the same time very interesting. We ate at local places—that was sometimes an adventure—and went to the cockfights. They aren't so cool. At night throughout the hillsides you could see many fires and if you stayed still and listened you could hear drumbeats and people chanting. Nobody would admit that they were voodoo—an ancient secret and sacred African religion, also known as vodun or vodou—ceremonies but we knew better. We were warned not to try to go to one of them because the people involved could possibly kill you. The people generally treated us very well with big smiles and a ready hand out—not to shake, but in hope of a few pennies.

Art the cook

Cock Fight

Leo

John the mate

Horses

**Mirve the rigger,
on our way to the Citadel**

San Cristobal Castle

Cannon on the trail

July 31. We got up early and drove to the town of Milot, where we got on some abused-looking horses to make the two-hour trip up to the Citadel—a huge fortress built by the dictator Henri Christophe, appointed by Napoleon to be the lord and ruler of Haiti in the early 1800s. All along the trail were cannons with the Napoleonic crest on the barrels. We were told they had been dropped by the slaves when they learned that as soon as Christophe heard of Napoleon's defeat, he committed suicide. All the slaves at that point rebelled and took over Haiti. At any rate, what remains is this huge fortress, high in the mountains, called the Citadel. We spent a couple of hours hiking through the miles of cool corridors and rooms that were once decorated. No longer. There must have been 10,000 cannon balls in neat pyramids everywhere. I took one and it resides in my living room to this day. There was a problem with the authorities about the return of our guns. We got them back the next day and we set sail the day after that.

August 2. As we were sailing out of the harbor, Keith and I were discussing some deep philosophical point of bullshit when the *Yankee* dipped her bow into a wave and about a bucketful of water hit Keith smack dab in the middle of his face. Maybe he pissed off King Neptune with what he was saying. We both had a hardy laugh—an omen for a great downwind run for Jamaica. A few hundred miles and the last port of call before Panama and the great Pacific Ocean.

As we turned westbound, we fell right into the trade winds and set all sails, including lower fore course, lower topsail, and upper topsail, plowing through the waters of the Caribbean Sea, great white foaming patches on either side laying in contrast on top of the deep blue sea and gently dissipating past our stern as we plowed our way to Jamaica at 8 knots, sometimes reaching hull speed of 10 knots. Standing at the helm and looking up gave me a very powerful feeling of pride, seeing her graceful, square rig pulling for all they were worth. The creaking and groaning of her rig was a symphony to my now sailor's ears, assuring me that I truly was the helmsman in charge of a ship of the line bound around the world as eight bells ended my watch. "8 to 12 on deck, Harvey on the helm, course 272° steady, I have the helm," shouted Harvey. I handed over the helm, repeating, "272° steady as she goes." Harvey replied, "272° steady, I have the helm." I shouted then, "Come right, come right, shee-it!" as the huge gaff head main started an uncontrolled jibe—*bang!* The anti-jibe vang parted with an explosion as the main swung wildly across the deck and exploded against the port limits. I looked up and saw the main topmast shaking to the limits. If she came down, it would be a nightmare, all 900 pounds of it crashing to the deck from a 100-foot fall. This is how you get killed on a sailing ship The whole ship's rig was lurching from the uncontrolled jibe of our 2,000 pound mainsail. Fortunately, nothing parted and we had minimum damage. Poor Harv, all he could say was, "Oh my God" as I grabbed the helm from him and steadied up on 250° to prevent a second jib. Now ol' Harvey was no sailor. He was a schoolteacher and a damned good one. He was as nice a guy as you would like to meet and I liked him a lot. I give him tons of credit for sticking to it and trying his best, but Harv was no sailor. About then came a stream of cusswords as Captain Kimberly raced up to the helm. He was a really good seaman and very experienced at that. Skipper assessed the damage and ordered us to "repair and make up another anti-jibe vang and prepare to jibe ship to come back to 272°." This time we heaved in the main sheet, taking six good strong sailors, including me, to bring the mainsail pretty much to the center of the ship. "Stand by to jibe ship. All hands ready," called out John the mate. Skipper eased the ship right and as the wind swung across the stern, the main this time gently swung to fill the sails left side at which point we eased the sheet line until the main was filled and pulling hard. We hooked up our anti-jibe vang and *Yankee* settled on 272° and was back on her downwind run. A beautiful maneuver when done right.

Leo on wheel trick

Bilge

In the early morning on August 5, after a dreamlike slide downwind, we brought up Montego Bay right on schedule and dropped anchor at Doctors Cave, Jamaica. All hands went aloft and harbor furled the square sails. It takes a crew of sailors to handle the sails on a ship like *Yankee*. When I was in high school, our family spent spring break every year in Montego Bay and I not only know well that part of Jamaica, but also increased my scuba and snorkeling skills on the awesome reefs around Montego Bay.

The English-speaking natives were all blacks as in Haiti but, unlike the Haitians, were friendly, happy people who made great companions very easily. God bless the British. Leo and I prepared to spend most of our time diving in the crystal clear waters of Jamaica, which we did. We were enthusiastically joined by Doc, the ship's doctor and humanitarian who used his skills at his own expense on many islands in the South Pacific, some so remote that they had not seen a ship in several years until we showed up. Jamaica is a mountainous island like Haiti and the Dominican Republic, with an abundance of mountain streams rushing to meet the Caribbean Sea on some lush tropical beach. One river worth mentioning is *Ocha Rios* at Port Antonio, a clear blue river that flows through the lush jungle, with deep blue swimming holes and rushing clear water. Genuinely an Eden in paradise.

Though early in the journey, there was already some tension developing on board between crewmembers. On many occasions we ran into Sam's group after they had been touring all day, some of whom referred to us as barflies, and not in a flattering way, as we made many dives during the day and, being young and full of energy, hit the bars at night.

On one dive we came upon a huge sea turtle who seemed to enjoy our company and stayed with us throughout the dive, his huge, friendly-looking turtle head looked like it would be something worth a little scratching but as soon as my fingers touched it, he immediately turned away and with incredible speed disappeared into the contact zone 150 feet away and faded in the blue depths of the sea. Good luck, old friend of the sea. We really had no intention of hurting you.

I love all of the contacts and experiences I have had so many times with the friendly creatures of the sea. On another dive, at 100 feet we ran into a giant sea bass (jewfish) and I do mean giant. I will bet he weighed at least 400 pounds. Leo stuck his hand out in front of his huge mouth. In the flash of a half-second, with a loud sucking sound, Leo's arm was buried up to his elbow in the huge mouth. Just as quickly the big bass spit Leo's arm out. I was looking at Leo when his arm got sucked in and for a second his eyes were all you could see. They were about as big as the fish. When we got to the surface, I looked at Leo and said, "Are you okay, Jonah?" We spent the rest of the day retelling the story and laughed and laughed until our sides hurt.

August 8. We set sail for Panama. Our spirits were still high as we beat around the west side of Jamaica into a nasty chop, making deck watch a wet affair. *Yankee* would climb the face of a wave, then slam down and into the next, which would bring her to a dead stop, spewing spindrift over her windward side and across her decks as the wind changed direction so we could maintain a southerly heading and be on a wonderful beam reach. Although not as comfortable as running downwind we nevertheless were bowling along at a great sea-plowing 8 knots straight towards Panama.

Eight bells, my evening watch was over. I went to my bunk and fell immediately asleep. "All hands on deck." Cripes, it is almost midnight. Bounding out of my bunk, I raced on deck and immediately heard continuous cannon shots coming from forward and aloft. I looked up and could barely make out the source of the explosions. The upper topsail had torn away from the yard and in the high winds it sounded like an automatic cannon. "Bilge, Jim, Mirv, lay aloft and secure the upper topsail," shouted the captain. With no hesitation we jumped up on the forward pinrail and began our climb up the rat lines to the lower topsail yard seventy-five feet above the rolling decks of our ship. As the upper topsail yard with its flailing sail was lowered to us, we three clung to and climbed the last few steel rungs and were able to hang our bellies over the yardarm and plant our feet firmly on the lubber line hanging across the bottom of the yard. In this manner we could hang onto the ship with one hand and with the other start heaving in this monster of a sail gone wild. Thirty minutes later we had her tied down and returned via the ratlines to *Yankee*'s heaving deck. There were no well dones or pats on the back. It was an expected duty performed on every sailing ship at all times and is an eternal duty performed by every sailor at any time for the safety of the ship. Even after tending to an emergency situation like that, the tension between us and other crewmembers was still present, with them subjecting us to some disparaging remarks.

Harvey signaling U.S. destroyer

Skipper

Binnacle

Square sails

August 12. We sighted Panama's east coast. It was obvious that we were coming into a large port. The ocean was changing from deep blue to green and then to an ugly brown. The shipping traffic was one after another, with ships of all shapes and sizes heading for all the ports the world has to offer. Adventurous, these seas on the planet Earth. After some time and in gloomy rain and dark of night we anchored offshore and looked at the universe of 100,000 lights in Colon, Panama, known as the crossroads and meeting place of thugs, thieves, pirates, and just plain riff-raff of the world. My heart was beating with excitement. We would go ashore tomorrow morning.

August 13. We ate breakfast and promptly left for shore. We had to go very slowly so it would look like we were paddling the launch due to some stupid Panamanian law about using our engine. We were all laughing when we finally tied to the dock. My first glance around confirmed my feelings about Colón. A very busy place, elbow to elbow people and lots of very unsavory-looking people. Crumbling down buildings and streets mostly filled with people. Outside food and fruit stands, one right after another. Everything looking dirty. On every corner was a dingy-looking building with people continually going in and out. I was told by a grinning local that it was an exhibition hall. "You can go eento and see for yourself for yust $6.00 Americano, Señor."

"Hey, Leo, let's check it out," says I. "Okay," says Leo.

Well, the exhibition was not pre-Columbian art but men and women doing very perverted things with each other. Colón is not only the crossroads of tramps, but it is depraved also. Just think, there was one of these dilapidated dumps on every street corner. Come on, Colón, where has your self-respect gone?

About this time Leo and I spotted a huge Naval transport ship called the *USNSS Baltimore*. She was huge, about 650 feet long. After our surprise at what the locals consider an exhibition, we decided to change pace and go have a look at her. She had a huge plumb bow, portholes on four decks, all in a perfectly straight line. Aft of the bow was the super structure topped by two tall stacks in tandem, a well deck, and ending up with poop castle and round stern laced with portholes. As luck would have it, the captain was standing right where we were and invited us to tour his ship. By this time, Mirv the rigger and Jim 2 had joined up with us.

The ship was very military, no niceties anywhere. Exposed pipes everywhere, all warnings painted in red block letters on grey metal walls and bulkheads. Her engine room was, to say the least, massive: 400 feet long and four stories high, filled with gangways going up, down, lengthwise, around and over massive boilers, engines, turbines, propeller shafts, and leading in and out of enticing exits and entrances to whatever. All of this below the water line. We then climbed nine decks to the bridge deck where her captain spent his time orchestrating this massive ship with her tons and tons of machinery. I was very impressed to think about what experience this man must have to know this ship so intimately as to be able to command such a vessel at 20 knots through the sea and be totally confident in his duties. Really impressive. *Baltimore* made *Yankee* seem like a toy in comparison. Although *Yankee* was no toy and our captain knew his business also.

We then had a lunch of garlic steak, chiles, and tortillas. Very good. I must say the only thing left was to spend the rest of the day bar-hopping and being good sailors. That's what we did and did and did until past midnight. We then made our way back to the dock way too late to catch the launch back to *Yankee* so the four of us laid down on this filthy dock amongst cockroaches and God only knows what else and actually went to sleep.

At about 3 a.m. I awoke to see this human figure standing in front of me. I sat up and was prepared to fight for my life when the person said, "Hola, amigo, eez the *Yankee* you sheep?" "Yeah," says I. "For a couple of yankee dollarios I take you to sheep, okay?" "Hey, come on guys, wake up, we got a ride out to *Yankee*." To this day I don't know how the five of us got into this tiny little rowboat but we did, and how we didn't wind up capsized in that filthy harbor remains a mystery. Captain José did a fine job and got us to our ship safely.

We were able to collapse in our bunks for a short sleep before chow bell at 6:30 a.m. and a long, hot transit through the Panama Canal that none of us four were very enthusiastic to do. But all that changed once we started.

I remember our transit clearly. It was unbearably hot and really interesting as we entered the huge lock chambers, always with a very large ship transiting either east or west. The water boiled and churned as we went up and was just the opposite on the other side—as we went down, the water in those locks was perfectly smooth. We transited the canal and came to Gaton Lake, a unique lake with huge chunks of jungle that had broken away from the shore and were floating around the lake, each one having its own ecological system with palm trees, flowers, and parrots squawking along with other animals trapped on their floating islands. We then dropped down the other side to Balboa and Panama City. On the way to Pier 18, an ocean-going freighter passed us and on her poop deck there was a Coke machine. Wow, could I go for one of those. The lucky crew on that ship could have an ice cold Coke any time they wanted. Anyway, we tied up at Pier 18 and guess who draws the first port watch? Me. Damn Skipper. This is a guarded dock. What the hell do we need port watch for? Anyway, Skipper demanded a port watch and he is the skipper. Aye, aye, sir.

I watched the rest of the crew depart, envying them their good fortune and spent a very boring evening aboard ship, all night and no sleep. Boy, was I happy to see the sun come up. Of course, the rest of the crew came back aboard about 4 a.m., all of them below and passed out until noon the next day. I even got a few hours of rest before we all left for shore again. Wow, what you can do when you are young.

Gatun Locks

Norwegian freighter

Gailard Cut

Harvey

Floating island

Art the cook

Jim1 sneaking a beer

Chart house

Forward hatch

3

Panama to Galapagos and Insanity at Sea

We spent four days in Panama, a big city but, unlike Colón, a pretty nice city and much cleaner. People were dressed well with lots of smiles and seemed to be very friendly. Panama seemed to be better off than most Central and South American cities. There were large areas of slums as there are in all big cities, especially in this part of the world. Two stories about Panama.

We were at the "New Orleans Bar" on Plaza Cinco de Mayo. They had a tattoo parlor and the old man who was doing the tattooing looked just like Charlie Weaver, an old American comedian that our generation in the 1950s just loved. I told my companions I was going to let that guy put an anchor on my left arm and he did. It turned out to have one fluke different than the other because I think he was as loaded as his clientele, but I love my anchor and I feel it confirms the sailor in me.

Mirve was with us and really tying one on. He said he was going to put a sailing ship on his chest and we dared him to put "Yankee" below the ship and he did. Now you got to remember that Mirve the rigger (Henry Coumbe) was from a wealthy family in England. I will bet his family saw this English boy when he got home and absolutely had a fit when they saw their son with a ship and the word "Yankee" on his English chest. I think my own parents were quite upset when my picture showed up in our hometown newspaper in an article about my adventure and there in the picture was my arm with an anchor firmly attached.

The other story is about a place called the "Casa Villa Mour" (the House of Love). Well, it was just exactly what the name implied—a huge mansion with 500 girls employed. Being young sailors, Leo and I were bound by maritime code to at least visit any place with a name like that. And it was a huge old mansion out in the country. We came into a nice bar and signed our names and addresses in the guest book. This place was first class. We settled in for the evening, just to look around, mind you. Well, the evening lasted a long time and Leo and I returned to *Yankee* at 5:00 the next morning. Fast forward to Christmas 1962 and my mother gets a Christmas card from—you guessed it. For years a card was sent every Christmas and my mother would always talk about how her son always made such good friends on his voyage. I never told her the significance of that place. Maybe she knew and was covering for me. It would be just like her. Anyway, please forgive me, Mom.

Sunrise

August 19. We set sail for the Galapagos Islands. I was particularly happy because my best friend Leo was made third mate on the 8 to 12 watch, me being still on the 4 to 8 watch. Guy was made second mate and he made a good one. In spite of his comments about the 4 to 8 luck in the Caribbean, we now were the best sailors on the ship (in his opinion). He might have been right. At any rate, we were now sailing my favorite ocean in the world: the great Pacific Ocean. I was psyched. Sailing into the Pacific we were faced with headwinds and had to tack into the wind for a short time. The wind shifted and for a day we actually sailed right straight for the Galapagos, about 700 miles away. As we neared the equator we entered the "Doldrums" or "horse latitude," where the wind died altogether and we drifted all around the compass rows. Now you would think that it would be really hot on the equator, but since the Humboldt Current comes up from the Antarctic, bringing its cold water north and then bending westward at the Equator, the temperature was almost cold and drizzly with fog. We stood our watches in foul weather gear and sou'wester rain hats on. The current also brings with it birds that you would not think that you would see in that part of the world, such as penguins. The nutrient-rich waters also bring whales, sea lions, and orcas. One day as I was sitting on the stern lazaret house I saw the biggest shark I had ever seen and to this day I have never seen another as big. He was eighteen to twenty feet long, and I guessed maybe 2,000 to 2,500 pounds. With the knowledge I have now of sharks, I am convinced he was a mammoth bull shark.

Gib sails no. 1 and no. 2

I quickly ran below and grabbed the huge deepsea rod and reel I had inherited from my grandfather. It was a large reel and short thick rod with a harness that I strapped on that would hook onto the reel. I quickly bent on a No. 10 silver spoon that had a hook as big as my hand. I ran back on deck and attracted a pretty good crowd as I lowered the hook to flash right in front of the shark's mouth. It flashed a few times and then it happened: the shark opened his mouth and took the spinner in. A cheer went up as I put all my effort into setting the hook in his tooth-filled jaw. The ocean literally exploded as my adversary reacted. The strength of this beast was unimaginable. I actually feared he would pull me over the side, but I dug in and the fight was on. Just as I was beginning to feel confident that I was going to have a long, exhausting fight before coming out the victor, I saw the captain with a knife quickly jump up on the lazaret and cut my line. At the time I was infuriated and let Skipper know. Skipper said, "Did you ever think what we were going to do with that devil if you did win that fight?" "Okay, okay, Skipper, but you could have let me win and then cut the line." I think our disagreement was a draw. I could see his point and I think he realized he may have acted a little hastily. Anyway, what a gigantic thrill. For the few minutes I had him, I felt, "Thank you, old denizen of the deep. Old beautiful shark, you gave me one of the many deep thrills I have experienced in my life."

The next morning as I was on bow watch and as the night was just turning to day, I sighted an island two points off the starboard bow. It was not supposed to be there. Oops. The lack of wind and the currents conspired against us to take us way north off course and the overcast skies prevented the use of our sextant so we could not determine exactly where we were. The island turned out to be the volcanic peak of Malpelo and rose straight out of the water to form a volcanic cone 1000 feet high. It could have been the home of King Kong. At least we now knew our exact position. Skipper was shook and I can understand why. If it had been the middle of the night in fog we could very well have been shipwrecked on this desolate and lonely island.

We had a shipmate we called Jim2 because we had two Jims on board. Jim2 was insane from the moment he came aboard. We believed the owners stuck him with us because they wanted his money. However, he had become dangerous on this passage and I began to carry on my person a brass belaying pin in the event I had to coldcock him. I almost did on the afternoon when he became uncontrollably insane and violent and tried to jump overboard. It took me and Skipper, Keith, Leo, Mirve, and Jim1 to subdue poor old Jim2. Doc shot him up with a heavy sedative, but to no avail. Crazy man was on watch the next morning at 4 a.m. Doc kept sedating him until in the Galapagos we got him on a transport and shipped home. It sure wasn't very comforting to have to live aboard ship with a maniac. We were beginning to realize at this point that we had a crook and cheat who was supplying *Yankee* with supplies and money. This would play a huge role and a very negative one as the months went by.

Our progress during this time was exceedingly slow. We had sighted turtles and had a marlin on the hand line.

September 2. Finally, after fourteen days at sea, we sighted a low island named Tower Island (also called Genovesa Island). As we approached it the sky became crowded with sea birds—so many that we had to shout at each other to talk because of the incredible noise being produced by the thousands of birds. I was trolling with a lure when this little booby sea gull got tangled in the line. I reeled him in and onto the deck to untangle him. He seemed to know we were helping him and was perfectly calm. We found out later on that all the birds were that way on the island. Wonder what it would be like if humans had never hunted for meat. I imagine animals would have no fear of us like the birds on Tower Island. That could be a bit risky with some of our animal friends.

We had some difficulty in anchoring and late that afternoon we got ashore. It took some time to be able to walk straight and not brace for the next lurch or roll of a ship's deck after fourteen days at sea. What a cool island: a circular desert island that is all that is left of its volcano birth with mainly cactus plants growing everywhere. The center of the island, which was the collapsed volcano caldera, was now filled with seawater and was where *Yankee* was anchored, protected from the winds. Very interesting ground features and easy to hike except for deep rifts scattered throughout the landscape. Since it is not a high island I wonder why the charts call it Tower Island. The best part of being on the island was the thousands of birds and their babies. They were incredibly tame and there was no problem in picking them up or petting them. Keith took a great picture of me holding in one hand a marine iguana and the other a baby frigate gull.

I have always been fascinated by the octopus, and lo and behold I found a beauty in a tidal pool. I hollered at Harv and we all fondled and played with ol' Eight Legs and watched him change colors several times. Octopi are incredibly intelligent creatures and I believe if we had evolved under the sea, the octopus would be our pet cats and the grouper our dogs. So many times on my numerous dives I have been personally entertained by these fascinating creatures, and even on some occasions have had them riding on my head and arms through my adventures in a different world on Earth. Have a good life ol' Eight Legs, and I am very happy to have made your acquaintance.

We returned to the ship late and Skipper had a couple of pitchers of rum swizzles and we got high and enjoyed a great fresh fish dinner, good company, and lots of laughs. We all felt very satisfied after a tough sail. Next day Keith and I went fishing and supplied the galley with five very large groupers that we ate under sail that night.

Leo and friends

Bilge and friends

We set sail that afternoon for Wreck Bay, a short 75 miles made long by contrary winds. Tomorrow we cross the equator and I will be inducted into the Royal Order of Shellbacks, leaving my lowly title of Poliwog north of the equator. A prized moment in any sailor's life.

4

Shellback Ceremony and The Galapagos Adventure

September 4. Bang, bang, bang, and through the main cabin came this gang of weirdos. I recognized King Neptune as a guy named Campbell, then came this big-breasted woman I recognize as our skipper in drag, and a clown who was really Guy. "All hands on deck!" cries somebody, and we assemble on deck. Several of the crew are ordered to sing to the rest of us as Art and Keith are put into the bosun's chair and towed alongside the ship. Keith later said all he could think about was that huge shark a couple of weeks back. I was accused of attempting to take a sun shot without the protective eyepiece on the sextant and damn near blinding myself, which I did indeed do. I was sentenced to climb the ratlines to the topmast, apologize to the sun, and return to the deck, which I did. When it was all over, we had a shot of rum and were issued our shellback certificates. I was now a member of the Order of Shellbacks, and crossing the equator in a 210-ton 'hermaphrodite brigantine' under full sail to boot. It don't get any better. What an honor and I am as proud of it today as I was then.

The next day in the evening we sailed into Puerto Chico and to the town of Wreck Bay. I was sent up to the lower topsail yard to watch for water color change and call out the position relative to the bow of the *Yankee*. As we entered the harbor, deep water was deep blue, and as it shoaled to shallow depths the water turned to turquoise. "Shoal two points off the port bow, three spokes to starboard," says I and *Yankee* responds almost instantly and passes safely the shallow water on our port beam and so on until we are in close to the shore and drop the hook. The town of Wreck Bay is basically right on the edge of the waterfront and is made up of quaint, nautical-looking wooden structures that appeared to be made of ship's planks and decking material. Anywhere a pole was used it appeared to be a ship's mast or a yardarm. I mentioned it to a local and he said, "Why you think eet ees called Wreck Bay, Señor?" I was amazed and I believed him.

Wreck Bay

Pelican

Lowland

Highland

Progresso

Yankee at anchor

    The few people who live on two of the seven islands equal the friendliest people in the world. They really went out of their way to make us feel welcome. The next day Leo, Keith, and I decided to walk the trail, not the road, six miles up the mountain to Progresso. We knew it was a town of just a few wooden shacks and would be hard to find if we didn't stay on the trail. The Galapagos Islands are amazing from sea level to about 3,000 feet. They are dry and fairly barren, and chilly below 1,500 feet. The air temperature warms up as you climb higher and higher and the landscape begins to change into a fairyland of flowers, trees, grass, fruit, and ferns interspersed with small lakes covered with beautiful floating flowers. Before long we had lost the trail and were pioneering our way through this awesomely beautiful jungle. We decided to keep going and if we had to we would spend the night and backtrack to the coast the following day. Oh to be young again. That's when it started to get foggy and the temperature dropped about fifteen degrees. I looked at Keith and Leo and said all we needed now is to have it start raining. That's when we felt the first drop. It started to drizzle more than rain and it was very cool, almost cold. It was also getting dark. We kept walking until we came out of the jungle and there was a fairly large wooden house across a pasture. We headed for it. We could see only the lighted windows and wondered what the reception would be like when we knocked on the door. The door opened and there was a very kind-looking Ecuadorian woman who said, "Vente, vente." Keith started to speak Spanish to her and she said that she could speak English. There were several small children, a couple of dogs, and her husband who happened to be the bus driver. We asked if we could warm up a bit and then we would walk by highway (really a dirt road) back to Wreck Bay. She scowled at us and said, "You certainly weel not, you weel eat some comida. We weel make you a comforatable bed then spend the night and een the morning my husband weel drive you een hees bus to town. Comprendo?" Yes, m'am, and we all had a good laugh with these great people. The house was so rustic-looking, no paint anywhere and natural dark wood beams and walls. A good dinner, good kids, a nice warm spot on the living room floor, good company, and a ride into town the next morning. Wow, what a neat place. We returned to the ship early in the morning and prepared to set sail for Academy Bay on Indefatigable Island, a big and actively volcanic island with the second largest population and town in the Galapagos Islands. We arrived six hours later.

We met Gust Angermeyer and his brother and their families. Gust was a German Jew who, with his brother, escaped Nazi Germany when Hitler took power and sailed a 25-foot sloop through the Atlantic and the Straits of Magellan to the Pacific and finally settled at Academy Bay. What a couple of cool guys. Gust had dark hair and looked very strong, with the tough look of a guy who knew exactly where he was and how to do it. He had the most loveable personality of anyone I have met. He would launch off on these intensely funny and interesting stories and would hold us spellbound with his German accent as he would spin fascinating yarn after yarn.

We got to know Gust very well as he went with us—or I should say we went with him—on a goat-hunting trip that lasted for three days. We did not go on a boat, but hiked along the coast for eight miles to a picturesque cove called Turtle Cove. As its name implied, the little bay was filled with sea turtles. Hiking the coast over and back from Turtle Cove was no easy task as even though a lot of it was beach, there were big areas of lava flows that proved very difficult to walk over. That portion of Indefatigable Island was a desert scene with mainly cactus and no fresh water streams or pools anywhere. The landscape inland began rising as part of a huge volcanic cone which we could not see due to a persistent cloud cover. Lucky for us, the temperature was cool, perfect for our long hike. At Turtle Cove there was the one and only spring we saw on the entire hunt. Around the spring was a small forest of trees just as green as could be. This is where we camped for the next two nights. As the sun was going down and Gust was spinning his tales, I could not help but think that life does not get any better.

The hunt went on all the next day and we all had our fill of culling the herds of wild goats. We brought two back and were fascinated as Doc dissected and described each organ and its purpose. We boiled the heart in salt water and cooked the meat over an open fire. It was delicious. We all again were mesmerized by Gust and his wonderful stories and slept well that night. Next day we retraced our steps and hiked back to Academy Bay and got there in the late afternoon, exhausted.

We sailed to a spot on Santa Cruz Island and anchored in a perfectly calm narrow bay. Ashore, Leo and I walked among a herd of sea lions. They had no fear of us. I sat down next to a mother and two pups. I picked up the two pups and cuddled and kissed these two darling fluffy and warm sea creatures, absolutely falling in love with them, and the mother looking at me with her beautiful shining black eyes. All of a sudden with a great bellow a gigantic bull sea lion exploded out of the water, obviously pissed off and headed straight for me. He probably weighed in the neighborhood of 450 pounds of strong muscle, fat, and flashing teeth. With beating heart, I dropped both pups and stood up. Unbeknownst to me, a sea lion bull will only attack when his adversary cannot stand taller than he, so when I stood up he immediately cowered, all his fierceness turning to wimpiness, and slunk back into the sea. The end of the story was that I inherited his females, most of whom followed us back to the ship where they hung out all night, making an unbelievable racket, probably bellowing to their new love to come back and do his duty. I think it was the skipper who told me, "Nice going, Bilge. Next time try to curb your desire to impress the girls." "Aye aye, sir," said I, looking at the deck.

On my watch the next morning we had a great following breeze and at 5:30 a.m. Skipper gave the order to set all sails, including the squares. We must have been a beautiful sight to the only inhabitants on the island—my harem. I was at the helm and marveled at the sight before me: all sails pulling hard in the predawn light, slipping smoothly and gently through the calm waters of our little bay, the land close on both sides of the ship slipping effortlessly by as we steadily plowed through and entered the open sea. Some of the moments I remember on the *Yankee* were true magic. This was one of many I experienced. So, good-bye to all you wonderful ladies of my new harem and thanks for the wonderful experience of having made your acquaintance. I have had quite a few more fine and adventurous experiences with these marvelous sea creatures since this one.

We were about two hours to Seymore Island with a following wind. Daphne Island is a sleeping volcano with a perfectly round and deep caldera in the center. We climbed down and into the caldera where there was a colony of blue-footed boobies, very tame birds.

Back on the ship we set sail to Borrero Bay. The bay itself is surrounded by jagged cliffs and high fingers of volcanic rock. A very wild place when it was active 30-40,000 years ago. I drew port watch but enjoyed it very much because I was the launches captain and spent the day ferrying people from *Yankee* and back again. Actually a great, relaxing day for me.

My harem

***Yankee* at peace**

Fresh meat for *Yankee*

Fresh meat for *Yankee*

September 14. We sailed to James Island and Sullivan Bay with its high rocky cliffs on the north end leading to a beautiful half-moon beach where we anchored at the south end. Leo, Jim1, Doc, Mirve, and I loaded our guns and went ashore to what turned out to be an unbelievable hunt for fresh meat for the ship. We climbed the steep slope to the very top to a sort of plain where before us stood several hundred goats. The war was on, and there was no limit. It was definitely a massacre but we supplied the ship with loads of fresh meat.

I climbed up to look at the crater of a long-extinct volcano and found the caldera filled with water. I later found out that it was seawater and is a geological mystery as to how the crater could have sea water when the bottom is several hundred feet above sea level. To this day I don't know the answer.

The next morning on my watch we set sail from Sullivan Bay bound for Isabella Island on a fine and fast beam reach, *Yankee* heeled and crashed through the chilly blue seas of the South Pacific. We tacked as she headed the wind, all sails setting up a loud chatter, her bowsprit pointing skyward and crashing down and into the next wave with enough momentum to literally explode that wave into billions of sparkling diamonds of spray before taking up the strain of the sails and heeling over to port as the wind filled the sails. We were now on a direct heading for James Bay.

We entered the bay still with the bone in *Yankee's* teeth, rounded up, dropped sails, and dropped anchor. We were looking pretty professional. Sometimes sailing is like being in heaven. Wow. That was a great sailing day.

I went fishing with Iggy as Doc, Leo, and Jim1 went ashore and got a couple more goats. Iggy and I caught enough fish for supper and it was delicious. This island also had a crater or caldera filled with saltwater. In this case the dead volcano was brought up from under the sea and was naturally filled so long ago that the salinity in the water was thick enough through evaporation that for a few years somebody was actually mining the salt deposits.

We put our gear on to dive and Leo and I being experienced divers didn't stay with the other group of divers. The water was chilly and Leo and I were equipped with heavy wet suits while the others had no protection against the cold water. Consequently, they came up freezing after about only twenty minutes.

Leo and I made two dives that day, each lasting about one hour and fifteen minutes. There are no coral reefs because of the cold water and everything underwater is formed from black volcanic basalt. Visibility was probably about fifty feet at best. The sea was abundant with life: every kind of fish swimming around and up to us by the thousands. A very busy and bustling world. We dropped down to about sixty feet and were instantly surrounded by sea lions who were delighted we were there and played with us as part of their group, even letting us pet them under the sea. I felt that we were in a land of make-believe as one clown put his nose right on my mask and turned upside down to look at me.

Suddenly, the sea lions were gone, and it wasn't long before we saw the reason. Just barely visible was a very large and dim silhouette of a giant sea animal, in the range of 5,000-8,000 pounds. We instantly recognized it as a big killer whale. We tried to swim up to it but it was moving steadily ahead too fast and we were getting low on air so we both reversed and swam back and surfaced near the ship. When we got on deck and shed our gear, the other group of divers excitedly told us that they had seen a killer whale and by their remarks it sounded to Leo and me that they panicked and made helter skelter for the ship. Leo said we saw it also. "Oh my god, what did you do?" they asked. I nonchalantly answered, "We tried to get closer for a better look." Their jaws dropped, eyes staring at us. We both had to check ourselves from outright laughter as being west coast divers both Leo and I knew that killer whales have a completely benign nature towards humans and have never attacked or attempted to hurt any diver.

After dinner we decided we had had enough of goat meat and dumped the rest overboard. I must admit, I prefer fish any day. We set sail for a very active volcano making up the island of Narborough, now called Fernandina Island.

The next morning we sailed into and dropped the hook in Espinoza Bay—a wild and frightfully jagged-looking place because it was basically still forming. We sailed later that day for Tagus Cove, another wild-looking cove with thousands of sea birds diving and fishing. Leo and I went ashore and captured the largest marine iguana I have ever seen, a monster about eight feet from mouth to tail, with a face only a mother could love. It was totally benign and did not fear us. CB 'Bulldog' Pace was asleep in his bunk and—you guessed it—that's where ol' 'Tail's a-dragging' wound up (with our help). You should have heard the commotion—screams, yelps, and cussing. The fastest I ever saw the Bulldog move, a blur of bodies half-human, half-lizard as they both vacated CB's berth with all haste. CB hit the ground, took a couple of steps back, and all he could say was "gol-l-l-l-ly." The iguana just sat there with the same expression on his unusually ugly face as if to say, "What's everybody so excited about?"

Guy and some others returned and deposited a really cool penguin on the deck. He was fairly friendly and I held him in my hands. I stupidly put him next to my face and without hesitation he grabbed my nose and to this day I still have the scar. I guess you can call it karma after our trick on CB 'Bulldog' Pace but we all got a big laugh out of it as we let the pair go over the side. So long you two wonders of the marine world, it has been painfully nice to meet you both.

We set sail the next morning and as we passed by a beach you could see sulfur vents just up the beach. As I had spent a lot of time in Hawaii and around the very active volcano of Kilauea Iki, I knew a little trick. You can take a lit cigarette and wave it in front of a sulfur vent and *voila*! It will magically produce volumes of steam. When I told the crew about the phenomenon I got some very skeptical looks so the group went ashore. To the great pleasure and joy of the group, I passed the first cigarette in front of the vent and steam came pouring out. The group spent the next 40 or 50 minutes throwing lit matches and cigarettes into the vent and marveling at the clouds of steam they were producing.

Bulldog's bunkmate

A pretty face

We motored all night trying to reach the island of Floriana. We anchored at Post Office Bay at 3:00 p.m., where I put some letters in the barrel post box. They reached their destinations one and a half years later, just like they did in the 1800s. It was here that I discovered the reason why the *Albatross* was lost in the Gulf of Mexico. All ships leave their names either painted or carved in the rocks. I even have a neat picture of a carving in a cliff wall that says 'Darwin's *Beagle* 1836.' Laying on the ground were four cement ballast bricks painted red, white, and blue and on the blue side it said 'Courtesy of the Brigantine Albatross.' The ballast bricks weigh about 100 pounds each and there were 20,000 pounds of them in the bilge that was called 'inside ballast' and kept *Albatross* upright in a strong wind. They were placed in the bottom of the ship in such a manner that they stabilized themselves by locking into each other. When the crewmembers, whoever they were, removed the four ballast blocks, they destroyed the integrity of the rest of the 20,000 pounds of internal ballast blocks. When the *Albatross* was knocked down on her beam ends by the fierce winds of a white squall, the rest of the ballast blocks let go and probably came crashing through the cabin floor and came to rest on the side of the ship that she was laying on, holding her down, and not allowing her to right herself again. She subsequently filled with seawater and sank very quickly. It may be the reason thirteen of her crew could not get out and went down with the ship. We all make mistakes and sometimes they cost us dearly.

I feel for the captain, he was exonerated in the trial that followed but it probably destroyed him personally. There was no mention of the ballast blocks being removed but there they were, laying on the ground right in front of me. Anyway, it is just my theory on what happened.

Ballast blocks

That night we were invited to Mrs. Whitmar's house for a home-cooked roast beef dinner. We all thought we had died and gone to heaven. Wow, was that good. Thank you, thank you, thank you, Mrs. Whitmar and family. I remember that our dinner at Post Office Bay was great.

Next evening we were back at Academy Bay and that night we had a slam bang party aboard *Yankee* and broke up at about 2:00 or 3:00 a.m. with Keith loaded to the gills and saying that he was "goin' to shettle down and live sha resht my life here." So we helped him load his stuff in a small rowboat and he set off on a crooked course to shore. We heard the clunk as his boat hit the rocky shore and we called to him, "You alright, Keith?" and heard him call back, "Yup." Next day Skipper was mad as hell and ordered us to go ashore and bring that idiot back before we sailed. So we did. As we got to shore, there was Keith's boat and most of his belongings floating in the water. A little ways inland there under a cactus lay "Keithie," sound asleep with four large marine iguanas laying next to him. He woke up and looked at us for a minute and then said, "Where the hell am I?" I said, "Come on, Iguana, we need to get back to the ship." The name stuck and he was from then on known to everybody as "Iguana" or to his best friends as "Iggy." The name has stuck to this day. My memory is bad concerning the date, September 22, only because I was deeply involved in the fun and drinks and thought it was all a great idea. Not to mention the Panama Red that 'somebody' smuggled aboard *Yankee*—my oh my. A good time was had by all. The next morning, after retrieving ol' Iguana and with very sore heads we hoisted anchor and set sail for Pitcairn Island, 2,500 miles distant.

5

A Grand Downward Slide—19 Days, 2,500 Miles

With sore heads and dry mouths, we winched in the anchor—a sweaty, hard job to begin with, made worse by our hangovers from the night before. We motored around the point and 220° was our heading on a port tack if we could hold it and was our great circle route to Pitcairn Island, 2,500 miles off the end of our bowsprit. It remained cloudy and chilly for the next two or three days and rainy on our 4 to 8 watch.

September 24. Gypsy (Pete Grant), one of the new guys on board (though not actually new to Leo and me as he was crew on two of the 10-day cruises we did before our round the world cruise departed), was a real thin, wiry guy who for the most part kept us in stitches. A fun crew mate for sure. In any case, on the second day of this run the sun came out in all its glory after most of a month without seeing it, except for our moments ashore in the Galapagos. Gypsy came up from below, looked up at the sun with a very bewildered look on his face and said, "Hey, what's that?" then started the 8 to 12, so we finished our 4 to 8 with a laugh. Good ol' Gypsy.

The next day was still chilly. After watch, I climbed out on the bowsprit and was entertained by a large group of dolphins riding the bow wake and blowing out just under me. What marvelous mammals they are and another sea mammal that I have had many good adventures with. So long you sleek speeders and have fun. A great way to spend the morning on what was the beginning of the best nineteen days of a down trade wind slide on our entire cruise. From Galapagos to Pitcairn, September 22 to October 12, a magical sail to be sure.

That night we were treated to a display of phosphorescence, or plankton, I should say. As *Yankee* slipped through the sea, plankton by the millions flashed their mysterious lights. If you would look into the universe on a clear night and see all the stars flashing on, off, on, and none flashing back on in the same place twice in a row, that is what the sea in the close proximity of our ship looked like. Further out, every once in a while I would see a big underwater flash I feel was magnified by the length of water I was looking through from my position on deck. I saw these same flashes occasionally on our cloudy, foggy cruise from Panama to the Galapagos. I mentioned it to Harvey and I think he thought I was nuts. Well, anyway, I think in the clear weather of this night I found the answer to the giant flashes I saw previously. They weren't the sea monster I was secretly hoping for but just itty bitty plankton turning on their tiny lights and the show being greatly magnified by the water in the wave that I was looking at fifteen feet away.

By evening, on the helm I noticed *Yankee*—on a beam reach, all sails set except the squares—was fairly bowling along at 10 knots. She responded to the helm like a racehorse, her creaking and groaning settling into an even and business-like symphony.

Skipper and I were the only ones on deck, the others being below. At dinner chow call, Skipper says, "Eh, Bilge, she has got the bone in her teeth and the women of Pitcairn are pulling on the line." "Aye, aye, sir," says I.

I am sure we are on the edge of the trade winds. I am right with the world. I planned my wheel trick to be 6:00 to 7:00 so for 30 to 40 minutes a day I would be the only one on deck and in direct command, as the others were at chow, on this beautiful sailing ship on an unreal sea at sundown. Later in the voyage it would pay surreal magical dividends.

On the morning 4 to 8 I was on the helm, *Yankee* bowling along at 9 knots. I was in my foul weather gear and cold when I felt a warm patch in the wind, and then it was gone. A few minutes later I felt another, then another, and the wind started to shift off of our stern and stayed warm. I peeled off the foul weather gear and shouted, "We're in the trades!" The wind picked up and we set our squares. I felt an incredible but mild penetrating vibration throughout the ship's keel as we raced past hull speed and tore through the ocean at 11, or even 12, knots. *Yankee* took one huge wave after another and tore down the face of these monsters only to plow into the back of the previous wave, slow down, and have the whole process repeat itself again for the next fifteen days or so. This is what it is all about.

Skipper ordered all sheets, braces, and vangs to have anti-chafing canvas sewn around the exposed lines that crossed over any edge of the ship so that the sewn-on canvas would protect the ropes from chafing through and parting at that point of contact—something you would never do unless you were planning to stay in the steady winds of the trades for a long time. Before you can move any of those lines you have to remove the anti-chafe canvas from them.

Day fed into day of great sailing. One day I climbed the foremast to the upper topsail yard and perched straddling the yard and looked down upon *Yankee*'s sleek lines and beautiful round stern, her deckhouses, and symmetrical lines of her deck planks. I was watching her plow through the ocean with ease, her shapely hull contrasting with the deep, deep blue of the South Pacific ocean as her bow would fall off the crest of our following wave and pick up speed then plow into the next sea with a surprisingly gentle motion but with great turmoil, causing the sea to part from either side of *Yankee*'s bow stem in a crashing, tumbling breaker on either side of the ship, spreading a great swath of white foaming sea on both beams. These giant patches of foam would dissipate almost as quickly as they began. I have never lost my fascination for the turmoil a ship's hull causes on the sea when said vessel is moving at speed. I probably spent the good part of the morning fascinated by *Yankee*'s ballet through the South Pacific and the power of the trade winds to make her dance with such perfection.

Our position was about 1,000 miles west of the Galapagos Islands when we decided to set the fore course, a big square sail that is harbor furled by tying furling lines from the top of the sail, about twelve of them reaching just about to the deck, and is then tied around the sail and mast. It is the lowest of the three square sails. The top portion of this big square slides on runners on the bottom of the yard out to the end of the yard on both sides. The trick is to have one sailor climb the rat lines to the fore course yard and then position himself clinging onto the sail with his legs wrapped around the sail itself and inch his way down the sail and untie the furling straps one at a time but leave the lowest one attached. At a given signal, port and starboard outhauls are heaved on to spread the top of the sail out on both sides of the yard by two sailors. I and three others were ready on the weather sheet with four other sailors ready on the lee sheet, and the top portion of the sail already filled with wind.

Skipper called, "all hands ready on the lee sheet?" As soon as the skipper gave the order to release the furling strap, we had seconds to manhandle the sheets to port and starboard pin rails and make them fast on their respective belaying pins or risk losing control of this monster sail. "All ready on the weather sheet," says I. "All ready on the lee sheet," says Leo. "Skipper, let go the furling strap and set the fore." At that moment, a hard gust hit us and I watch in disbelief as my three sets of extra muscle are hurled butts, legs, heads, and torsos onto the foredeck in a human pile of wreckage as I am becoming airborne and picking up speed on course for the lee rail. Shortly, I am dangling ten feet over the rushing sea and my mesmerizing foam is definitely not as beautiful to me that close up. The thought crossed my mind that if I let go, the crew probably could not ware ship in time to rescue me. I could see the headlines: "Chi Sox Owners' Son Lost at Sea, The Last Thing Seen of Him Was a Clenched Fist and Middle Finger Disappearing Beneath the Waves."

Back to reality. Skipper, Leo, Jim1, Mirve, and Harv had a hold of the portion of sheet that was still on deck. Skipper hollered, "Hang on, Bilge!" I hollered back, "Is that an order, sir?" as the gang pulled me back. All faces had broad grins, Skipper's the biggest.

Once belayed and secured, I was surrounded, hugged, and banged repeatedly on my back. Thanks, brothers of the sea, you freakin' saved my life. Thanks.

The days melted into each other as we flew through the sea, averaging 180 miles a day. Harvey, bless his heart, pulled a practical joke on those below deck. Being a signal flagman in the Navy, ol' Harv placed himself over the main cabin skylight so everybody could see him. He looked at me (on the helm) and winked. I got the message. He began signaling "AA AA AA" (what ship are you?) and then quit. Sometime later, Eileen Dickey came on deck, obviously in a state of distress. "What's the matter, Eileen?" says I. "Oh that damn Harvey saw a submarine and didn't tell anybody at the time. I am so mad at him," she replied. I blew it right then as I could not contain my laughter. Eileen says, "Ooooh you," mostly directed at Harvey and turned to storm below decks. "Look out below," says I, our spirits definitely high.

4 to 8 finished up the starboard lifeboat and she looked very neat and seaworthy with her new paint and emergency supplies stowed on board. Guy did most of the work.

We rigged up the bosun's chair and I was elected to ride it first since I was the biggest (the first mate started calling me 'Tiny,' a name some of my friends still use to this day). I was perfect to test the chair (thanks, guys) being hung by block and tackle to the inward portion of the fore course yard. I was hoisted about ten feet high and as *Yankee*'s bow fell over the top of a wave and started down by gravity, the chair and I would swing almost even with the bowstem and the crew would release their grip and I would plunge into the warm blue South Pacific sea, surfacing shortly and was then treated to the awesome sight of our beautiful white-hulled sailing ship moving by me while sitting in the bosom of the sea. Just past the stern of our lifeboat sitting on deck, the line attached to the bosun's chair would come taut and the crew would heave. I would again be hoisted high and swing forward again to splash into the sea. I repeated this fun sport three or four times. In an hour or two, everybody had tried it. Great way to spend the day. Guy later tied off the chair to the bowsprit and would go out by himself and get into the chair after crawling down the dolphin striker. The motion of *Yankee* would jerk him out of the water and swing him way out in front of the ship, where he would splash into the sea and watch the bow stem coming right at him. Just before the bow stem would hit him, he would be jerked out of the sea and repeat it time and time again. It worried me so that when I saw Guy heading for the bow, I assigned myself life guard duty and would stay to keep an eye on him. My thinking was that if the rope attached to the peak of the bosun's chair were to part, Guy would be hit dead on by the bow stem moving at him at 8 or 9 knots. That, coupled with the 210 tons of sailing ship, Guy would be lucky to survive. At least I could yell out the alarm, "Man overboard!" We tended to look out for each other no matter what.

That night on the 4 to 8, me on my 6 p.m. wheel trick, I was to have a moment in time that would engrave 'beautiful' into my mind for the rest of my life. I think about it today and it comes back as beautifully and clearly as if I were again standing on *Yankee*'s afterdeck, gripping her helm. I was enjoying my position as the only man on deck, the others below and having dinner and discussing Pitcairn Island. I was engrossed, as usual looking forward, the whole ship being in front of me, and marveling at her yards and square sails filled and pulling and feeling I had stepped back in time to the 1800s when all ships looked like this. I was aware of a sky full of cotton puff clouds when the sea all around and in front of me began to turn gold. In a few minutes the clouds were gold then the sky was gold. I stood in awe, not being able to move or look away and then realized the sails and decks were also a deep gold. This lasted for four or five minutes, then disappeared as quickly as it began, sky and clouds turning red and slowly turning to grey just before nightfall. I had not looked at the compass for the entire time and five minutes later when I looked at the lubber line, she was still on the course I last remembered her to be on. An astounding time for a sailing vessel to remain on course in a following sea and wind, with no one assisting her wandering. I realized at that point that I was the only man on planet Earth that saw this beautiful thing happen and it has evoked many deep thoughts in my life ever since.

The trades

Next day Skipper came down sick. He was in good hands and the ship faithfully sailed on. No beautiful sunset on my p.m. wheel trick but I was sure hoping for another. On the morning 4 to 8 watch, around 6 a.m. we heard a 'whoosh whoosh' around our moving ship. As it became light, we were amazed to see pilot whales by the thousands all around our ship. I climbed halfway up the mast and I could see spouts all the way to the horizon. They continued to pass us until just before noon sight was taken. I won't even guess how many whales were out there, but it had to be in the hundreds of thousands. Was this connected to the golden sunset? Who knows. I read Guy's account and was astounded at the lack of enthusiasm, maybe he didn't realize or see the extent of what was going on out there.

October 12. We sighted Pitcairn Island, at first a half-dome shape. We laid off all night and at sunrise we were close and in calm seas and wind. I breathed in the heavy scent of land laced with fire smoke and the sweet scents of flowers and food cooking. We could plainly hear dogs barking, children laughing and screaming joyfully as they played, and a large crowd of people (the descendants of Fletcher Christian, the leader of the mutiny against Captain Bligh and HMS Bounty). They appeared very excited and we were to find out they had not seen a ship in quite a long time.

6

Living With the Ancestors of *The Mutiny on the Bounty*, Pitcairn Island

October 13. Skipper set sea watch time and shore liberty. Of course, guess who drew first sea watch. Oh well, it will be really nice to sail *Yankee* with only one-third of the crew aboard. Skipper even seemed to relax. I remained aboard *Yankee* for the next three days, wondering what these ancestors of the most famous mutineers in history would be like.

Pretty soon two longboats, each with six oarsmen, came around Bounty Bay Point and made for us. It didn't take long before they came alongside. They were very muscular and, having been around Polynesians before, I instantly recognized that half, with the other being Anglo Saxon-English. They were a rough, tough-looking gang that were boarding our ship. They introduced themselves and I got a chill when I heard the names Christian, McCoy, Adams, Young, and Brown—all of them directly related to the mutineers of the *Bounty*.

At this point, looking over this crowd of ruffians, I was convinced we were about to get our throats cut and they would take our ship. Instead, they politely offered us their homes to live in while ashore and spoke the most charming old English, the first I had actually heard in person. They redeemed their rough looks by their gentlemanly and kind behavior. The first shore crew boarded the longboats. Skipper surprised all of us by ordering the shore crew to be back aboard tomorrow. What the hell, Captain? With stunned and angry feelings the shore crew pulled for Bounty Bay.

We spent the rest of the day sailing *Yankee* slowly, with No. 1 jib sail, fore sail, main stay sail, and the main set our speed, down around 2.5 to 3 knots, just loping along, going nowhere in particular. At midnight, we tacked ship and took up our reciprocal course, still with the same sails set and our speed slow. At daylight when I could see Pitcairn, I was shocked to see the island was not where it was supposed to be but on our starboard side. This meant we had been forced off course by some weird current and wound up to the west of the island, a place we did not want to be. An area of shoals exists on that side of Pitcairn. I hollered, "Skipper! Skipper! All hands on deck!"

Skipper was on deck instantly and sized up our situation immediately. It was getting light now, and all around us I could see great patches of turquoise water, indicating shoals. A string of very salty words growled out of Skipper's mouth and he instantly went into action as he was taking the helm. He shouted orders: "Mirve, Leo, wind sheets; Bilge, Jim1, lee sheets. Stand by to tack ship." "Ready?" "Ready." "Coming about." Skipper jumped in front of the helm and expertly spun the wheel in a blur. *Yankee* slowly responded as the jib, fore sail, stay sail, and main headed the wind and set up their staccato chatter at the perfect moment so the wind was actually just beginning to fill the other side of the sail. Jim1 and I frantically heaved in our sheets and made them up on their respective belaying pins on the now lee pinrails. We could feel the steadying power of the sails as they filled and took the strain, the island now on the port side and our bowsprit heading for the healthy blue of deep water. Phew, don't want to repeat that, but then we had an even closer call later at the Tuamoto atoll of Tema Tangi.

Pitcairn Island

***Yankee* rounding Bounty Point**

I felt pride at our ability to handle the ship and the skipper's rare compliment ("Well done, Tars"). I still remember to this day how I definitely felt like a real sailor. We rounded the south end of Pitcairn and saw the native launch rowing out to meet us. Better late than never. Just then, the giant US Coast Guard *Eastwind*, an icebreaker on her way to Antarctica, appeared on a heading for us. Skipper, knowing that the islanders wanted to trade with the *Eastwind*, continued on course. We did not know that the launch had our crew and were chasing us because the islanders wanted to talk to us about going to Henderson Island, 176 miles south to cut *mira* wood. They use *mira* to make their very fine carvings. I still have my fish carved by Ivan Christian. Anyway, it worked out fine as the *Yankee* crew instead wound up aboard *Eastwind*, where the US Coast Guard rolled out the red carpet for them. Even gave Harvey and Guy a helicopter ride. After a while I saw this helicopter lifting off the deck. I scurried up the main ratlines and perched myself on the main spreaders as the chopper flew in real close and I could see two helmeted figures sitting in the open doorway photographing *Yankee* and me standing on the spreaders. When I found out that it was Guy and Harv I couldn't ask enough questions, being the aviation nut that I am. I certainly thought it was way cool.

When the shore crew returned to *Yankee*, it was our turn to go ashore with our new friends. As we rowed toward Bounty Bay, a huge wave loomed up behind us. I photographed what turned out to be one of my favorite pictures. In the foreground is the tiller of our longboat, a mass of blue water, and very small behind the crest of the wave are the sails only of *Yankee*. The picture hangs in my kitchen to this day. The islanders, being expert seamen, timed just right a monster breaker looming up behind, the helmsman hollering, "Away, lads, all together!" The six oarsmen in perfect unison rowed hard. I knew this was the end. The crest of this monster was at least ten feet above our stern. The stern began to rise and our speed increased to just below supersonic. The giant wave was breaking all around us, rushing us at great speed directly toward a cliff. We're all dead! At the last moment, our helmsman came hard left and we careened behind a seawall and into perfectly calm water and a dock. In the meantime, the furious wave that we were just on exploded with a deep *frump* against the cliff face. Wow, what a ride.

Looking back toward *Yankee*

Coming into Bounty Bay

Definitely cool guys, these mutineers. Bligh probably had it coming to him anyway. One thing I will say about Captain Bligh is that he was one of the world's greatest sailors. To sail a small open boat with little food or water 4,000 miles to Timor was definitely a super-human feat and says a lot for his ability at gaining the respect and loyalty of the crew in the overloaded lifeboat.

When finally I got ashore, I stayed at the home of Ivan Christian, the great-great-great-grandson of Fletcher Christian himself. We climbed the steep trail to the top of the same cliff our wave used as a violent brake. I was introduced to Ivan Christian, his wife and two daughters and was given a bedroom in their own home. They were a marvelous family that put me at ease and accepted me as one of their own. I was pleasantly surprised to find out *Yankee* was to sail to Henderson the next day and we were to stay at Pitcairn for what turned out to be just short of two weeks. Alright. I seem to be on the right side of luck in this life. The beautiful ladies of Tahiti played as big a role in *Bounty*'s adventures as they did with ours, as we were to learn.

That night I asked Ivan if it was possible to take a fresh water bath so we set to the task of heating water over open flames and filling a wash tub in a separate little shack just outside of the main house. The houses on Pitcairn look very rural England and are all hand built. For the first time in two months I was able to wash the salt off my body. Oh, did that feel good. I was just getting relaxed when I focused on the raw wooden walls of my private bathroom. That is when I noticed the walls were covered with great big grey, terrifyingly ugly banana spiders. I hate spiders. I was afraid to move fast so I slowly vacated the bathroom. I wonder if the Christians ever wondered why I never used the washtub again.

The next morning Iggy and I walked down a trail to the shore and there we found an Olympic-sized swimming pool cut out of the surrounding lava cliffs by wave action. It was a great place to swim. The waves would break outside the pool and would cause just enough disruption in the pool to make it exciting for us. This would become our daily bath for the rest of our stay. Salt water be damned. Before we left Pitcairn, Iggy and I hiked every inch of this lovely, lonesome island.

As *Yankee* set sail for Henderson, we were psyched to spend the next eleven or twelve days hiking this island. No roads, only hiking trails. Just the way I like it. In some spots the jungle was very thick but all in all the walking was a great change. Tall coconut palms and flowering bushes and trees everywhere. Every place you looked were bananas and oranges sweet as pie. No wonder Christian and his crew of mutineers decided this was their new home. The climate was perfect, mostly in the 70s.

Next day Iggy and I made a very strenuous hike over a steep ridge and down a treacherous trail on a cliff face, starting about 1,000 feet up, at a place called the 'Rope.' After a scary hike on this trail we ended up in a half-moon bay surrounded by steep cliffs. At the base of the cliffs the walls were covered in ancient Polynesian petroglyphs—a fascinating sight to see, well worth the dangers of getting there. Iggy took a picture of me in full beard standing next to a cliff base surrounded by these ancient carvings. I learned later that Guy, Harv, and their group declined the treacherous hike down this intimidating trail. I really don't blame them.

Climbing down a treacherous trail

Ancient petroglyphs

Iggy enjoying himself

Christian's Cave

Carving a fish

Windward side

We returned to the village just in time for a fabulous feast. The islanders are all vegetarians due to their Seventh Day Adventist religion, but what they could do with vegetables was astounding, not to mention delicious. The kids entertained us with their singing and a little girl named Melva played a guitar and was really good. We felt our friendship with these great people blossoming and felt totally at ease with them. It was

Nancy Christian's birthday and everybody was there. We went to bed that night with full bellies and fell into a deep sleep. Wow, that felt good.

Doc did several operations and Guy was his assistant. The things Guy had to do would scare hell out of me and I still respect him for his ability at learning these complicated skills. Good ol' Guy.

Yankee finally returned and anchored in Bounty Bay. After a couple of failed tries, we made it back aboard. Leo, Iggy, Mirve, and I made several dives trying to locate the remains of *Bounty*, but by now it would be just a pile of ballast rocks as all of the wood would long ago have rotted away. We did not locate her but one of the dives is worth mentioning. We had just reached the sandy bottom at 110 feet, visibility a sparkling 100 feet. Just as we were to begin our search, I looked out in front of us and noticed a fast movement at the contact zone about a 110 feet out, moving very fast one way, then reversing course and moving the other way. I knew from experience that this was the action of a deep sea predator trying to make his mind up whether to take the chance or not. Quickly he moved into view and my heart froze—definitely a predator, a very large mako shark on the hunt and knowing we were there and maybe edible. The mako is a fierce and dangerous shark known for its ferocity and has been known to attack humans. I got the other divers' attention. Leo already knew and I gave the signal to abort the dive and put my hand to my forehead, the international signal for shark. Leo and I got everybody back to back in a defensive position and controlled our ascent to the surface so as not to rise too quickly. We never saw the shark again to our great relief. Mirve, who without his glasses couldn't see very well, asked why we came up. I said, "Because of the shark." Mirve looked at me with wide eyes and said, "Shark, I didn't see any bloody shark." After we all stopped laughing, I said, "Believe me, Mirve, there was a shark, a bloody big one."

That afternoon Skipper asked Leo and me if we could take a couple of barnacle scrapers and see if we could scrape our accumulation of barnacles from the underwater portion of the ship's hull. We refilled our tanks with air, and worked for a little over two hours. It was not as easy as we thought. We were on our backs most of the time. *Yankee*, all 200 tons of her, was constantly in motion due to wave action. You definitely did not want to get hit by her. So we did a balancing ballet, rising and lowering in the water under her keel as she rose and lowered. It was all done by muscle and timed breathing: in to rise, out to lower. At the same time, we handled our long-handled hoe-looking device like a rake, keeping it in contact with the hull and barnacles. We would then push and the barnacles would come off the hull with ease. At one point I became fascinated with this curtain of thousands of barnacles drifting down through the light blue depths of this underwater world to the sandy bottom below where only a couple of hours before we had our encounter with the mako. Hmmm, I wondered if makos are attracted to barnacles being scraped off of ship hulls. I guess not, as we never saw him again. We scraped off about eighty percent of the barnacles and *Yankee* benefited by picking up 1 knot of speed, which translates to an extra twenty-eight miles a day if the winds don't fail.

Listening to the farewell songs sung by the men of Pitcairn, we said our thanks and good-byes. Our friends loaded on their longboats and said good-bye as they pulled for Bounty Bay.

October 28. We set sail and rounded the point to be instantly set on by a very windy and rainy squall. We shortened sail only to have the squall pass quickly by and leave us in fluky winds and having to reset the shortened sails, *Yankee* rocking and rolling and basically going nowhere. We were bound for the island of Mangereva.

We had a couple of fairly major problems in that we were short on fuel and our 110-volt Lister generator had failed. Our stop at Mangereva was questionable. It rained a lot at the beginning of our trip and there was a lot of sail handling to do on all watches and several "All hands on deck" in the middle of the night. Next day, after trying to get our Lister to work but failing, we had to make the sad decision to bypass Mangereva. Oh depression. Come on, you guys, think if we were shipwrecked at Mangereva we would be instantly in paradise, seeing as how there are ten women to one man. It is the island of your dreams, but no, we sailed for Tahiti and I mean sailed. We had no engines, no electricity, and we had to rely on fluky winds to navigate the Tuamotus (*tua* means danger, *motu* means islands), a group of low atolls. Some have no people living on them. But wait, aren't we going to Tahiti? Isn't that place supposed to be even better than Mangereva? Well, what are we waiting for? Depression gone, excitement back, alright.

Skipper ordered the bulwarks to be chipped, scraped, and repainted. Man, was I happy to be on the 4 to 8, we don't have to sit there in the heat of the day and beat the bullworks constantly with chipping hammers. We left that to the 8 to 12 and the 12 to 4. Hardy har har. My joy is short-lived because the noise created by the watch mates was so loud with no place aboard to escape it that I finally got a hammer and joined in. The job took a week. Wham, bang, carumptf, slat, creak for the next two days, absolutely becalmed, is all we heard and made no headway. Bored to death and sick of slatting and banging. Little did we know that later in our journey we would be forced to put up with twelve days of this in the Coral Sea. The wind freshened on our watch and it was pure pleasure to be moving again, even though with tear-soaked eyes we watched Mangereva go by on our port side and slowly disappear off our stern. Good-bye, all you brown-skinned, hula-skirted ladies of Mangereva. It is truly sinful that we could not stop even just to say hello. Just to get even with us, I think the ladies cast an evil spell on our upper topsail and it shredded itself right before our eyes. Just for that, we will be consoled by the ladies of Tahiti and they are pulling on the line. 120 miles noon to noon, not the best but instead of 850 miles to go we only have 730 miles to paradise. From dead calm to raging storm, rain, lightning and all, I lay awake in my bunk awaiting the frantic call "All hands on deck," but it never came and I drifted off to sleep with the moan of the gale in the rigging in my ears, only to be poked in the shoulder. The mate was telling me it is 3:30 a.m. and to make ready for your watch.

I was proud to be on the 4 to 8 as Skipper recognized us as the best of the three watches, with 8 to 12 next and the 12 to 4 completely useless. I was in high hopes that some of these non-sailor types would leave us in peace in Tahiti, take their consuming lack of enthusiasm and go. I was not to be disappointed, although the effect it had was an unwelcome watch change at Rorotonga. Becalmed again, we took advantage of the time and went swimming. Earlier in the day Leo shot a big tiger shark. We fearlessly jumped off the bowsprit and started a game of water polo with an old rag. At least we had a fun day in spite of being dead in the water all day. Next day we paid for it as we were struck by a black squall and gale force winds. We wrestled in the forestaysle and Skipper ordered Gypsy and myself to the fore course yard to stand watch for the atoll of Tema Tangi. "Land ho!" says Gypsy. "Water color change dead ahead!" I holler. "Tack ship hard over the helm!" hollers the skipper. As we tacked around, I saw turquoise water and I was sure we were going to hit, but *Yankee* did her thing and we missed. A close miss in a place you don't want to be shipwrecked: uninhabited, no water, and off the shipping lanes. To this day, I don't think the crew on deck had any idea of how close we came. More squalls and sail changing the next day, at least it was cool from rain being with us all day. Fifteen days at sea that should only have been six.

Electra and Irving Johnson, the well-known previous owners of *Yankee*, made seven trips around the world—five of them on *Yankee*—and always had good winds, leaving Connecticut in November. I think our backers in Miami can be accused of poor planning. They neglected to supply us with what we needed and this would become a serious problem in the coming months when we reached the western South Pacific and the Coral Sea. We finished painting and Skipper and Gloria painted all the scuppers bright red. I must say *Yankee* looked real spiffy. As if a compliment from King Neptune, the wind picked up and we went bowling at 9 knots, and for the first time during our bedraggled slow passage from Pitcairn we were again in high spirits.

November 14. 4 to 8 watch and I could smell Tiare Tahiti, gardenias famous for the smell of Tahiti. My heart was racing at daybreak. Mirve on the helm said, "Bilge, look at the horizon, do you see what I see?" I focused where Mirve was pointing and after a while I saw, high in the sky, a faint outline of a high mountain. The commotion we were making brought everyone on deck and they chimed in with yells of joy. We sailed all day and night and made our final tack in the channel between the island of Moorea on our port and Tahiti on the starboard. We rounded out for the approach to the channel, and shortly we were tied up to the dock in the town of Papeete. The sweet smell of Tahiti filled our nostrils, the sound of Polynesian music penetrated our ears. We were in paradise and a paradise it proved to be.

Skipper contemplating near miss

Sunset

"All hands aloft to set squares"

Women of Tahiti pulling on the line

7

O' Tahiti
Paradise Found

November 15. Tied to the customs dock, we impatiently waited for our clearance. When the French gendarmes and customs people found out that we had been 98 days at sea, only on basically uninhabited, thirst-producing dry islands, and that we—with the exception of old man Chaulker, were young sailors bursting with lust, er, I mean enthusiasm, to go ashore, sped up the procedure as fast as they could, but then informed us we needed to tie up stern first to the commercial quay. We maneuvered *Yankee* stern first, dropping our anchor as we backed in and tied two hawsers port and starboard to two samson posts ashore.

The 110-foot wooden schooner tied up next to us belonged to Sterling Hayden, captained by Omar Dar. She was *The Wanderer*, and the movie star Hayden had kidnapped his children from his hated ex-wife in Hollywood and was hiding them here in Tahiti. Ah, the adventure had just begun.

Bursting at the seams, awaiting Skipper's permission to go ashore, a big sigh escaped from all of us when Skipper assembled us on the stern for a talk from Doc. "Come on, Doc, make it fast," says I. So for the next painful ten minutes, Doc told us all about how to avoid venereal diseases, and was really enjoying himself with detail. (The funniest part of this was that we later found out Doc was the only one who got one of those diseases.) Skipper said, "O" and we tore down the gangplank so fast we never heard the "K" part. Papeete is a bustling small town, complete with open-air buses and Vespa motor scooters, most topped with beautiful, dark-skinned *vahines*, which means women, with flowers behind their ears and dressed in a *pareu*—a one-piece cloth skirt wrapped around their thin waists. Glancing over at us as we raced for Quinn's Bar, they flashed sparkling smiles at us. Little did we know then that the women of Tahiti made dates with the guys and always got what they wanted.

The undulating tones of a steel guitar weaving its way through a lively Tahitian song drifted out of the famous Quinn's Bar, a place of legend which Sadie Thompson called home, where many South Sea legends were made, where Gaugin was a household word, and Leeteg (the father of modern velvet painting) was a brother to all. We stepped inside and our Tahitian party and adventure began in earnest. Besides the sailors like us, seated everywhere and dancing to the music were astoundingly beautiful girls. Not a rowdy place, everybody just having fun.

We were instantly surrounded by these lovely creatures wanting us to dance with them. Of course, we could not refuse. We definitely did not want to hurt their feelings.

I fell in with Black Black (Juliet), Suzy (to be nicknamed by me 'Suzy No Pants', and the name stuck), Angel, Vaima, Antoinette, Moia, Maria, and a transvestite known as Tané Amu, dressed like a woman and very beautiful. I didn't know for two days that Tané was a man. I found out in 2009 that Black Black and Suzy No Pants are still alive and kicking in Papeete.

Yankee entering Papeete Pass

Fare (faray)—name for house or hut

My newly acquired harem, including the friendly Tané, fed me drinks until I could not stand anymore, at which Black Black looked at me with a fierce look and said, "Fin'e you pig all over you go ship sleep when you no pig all over you come back what's a matter you capitain?"

After 75 days with nothing to drink, it didn't take long for me to get in that condition, so with my tail between my legs I went back aboard *Yankee* and vowed never to get in that condition again. Passed out. Later, maybe four hours and late afternoon, I awoke to the feeling that somebody was sitting next to me on the bench next to my bunk. I turned over and to my delight saw lovely Black Black and Suzy No Pants. Black Black smiled and asked, "You no pig all over?" I said I felt much better and she replied, "Goo you come me and Suzy we have much fun now." I was charmed. I found out later that this was a custom that the girls would take up with a newly arrived sailor and make him drunk and let him sleep it off to get it out of his system. I am really beginning to love the way these people think. Well, we really had fun and it lasted every minute of our stay.

I will tell the story of sweet Suzy and how she got her name, Suzy No Pants. I was a young sailorman and doing what all sailormen have done when finally reaching the shores of the paradise known as Tahiti. It has been done by every sailor since Captain Cook stepped ashore in the 18th century. The Tahitians are known to be the friendliest, most charming, and most hospitable people in the world. And probably the cleanest: they bathe two or three times a day. They greeted any newcomers with open arms, like every Polynesian native on every island in Polynesia. They were known for their generosity and hospitality anywhere you go. I hope it has stood the test of time.

So, Suzy's story. In one corner of Quinn's is a door that leads to the communal bathroom, known as 'the wall.' No privacy. Just a wall with a continuous stream of water where men and women alike relieve themselves of used booze. There is no place for the other function, and being a good Tahitian means going someplace that also has a shower so they can wash all over. If not, "you pig all over." Well, as we were laughing and dancing and having a great time, I noticed that Suzy was getting very drunk and could hardly keep her head up. She disappeared into 'the wall' and after a while I became concerned. I went in to see if she was all right. Well, there was Suzy sound asleep in the corner, her *pareu* nowhere in sight. She had nothing on from the chest down. I got Black Black's attention and she said, "Pu her on shoulder we take her bed she pig all over."

So, following orders, I picked Suzy up and flung her over my shoulder and started out the door with her bare bottom for everybody to see. When I entered the dance hall, the band broke into a loud and lively song and everybody began to cheer. We were definitely a big hit at Quinn's. The bandleader got on the mike and said, "Where you go with big fish, Captain?" I hollered back and said, "I got to take Suzy No pants home!" The bar broke into hilarious laughter and Black Black fell to the floor in uncontrollable laughter.

We got Suzy home just around the corner and tucked her in bed and went back to Quinn's where everybody bought me drinks until Black Black informed me, "You pig all over," but this time she escorted me to the ship, giggling all the way, and tucked me in bed. As she left, she said, "I see you tomorrow rover boy." Wow. What a great first night in paradise. It never let up our entire stay and we made many great friends. Suzy forevermore was known by everybody as Suzy No Pants.

Next day, Leo and I rented two Vespa scooters and went for a ride out of town. There was only one narrow road that went completely around the island, with the exception of a cut-off dirt road at the southeast end of Tahiti. It leads to Tahiti Iti (Little Tahiti) and ends at a real old wooden mansion that any movie about the South Seas would drool to use. And it actually has been used several times. The property is home to Pepe, his wife, and six lovely daughters and all their friends. If you happen to go there, you will become an honored houseguest. Plan to be there for two to three days, whether you want to or not. The family's hospitality is unlike anywhere in the world. They always have a pig cooking underground and the table has food of every description ready to eat all day and well past midnight. Guitars, singing, dancing, and drinks are the name of the game for this marvelous family. It is set in the jungle at the base of a tall volcanic mountain and faces the lagoon with waters that are always calm. Diving in these crystal-clear waters (visibility 120 feet) with coral reefs everywhere is to experience millions of unmolested fish of every kind busily moving and doing their fish thing. Pepe has all the diving equipment you could need. Pepe's family go back to royalty and is a highly-respected family, famous all over Tahiti.

After our charming visit with Pepe, we headed back towards Papeete, but did not quite make it as we stumbled across Bel Aire at Faa about three miles before we got there. Bel Aire is a group of grass huts situated on Faa lagoon inside the barrier reef, where huge breakers boom and hiss all day long. For $3.50 a day, Leo and I based here for our stay in Tahiti. We moved our clothes and diving equipment to our grass hut, or *fare*, and made many dives. Every evening we rode our Vespas to town for great late evening fun with our local friends.

Tahiti is a great and high extinct volcano whose caldera has filled with sparkling, clear, fresh water loaded with fresh water eels that have big fins just behind their heads. The eel is known locally as ear fish and their fins do look like ears. They are very curious and friendly and, for some reason they remain unmolested. Maybe they don't taste good. We never had the chance to find out. The main mountain is Aori, and that is where the lake is. We never actually saw it because it is a two-day hike through dense jungles and very steep ridge-like slopes through dense fern forests. It rains constantly once above 2,500 feet altitude. The mountain peak and caldera lake are 7,000 feet above sea level. Since we carried no warm clothes, we didn't go. Besides, the diving and nightlife was not only fun, but comfortable and warm.

Venus point

War canoes

We all knew that Skipper and Gloria were going to get married and that they were having lots of trouble with the French officials, so on November 19 they left for Hawaii.

For six days we were jumping for joy, celebrating an extra six days in paradise. We all had the same feeling about what it would be like with Skipper and his former-crewmember-turned-wife Gloria on board *Yankee*. Our feelings for the most part were very negative. We did not know then how right we were. In the meantime, we intended to enjoy Tahiti to the max and that is what we did. Every night we enjoyed spending at Quinn's or Vaima's. Due to some French ordinance, Quinn's and all other establishments had to close down at midnight, at which time the open-air buses were waiting to take us out to Lafayette's, which stayed open until 3:00 or 4:00 a.m.

One day we loaded our diving gear on board an open-air bus and headed for Venus Point with the intention of diving the big lagoon at that location. We made arrangements with a local native to take us out to a dive site of our choice. We gave him instructions to wait right there until we came up one-and-a-quarter hours later. We dropped down in crystal-clear water to 120 feet to the face of a reef to a white sand bottom. I glanced up and noticed quite an unusual number of sharks milling around between the bottom and the surface. I pointed it out to Doc and Leo and they gave me the OK sign. We continued our underwater glide along the base of this beautiful reef. As usual, thousands of fish were busily going about their routines, darting in and out of the reef, chasing each other around in circles at amazing speeds, all brightly-colored and representing every part of the spectrum, and every size from tiny to the big groupers and giant jewfish to the silver bullet bodies and fanged mouths of a group of barracudas sitting perfectly still in perfect formation, observing the goings on and waiting for the perfect moment to snatch a good meal. Also included on just about every dive were one or two sharks, slowly flying their aerodynamically designed bodies effortlessly through the blue depths.

We planned to spend ten minutes at depth and then begin a gentle climb, or ascent, up the face of the reef to take up the next hour of our dive, to reach the surface so as to not exceed our 'no decompression limits.' At ten minutes, I signaled the others to begin the ascent. I looked up and my heart stopped as I realized that I was looking at a curtain of silvery bubbles, which were coming from us, disappearing through an overcast of sharks right where we needed to go. The last time I had looked up I had seen about ten or twelve sharks, but this time there were more like 150 or 200, all milling around each other. I knew instantly that there was no feeding frenzy going on. They were not agitated in the slightest so I guessed that it might be a breeding thing, which turned out to be right. Not knowing how territorial sharks are, we decided not to tempt an ascent through the pack. There were some real monsters among a majority of smaller sharks. We all know that if we stayed with the reef it would lead us to a small island, but we still had to ascend with the rising bottom and pass through a level that was filled with sharks. As we approached that level, the sharks were looking at us with expressionless eyes, their mouths displaying meat-ripping teeth and opening and closing as they breathed. They politely moved aside and let us pass. As we did so, I realized that my heart was beating very hard and hoped our friends could not hear that. Later, on shore at the little island, Doc and Leo confirmed that their hearts were beating just as hard. Wow. What an adventure. Thank you, old denizens of the deep, for allowing us to join your tribe and learn something of your wild ways.

"Where in hell is our boat?" I asked. Well, okay, maybe our man decided to go ashore while we were diving and drink a few Hinano beers and simply abandoned us to our fate. But he was watching for us and soon he saw us waving from the island and motored out to pick us up. We couldn't get too mad at him as he brought six ice cold Hinanos for us. Since we decided to cancel our diving activities for the day, we drank the beer and arrived ashore at Venus Point, all laughing and grinning and enjoying our own company and that of this large friendly *tane* (man). We all wound up at Lafayette's until closing time.

Skipper returned from Hawaii a married man, like it or not. We arranged to have a pig and other food cooked underground in the traditional Tahitian manner. As well, we had the lead dancers from the Marlon Brando film *Mutiny on the Bounty* for Skipper's homecoming. In Hawaii they call this a *hukilau*, in Tahiti it is called a *tamaraa* and the accompanying dances are *tamure*. The lead dancer was not only beautiful but danced in the most suggestive way, all the time smiling at me and never looking away. I was in love. She danced up to me, put my hands on her hips, and although I could see no movement, I could feel her vibrating as the drums beat out the old Polynesian rhythms. Under a star-filled sky, the moon lighting the tops of coconut palms, I thought this is what it is all about, this is the personification of true Polynesia and I am here.

The LeTruk family came with their four daughters, Antonina, Elaine, Jacqueline, and Moya—four lovely Tahitian girls full of smiles and friendliness, and also full of teenage beans. Most charming. Little Jacqueline we called Ricky Nelson because she entertained us all with Ricky Nelson songs with a definite Polynesian flavor for the rest of the night. We became good friends of the family and the girls hung out with us all the rest of our stay. The evening over, Skipper and new wife Gloria left. I hope they had a good time. I was preoccupied almost all evening with one fantasy after another, hopelessly taken by the charm of Tahiti. I heard through the grapevine that another non-sailor in Sam's group was leaving. I felt the deck work would be a little safer. She will be out of harm's way. *Hari maruu*, have a good trip home.

There was a wreck just offshore in front of my *fare*. Leo and I went out to look at it. As a wreck, it wasn't much of a dive site. The French mine sweep had gone aground and sank bow first, with most of her stern sticking high out of the water. The depth at the bow was maybe eighteen or nineteen feet. Her stern rested on a big coral head and there was a little room between her keel and the sand, just enough so a diver could get him or herself in a lot of trouble, either by getting the tank or airlines hung up or if the old vessel decided to shift and slide off the coral head. A crushing thought to say the least.

Cooking underground Tahitian style

Cooking underground Tahitian style

Anyway, Leo and I cancelled the thought of exploring the old wreck in favor of deeper coral reefs further out. I therefore was surprised when I saw Guy, Little Gloria, and Chris about to dive this same wreck. Guy mentioned to me later that it was the deepest he had ever been since his training. Eighteen feet?! And that he took Chris the first time under? Little Gloria had a cold and could not clear her ears. The chief pilot does look after fools. I wonder if good ol' Guy ever increased his novice skills later as I did. I hold seventeen underwater licenses, Dive Master being the most advanced. I have done many, many dives: reefs, ships, night, cold water, warm water. I shudder to think of some of the dumb things I did as a novice. It is the most unforgiving atmosphere and if you don't learn fast, you die. I hope Guy did grow with his diving.

Guy's wreck

Sunset on Guy's wreck

The Tahitian language is such a beautiful and almost musical language. I naturally learned as much as I could and though not in any way fluent, I can make myself understood a little. The first thing I learned that was a big help to me—besides *iorana*, hello, or *hare maru*, good-bye—was *"eha te eroa a Tahiti?"* or "How do you say this in Tahitian?" The people really love it when you can say something in their native language. If you say something in French, they usually ignore you even though they are governed by France. Most Tahitians don't like it. You say something in Tahitian, and they are all smiles and open their hearts to you.

The days and nights melted into each other and one day it was announced to us that we would leave the next day, December 1st. We were all down and feeling that we did not want to leave Tahiti and all the wonderful ladies and some gentlemen we had the good fortune of knowing. That's when the good ol' Lister generator and the wonderful freezer broke down. *Ouay tata ouay maitai roa ouay!* Hip hip hooray! in other words. Guy, Harvey, and a couple of other men took the inner island ferry over to Moorea and waited for us there. Our good luck lasted for another eight days.

Tahiti was also to work her magic on Guy. He began to get over his uptight ways, much to the delight of the rest of us. Guy and the others came back a few days later and the story of his return and first night back is worth mentioning. It was to turn Guy completely around.

Guy met a beautiful Tahitian girl, Melanie, or as the natives pronounced it, Merany. She brought him home to her parents for dinner and, to his complete surprise, asked him to stay the night with her, Mom and Dad giggling with delight. When Guy returned for our departure, he was a delightfully changed man. All the tensions between us evaporated into thin air and I think Guy, pleasantly surprised, found we accepted his friendship with no mention of past tensions. Welcome aboard, Guyster.

One last event before our tearful departure at Faa, where the new airport was still under construction (something we knew would ruin our paradise). In the lagoon sat a beautiful 'Shorts Sandringham, a big four-engine flying boat operated by R.A.I. (Riataian Avion Internacional). (Little did I know that when I returned to Tahiti after becoming a commercial pilot, I would be granted the opportunity to fly this beautiful seaplane. I also learned that you can only take paradise for so long before you become completely 'rock happy,' and I was only too glad to leave paradise, never to return again. My next flying assignment was to be to Germany. Talk about culture shock.)

The day finally arrived and the shore behind *Yankee* was crowded with all of our friends: Vaima, Angel, Black Black, Suzy No Pants, Moia, Jacqueline, Elaine, Merany, and many more. I have tears in my eyes as I write this, as I did then. I called out, *"Haera maru ua here vau ia oe. Ma nau nau noa vau. Et e po et e au mauee tau mafatu."* "Good-bye and I love all. I will think of you night and day. Oh my aching heart!" That's when they all broke into the song *A Maruru a Vau'a Maruru Oe*. Tears rolled down their cheeks as they sang the song of departure and we slipped our hawsers and slowly drifted towards the pass, bound for Michener's "Bali Ha'i"—Moorea. They sang until we could no longer hear them, the green mountains of Tahiti slowly diminishing in size as we split the blue seas, our bowsprit pointing at Moorea. I will never forget you, Tahiti. You certainly lived up to your name 'Paradise of the South Seas.' I am blessed to this day to have known Tahiti when she was still in the 19th century.

Moorea framed by palms

Moea's guitar

We drifted to the pass from Papeete and inched our way to the open sea and the Tahiti Straits, a body of water between Tahiti and Moorea eleven miles wide. As we entered the straits, the wind died completely so we started both iron mainsails and made like a stinkpot and began motoring for Moorea and Pao Pao Bay. We had two 6-71 diesels that at 1,500 rpm burned copious amounts of fuel, were very noisy, were great in the chilly climate between Panama and Galapagos but in the tropics they turned the main cabin into a sweatbox. For all the negative aspects of our engines, it added one more negative for all the heat, smell, and noise. They pushed *Yankee* ahead at a mind-bending pace of an astounding 3.5 knots, or about four miles per hour. I think I could swim faster, and could definitely walk faster. Man, I do love the wind.

We left Tahiti late in the afternoon and at our galloping pace we should arrive off the entrance of Pao Pao Bay—or fjord, as it properly is—an intensely beautiful place with tall, steep, green cliffs all the way around, sometime after dark. "Hey, Leo, isn't that when the evening storms usually hit?" "I think so," he replied. We arrived right on schedule, and so did the storm. It was an intense devil with loads of wind. So windy it drove us back out to sea. "All hands on deck!" says I. We crashed into each other in the dark, frantically laying off sheets and halyards, and making them ready to run. We had two greenhorns on board, Bert and Lisa, who were riding with us to Moorea. We were slapping rope ends in their hands and telling them to pull when told to and let go when told to and, even though confused, they both did a great job. I was surprised when somebody said that they had done what many of the regulars on the ship had not yet accomplished and learned the ropes in two days. They learned the ropes? Hell, they just stood there and took hold of the ropes we gave them, and they followed orders. In defense there really were a few regulars that you definitely could not rely on. But not many. We set a couple of storm stays and let *Yankee* lay to for the night. As usual, our tempest was short-lived and in a short time the stars were out and the night was balmy and brightly starlit.

The next day we made the cut to Pao Pao, a one-and-a-half mile long, narrow fjord and bay with crystal-clear, deep blue water all the way to the end. We dropped anchor and felt very secure surrounded by high cliffs, storm-proof and protected. Just a short launch ride to the 'One Chicken Inn,' owned and operated by this craggy, toothless, Chinese-Polynesian character who we immediately fell in love with. When asked what was on the menu, he broke into a wide, toothless grin and cackling laugh, and pointed to his sign, saying, "*Rots o Hinano too*," chicken for breakfast, lunch, and dinner, true to the name of his place. But I am getting ahead of our story. Skipper announced the resuming of port watches and appointed Mirve for port watch, who was visibly pissed. I said, "Mirve, are you getting paid?" "No," he answered. "Are we in a protected harbor?" "Yes." "Then load up and come ashore with us." "OK."

Guy stepped in and graciously offered, "I have been here, so you guys go ahead and I will stand the watch." By his generous offer, he diplomatically avoided a confrontation with Skipper. "Thanks, Guyster, you are a good chap," said Mirve. So, off we went. Later, we found out that Skipper reprimanded Guy very harshly. What the hell, Skipper? We are here as unpaid crew and to learn sailing and have a great time exploring islands and ports. We never have been or are we ever going to be a commercially-paid ship or crew. The rift between crew and Skipper and Gloria began right then at Pao Pao and continued for the rest of the trip. Leo, the rest of the guys, and I continued to enjoy ourselves in spite of this new development. We all understood port watches in an unprotected area but not in any area like this or tied to a dock in a harbor.

We went ashore about 9:30 or 10:00 a.m. just as rain clouds moved in and obscured the mountains shortly thereafter. It started to rain. Iggy, Leo, and I wound up, after hiking through the now heavy rain, taking shelter under an awning attached to a very large and expensive home on the shore and surrounded by the beautiful green jungle of Pao Pao Bay. Shortly, a portly *huahine*, a Tahitian term for an older *vahine*, motioned us to come in and stay until the rain was gone. We all wondered whose home we were in. The large table and larger room we were in turned out to be part of the famous artist Leeteg's mansion the 'Villa Velour.' In 1953 Leeteg was killed on a Vespa motor scooter when returning from a drunken spree at Lafayette's in Papeete. He was famous for his bright drawings of Polynesia and its women, among other scenes, painted on black velvet. His paintings caught on in the U.S. and Leeteg was destined to become very rich.

Our beautiful *huahine* hostess came in with delicious escargot—cooked snails—and some marvelous *poisson crue*, raw fish marinated in lime juice. Wow, We hit the jackpot. Our wonderful hostess also supplied ice-cold Hinano beer and played the guitar and was joined by some of her friends. So we drank beer and sang and danced all afternoon. We listened to exciting and hilarious stories about Leeteg and laughed until our sides hurt. I felt he was in the room himself, grinning down from his own paradise and enjoying the afternoon with us all. Thank you, Leeteg, for the wonderful hospitality. Your painting is still a thing of wild beauty, as you were yourself. I would dearly loved to have met you in person.

The clouds parted late in the afternoon and revealed the awesome beauty of Pao Pao with her steep green ridges and the sparkling white ship called *Yankee* anchored peacefully at the end of the fjord.

The three of us were properly laced to the gills and made our way to the One Chicken Inn and more celebrating. We found Guy and some other crew also well into their celebration amongst a group of local Mooreans. They all decided to get aboard an open-air bus and go out to another spot. Iggy, Leo, and I were enjoying the company of our Chinese-Tahitian friend and decided to stay there. We drank copious amounts of Hinano, sang, and danced with some locals until the wee hours of the morning.

Finally, when I told my companions that I didn't think the launch was running shore duty anymore, our host volunteered his outrigger canoe for us to paddle out to *Yankee*.

We found the outrigger on the beach and piled in for the short paddle to the ship. We started to paddle and in our blind state it seemed that *Yankee* was getting no closer. We paddled harder. I was getting really sweaty and tired so Leo took over until he couldn't stand it any longer. Still, blurry-looking *Yankee* was no closer. Iggy dug in, condemning Leo and my ability at paddling a canoe. Soon Iggy was breathing hard and sweating, and *Yankee* was still there and no closer. Just then, Iggy said, "Hey, fellash. Look." He was pointing behind us. We looked, and sure enough there was a chain around the tree the canoe was next to and it led right to our stern, where it was still attached. We broke into uncontrollable laughter and almost flipped the canoe. We bedded down on the sandy beach and fell fast asleep until morning arrived.

Next morning we made it back to the ship and had our usual bland breakfast. Leo, Iggy, and I caught the first launch to shore. Jim1 was given the day port watch but he made a deal with Chris (CB 'Bulldog' Pace) to cover for him. We got to shore and Guy and some others decided to sail, or motor, around the point at Pao Pao to the neighboring fjord called Papatoi Bay. As it turned out, I wish we would have gotten our dive equipment and followed them as I heard later that the reef diving at Papatoi was spectacular. As Guy, Jim1, and the others were getting ready to depart, we noticed the ship's launch heading for shore at full throttle, with only the skipper on board. Uh oh, this can't be good. Skipper hit the shore in a rage and demanded Jim1 return to the ship and stand his day watch. "What the hell, does he think we are his paid crew?" says I to Leo. Leo just shook his head as did Iggy. "If I were Jim1, I'd tell Skipper to go to hell," says I. "I mean, after all what's Skipper going to do, keel haul you?" Jim1 went back to the ship.

We were all trying to figure out this startling and negative change in our once gung-ho skipper, and we started to put two and two together. It added up to Skipper's wife, Gloria. How right we turned out to be. Skipper always was a loner and a free man. Now he had an equal, or even superior, partner who seemed to be infected with control and power and considered herself equally in command of *Yankee* and her crew. Not a good sign. The storm was freshening. As a result, Skipper posted a notice that if you want to swap port watches you had to get the 'OK' either from John the mate or Skipper.

We spent most of the day hiking around in the enchanting jungles at Pao Pao Bay and hanging out at One Chicken Inn. We were scheduled to leave that afternoon and at the scheduled time, the launch came to pick us up. There was a port official who had to come out to sign papers for our departure. Dave, the assistant cook, stayed ashore and we would have to return with the port official and bring Dave back to the ship. As we started for *Yankee*, we noticed the anchors were up and *Yankee* was moving towards the inlet and the reef. Outside the reef there were pretty big comers rolling in and exploding on either side of the pass. We finally made *Yankee* and climbed aboard. It took some time for the paperwork to be cleared and all the time we were getting closer to the pass and the launch had not started back with the official to pick up Dave. The paperwork finally done, the launch began its now long haul back to shore, all the while we were heading towards the pass and the open sea. This was not a safe situation. I mentioned something to Skipper about maybe coming to a stop and waiting. He growled, "When I say departure is at 4:00 p.m., that is what I mean." I felt like saying you mean when Gloria says it. Instead, I said, "Are we on some kind of schedule?" He growled something in return. Hell, Skipper, this whole thing wasn't our fault. You should have gotten the official out to do the paperwork at 3:00 p.m., I was thinking.

Jim1 and Dave finally made the ship as we were entering the pass. We hooked the boat hauls to the launch and had to scramble to get the launch on deck and secured. This is how good sailors get hurt or even killed. The whole crew, including Guy, wondered what the Skipper's inflexibility was all about. Once out of the cut, we raised sail and pointed our bowsprit towards Bora Bora, about 150 miles to the northwest. The wind died for about two hours and then picked up slightly and set *Yankee* on a ghosting and gentle ride through the rolling blue sea.

December 12. Skipper called for watch change. I was now on the 8 to 12, and the only good thing about it was that Leo was the mate of the watch. On the 8 to 12 you come up for your watch at 8:00 a.m. when the sun is already up and the day is getting hotter by the hour. At 12:00 noon you are off until 8:00 p.m. and the sun has already set. The 4 to 8 is still in my mind the privileged watch and I missed it dearly. I stood my first 8 p.m. to 12 a.m. that evening and Leo, being my buddy, put me on the first wheel trick, 8:00 to 9:00, and then bow lookout 9:00 to 10:00. Unless there was sail handling to do, I would spend the next two hours lying in the emergency raft atop the lazaret, aft of the helm, and watch the universe or even drift off to sleep. Nobody on land has any idea what the universe really looks like. Only at sea at night with no moon can you really see it. A privilege, to say the least. The universe can be seen three-dimensionally and in depth: you can see the different colors in the stars and when a meteorite tears through the atmosphere and explodes, it puts Fourth of July fireworks to shame. I have seen meteorites in bright red, loud yellow, deep blue, and startling white, and it's always a joy when one startles you with its fast and unexpected appearance—especially when they explode.

There are some advantages to the 8:00 p.m. portion of the 8 to 12. Not so on the a.m. portion because you have a one-hour wheel trick and a three-hour work period. Again, Leo, being my pal, put me on the helm from 11:00-12:00, which is a hot time on any tropical day, but it beats sweating it in the heat on some always-to-be-done job on board a sailing ship.

The further northwest by west we went, the hotter the days got as the influence of the Humboldt Current receded further south mile by mile. Guy had really learned to appreciate the crew he had on his 4 to 8 watch (that was us) because he became heir to the former 12 to 4 watch and about 90 percent of that crew could care less about rigging lines or sails. Consequently, the call for "All hands on deck" came more often while the 4 to 8 was on duty and there needed to be sail handling because of the 'slackers' on that watch. We all had to cover for those who weren't of a sailor's mind. Alas, I didn't hear anybody from that watch complaining.

Yankee continued on her course at an easy pace of 3.5 to 4 knots, gently rolling and creaking her rig's symphony. Later in the day we brought up and slowly passed the islands of Huahine and Raiatea. Our progress was moderate, as these islands are only 30 miles to the south of Bora Bora. We ended up making 120 miles in 24 hours, not too bad for the old ship on wind power alone.

December 13. We entered the pass around noon. The island of Bora Bora is without a doubt the most beautiful of the Polynesian Islands. From the pass leading to the lagoon you look straight on to two 1,000-foot high magmatic upheavals, one very flat on top and the other with a rounded top, one end higher than the other. The cliffs are bare and grey as they are so steep that very few plants can grow or cling to them. The cliffs rise from the deep green jungle of coconut palms that lead to a brilliant white line of beach surrounded by sparkling turquoise clear water and ending where we were in deep blue water. About halfway into the lagoon, a powerful speedboat came roaring out to meet us. It was Jim Kelly, the owner of the Tiare Tahiti Hotel (that's what Guy called it but I remember it as the Bali Hai Hotel). Jim pulled up alongside and handed myself, Leo, and the others cans of Hinano beer that was so cold that when you opened them the foam that came out would freeze on contact with the warm air. In spite of the dry ship policy imposed by Skipper, we really enjoyed downing our Hinanos and disregarded the cold stares from Skipper.

We told Jim to book us in for two nights as we were going to leave in just two days. Leo and I grabbed our diving gear and planned to spend the next two days diving the crystal waters and reefs of Bora Bora. The nightlife on Bora Bora was as good as Tahiti, we were told. We never found out because there was a very large group of local dance *vahines* practicing for the maiden arrival of the huge Matson Lines steamer *Mariposa*. Our wild evenings were there in our backyard.

That afternoon we made several dives and I had my second experience with the extremely intelligent and friendly octopus. On one of our dives, I came across an octopus peeking out of a crevice in the reef. I had a bag full of cut fish and offered him one in my hand. At first, he was very timid but pretty soon he crawled onto my hand and took the fish, eating it with his parrot-like beak, all the time watching me with his big octopus eyes. I guess he decided I was all right and proceeded to expertly open the bag and feast on the rest of the fish. He stayed with me for the rest of the dive until we went by his crevice and he departed. A couple of hours later, we repeated our dive with a bag of fresh fish. When we were about twenty feet from the crevice, all of a sudden this bullet with eight legs in trail came right at me at very high speed and displayed great pleasure at my return. ol' 'Ocky' feasted again. Every dive we made after that, even in different areas, Ocky would show up and ride on me. Ocky, you eight-legged wonder of the deep, thanks for educating me and allowing me into your world. Most people, unknowing people, think you are some kind of monster. You showed me the exact opposite and it was a pleasure getting to know you. I will always feel friendly towards octopi, thanks to Ocky of Bora Bora.

When we got up the next morning we ran into a very glum Guy. "What's up, Guy?" I asked. It turns out that it was Harvey's turn for port watch but he had already made plans to do some things so Guy graciously told him that he would stand his watch. Guy asked John the mate who okayed it. Well, when Skipper found out, he had another one of his now famous explosions and I heard that Guy and Skipper had quite a row. Guy was mad because the written order said mate *or* Skipper, and guy could not understand Skipper's tirade. "Something ain't right in la-la land," says I. Well, we ate breakfast and about six of us agreed that the crew—the sailors among the crew—had to under any circumstances stick together. This policy we adopted was to pay off later in Pago Pago (pronounced Pango Pango), the capital of American Samoa. For the rest of the day, Leo, Iggy, and I hiked into the small village of Vaitape, a real South Pacific town that time had not yet caught up with. The beautiful Polynesian *vahines* with their light brown skin and sparkling long black hair passed us by, all of them with stunning smiles on their faces. Man, these Polynesian people are the best. Even the men would come over just to say hello, *iorana oe*. Leo and I decided to get one more dive in before returning to the ship for a 4:00 p.m. departure. Guy was given port watch and basically never got ashore at Bora Bora. When we came aboard, Guy told us that he had gone to Skipper and said he would like to change watch with Harvey and Skipper growled that he was sick and tired of watch changes and refused Guy, at which point there was another row. I guess Guy was no longer the captain's pet. Actually, it was probably a good thing because it brought all of us closer together.

We set sail at 4:00 p.m. on December 14 and tacked *Yankee* twice as we sailed a big circle around the lagoon. We really must have been a sight to the hundreds of people on shore waving good-bye. As we tacked about the second time and fell off on a heading for the range markers that would put us into the cut and the open sea, the wind fell aft and we went aloft and unfurled our square sails. A real square rigger under full sail outbound from the most beautiful island in the South Pacific. Talk about emotional.

As we passed the reef entrance, *Yankee* began to gently rise and fall to the rhythm of the sea. It actually felt good to be at sea again. We were basically on course for our next port, Roratonga, 500 miles off the bowsprit. With tears in our eyes, we bade farewell to French Polynesia and with adventure in our hearts and high hopes we tried to guess what British Polynesia was going to be like. We weren't disappointed. We made 130 miles a day for the next two days and we estimated a four-and-a-half day run to Roratonga.

The second day out we bent on a new main sail, not a small task, to say the least, as the sail itself was 1,200 square feet of very heavy canvas. We then bent on our fisherman stay sail to replace the old one, which was about used up. Another tough job. Sailing ships are never ready for sea and must be constantly worked on. Between watches, I decided to climb aloft on the foremast and go above the lower topsail yard to the upper topsail yard, where I planned to perch myself and enjoy the view of *Yankee* plowing through the blue sea from the highest point on the ship. I was about three-quarters of the way up when *Yankee* took a hefty roll to starboard and my feet slipped off the rung. I wound up hanging by my hands 110 feet above the deck, my heart in my mouth and beating faster than Gene Krupa could play the drums. It seemed like years before *Yankee* came up and settled back to her port list and I could regain my footing. I quickly descended to the lower topsail yard and sat down holding on to some halyards for safety. Okay, King Neptune, lesson learned. Never go aloft alone. Always go with another shipmate. Hell, I hadn't even told anybody I was going aloft. I will never do that again.

Sitting on the yardarm, my heart still beating and my breathing still heavy, I couldn't help but totally enjoy the sight of *Yankee*'s trim hull slicing through the sparkling blue sea so gracefully by wind power alone. Everything about hull, decks, and deckhouses were in perfect order with no ornamentation whatsoever. Looking down on her from that height, the crewmembers on deck looked small and she looked in perfect ship order, nothing wasted.

We now had an unhappy crew as Gloria, Skipper's wife, had been relieved of all sea watch duties and worked during daylight hours on deck when she wanted to. This did not sit well with some of the crew. It didn't bother me that much, but I could see why there were objections to it by some members of the crew.

December 17. We arrived at Roratonga at night and hove to outside Avarva Harbor. We entered the pass and anchored just off the dock. Roratonga is also a high island with a central extinct volcano and thick jungles in the surrounding lowlands, as well as the usual forests of coconut palm trees along the coastline. Leo, Iggy, and the rest of us found this great old wooden hotel planted in the middle of the palm forest. I swear it was used in the 1930s movie 'Sadie Thompson of the South Seas.' We settled in and took a hike to town. On the way we noticed the wreck of a 19th century sailing vessel upon the reef. She appeared to be about 300 feet long. We found out she was *The Princess of Scotland* and was driven ashore by a typhoon in the late 1800s. Little did we know then as we explored her bones that *Yankee* would join her a couple of years later on her final cruise.

We continued our walk into the small village and down the road came four bicycles topped by four dark-skinned, shiny black-haired, beautiful *vahines* with sparkling wide smiles and dressed in *pareu* cloth tied around their thin waists. I hollered out, "*Ia orana oe*," hello, and they all stopped and said, "*Kiorana oe*," then "*Oe parou Tahiti?*" You speak Tahiti? "*E*," yes, I replied, "*Ma nau nau noa vau. Et e po et e au mauee tau mafatu.*" the same line I used in Tahiti and translates into a local joke. Screams of joy as they dropped their bikes and came laughing up to us. Our fears about British Polynesia were gone once and for all: the only difference between these lovely ladies and the French speaking Polynesians was that these people spoke English as well as Maori or Polynesian. Maori uses the letter 'K' more often than Tahitian, but basically the words are the same.

The girls asked us if we would take them to see the 'Johnny Frisbee Dancers' perform that night. Well, we certainly did not want to hurt their feelings and so enthusiastically agreed. We hadn't been ashore one hour and we were set. Leo told one of the girls that tomorrow was Bilge's birthday. They grabbed us by the arms and hurried us back to the Roratonga Hotel, where we were staying. It turned out that one of the girls was related to the owners, they were her Grampa and Grandma. She came back and told me not to worry, that there would be a big birthday for me. I love these people. *"Ou'a tata ou'a,"* says I, using a local expression of happiness. So we all met that evening to eat, then went to a big exhibition center. Johnny Frisbee was an outstandingly beautiful woman from the island of Puka Puka, just north of Roratonga. Her father, Robert Frisbee, was a real South Seas trader, hence the last name. Johnny is not an uncommon name for a woman in these parts. She formed a group of native dancers (old Polynesian style drums only) that are so perfect in their many different forms that they became world-famous, even performing before kings and queens, presidents, and heads of state all over the world. We were not to be disappointed.

As the drums—made of hollow bamboo with different sized slits cut into them—beat their very Polynesian rat-a-tat-tat beat, the men and women, dressed in lava lavas and traditional grass skirts, performed impossible movements, impossibly fast. For the next four hours, their magic wove itself into our deepest being. When it was over, I literally had a hard time coming to the reality that I was a white guy living in the 20th century and not a native on an island in the 15th century having just gone through some rite of passage to show the chief, talking chiefs, and fellow warriors that I was capable of joining the adults in the tribe. Wow, that was the greatest show I have ever seen and still is to this day. It was the beginning of my twenty-first birthday. Is there some kind of coincidence here? Well, my good people, my party was just starting at 12:00 midnight on the island paradise of Roratonga. We danced, drank, and laughed with many local people and didn't know any of them but for the time being we were all brothers and sisters. We partied until two hours after departure time, refusing to return to the ship until we were through at 18:30, or 6:30, in the evening. Skipper never said a thing. After all, we consisted of the only crew that could sail the ship. We were way too wasted to set sail so Skipper started our two iron main sails and motored the rest of the evening and we went below to sleep it off.

Next day some of the other crew said that Skipper should have left us. "Isn't it interesting that Skipper wouldn't wait in Moorea but didn't dare leave Roratonga without us? Think about it, people," I said. Revenge is so sweet if you have patience.

I awoke to the steady roar of the engines. "Oh, shit, turn those bloody things off.

Oh, what a head," I moaned. I came on watch and we were to change the big main sail again and replace the heavy canvas sail and bend on a much lighter Dacron sail. It was a tough job made tougher by the 'day-after' condition we were all in. After this job was done, we unbent and bent on another fisherman stay sail again. To this day, I wonder if Skipper was just getting even with us. After all, in spite of the situation, the old man definitely had a great sailor's sense of humor. I can tell you from experience that it is no fun if you happen to be on the wrong side of Skipper's humor.

Even though we all really wanted to go to Puka Puka Island, the islanders have rejected white man's ways and are very careful of who they allow on the island. I can't but admire them for their strong will. Consequently, they live in the old Polynesian lifestyle and reject fiercely any interference, especially the narrow and closed minds of missionaries. I would really have loved to meet these great people. Instead, we were bound for Palmerston Atoll, a 170-mile run. Palmerston is a small, very low atoll. I believe before the 1860s nobody lived there. In 1863, an old man of the sea named William Marsters settled this very remote island with three Polynesian women and proceeded to populate it. Apparently, the Marsters family have 2,000 members today, all with the Marsters surname. They live throughout the French Polynesian islands and when we arrived, there were about a hundred people, maybe even less. We had a young islander by the name of Joel Marsters sailing with us to get home by Christmas. The sail over was sort of a drift with little wind but we made it Christmas evening.

We had *Yankee* decorated belowdecks and had a really good Christmas dinner, thanks to Art the cook. We ate at about 16:00 and a launch from shore came out through the very narrow pass handled by a group of tough-looking natives who were obviously in the midst of Christmas celebrations. Hey, things are looking up.

We filed into the launch and made it to shore, where we met Amu, a huge Polynesian guy. I hoped his name (which means to eat in Tahitian) didn't indicate anything peculiar about him. Amu took us to the meeting hall where the party and residents of Palmerston were really getting it on. Ol' Amu started making long drunken speeches that went on all night about how happy he and the islanders were to have real Americans visiting their small atoll and how his people were very religious, or "werrrry relishoush" and that they only drank on Christmas, or "cherishtmash." "The holiest day of the year," said I. Now, you don't suppose ol' Amu was lying to us, do you?

One thing we all noticed was the total lack of women. You know the beautiful dark-skinned, thin, black-haired beauties with the big smiles that we had gotten so used to? Well, we saw the hair and the smiles directed at us but they were all men. "Hey, Leo, you feeling the way I am?" "Kind of weird?" said Leo. "Yeah, man," I said. So we slipped out and began walking around the island village in hopes we would chance upon some of the prettier of the species of Palmerston. Not to be. The women apparently were rated as second-class citizens and were put to bed and only show up when the cooking had to be done. Very un-Polynesian, to say the least.

Sunset at sea, bound for Palmerston Atoll from Roratonga

Palmerston party launch

Several young boys were walking with us and it became obvious that they were all trying to make time with us. So we sat them down and tried to explain to them the marvelous and wonderful differences between men and women. But that made no sense to them and they figured we were sexually inept so we let it lie at that. I was really beginning to miss Polynesia. As we bedded down in our own native hut we discussed the possibility of standing watches, just in case. Alas, we all woke up unmolested to a bright, sparkling South Pacific morning in the midst and shade of a tall palm forest. The rustling of the palm fronds is a familiar sound to all who have been on a low atoll anywhere. We had brought our fins, masks, and snorkels, so we cornered a few of the boys and asked them where we should do some diving. Well, the demeanor suddenly changed—joy, squeals, and smiles broke out as only true Polynesians can exhibit. The boys were very excited but first we went to the town gathering place—held up by timbers from the old ship—where we ate a breakfast of dried fish and a very tasteless vegetable that I still do not know what it was. This was all we got until dinner.

The young boys showed us their favorite diving spots and, as usual, it was awesome. We saw the biggest coral heads I had ever seen, all of them covered by thousands of busy fish of every color and description. The playing field was suddenly even. We spent a great morning with our new friends. I love diving. It is a world-wide language, like music, to all who dive.

The boys took us for a hike all the way around the island, which took all of one hour. Palmerston was like all atolls—blue ocean, white sand, thick palm tree forests, and very little else. A very beautiful place for a day or two and then extremely monotonous. I still cannot understand how you can be born, grow up, live, and die on so small a spit of sand, blue sea, and palm trees without going completely bonkers. I guess the only answer is you have to be born there to understand.

The men of Palmerston

Palmerston gathering place

Breakfast on Palmerston

Two lost headsails

December 26. That evening we set sail—actually motors—for Pago Pago in a dead calm. We had a marvelous sunset as if we were to have one last look at paradise: Polynesia. Samoa is Polynesian but nothing like we were used to. We had light winds for the 380-mile passage to Pago Pago and for the first time set our stun sails—light air sails that ride outboard of the end of the yardarms and between fore course yard and lower top sail yard on extended and portable stun sail yardarms. It is a very light weather sail, but not very practical. You must be very careful not to get caught with your pants down and constantly keep an eye out for any weather changes because if caught, they will definitely blow out and cause serious damage to the standing rig. They were out of use by most sailing ships by the 1860s so we were proud of the possibility that *Yankee* was probably the only sailing vessel in the world at that time using them. It was the only time we used them, and it was just for the day.

That night, Art served a terrible meal of Spam (not the first time). John the mate became enraged, as we all were, and took the tray to the galley and threw it in Art's face. This sparked a whopper of a heated discussion, the result of which was that our warm water and bug juice would now be cooled in the fridge and that made a huge difference. Nothing like something cold on a hot day. We were also promised that we would be supplied with fresh meat in the next port. That never happened and we continued eating cheap canned food. Try it sometime and see how long you can put up with it. Remember, this canned food was far from quality food. I know that Guy said that he didn't think that the food was the real reason for the problems we were experiencing and he is right, but it sure was the catalyst that sparked further and deeper problems aboard ship.

The next evening, as I was coming on deck for the 8 to 12, I took the wheel and steered 282° for Pago Pago, still a few days out. I noticed it was unusually dark, and no stars were showing. We had No. 1 and No. 2 jibs set, foresail, main stay, fisherman, and the main sail set. I thought that maybe we should shorten sail as a precaution as we were under thick clouds and to me seemed we were taking a big risk. About ten minutes later, I felt a cool wind hit me and I could smell fresh water. I stood ready to lay off the wind if we got hit hard. Skipper told me to stand by as he knew also that things weren't looking good. He also told me stay on the helm until he released me. The third of only three compliments I got from him the whole trip. Compliments from Skipper were more than rare, as it should be.

Skipper called the remainder on watch to douse the fore sail and it was a good thing. As soon as it was furled, we got hit. And we really took a hit. The wind exploded, and even the sails made a report like a cannon. "Hold your course!" says Skipper, and, "All hands on deck!" as *Yankee* took a knockdown, her lee rail under water, and was literally roaring through the night sea. Tons of white water was pouring over the lee rail and piling waist deep along the port side scuppers. Her freen ports could not release the boiling mass of water faster than it was coming on board. "Six spokes left rudder and steady up on 255°," called Skipper. "Left rudder steady 255°," I responded. When we steadied up on 255°, *Yankee*'s motion eased a lot, but the wind held steady at about 50 knots, the spindrift hitting the rail like BBs fired from a gun. I could not look into the wind because it stung so badly. We weren't too sure of our position but knew we were north of the island of Manua, and were now heading basically towards her outer reef and the windward side, to boot. Skipper was pacing back and forth and considering his next action.

Yankee settled in and, as heavy as she was, she literally made her own space in the raging seas around her. Any other vessel would be pounding and rolling heavily in these seas but not our seaworthy vessel. *Yankee* would muscle her way into a sea and split thousands of tons of seawater, sending vast amounts of spray and glowing fields of white foam right back at King Neptune's backyard. She was heavy enough that her motion was smooth with no slamming or jerking. She was a real weather-wise ship and filled us all full of confidence in her seaworthiness at handling anything Mother Nature could throw at us. I felt proud of my ability to handle her helm in such chaotic conditions as these, and having it confirmed by the skipper's trust in me. "Bilge, you and six others man the wind and lee jib sheets and prepare to tack about," said Skipper. My first thought was that these squalls don't last that long, maybe we ought to ride it out rather than risk a tack in these high winds. But that's probably why I am not the captain, so I jumped to it. Three each on the wind sheets, three each on the lee sheets, a total of six strong young men. I was on the lee sheets about to become the wind sheets after the tack. Guy, the second mate, was with us, and Leo, the third mate, was in charge of the wind sheets. Skipper was at the helm, two sailors amidships on either side necessary to relay Skipper's commands to all of us forward and ready because of the howling of the wind through the rigging. "Ready about?" hollered the two relay sailors. Both Leo and Guy hollered back, "Ready!" "Coming about!" we heard, as *Yankee* pointed up and I thought there were at least ten machine guns going off in my ears as the sails headed to the gale. Leo's gang threw off their sheets and we started hauling for all we were worth to bring these monster thrashing sails under control. We were about to tie off on the deck cleats when No. 1 and No. 2 filled, literally ripping the sheets out of three pair of hands. Both jibs instantly tore to shreds and the clew cable that attaches to double blocks where the sheets pulled through began thrashing furiously and banging against *Yankee*'s steel bulwarks so hard that they were making sparks every half-second or so. The noise was ear-shattering. It was then that I saw Guy moving forward, I guessed to try to regain control of the sheets. I dove for him and tackled him, hollering, "Leave it be, Guy, you're going to die if you get in range of those blocks." I think he realized then that it was humanly impossible to regain control and he relaxed.

As if by magic, the wind died to nothing and the storm vanished, leaving our head gear a total shambles. "Well, King Neptune had a good laugh on us," said Leo. Whew, what a mess in just a few seconds. The seas became very confused and *Yankee* began to wallow, rocking and rolling.

I remember hearing the main gaff head banging and booming with every roll, slamming back and forth to her stops on either side. The gaff is the boom that rides on top of the main sail and gives the sail the high-peaked look. It weighs about 500 pounds. Attached to the peak of the gaff is a thin vang line that can be used to trim the peak. The noise got my attention and then I saw Skipper's right arm raised high and every time the gaff shifted and slammed against the stops, Skipper would leave the deck and go straight up in the air an astounding seven or eight feet. I couldn't believe what I was seeing. Somehow, the old sea dog had got the vang line twisted around his thumb and it was jerking him by his thumb into the air every time the gaff would hit its limits. Nobody saw it but me, and the tough old skipper wasn't even shouting with the pain he must have been in.

I raced to the aft deck and leapt up to grab the vang line just above Skipper's thumb. I got it and my weight forced the vang down and freed Skipper. As soon as I got the vang secured, Skipper growled, "Bilge, what the hell are you doing aft?" "Trying to give aid to a helpless sailor," I replied. Skipper's eyes got wide and he actually smiled, the crusty old salt.

Well, you don't want to get on the wrong side of the King. First, we didn't heed the signs that were all around us, then we didn't shorten sail quick enough. We got impatient and needlessly worried about the reef at Manua, and then instead of riding the tempest out, we panicked and tacked into the teeth of a full gale. We paid for that by losing both head sails. Just for laughs, the old King called a halt to the storm and left us wallowing in a flat calm. Then, just so we wouldn't forget, he left Skipper hanging by his thumb tangled in the gaff peak vang line. Jeez, what a grouch! It is compounded emergencies like this that sink ships and crash airplanes. The all-time rule that works everywhere is the genius of the Boy Scout motto: "Always be prepared."

Next morning, with spikes and knives in hand, we all grimaced at the mess on the bowsprit. We set to work unbending, cutting, unwinding, cutting, sweating, cursing, pushing, pulling, and cutting those symmetrically perfect sails, so nice to look at when they are up and doing their job, turned into an unrecognizable mess within five seconds of one moment in time.

By noon we turned the job over to the 12 to 4 and by 18:00 we had two more jibs bent on, two blocked and looking as if nothing had happened. It took us all day in the now real tropical heat. We were only twenty-five miles from Tutuila and Pago Pago.

December 29. In the morning, we raised the high, clouded volcanic mountain of the very densely-jungled island of Tutuila, or American Samoa. The mountain name translated to English is 'the Rainmaker.' True to its name, it rained all day as we entered the L-shaped fjord and anchored at the dock in Pago Pago, back on American soil for the first time in six months. My camera broke in Tahiti, so I have no pictures from Moorea, Bora Bora, Roratonga, or Samoa. Leo supplied me with pictures of Palmerston, Tokelau, Fakaofa, Atufu, Guadalcanal, and Australia.

8

Samoa and the Polynesian Atolls of the South Pacific

Pago Pago had not changed one bit since the last time I had been there, about three years before. The old wooden Rainmaker Hotel looked the same, as did the town itself. The big Samoan men still dressed in their *lava lavas*, sometimes with shirts, most times without, and no shoes. The chiefs and talking chiefs all seemed to be in excess of 350 pounds, wearing their bead necklaces and carrying big, thick war clubs—used as canes—as symbols of rank, not to mention the tattoo designs around arms, legs, head, chest, and waists. The tattoos are very painful to receive, and are only allowed if you have proved your bravery. They also denoted stature and rank in the village tribe. So the chiefs and talking chiefs were usually tattooed from head to toe. The pain they endured is unimaginable to me. The intricate Polynesian designs went completely around arms, across foreheads, cheeks, chin, neck, and covered some very sensitive spots. The tattoos were put on tap by tap, using a bamboo needle and tapper and ink. A small design, for example a thin design around a forearm, would take all day. The recovery time was spent soaking in a sacred pond of spring water for the night. As a young man in this culture, the first tattoo signals the move to being an adult member of the tribe. All villages are traditional Polynesian ones, with grass huts, and all have a large central meeting hut, a chief, and a talking chief.

I hiked out to the one grass runway, which I suppose is now an international airport, and watched with awe as the huge Pan Am Clipper, a Boeing 337 4-engine Stratocruiser, completed its long final approach and gently touched down.

Later, I visited a few old haunts and spent a great afternoon at the old Rainmaker Bar and Grill, which is when I found out that I had the night watch. It's a good thing, because I was about used up on things to do and tomorrow, December 30, we were to make sail for Upolú and the town of Apia for New Year's and their independence from England on New Year's Day. I thought about expressing my anger to Skipper, but being a loyal member of this great sailing ship's crew, I thought better of it and stood my watch like a good sailor should do. Actually, it turned out all right. I had a great meal at Rainmaker Bar and Grill in sight of *Yankee*. In the early evening, the Pan Am crew stopped by and I invited them aboard to have a look. They were very excited about our adventure and when they found out about my intense interest in aviation, the hanger flying session was on. The captain was an old B-17 pilot with the 8th and the co-pilot was a Navy flying boat pilot right here in the South Pacific. The engineer was a navigator on B-24s and then an engineer on B-29s over Japan. Man, I was in heaven. The conversation went on until after midnight, long after the stewardesses got bored and left. I was thrilled to meet those guys and pass the time with them. It confirmed my ambition to fly airplanes after *Yankee* and that is what I did.

After the crew left for the hotel, I sat bored, watching big banana spiders hunting on the grey cement walls surrounding the church right at the dock until I was relieved at 6:00 a.m. We left the dock on December 30 for the short sail to Upolú and the town and bay of Apia. The independence party promised to be a good one, and we were not disappointed. I mentioned the fact that I saw no fresh food come aboard and this started another ruckus between the crew, and this time Art the cook took it personally. Art really wasn't to blame, as he had no control of the money to buy food. I felt sorry for him. Art tried to be a good cook, but with what he had nobody could produce fit meals for anybody. That didn't help the emotions of the crew. Before we left, we had another whopper of a battle. We threatened to leave the ship until we got our point across. The few remaining members of Sam's group piped up and said, "Then we will leave without you." That's when Skipper piped up and in a pointedly angry tone said, "We can't do that, you damned fools. They are the only reliable crew I have that can sail this ship." With a few red faces on their side, Skipper effectively broke the stalemate and we would stay aboard. It also seemed to put a stop to their arrogant and superior attitudes. At least for the time being.

We did not make Apia for New Year's Eve, but did for Independence Day. Upolú, or Western Samoa, with its rolling mountains and thick jungles was different from the other Polynesian islands we visited. There were none of the abrupt sheer cliff walls we were used to. It was hotter here, and the jungles were much thicker. All around the island were orderly grass hut villages, each one with its own chief and talking chief, and everybody wore the traditional *lava lavas*. The children are never orphaned in Samoa, much to the people's credit. They are cared for by every member of the village. Nobody has more than someone else and the land they own cannot be sold by Samoan law. The people still hold to Polynesian tradition and are ready at any time with a welcoming smile and are genuinely happy to have you stop by for a visit. The children are polite and will play with you in an instant—no bashfulness here.

The Samoans are known throughout Polynesia for their ferocity in battle and throughout history have been fierce warriors when called upon to defend their island and homes from marauding tribes. They are trained to defend almost from birth. I have heard them called the protectors of Polynesia. The men are huge, probably the most massive natives anywhere. I might add that they also probably have the biggest feet of anybody in the world. I had a Samoan girlfriend who was petite in every way except her feet: she couldn't get her feet in my size 10½ shoes. They are known throughout the world as leaders in any martial art and a Samoan held the title for World Champion Jujitsu fighter in Japan for many years, and was very respected by the Japanese. Despite their potential ferocity they are all ladies and gentlemen, and display friendly hospitality. The Polynesians are definitely cool people.

Having been to Upolú before, I grabbed Leo and Mirve and introduced them to Aggie Grey, who had us over to her hotel, Grey's Hotel, and cooked a wonderful dinner for us. She was a personal friend of Robert Louis Stevenson and set us up the next day for a hike up to his grave on a mountain overlooking his beloved South Pacific Ocean and surrounding hills of Upolú. Our guides were a group of young boys who were very happy and excited to show us the way. We set out early the next morning for the strenuous hike through the thick jungle and up the mountain. We followed a crystal-clear tumbling stream, which about halfway up formed a big, deep pool that was clear enough to be blue. The heat was intense and we were sweating profusely, so we all took a break and en masse dove headlong into this paradise of cool clear water. We swam and jumped, the surrounding cliffs echoing the joyful screams and laughs of our great young guides.

Cooled off, we continued our hike and eventually came to Robert Louis Stevenson's grave. What a peaceful place it was. We broke out the sandwiches that Aggie had made for us and enjoyed our picnic lunch. We were all tired and lay down under the shade of a huge banyon tree and soon all were asleep. About an hour later, we woke up feeling refreshed and reluctant to leave this paradise but the boys insisted we must get started. Hiking down was really easy and soon we realized that the boys had disappeared. We thought the little brats had left us, but really weren't worried.

I was in the lead and came around the corner and onto the cliff top above our pool when all of a sudden, out from the jungle jumped the boys, pretending to be shooting at us. I grabbed my chest and fell of the cliff, moaning, "Arr-r-r-r-r-r-r," and fell into the pool as if shot. The gun battle was on and even our English lord Mirve the rigger was prancing from jungle to rock and blasting away at the boys. All of us had to get shot off the cliff at least ten or fifteen times, the boys even more. The squeals of joy, laughter, and gun shots lasted for the next thirty minutes or so and Leo, Mirve, and I were for the time big kids playing with these Samoan kids, all of us acting nine or ten years old. I will never forget those great kids and even today I smile when I think of them. What a great and special day that was.

A day or two later, Leo and I boarded a native ferry boat and cruised over to Savai'i (Western Samoa), an island like Puka Puka where the Samoans live in their traditional way, Leo and I were honored by an invitation to have lunch in a meeting hut as guests of the chief. Before we went in, we were briefed by the talking chief, "Do not talk directly to the chief. Talk to me and I will talk to the chief. Never sit so your toes are pointing at anybody, it is considered an insult. Enjoy your meal, and feel free to talk to me or anybody else. Conversation during a meal is traditional, but not directly with the chief. When finished eating, if you enjoyed your meal the louder you burp the happier you make everybody around you."

So in we went, the chief a huge gentleman dressed in his finest native garb (*lava lava*) with a woven grass belt, many strings of shells and brightly-colored beads, a woven headpiece, and his ever-present walking stick club. His face, covered with many tattooed stripes, was very fierce-looking. As soon as we entered, his fierce face broke into the great and famous Polynesian smile, and he shouted to the talking chief, "*Talofa*" and "*Welcome*." The talking chief repeated to us and we returned the greeting. The chief then motioned to us where to sit and Leo and I were careful to sit on our legs so our feet were pointing at the wall behind us. The feast began, and wow, was it good. Foods I still have no idea what they were besides fish and some familiar and unfamiliar fruits. The conversation came very easily as we wove from one subject to the next: about us, Americans, about them, and Samoa. I asked our talking chief how they become chief. He became very serious and began a quiet conversation in Samoan with the chief. Soon, the chief looked at me and smiled, and indicated that the talking chief will speak. The talking chief very seriously told us that "there are many sacred secrets involved but the chief feels you are trustworthy and has given me permission to tell you a little about the subject so you will have an understanding." We found out later that it was a great honor for the chief to allow us to hear the following story.

The talking chief began by standing up and focusing his eyes on the two of us, his gaze never wavering. "When you are a young man in Samoa, you spend your whole life proving your bravery on land, in the sea, and in fighting. As you prove your bravery, you are rewarded by a tattoo. As in all people, some get very few tattoos but others are very brave. When the chief dies, the bravest of our men carry the body into the hills. At a certain spot only known to us, the warriors go into battle with each other. The last warrior left standing is now the chief. In the old days, this warrior would cut out and eat the chief's heart, but we do not do any of this today. Our chief is brave and loved by everyone."

Leo and I asked the talking chief to thank the chief from our hearts for letting us in on such a sacred tribal tradition and tell him that we were honored to sit with such a brave man. This seemed to please the old chief, but something was missing. Everybody seemed to be looking and waiting for our next move. Then it dawned on me what they were waiting for. I built up as much pressure as I could, then let out a huge belch and everybody broke into smiles and laughs and competed to see who could belch the loudest, laughing and patting each other on the back. Man, I love these Polynesians.

Later, I was talking to Aggie Grey, the widow of Zane Grey, and told her about the experience with the chief. She smiled and said, "Dave, they still do it." I don't know for sure, but I don't want to dispute this famous woman of the South Seas.

The time to leave came too quickly. When we got back to the ship we discovered that Harvey had gone native and was planning to leave the ship and go back to French Polynesia. I can't say I blame him. I almost envied him but our new adventure was awaiting at Tokelau Atolls.

The morning broke and before departure, Harvey being Harvey could not just say good-bye but had to have a whole theatrical performance, planned for the benefit of himself, I think. This is the guy who in mid-Pacific, halfway to Pitcairn, decided we should all perform in a shipboard play. "Okay, Harvey, what's the play about?" I asked. "The play," said Harvey, "is about Winnie the Pooh." We all stood there with our mouths open and astonishment on our faces. Being a Boston schoolteacher, we figured he must think us kindergarteners. Needless to say, it never went past that point. I always thought Harv was living in a dream world, which is alright, just don't put it on us.

On the port side of the ship, about twenty outrigger canoes were lined up beside each other, apparently pre-arranged. Harvey came on deck, dressed in only a *pareu* wrapped around his waist, barefoot, and with shell necklaces draped around his neck. He dramatically stood up on the rail with one foot and, balancing the other on the pinrail, launched into this dramatic speech right out of Hollywood. At the planned moment, he turned to face the canoes, threw his arms out, thrust his chest out, and began his swan dive ala John Wayne in *Wake of the Red Witch*. As he dove, a hand (not mine, but I will not say whose) reached out and pinched one loose corner of the *pareu*. Harv departed the rail as the *pareu* departed Harv, leaving him totally naked in mid-air. Well, old Harv was frantically trying to cover his private parts just before he belly-flopped into the lagoon. We hit the deck in uproarious laughter and the natives were doing the same in their canoes. Harv broke the surface, completely pissed off. He shouted, "Bilge, you son of a bitch!" I raised my shoulders and arms in an innocent gesture, but was laughing too hard to defend myself. I can't say he wasn't asking for it. Later, Leo said, and rightly so, in my opinion, "You know the only thing about that guy that was real was when he called you a son of a bitch." With sporadic laughter and happy hearts, we hoisted anchor and set sail for Tokelau Atolls and another adventure.

The Tokelau Atolls, 380 miles and hopefully a four-day sail from Samoa, consist of Fakaofa Atoll, Nuku Nanu Atoll, and Atufu Atoll, lay 9° south of the equator and 171° west. I was particularly anxious to see these very remote Polynesian atolls. They are home to very real atoll-dwelling Polynesians, living the way they had since they first populated them. It was to be our final visit to Polynesia. Nukufatau Atoll is where Eddie Rickenbacker finally, after twenty-four days in a life raft, reached safety and was rescued by the good natives. His B-17 was forced into the sea and Eddie, through force of will, kept everybody alive and hopeful until finally washing up on the beach at Nukufatau. He was picked up by a Navy seaplane and flown to a base on Funafuti Atoll that we were also to visit. I had the great honor of talking with Eddie on the telephone and expressed to him my adventures on Funafuti.

Atufu is also where I made the most dangerous dive of my life. We started for Tokelau on a north by northwest heading, about 320° on the binnacle compass and began our 380-mile drift. *Yankee* barely kept steerage, making slow swirls from her stern and light ripples in the calm blue sea as her bow slowly split the sea apart. We drifted along at just less than 1 knot—not even one mile per hour. We had every stitch of canvas set and there was not even enough wind to keep her sails asleep. Instead of her creaking and groaning of the rig at work, the symphony was replaced by crack, boom, chatter as all the sails would reach their swing limits with every pitch and roll, constantly, all day, all night. There wasn't enough wind to hold the sails in place and they endlessly slatted and banged with no letup. Of course, the sea is relentless in any kind of condition, you just learn to live with it. It was also very hot on deck in the daytime as we were getting closer to the equator. It would cool off some in the wee early hours but not much, and as soon as the sun rose 1° above the horizon, the cooling effect was instantly gone. By the time

I came on watch at 8:00 a.m., it might as well be noon. The heat was oppressive, to say the least.

Two days later, *Yankee* was in irons—in other words, completely becalmed. Her rudder was useless and *Yankee* just floated in one spot, all sails hanging limp, the sea mirror flat, and no shade on board. It was even hotter in the main cabin. We rigged a canopy under the main boom so at least we could have shade over the helm, but even in the shade it was hot. Better than nothing, however. We were in the Doldrums, for sure. The Doldrums are 10° north or 10° south of the equator, areas that produce no wind or fluky winds at best. When we crossed through the Doldrums from Panama to Galapagos it was different because of the influence of the cold Humboldt Current. This truly was the meaning of the Doldrums, or horse latitudes, that the sailors of the past were so leery of.

We happened to go into irons in the middle of forty or fifty Japanese glass ball floats, a long and deep line attached to each one. All of a sudden the old light bulb flashed on in our head when Mirve said, "I wonder what they are fishing for?" We all looked up with forefinger and thumb cradling our chins and one eye closed. "Did he say fish?" I asked. "Sounded like it to me," said Leo. I asked, "How far is it to that first buoy, do you think?" "Oh, an easy swim," said Leo. "Hey, Mirve, run down to my bunk and grab my 30.30 and go up to the lower top sail yard and give me shark watch, I think I am going for a swim." Mirve did not hesitate and soon he was perched on the lower top sail yard, rifle at the ready.

I dove over the side—not as pretty as Harvey, but just as naked—and hit the water. Oooh, did that feel good. I swam out to the glass ball and got hold of it. It was mightily weighted down and I could feel struggling coming from the line so I knew we were going to have fresh fish for dinner. I was thinking this will teach those Japs to attack Pearl Harbor when a loud pop, sheeuw, bang startled me. The pop was the bullet hitting water, the sheeuw the bullet tearing through the air, and the bang coming last was the report from the gun itself. Hell, that's what it sounds like when somebody is shooting at you. Now I understood why you never hear the shot that gets you. "Hey, Bilge, there is a shark right behind you," hollered Mirve. Oh shit, this must be the sneak attack part of this deal. Almost afraid to look, I turned my head and, sure enough, there was a big brown spot in the water about twenty yards behind me. Once in a while just the tip of his dorsal would break the surface. Pop, sheeuw, bang. This time I was looking at Mirve. The pop came before I could see the smoke, and the bang came after I could see the smoke. The bullet actually hit the sea and beat everything out of the barrel, including the smoke. I found it fascinating, but he missed the bloody shark. "Put on your damned glasses, Mirve!" I hollered. The shark did move further away, so he must have been mystified by the impact I am sure he must have felt.

I made the ladder and four hands reached out. I was so relieved that my pals and bosom brothers of the sea were so concerned for my wellbeing, and that's when all four hands went right by me and grabbed the ball and then disappeared over the rail. "Hey, you freakin' bums, remember me?" "Come on up, Bilge," hollers one of them. Well, I got up the ladder and on deck while my pals were eagerly hauling in the line. I looked and there was sharky-poo lying right alongside. "You're mine," I said, grinning. I leapt below and grabbed my heavy rod and reel, hooked on a spinner, and was back on deck in a flash. I dangled the No. 10 spinner and hook and tried to make it look very enticing and it worked. He took it in his mouth. I held my patience and then the big dummy took it into his mouth further and with a mighty pull, I set the hook home. Ka pow. The ocean exploded and the fight was on. The line ripped out 'zinnngggg.' I got worried for a little while that I didn't have enough line. He finally stopped and the heavy tug of war went on for the next hour and a half, my muscles aching so badly I almost wished Skipper would cut the line. But Skipper said, "Get him in, you deserve him."

I started making headway soon and in another half-hour we had the 'tiger' on the surface. Tiger sharks are not a friendly type to be in the same puddle of water with. This time Leo leveled the rifle and fired. Bulls-eye. The big tiger quit moving altogether. We hooked on to him with block and tackle and worked him on to the deck. He measured 8 feet, 3 inches. We figured his weight at around 250 or 300 pounds. Doc got his spike knife out and proceeded to give us shark anatomy lessons, making it very interesting as he expertly removed organs and laid them out so everyone could see. He explained what each organ did and the differences between fish and mammals. You're cool, Doc.

While I was reeling in Tiger, some of the other crew were handing in the line and wound up retrieving five tuna for a total of about 250 pounds of fresh tuna meat. Thanks, Hirohito, we sure appreciate the fresh meat. Actually we did feel a little guilty, so we rebaited the hooks with shark meat and threw it all back in. All sweaty and very hot, we were all glad when Art showed up with three pitchers of cold bug juice. Boy, did that taste good. We had fresh tuna this and that for the next two-and-a-half days.

Our luck with the wind changed slightly and we picked up enough wind to give us about 3 knots. The atoll of Fakaofa was close on our starboard beam.

January 12, 1962. In the morning, we started to see several small native sailing canoes coming from shore and heading towards us. Before long, our decks were crowded with natives of Fakaofa, all dressed in traditional clothing and very happy to see us. The head of this group acted as our pilot and helped take us through the pass to our anchorage. The Tokelau Islands are very low, palm-covered atolls. Fakaofa, the first atoll we came to, consists of many very long islands and they form a perfect circle with a sparkling and huge shallow lagoon in the center of every shade of blue from turquoise to deep indigo. These islands had much more land mass than Palmerston did. Underground fresh water was abundant, though there were no rivers or lakes on the surface. No wonder these islands have supported the Polynesians for so many centuries. A big difference from Palmerston.

Polynesian canoe

Fakaofa natives on deck

We already had an idea of some of their customs, and one was the greeting and gift-giving ceremony for all newcomers. We were all prepared and brought gifts from cloth to fishing gear, things they really needed for survival. I know, I know, in Hollywood it's glass beads, but remember Hollywood has always stayed afloat on a sea of B.S. As soon as we all were ashore, we were escorted to the ceremony field and lined up on one side, with all the natives on the other side, their chief in the center. I might add that the chief and the people were dressed in their finest grass skirts, *lava lavas*, and shell necklaces. The chief was the only one with fine headgear consisting of feathers interwoven with palm fronds.

The chief stood up and in a Samoan dialect spoke the traditional welcome speech with the huge grass central meeting hut in the background. Once again, we were transported back in time. When he was through, the bamboo drums began their Polynesian beat and several men began their intricate dance towards us, holding their handmade gifts for us. The skipper had to make up a dance, as delicate and professional as the native one, as he moved towards them, carrying his gift. We must have looked like blithering idiots, but this was very serious and nobody cracked a smile, much to our relief. As each one of us danced, one at a time, to present our gifts and receive theirs, the drums tapped out their complicated rhythms. Wow, is this cool or what? When all the gifts were exchanged, the drums abruptly stopped.

Atoll of Fakaofa

Atoll of Fakaofa

Drying fish and copra at Fakaofa

The chief stood up and welcomed us as members of the tribe. The natives threw up their arms and with huge smiles raced towards us, shouting in glee to personally welcome us. You know, if the whole world acted as the Polynesians have every place we have visited, the world would be a hell of a lot better place. Where else in the world would you get a welcome like this?

They had known we were coming, since we contacted them by radio, so they had prepared a big feast, cooked underground, consisting of pork, fish, shellfish, fruits, and vegetables, the likes of which nobody has eaten unless you have been here. We gathered at the talking hut and began our feast, eating with our hands, at sundown. It was totally delicious. We were expected to eat, dance, and sing all night. Throughout our feast, the native men and women would spontaneously break out in their own personal dances and soon the guitars came out. Art showed up with his accordion (a big hit) and we had a great night. No booze, as the people in these islands did not partake in that sort of thing—probably why they are so healthy. We made it back to the ship around 4:00 a.m.

The next day, Leo and I did some snorkeling and Doc tended to some locals in need of medical attention, which made us all heroes to the natives. That evening, we hoisted anchors and sails.

January 14. We headed for the atoll of Atufu, 100 miles away and the furthest out of the Tokelau Atolls. The winds were still down but not dead so we motorsailed most of the way. By about 10:00 a.m., we had Atufu dead abeam and native canoes outbound to meet us. Again, our decks were crowded with native people. We noticed right off that they were not dressed the same as the Fakaofa natives in that they had shorts, shirts, and shoes or sandals on. They were friendly to us, but the exuberance did not seem to be there. The leader of the group acted as pilot and showed us a protected spot just off the reef where we anchored. I noticed the depth finder was indicating 250 feet to the bottom directly below *Yankee*. Leo and I plotted a dive to that depth and according to the U.S. Navy dive tables, we had a 12-minute bottom time and it also was the no decompression limit. Leo and I planned a 25-minute decompression dive and came up with a 1 hour 15 minute hang at twenty feet and a 30-minute safety at ten feet for a 1 hour 45 minute decompression stop. We were young and in good shape so we planned the dive for noon the next day. In the meantime, we offloaded some supplies for the Atufans, as they had no welcoming ceremony planned. We figured it was because we had already had the ceremony and were officially welcomed to the whole Tokelau Group of islands.

Doc and kids

Atufu meeting place

Atufu Atoll is a little different from the others in that the island itself is round and sits squarely in the middle of the surrounding barrier reef. There is no pass, so we had to anchor outside the reef and keep a weather eye out on the conditions. Definitely an anchorage requiring an anchor watch. Skipper stayed aboard and assigned four of us for day and night watch. Fortunately, Leo and I were not among them so we went ashore. An atoll is an atoll, no matter how you look at it or what shape it is. Atufu was no different: green palm forests, white sand, and blue water.

The ladies of Atufu

Young Atufan girl

The people planned a dance in the afternoon. The time came and the women lined up in front of us, all dressed in long dresses from neck to toes. One man on each end dressed in the traditional *lava lava*. They looked Polynesian but nothing else did, including the tin-roof, metal girders and posts that held up the obviously military-built shade structure they called 'The Hut.' There were no drums, but they performed spoken chants and we found it interesting to watch and listen to. We watched for about an hour and then Doc went to work caring for the island's sick. Also, none of the Tokelaus had seen visitors in a year so this was very special. A tall gentleman we presumed was chief asked us if we could put on a US military marching demonstration. Well, Leo and Mirve were the only two that had been in the military, so they briefed us on what to do. The Atufan men brought down their arsenal of World War I bolt-action M1 rifles and gave one to each of us so we looked like real soldiers. The entire native population was there watching, very excited and interested in what we were doing. I was tail end Charlie and after marching and doing a few maneuvers, Leo brought us to a halt and left face and looked at me. His back was to everybody but me and he gave me a puzzled look. I said to do a rifle inspection and the same march again and then I would do a Laurel and Hardy routine. So when it got to me, he grabbed my rifle and threw it back to me, and I threw it back to him. Leo did great: he very professionally reamed me out and threw the rifle back to me. The natives did not know quite what to think at this point. When he threw it back, I faked that it was too much and fell backward into the sand and gave the ol' Three Stooges brush of the hand and a high-pitched 'mmmmm.' Next Leo gave a right face and I, of course, turned left and crashed into the others to the screams and laughter of the people watching. We kept this silly behavior up for about another fifteen minutes to non-stop laughter. It felt really good to be a star comedian and broke the ice with everybody.

That's when I met 'Crazy Charlie,' a small but very well-muscled Polynesian man dressed in traditional clothes—*lava lava*, criss-crossed snail necklaces, woven palm frond hat, and carrying a spear. He immediately put us at ease with a big bear hug and told us he would show us around. He told us he refused to obey those idiot missionaries and that he is and always will be a Polynesian. We liked him right away. It turned out Charlie was no teller of tales. He lived in his own grass hut that he had built in the traditional way. He lived there with his two wives but assured us he had many girlfriends. He dived deep in the lagoon, sometimes 100 feet down, hunting fish and pearl shells. He carried a big knife that had been handed down for generations and was given to his great-great-great-grandfather by a white sailor on a clipper ship about 1865. Charlie used the knife to hunt wild pigs that lived on Atufu. That's how he got the name 'Crazy Charlie.' Usually he would ambush the pig and kill it by hand by breaking its neck. Only if he lost control would he use his knife. His family were all chiefs and Charlie felt he needed to keep the tradition of bravery alive. He seemed to be doing a great job of it. He wasn't the only native who shunned the missionaries, but he was definitely the chief of his large band of followers. After our dive, Charlie was so impressed that he gave me his knife and I still have it to this day. It is a real piece of sailing art with a twelve-inch handmade blade, a six-and-a-half-inch handle wrapped in painted marlin and topped off with a cats paw knot. A very intricate piece of 19th century sailor's art. I accepted with tears in my eyes. After our dive and just before we left, I went ashore with a big bowie knife I had on board and presented it to Charlie. He took it with a big smile and hug and told me we were friends for life and I always had a home on Atufu Atoll.

The Dive

Next morning Leo and I prepared for our deep decompression dive. We made our dive plan according to the then current Navy dive tables and made it a mandatory decompression stop dive by adding ten minutes to our no decompression stop limit of twelve minutes bottom time, minus our descent time. The old tanks had what they called a 'J-valve'—a device on the pressure regulator mount attached to a long stiff wire with a ring you could stick your thumb into and pull down, opening a valve that would give you another 200 pounds of compressed air. In my case, it was another 400 pounds as I used a double tank system. At that depth, the 400 pounds by outside pressure would be reduced to about 200 pounds but would expand on the way up, giving me plenty of ascent air to reach the tanks hanging at twenty feet for the decompression stop required for the dive. The reason for the J-valve was simple. In those days, very few divers had pressure gauges and relied on taking a hard breath as the air emptied and as soon as you would have to suck hard, you would reach down with your hand, hook your thumb into the ring at the end of the J-valve wire, pull it down, and voila! You had 200 more pounds of air—plenty to get to the surface and even make a safety stop for five at twenty feet.

Thinking I was real smart, I filled my tanks to a short fill, 2,000 psi, the night before. I went with 2,000 psi because the way Leo and I figured, we would start sucking hard two to three minutes before abort time was up and have to start up a little early. Very foxy move, and it worked perfectly and probably helped save my stupid life. You always fill a tank with a J-valve with the valve in the open position, which I did. Before putting on the tanks for the dive, you always check to make sure the J-valve has been closed again, which I didn't. Leo didn't catch it either on the pre-dive check. "Ready?" Leo asked. "Ready," I answered. A backward drop to the sea and splash. Being already negative buoyant, I was instantly starting down and pre-clearing my ears. I took a breath and felt the rushing air accompanied by that reassuring breathing sound emitted by the regulator itself. Everybody who dives recognizes that sound. I was again thrilled and mesmerized by the intense world of blue water and silver air bubbles I was surrounded by and delighted at being able to breathe in this hostile atmosphere called water. I looked up and there was Charlie watching us as he floated on the surface with his handmade goggles. I looked around and there was Leo at my depth, about twenty feet. The sea conditions were crystal-clear and I recall that the visibility was at least 130 feet. We passed through one atmosphere (thirty-eight feet), and I checked my depth gauge carried on my wrist. It's the only gauge I have and is an ancient one at that. As we passed two atmospheres (seventy-six feet), I was startled to see the smiling face of Charlie cheerfully waving at us. Man, this guy is a real South Sea pearl diver. I am impressed as he follows us down to three atmospheres (114 feet). He waves good-bye and heads for the surface. That was one hell of a dive with no equipment, I was thinking.

The sea was still bright and there were still lots of fish swimming around at this level. But it was slightly less bright as we continued our descent and at four atmospheres (152 feet), there was a definite decrease in the brightness of light and the fish were gone. I also began to feel the effects of 'rapture of the deep,' as we called it in those days. Today it is called 'nitrogen narcosis' and the dangers are well-known. At five atmospheres (190 feet), it was visibly darker but still fairly bright. I was cloaked in 'rapture,' feeling overly safe, and with a never-before-felt euphoria. Keep your shit together, Bilge. This is serious business, I scolded myself. This tactic worked and literally kept me thinking through this carefree attitude I was deeply entrenched in.

At six atmospheres (228 feet), and almost at depth, I couldn't find Leo and, worst of all, I didn't care. A little over seven atmospheres (266 feet), I kept it together enough to halt the descent. I looked to my left and saw a huge barracuda and thought, ha ha, I have made a new friend. Okay, Bilge, that's enough. Think through this rapture. That's when I started sucking hard. No sweat. I reached down and hooked my thumb into the ring and pulled—nothing. I pulled again. Again—nothing. Oh shit, I am at over 250 feet and no air. It is amazing how the rapture disappears when you know you are about to die. I started slowly up, keeping my hand down on the urge to panic and hoped the laws of physics were right. The law says that when pressure gets less, the remaining air in your tank will expand. So as I got back to seven atmospheres, sure enough I took about a one-quarter breath. Not much, but now I had a little hope. I must keep the urge to panic locked in place and concentrate on making the next atmosphere at six. Fighting desperately to not speed up my ascent, I took another small breath at six atmospheres, but I still had a long way to go. At five atmospheres, another small breath, but I was really becoming scared and had to keep telling myself to keep it slow. At four atmospheres another one-quarter breath, and panic was getting very real. I managed to keep it together and stay under my smallest bubbles, the rule in any ascent from depth. At three, another breath, but it didn't at all feel enough. Still, I fought harder than ever to not panic.

I kept a slow ascent but my lungs were screaming for air. At two atmospheres, I could see the decompression tanks and fought the panic that I would not get there in time. Still, I kept my ascent slow and at one atmosphere I was finally within easy reach. I slacked up a bit to reach the regulator hanging just above me. I was starting to feel a buzzing in my head due to oxygen depletion in my system. I grabbed the regulator and jammed it into my mouth, sucking hard. The greatest joy in my whole life was when I got that whole lungful of air. How sweet it tasted when I needed it so badly. I enjoyed the feeling for at least ten breaths and then thanked the diving gods for giving me the strength and cool head that saved my life. Leo was already there and we spent the next hour and a half enjoying the peaceful life-filled sea at twenty feet.

When we got on deck, enjoying our friendship and diver brotherhood, we went over the dive about a hundred times. Somewhere in our jubilant conversation, I asked Leo if he had seen the giant barracuda and he said he hadn't. I said, "Where the hell were you at 250 feet?" He answered, "Right next to you." I realized that my barracuda was Leo, and that 'rapture of the deep' is a very, very dangerous friend. It happened because of one very simple reason—no equipment check before the dive. I learned a lesson for life.

Atufu Atoll

Charlie and his two wives

January 15. That afternoon we upped anchor and set sail for a 550-mile to the west-southwest for a group of very remote atolls called the Ellice Islands. We were headed to the capital, Funafuti Atoll. There are eight islands in the Ellice group, all atolls and at the time controlled by the British. During WWII, Funafuti was a radio and PBY patrol base located about 650 miles east of the Solomon Islands and the main war zone. It was considered a backwater base, but also all passes were mined. By the time we were there, all passes had been cleared but for one, and we had to be very careful to not enter this one pass. In 1964 I heard that a PBY flying boat landed in the wrong pass and was blown up with all hands lost.

The winds were fluky at first, and the group of atolls lay 174° west and 8° south. We didn't have high hopes for any fast sailing and set our minds for another slow drift. We figured for about six days at sea. We were wrong—it took seven days. The almanac said that a full eclipse of the sun would take place basically on our course two days after we left Atufu. Everybody was excited about that. The sky had been cloudless since we left Samoa. I came on the 8 to 12 the morning of the event and would you believe our luck? We were under a complete overcast.

The eclipse was supposed to happen at about 11:30 a.m. Gypsy and I went below and dressed up like a couple of natives, complete with grass headdresses, *lava lavas*, shell necklaces, and drums. We came on deck and beating the drums did a made-up weather dance. The weather gods didn't approve, and the skies remained overcast. The time came and on cue it started to get darker and darker. As it became darker, we noticed that the few sea birds around our ship landed on the surface of the sea, tucked their heads under their wings, and went right to sleep. The sea terns landed in our rigging and did the same thing. Like magic, day turned into the dead of night. This lasted for about one minute and then it started to get light again. The birds woke up and started flying as they were doing three minutes before, as if nothing had happened. I have always wondered if our feathered friends and birdbrains thought that they got a full night's rest.

January 22. We sighted the low atoll and began taking sights off the atoll itself to navigate to the proper pass. Skipper sent Leo and me up to the fore course yard to keep a sharp eye out for anything that might look like a mine. We were right on target and sailed through the pass and into the lagoon with ease. There is still a radio station on the atoll, and soon a motorboat with a couple of the personnel from the station and the local native constable arrived alongside and boarded *Yankee* for customs formality. The constable was dressed in western clothes and nothing about him looked native except his Polynesian and Micronesian facial features. He spoke with a slight British accent but still couldn't get away from the natural friendliness of all the native people we have come to admire.

The paperwork did not seem to be as important to him as the basket full of fresh tomatoes he brought us as a welcoming gift. These people are definitely the best. We all sat around the table, including our guests, and ate the sliced tomatoes that Art prepared for us. A little sugar on them and did they taste great. When we got through, the constable informed us that those ashore were very anxious to meet us so we took the launch ashore.

The natives here were very different from what we were used to in that they were dressed in shorts, shirts, and shoes and lived not in huts but small framed houses. There was also electricity for lighting instead of the familiar kerosene lanterns in use in the Tokelaus. The atoll of course was exactly like all the other atolls—green palm trees, white sand, and blue sea. The folks at the radio station invited us over for some beer and a home-cooked meal that the wives had prepared. What a nice evening we had and the conversation with the Brits kept us all interested for the evening.

Next day, some of the kids wanted to walk us around the island, which we did. At one spot the youngsters stopped and told us that this was the spot where Eddie Rickenbacker was dropped off by the Navy seaplane. I read his story when I was twelve—little did I know I would stand on the very spot my boyhood hero had stood after his rescue. It seemed to send chills through me as I looked out to sea and at my feet standing on the spot. I can still describe that spot today, as if I were there again.

January 24. After staying on Funafuti for two days, we left in the morning and pointed our bowsprit towards our next destination, the famous war island of Guadalcanal in the Solomon Islands, 650 miles to the west, 180° west and 10° south, right on the international dateline. We held a heading of 270° and estimated a seven-day passage. We said good-bye to Polynesia and looked off the bowsprit, wondering what the Melanesians were going to be like. We had pictures in our minds of short, black people, with bushy hair and scarred designs on their faces, and a cannibal past. You know, those rumors proved to be right, not to mention the famous bones through their noses.

9

"You Him Big Fella No Smart" and An Operation on the Dinner Table

We were on our usual drift, very little wind but we still figured seven days for our 650-mile run. I was very anxious to get to Guadalcanal. When I was younger, I had an intense interest in World War II and especially the Pacific War. Of course, I saw every movie produced about the subject and still like to watch them. The island names in the Pacific fascinated me: Rabaul, Tulagi, Munda, Vela la Vela, Pavuvu, Tarawa, Pelelu, and so many more. It gave me a great desire to actually see what they were like.

On this trip, we were going to see Guadalcanal, Savo, Tulagi, and Pavuvu. I was very excited. I have read copious amounts of literature about WWII in Europe, Russia, Africa, and, of course, the Pacific. In later years I would not only see most of the islands but had the great adventure of diving the many shipwrecks strewn around the North and South Pacific. I also have experience in just about everything we flew in those days and am still convinced that the aircraft built from the late 1930s to the middle 50s are the toughest and best-built aircraft the world has ever seen.

About two days out, we picked up a steady northerly that put us on a beam reach and lifted us through the water at 4 knots. A nice leisurely pace and the rigging, being content, began its wonderful symphony of creaks, groans, and squeals we hadn't heard for so long. It sounded great to hear it again and made falling asleep in my bunk a joyful thing again. The seas were steady and fairly small, causing *Yankee* to gently ride up and down, and the steadying effect of the beam wind caused *Yankee* to heel no more than one or two degrees and eliminated all rolling.

Making a wake

Sunset

Guadalcanal

Jap wreck

Not everything was happy on board as we were eating canned beef stew, canned chili, canned everything and it tasted awful. For breakfast it was either oatmeal and hot coffee or powdered eggs and hot coffee. Lunch wasn't even worth going below for. We had a freezer on board but no fresh meat. The tension between Art, Skipper, and Gloria was becoming a problem with the crew and would come to a head in the Coral Sea inbound to Cairns, Australia.

We trailed a line and feather plug behind *Yankee* and one night as I was on watch we heard the line slapping the gunnel and knew we had one on. I grabbed hold and it felt like a nice fish. As I started to hand in the line, there was an explosion on the surface about fifteen yards out and the line started to tear out of my hands. Stupidly, I tried to hang on and my reward was a painfully burned palm where the line pulled through my hand. I let go and the line came to its limit and didn't even hesitate to part with a snap. To this day I don't know what the hell it was and guess it could have been a big mako shark or another big deepwater shark.

The days went steadily by and on February 2nd our bowsprit was pointing directly at Honiara, Guadalcanal. An overcast day, but high enough that we could see the high mountains behind the town of Honiara. The mountains were rolling like Western Samoa and the thickest jungles yet. By 10:00 a.m. we had cleared customs and Leo and I were ashore and looking around this strange place. It looked as if the war was still going on because the whole town of Honiara was made up of the remains of Quonset huts left behind by the 1st Marine Division.

The culture shock was immediate. It was instantaneously clear that somewhere between Polynesia and here we had crossed an invisible barrier into Melanesia and a totally new and very different culture. The friendly smiles and feeling of hospitality were no longer apparent. The people were indeed short, black, bushy-haired, and some had carved designs on their faces and/or a bone through an ear lobe. The language was a pig English, very difficult to understand. Their native language is a harsh-sounding language and impossible to understand for us anyway. In all of the restrooms, for the benefit of people who come in from the jungle and don't even speak pig English, there is a picture board with four or five drawings showing the right way and the wrong way to use the toilet. The people rarely smiled, but were not unfriendly. All were dressed in *lava lavas* and beads and went barefoot. They were usually carrying a machete.

We discovered the Honiara Mendana, a hotel. Leo and I figured we had been aboard *Yankee* since Bora Bora, so it was time to take a break and get a room here. This was no luxury hotel but was made up of several Quonset huts left by the Marines. But it was comfortable and air-conditioned, which was hard to get used to after not having it aboard ship. One thing the hotel had that nobody else in the world had was their cook, 'Hong Kong Charlie.' And, man, could that Chinaman cook. Leo and I walked into the dining room when out of the kitchen rushed this slight and middle-aged Chinaman, hands outstretched and big smile on his face. Grasping both our hands at once, he said, "Me Hong Kong Charlie. Me vely vely good cook. You eat me cook you no eat anywhel else. Me Hong Kong Charlie." That guy could not only cook the best Chinese food I have ever eaten, but French, German, Mexican, and delicious American hamburgers. And he was right—we didn't eat anywhere else.

Next day Leo and I scored an old WWII Jeep from none other than Hong Kong Charlie's brother. Every Chinaman and woman we met were somehow related to Hong Kong Charlie. Seemed to us that ol' Hong Kong has it made in Guadalcanal. We drove out to Henderson Field, famous during the war. We took the field from the Japanese after a bloody fight. Our Marine and Navy pilots were flying F4F or FM2 Wildcats from sunrise to sunset, flying combat against the Jap A6M Zero fighters. Most of our guys, and I suppose the Japanese as well, were sick with jungle rot, diarrhea, and 101° or 102° fevers. I don't know how they did it. The natives in the Solomons were our greatest allies and saved thousands of Aussies, New Zealanders, and Americans from the horrors of being taken prisoner and barbaric treatment by the Japanese. Thank you, him little fellas.

We hiked all around Fighter One and Fighter Two. Aircraft wreckage littered the areas all around both bases and I recognized several American types that either ran off the runway or were pushed out in the jungle because they were used up. Every once in a while, we would find a splattered wreck that obviously went straight in and showed evidence of burning. They were all Japanese aircraft. Not too healthy a place to be if you were a pilot for the Emperor.

Although the clouds were out and shaded us from the intense sun, it was sweltering and soon Leo and I were dripping wet. We hiked down a two-lane dirt road shaded over by huge trees and found lots of evidence of heavy fighting–helmets, fragments of artillery, and bits and pieces of things that would only come from an army. We were to learn that this was the initial stage of 'Highway One' that the Marines fought to build inch by bloody inch until they ran the Japs into the sea at the northwest end of Guadalcanal. At Tangararo, just a short ways down Highway One, was the famous ridge called 'Bloody Ridge,' where the Japanese took a real beating. It started to rain, so Leo and I drove our WWII Jeep back to town and spent the rest of the evening at the hotel bar, talking about the day, drinking cold beer, and eating Hong Kong's delicious food. The next day we decided to spend the day hiking Bloody Ridge and the surrounding area.

The next morning we left Hong Kong's great breakfast table after a meal of kippered herring, scrambled eggs, bagels with cream cheese and lox, with Hong Kong looking out of the kitchen with his great smile, watching us as we dug into our Jewish meal. "Now where do you suppose ol' Hong Kong learned Jewish cooking?" I asked. Leo said, "I don't know, but he sure is good at it." We told Hong Kong that we were going to hike around Bloody Ridge. He said, "Wait. You wait light here," and hurried off. Pretty soon he showed up with two machete knives. He said, " You need these, glass very hard. Hong Kong take plenty good care you."

When we got to the area, we instantly found out why they call the grass, or glass as Hong Kong says, 'saw grass.' If you try to walk through it, it will cut you to pieces. We sure did need those machetes. We cut through it fairly easily but it was very hot going as the clouds had not formed yet and the sun, even at 10:00 a.m., was broiling hot. As we got closer to Bloody Ridge, the grass got lower and much easier to walk through. There was evidence of battle everywhere you looked. We continued hiking the ridge and I noticed at my feet a heart-shaped aluminum wristband, obviously handmade. I picked it up and was astonished to see written on the face of the heart "Charlie Barnz, 1942, Fiji, Sydney, Guadalcanal, 1st Marines." I couldn't believe my eyes. I brought it home but never could get the Marines to give me any information on Charlie Barnz. It is one of the things I regret in my life and wish that I had tried harder. But anyway, thanks, Charlie Barnz, for your efforts and successes that have given me the freedom to come here and stand on the spot where you may have given it all.

We then dropped into the jungle and immediately found the splattered wreckage of an A6M Zero, the red ball faded, though still visible, on one wing. A little further on we found a battered tank and identified it as Japanese. This must have been a big battle. We spent most of the day hiking around the area and could not help but wonder as to how the soldiers on both sides could take the heat and the very dense jungle. Inside the jungle, there were times that you felt that you couldn't breathe, although when we stopped to rest and sit down, the jungle itself was beautiful—trees, ferns, vines, and flowers everywhere you looked. And up in the trees were birds of every color you could imagine, all talking and busily flying about like the reef fish. It was noisy, but a peaceful kind of noisy. It was natural and belonged. We saw white cockatoos everywhere and heard their raucous voices chiming in with the others. I thought of Dad because everywhere we looked there were thousands of butterflies of every size and color. Dad would have loved it and would have spent most of the time prancing through the jungle with his ever-present butterfly net. I don't remember bugs being much of a problem, although they were buzzing away so they were there. I thought how peaceful and beautiful this tropical jungle was and how man in his lowest and most deranged greed could have turned this paradise into the living hell it was in 1942-43. Thanks again, Dad, for giving me this wonderful adventure that I was on.

We were brought back to reality when the peace was shattered by a series of very large and muffled explosions. We found out later that there was a huge dump not too far from where we were, where all the unspent ammunition had been dumped. It was a daily routine that a few of the shells would still, after all these years, spontaneously detonate.

Tangararor

Relics from Bloody Ridge

We hiked back to the Jeep and drove back to town and our great Quonset hut hotel. That evening we enjoyed a wonderful French dinner prepared by the best chef I have ever known, Hong Kong Charlie. After dinner while enjoying a few cold Foster's, we met a young guy our age by the name of Timmy Georgeti who was an acquaintance of none other than Martin Clemens, a famous coast watcher who risked his life to spy on the Japanese and pass the intelligence information back to the allies. I definitely wanted to meet him so Timmy took us to his house and we spent the most interesting evening, fascinated by Martin's and his exciting stories and adventures. He related one that I still laugh about. Now Martin was a big guy even then, with a big bulge at the waist. In Australia, when you are sick, you are not sick but 'knocked up.' So Martin in his jungle hideout became very sick and sent a couple of native runners to get a medic from the nearby Marines with a message that he was "a bit knocked up, send help." Pretty soon, a squad of U.S. Marines and a medic showed up and this tough-looking Marine Sergeant came in and with wide eyes and mouth hanging open, pushed his helmet up and said, "Jeez, this guy really is knocked up." Lots of laughs and a great evening. Our new friend, Timmy, stayed with us and showed us the Guadalcanal that only somebody who lived there could have done.

Next day I told Hong Kong that we needed steaks and beer and that Timmy, Leo, and I were going to cook the steaks on the banks of the Lunga River. Hong Kong said, "I know dese peopr here I give you extla steak no cost you nothing and plenty beer and ice. Hong Kong Charlie he know everything." So we packed up the Jeep and headed up Highway One about fifteen miles to the muddy, crocodile-infested Lunga River. It was not the prettiest of rivers I have ever seen, but the intense jungle it ran through was beautiful and added greatly to the charm of this river.

We got a fire going and relaxed with a couple of Foster's. I opened the big icebox and couldn't believe the number of steaks ol' Charlie had put in there. We three couldn't possibly eat all those steaks. So we started cooking, and then I felt their presence before

I saw the old native and his grandson silently standing in the jungle. I said in my own pig English, "Hey you little fellas have big freezums and good eat with big fellas." The old gentleman, who was also carrying a big machete, came over with his grandson and joined us. He wouldn't drink beer but immediately started to help cook our steaks. He said something to his grandson and he took off into the jungle and soon returned with dad, uncle, mom, and baby. They also brought big, beautiful, jungle-grown sweet potatoes.

We all cooked and I felt very privileged to be keeping company and communicating with our new native friends. They were all very polite, but not one of them smiled, as much as I tried to make them. Timmy later told me that it is not in their custom to smile or laugh because they think that it might be taken as an insult, as in laughing *at* somebody. They showed their pleasure by being respectful and would not eat until we had eaten first. Then they enjoyed their steaks and sweet potatoes. The sweet potatoes were more than good. I asked the old man, "You no likum freezum?" "Me no likum you drink make you no smart." That was probably some real good advice from our gentleman friend of the jungle. We found out that he was a runner for the coast watchers and was captured by the Japanese. Before the four Japanese soldiers could get their hands on him, he killed all four with his machete. Whoa. I would not want to be on the wrong side of this guy. To look at him, you wouldn't think he could do anything like that, but then again, he did look very serious.

He then broke into a story about that and other incidents in his life, all translated to us very professionally by Timmy. We all sat spellbound as this old jungle native proceeded to weave us together with his adventurous stories. Even though we saw no smiles, we felt their honest and real warmth as we said our good-byes. That day, even as hot as it was, was also real cool. I looked at Leo and Timmy and said, "You two big fellas no smart?" They both laughed and then said, "You big fella no smart also?"

Lunga River

Him fellas

**Friends from the jungle
and more friends from the jungle**

"You him big fella no smart"

"Him big fellas even more unsmart"

Thirsty Jeep

We gathered up our trash, loaded the Jeep, and feeling great, proceeded to the end of Highway One and past wreckage of all sorts, including rusting shore batteries and a ship with her bow sticking straight up out of the water. The Japanese writing on top of English lettering proclaimed her to be *The Kinugawa Maru*. We drove all the way to the beach at Tangarare, where our 1st Marines drove the remaining Japanese into the sea. Standing on the very spot, I felt a deep respect for the men of the 1st Marines, and definitely felt this a place of honor. As we drove back, we stopped once again at the Lunga River and enjoyed this peaceful spot. Again, I couldn't imagine it being a place of man-made hell in 1943, where we lost 1,100 Marines when they were ambushed by the Japanese.

Leo and I stopped in at a local bar for a cool one, as it is really hot in Honiara. The bartender was native and had no indication of even a hint of a smile. We asked him if we could have a beer. He said to us, "You him big fellas talk him two big freezums." While we were there, a newspaper was lying on the bar and told of John Glenn's February 20, 1962 flight around earth in Gemini. I looked at the native bartender and told him about what I just read. He looked at me like an errant child and said, "You him big fella talk him little fella big lie," at which point Leo looked at me with that grin of his and I looked at the gentleman behind the bar and said, "No, not me," and held up the newspaper and said, "This tell big lie." The bartender actually smiled and said, "Two more big freezums?" "Yeah, OK." The ice was broken and we learned that like everybody, deep down, they were probably pretty good people. And they really turned out to be so.

After our refreshing stop, we walked to the other end of town where, because the international dateline cuts right through Honiara, we had walked into yesterday. Didn't seem any different but was a fact. I read about a ship that planned to be at the equator at the same time as crossing the dateline, N-S 0° and 180° W. Technically, you could walk from stern to bow and go from today to tomorrow and from port, where it was summer to starboard, where it was winter. It probably was a very interesting log entry.

That evening back at the hotel, we settled in to an absolutely delicious Chinese dinner cooked by the master chef and true artist Hong Kong Charlie. I still remember that day with good feelings. Timmy became a good friend, and I stayed in touch with him after our adventure on *Yankee*. But the story of Timmy is not quite over.

Iggy had left the ship to stay in French Polynesia. I believe he left in Bora Bora. A couple of nights after our steak cookout at the Lunga River, while enjoying a couple of cool ones (big freezums), in walks Iggy, to the great joy of us all. Of course, that started a huge celebration that lasted most of the night. After eight days and nights of Guadalcanal adventure, we set sail in the late evening for Savo Island. About two hours out, I heard a commotion in the main cabin and rushed down as Leo, laughing his head off, comes the other way. "What the hell is going on?" I asked. Leo, between laughs, said, "We got a stowaway." I couldn't imagine. Leo continues, "Check out your bunk." I tore down to the main cabin and ripped open my bunk curtains and there, with a stupid grin, lays Timmy and thirty or forty Foster's beers ready to party.

Wow, was Skipper pissed. We turned around and headed back to Honiara and docked. Skipper, in a rage, declared, "We will depart in the morning." I looked at Leo and Iggy. "In the morning?" "That's what I heard." "Okay, we need to get Timmy and all those beers off the ship and home." Well, naturally, we couldn't let those Foster's go to waste and we had another farewell party with Timmy and Martin Clemens at their house.

February 28. We returned to *Yankee* about 5:00 a.m. to get a couple of hours of sleep before shoving off at 7:00 a.m. This time, after a short sail, we were laying off of Savo, a volcanic peak that lays between Guadalcanal and Tulagi, where we planned to spend a few days and also the base where John F. Kennedy commanded PT109. The island of Savo is very small and we laid off for most of the day. I went ashore on the first launch and met a few inhabitants that were basically the same as the people we had just been with. They still lived the way they did for centuries and were happy to see us. There was no electricity or running water except that which Mother Nature had provided—a nice, clean and crystal-clear rushing stream that went right down and emptied at the beach. Iggy and I spent our two-hour shore leave joined by laughing and screaming young Melanesian kids of both sexes and naked as j-birds (not us, of course). We all ran countless times up to the village and rode the stream back to the beach. I think the elders probably thought "Him big fellas maybe him little fellas," but they didn't seem to mind and were always polite and friendly, offering us coconut milk in the shell on several occasions.

We got back to *Yankee* in time for fresh salad for lunch. Art had spent his own money to buy the ingredients for it. It was great. Thanks, Art. I threw on my tanks and made a solo dive. I know, I know, today we think it a cardinal sin to do such a thing but in those days we did it all the time. We have come a long way in safety since those days and even I would never consider the risk of solo diving today. Unless you dove in the old days, you would not believe the equipment available to all divers today. I don't know how we survived those pioneering days. I dropped over the side into the crystal-clear waters of the South Pacific. I wasn't planning a deep dive, but just deep enough to examine *Yankee*'s underwater hull. She was covered in barnacles that had grown and reattached to her since Leo and I had scraped her clean back at Pitcairn Island. I knew we would probably pay a knot penalty because of our hitchhikers. I hung out at thirty feet for a while but the ocean was deep, I could not see the bottom, and it seemed to be devoid of fish, so I surfaced and climbed back aboard. About 3:00 p.m., Leo and his group went ashore and, judging from the shouts and screams of the native kids, they were having a repeat of our earlier visit.

When they returned, we motored to Tulagi, a very short distance, and pulled into the same well-protected harbor as our PT boat force used in 1943. There was not much left of the base except a rickety dock and a few Quonset huts, all owned by the Chinese merchants, none of them anything like Hong Kong Charlie, but they all knew him. We did not trust the old dock, so we dropped a bow anchor and backed in close enough to the shore, being deep water all the way, and tied the stern to two hefty trees. A couple of Chinese folks brought us a stout plank to use as a gangplank. Unlike Charlie, they didn't do it for free. They also had basically nothing in their shops, Tulagi being fairly remote.

It was unbearably hot because no wind could get in to cool off the harbor. We met a native man who spoke perfect English, who took us for a hike down the unimproved road to the face of a cliff. He was dressed in traditional native style, and turned out to be college-educated in New Zealand. Man, it's an amazing world. He was a walking history book, and kept us spellbound as he recited historical facts about his people, the islands, slave traders, and the Japanese during WWII. It turned out that Bully Hayes, a notorious South Sea pirate and blackbirder slave trader, was based here in the mid-1800s. He made his slave-capturing raids of the Solomon Islands posing as a missionary and gathering his flock together. His men would spring out of the jungle with big nets and capture as many natives as they could to be sold as slaves in the world slave market. Their ship, the *Leonora*, was shipwrecked in 1874 at what is now the Utwe-Walong Marine Park on Kosrae. Bully Hayes was murdered in March 1877 by former crewman Peter Radeck, or "Dutch Pete", after a violent disagreement, his body thrown into the ocean.

The cliff where we stood used to be a large cave system and is where the Marines cornered the Japanese in 1943. Instead of risking their lives in combat, they came in with many Caterpillar bulldozers and sealed the entrance, blocking in 12,000 Japanese who are still there. We were told that when the war moved north, the U.S. soldiers were ordered to push everything left behind into the harbor at Tulagi so the natives would not wind up killing or hurting themselves on the potentially dangerous equipment. Some trucks and other equipment were brand new. I hate war. A sobering thought for all of us as we returned to *Yankee*, where Leo and I donned our dive gear and dropped into the 90 degree water.

As we descended to thirty feet, we hit a thermocline and the water became noticeably cooler, almost chilly. The visibility was only about thirty to thirty-five feet. There were no reefs, and the volcanic structure continued right on down with little growth and the walls sloping towards the middle of the cove. Sure enough, we saw the headlights of what was a truck. At that moment, I saw a large shark and, being an uncomfortable dive to begin with and feeling leery of sharks, we aborted the dive and returned to the surface. Later, we saw the shocked expression on our English-speaking friend's face when we told him of our dive. He emotionally told us to "never dive there again," and related the native history of this particular spot.

It appeared that the natives were all members of the shark clan and would sacrifice live victims to the sharks in the harbor and also feed the dead to the sharks. This practice supposedly halted only when the war came to them. Still, people are taken by sharks to this day. That is why we never saw anyone swimming in these waters. It seemed our friendly native people had a dark side.

Our English-speaking guide

There is another dark side that is more commonly known. If you look up 'cannibal' in a picture dictionary, the picture would closely resemble a Solomon Islander. And, in fact, the Solomons are listed as formerly being among the islands infested with cannibals. One island in the group that I read about accepted with great kindness the two missionaries that were sent there and a year later when another ship stopped by, the chief personally came aboard to talk to the captain. He told the captain that "the missionaries were very good for his people and that he would like to have more missionaries come to help his people." About another year passed, and another ship showed up with four more missionaries and left. A couple of years later, another ship showed up and the old chief again asked to speak to the captain and proceeded to praise the wonderful missionaries and how good for his people they are. He requested more missionaries. Well, the old captain, knowing these islands, said, "Isn't six missionaries enough?" The old chief said, "Oh no, missionaries good for people and taste good, too." Whether or not it's true, it makes a good story.

One documented story that came out of these islands is the story of a black private in the army who was stationed on Guadalcanal. Of course, being black in those days was unfairly unpleasant, to say the least. This particular man was not only black, but also extremely intelligent. One day as he was busy at some backbreaking menial dirty job, he thought to himself, "This is enough. When I get home to the good old U.S.A., I will basically do the same thing I am doing now. I have had it. So he learned not only the native language, but pig English as well. As he became fluent, he made many native friends. When his battalion was ordered to get on the ship and move north, our friend put on his native finery and stood on the dock with the other natives and waved good-bye to his troop ship. His knowledge of handling big machinery put him in tight with the local natives, and with his ability to argue politics with the white overseers, he soon became a major chief of the tribe. To this day, I have wondered if he in reality was not our English-speaking native friend whom we had met on Tulagi. If so, good on you, pal.

March 12. We dropped our stern lines and upped anchor and sailed away from hot Tulagi Harbor. Once we rounded the point and entered Iron Bottom Sound, the air, although still hot, seemed much more refreshing and we pointed our bowsprit towards our next stop—Russell Island, or Pavuvu. There was a great sea battle in 1943 and many U.S. and Japanese ships were sunk here, hence the name "Iron Bottom Sound." It has officially been called this on all charts since that day in 1943.

We had left late in the afternoon for our 185-mile run to Pavuvu. We would sail overnight and reach the island the next morning. As we tacked on a northwest heading of 295°, the wind picked up to about force 2 and gave us about a 10-knot breeze coming directly from the west and in the direction we wanted to go. After my wheel trick at 9:00 p.m., Skipper ordered another tack and we tacked around to 195°, which put us on a heading for the northwest tip of Guadalcanal, only about twenty miles south of our position. Skipper told Leo to make sure John the mate would wake him at 2:30 a.m. for our next tack that should put us within range of Pavuvu. *Yankee* was ghosting at about 2.5 knots on an easy tack. Leo was in the navigation cabin and I was on bow watch.

The night was very dark. I was thinking about the millions of things one thinks about on bow watch and looking for shadows that should not be there—ships, lights, or fast-approaching clouds—when Leo came up and said, "Dave, I think Skipper has made a mistake. If John gets him up at 2:30, we should probably be grounding on the beach at Aruliho." "You better get him up," I said. "Shit," Leo said, "This is going to be fun."

We were all leery of not just Skipper's mood, but everyone else's as well as we still had nothing but canned food and not a word of money from home base in Miami. The crew was rightly pissed off. Not only that, but we had one lifeboat that would probably go down if launched. *Yankee* herself was badly in need of repairs at a shipyard dry dock, yet the owners continued their irresponsible silence. I don't blame Skipper for being edgy. So I looked back and saw Skipper and Leo through the charthouse porthole, going over the charts. Pretty soon, Leo came forward and said, "Skipper showed me where I made the mistake, and I am sure that he is right." "Was he mad?" I asked. "No," said Leo. We agreed that, in spite of our problems, Skipper was a damned good captain, and that his whole being, heart and soul, was in the operation of the ship. I went to my bunk feeling almost good. I was shaken awake by an excited first mate at 2:30 a.m. He excitedly exclaimed, "The boat is sinking!" Oh, shit, I thought. Leo was right.

As I dove out of my bunk and hit the deck as fast as I could, I saw everybody hanging over the stern. John the mate handed me the loose end of the thick rope that we were towing our launch with and all sails were feathered or sheets loosed so the sails would feather into the wind, bringing *Yankee* to a stop. John said, "Take this up to the davits, and when I tell you, start heaving it in." Pretty soon all hands were on the rope, slowly bringing our water-filled launch to the portside davits. "Jeez, John, I thought you meant *Yankee* was sinking," I said. "I said the boat was sinking." He was right, of course it was the boat but he could have said the launch instead. We had been towing the launch behind *Yankee* and she filled with water for some reason. We got her in position alongside *Yankee's* port midships and over the side I and two others went to begin bailing her out. We got most of the water out and attached the deadfalls to her. It took the rest of the crew to haul the launch on deck. We could see the leak by the steady stream of water pouring out of her right at the forward end of the keel.

Great, now we have one lifeboat that will sink, the other in need of repairs and the only other means of flotation is an old WWII balsa wood life raft strapped to the top of the lazaret in the stern. The emergency supplies that Guy had sewn shut in a waterproof canvas sack proved good and we still had our other emergency supplies intact. Upon inspecting the launch, we found the fiberglass coating at that point had separated and the wood seam had spread enough to let water into the launch. It turned out to be an easy repair. The 4 to 8 watch was on as I went below to continue my sleep until on watch the next morning at 8:00 a.m.

As I came on watch, the wind had died and we were under power and passing a low palm-forested island that belonged to the Palmolive Company—their source of coconut oil for making soap.

March 13. Late in the afternoon we made the harbor of Pavuvu and tied alongside a large freighter tied to the dock. Her name was *Southern Trader of Hong Kong*. Her very friendly crew and captain were all impressed with having such a famous sailing ship as *Yankee* tied next to them. They opened a door in the side of their ship to allow us access to the shore through their ship. We were all offered a tour of the entire ship and she was impressively massive and even the engine room was sparkling clean. The mate, engineer, and captain had us over for a great, freshly-cooked dinner and ice cream sundaes for dessert. You know, these freighter guys have it made, I thought.

We went ashore to the Palmolive Company recreation center where we drank ice cold Foster's and were introduced to the game of snooker, which is played on a pool table with no pockets. The object is to hit all four red balls by banking shots with the cue ball. After copious amounts of beer and many games, we called it a night and were invited on a crocodile hunt the next evening. But first we had to stop at the ship's PX for a few more ice cream sundaes in the company of a group of Chinese able-bodied seamen. They were very friendly and we spent the rest of the evening talking and laughing in good company.

The next day dawned hot and sticky and we spent most of it on board the *Trader* and in the air-conditioned recreation center. I wanted to hike out to the old Japanese fighter base but couldn't tear myself away from the air-conditioned comfort that we were all enjoying. I have lived to regret that as fate and circumstances were to intervene and I never really got a good look at Pavuvu. Just before boarding the company powerboat to go on our crocodile hunt, I noticed a slight pain at the end of my spine. It didn't hurt very badly and off we went into the night, shining our spotlight at the base of the mangrove trees and looking for the telltale orange glow of the croc's eyes. About two hours into the hunt I was in great pain and getting worse. I hated to say anything but finally had to. We motored back to the ship and I literally had to put my arms around Leo and Mirve's shoulders and be helped back aboard *Yankee*. I was relieved to see Doc, and after he inspected the area at the base of my spine, he proclaimed that I was suffering from a pilonidal cyst and that he had to surgically open up each side of my spine. Great! Leo, my best friend, would assist Doc, and that relieved me some. Doc gave me a shot of some kind of drug that made me feel great and I had no problem sleeping.

The next morning, I woke up to another one of those great Budweiser hypos and noticed the gimbaled table had been sterilized and all kinds of tubes and plastic bags were in place where Doc and Leo would be working. The ship was empty and I asked where everybody was. Doc said they all went aboard the *Trader* until the operation was over. "You scared?" Leo asked. "Nah," I said, neglecting to finish the sentence ("Just terrified."). Leo then handed a book to Doc. As Doc opened it and studiously read the pertinent section, I saw that the title was *Basics of Surgery: Instruction Manual*. "Doc, you sumbitch," I said and we started the procedure with a healthy laugh, which did a lot to put me at ease. Soon I was hooked up and Doc said, "See you in a second." He wasn't kidding. The operation took an hour but all I remembered was waking up, the pressure causing my pain gone. Doc asked, "How you doing, Bilge?" I said drowsily, "OK." In a while I was drugged out again and in my bunk wishing that I could be ashore with the rest of my buddies. They weren't far, and all came to say hello. I really had a great feeling of being a part of this crew. Little Gloria (not wife of Skipper Gloria), who much earlier in the journey I had had a shouting match with, both of us being unreasonably pissed off about something that neither of us could remember, came by and told me she was going to be my nurse and she did a great job of it. I don't think I ever had a good chance to really thank her. So, thanks, Wild Little Gloria, you got a temper like a wild tiger and a seaman's great sense of humor. Thanks for your support.

I spent the next couple of days in a groggy state as Gloria kept me hyped up on whatever that magic brew was. Doc slowed up the dose and in three days I didn't get anymore.

We had gotten underway, and for the first time I missed our departure. We pointed our bowsprit towards Cairns, Australia, and a 620-mile crossing of the Coral Sea. After many great adventures while crossing the Pacific, now we were in the Coral Sea and about to cross another social barrier to be with our own kind in Australia. Little did we know then that we were embarking on the most trying passage of all, and that it would be my last.

10

Becalmed in the Coral Sea

March 20. After being at sea for two days, I was feeling well enough to spend some time on deck. I was bored with nothing to do and was anxious to get back on watch. That's when Doc told me that I could not go into the rigging or do any kind of strenuous work. Well, that was okay, but could I stand a wheel trick? He said, "Yes, but if you stand a bow watch then you must do just that. I don't want you to sit for more than five minutes until the incisions have a chance to heal from the inside out." I could live with that. Then Doc told me I would have to leave *Yankee* and get the definitive operation in a real hospital. Say what? "Why can't I continue the cruise if the incisions heal?" Doc said, "Well, you can take the chance, but if the cavities get reinfected, it could be fatal. And the operation will eliminate that possibility."

Doc knew I was down and put his hand on my shoulder, and with a very intelligent and concerned look in his eyes and a smile on his face, he said, "Hell, Bilge, it ain't the end of the world. Shit, you are just starting out!" Doc was always a good pal, hell, he was the best, so I decided I would get to Cairns and figure out what to do next.

The wind had died to zero and *Yankee* sat frozen in time, sails hanging totally limp. The Coral Sea was a mirror, not a ripple anywhere. It was downright eerie. The next ten days would be a repeat of the first time we were becalmed. We did not have enough fuel to motor out of our situation because our people in Miami had sent no money and we could not replenish our fuel tanks. We were stuck. I guess we should not have left the Solomons, but we were all so anxious to get back to the comforts of civilization that we neglected to use good sense and decided to take the chance of making a reasonably quick passage in seven days. The best laid plans... In the next four days we moved seven miles backwards the first day, fourteen miles forward the second day, the third another six miles back, and the fourth day brought us six miles forward, for a grand total of seven miles to the good.

The heat was unbearable, being 100 degrees in the shade and 115 degrees belowdecks. All watches were done by sitting and waiting, letting *Yankee* fend for herself. The previous day's garbage floated aimlessly around the ship, not even enough motion in the sea itself to disperse it. On the fourth day, Iggy announced that he had had enough and was going for a swim. So we dropped the port boarding ladder and all, except for me, stripped down to go in. Iggy was first on the rail and began to make his headfirst dive when he, and the rest of us, saw the nine- to ten-foot shark laying alongside in the exact spot Iggy's head would first make contact. Iggy was already in the first stage of his dive and leaning pretty far out. Like a classic cartoon sequence, he let out a high-pitched "EEE-E-E-E-E!" and literally reversed direction. With our rough help, he regained the deck in record time, at which point Iggy said only, "I changed my mind." We all hit the deck in uncontrollable laughter, welcoming Iggy back to the world of the living. Soon there were several big sharks around *Yankee* and they stayed with us from then on. We watched these giant, fang-filled monsters devour five No. 10 tin cans, chewing them up and swallowing them. I don't think Iggy would have stood a chance had he made it into the shark-infested sea. This turn of events changed our minds about swimming, so we got out our rifles for a little target practice until we ran out of bullets. We didn't hit a single shark that we could tell.

We spent our watches dousing the hot, dry decks with bucket after bucket of water, but it didn't seem to make much difference. The relentless heat and mirror sea continued on unabated. That's when we found out we were almost out of fresh water and started rationing it to one cup morning, noon, and at dinner. Apparently, in our haste to put to sea, nobody remembered to fill our 2,000-gallon water tanks. We had only ourselves to blame, but a couple of crew were dead set on blaming somebody, which led to some arguing amongst the crew. There was a faction that wanted to blame Skipper, and I guess they were probably right, but what the hell difference did it make now? We were here and must deal with it. In the meantime, the food not only tasted bad but became unbearably monotonous. Here was our situation: one lifeboat out of commission, another fairly unreliable, only an untested WWII life raft; no fuel; running out of drinking water; bad food; *Yankee* herself needing major repairs and on the verge of being unseaworthy; an unhappy crew; and, to top it all off, we found out that our radio did not work. It was a real recipe for disaster. We could not run the generator for fear of using too much fuel. This meant that we could not use the fridge or freezer. At night we had to use kerosene for our lights. Every day broke the same and stayed the same all day and all night.

On the tenth day in the afternoon a really old freighter—she must have been built in the teens or earlier—her bow rose absolutely plumb straight up out of the sea, her upper deck led in a flat line straight back to the perpendicular bridge that was open and covered over with a canvas tent for shade. Her funnel had no rake, and was as plumb straight up as her bow, her aft deck led to a stern castle that sat on top of a stern that looked like belonged to an old Cape Horn sailing vessel. She was a ways off but she came to a dead stop, as I suppose her crew was totally surprised to see what looked like a ghost ship with all sails hanging limp, and a square rigger to boot. We gathered our signal flags and were about to send up the signal that "We need assistance" when copious amounts of pitch-black smoke raced out of her funnel and we watched her slowly disappear over the horizon. I guess we must have scared hell out of them and we supposed they would report the sighting of the ghost ship *Mary Celeste* at their next port of call. "Hey, thanks, you guys!" I hollered. Skipper was not in a good mood and would diplomatically disappear when the arguing started. Strangely, we did not see Gloria, Skipper's wife, much at all during this time. How she could keep below decks was really hard to figure with the heat.

On day 14 we saw clouds forming to the southeast and the barometer began to fall. We prepared for a blow and that night it blew Force 7, or full gale, for the next ten hours. It also rained heavily, and we put our lips to rope ends and drank lots of fresh water. We were enjoying immensely the cool air and rain and even Skipper was a changed man and back to his old seafaring self. We made good time towards Cairns, for a change, and the next day, the winds died, leaving the sea totally confused.

Each wave was crashing into the next and forming huge crown-type seas with fifteen to twenty-foot crowns. It was an amazing sight, and even though we could hardly walk because of *Yankee's* violent motion, after fourteen becalmed days we sat mesmerized at the magic and tumultuous scene that lay before us. This lasted until early afternoon when the sea began to calm and we actually picked up a light Force 2.5 breeze on our port beam, and began to make steady headway towards the Thursday cut, named by Captain Cook, that leads into Cairns, Australia.

Coral Sea

Cairns, Australia

March 16. After sailing all night we made the cut in the morning. By 12:00 noon we were tied to the municipal dock and had cleared customs. Somehow, the newspapers had gotten hold of our hard sail and published the most ridiculous trash articles about us, none of which even came close to smacking of the truth. "Mutiny on the *Yankee*," read one headline. "Girls Fight for One-eyed Captain," said another. I guess to be a good journalist in Australia, you have to know how to make a good story out of a lie.

Roo

Koala

Many of us left the ship at Cairns, disgusted with the lack of support from our Miami backers. Poor old Skipper got beat up bad in the lying Australian press and many years later, when he and Gloria were running a square rigged schoolship very successfully, I wrote and told him how much I respected him and his seamanship skills, and that I had learned an incredible amount thanks to him. He wrote a letter back to me that made me feel great. I read in *Yachting Magazine* that Captain Arthur M. Kimberly had died in 2011. So long, you tough old seadog, a bone in her teeth and the women pulling on the line forever. He's got no idea how much he gave me.

And so my sea adventure has come to a close. It did not end the way I thought that it would and after a lifetime of experience, I don't think that I am alone in that respect. I came away from *Yankee* with a solid confidence in my own ability as a sailor and a deep love for the sea and sailing long distance or port to port in a sailing craft. My love for sailing craft leans towards long bowsprits, gaffhead sails, seaworthy sheer lines, portholes, and wooden decks. I have continued diving ever since and have dived many parts of this adventure-filled world, wreck diving being my favorite.

I left *Yankee* and went to American Flyers' School for Airline Pilots.

I lost track of Mirve the rigger, and most of the others. Iggy and I became life-long friends and had more sailing adventures together and still today we stay in touch. Leo loved his drinks in the evening and would continue drinking until it finally got him. He was not sad, mad, or even considered it a problem. He just loved getting wasted in the evening. So I think ol' Leo went out with that great grin on his face he would get when things were beginning to get funny, which was most of the time. Hop a ditty, ol' Leo. I sure had a great time with you. And to quote my great friend, "Man, that was kicks!" I will never forget you, Leo.

Yankee sailed on with a new captain from Cairns. Most of the old crew had left. Iggy, Mirv, and Gypsy made it to Singapore but, finally, even they could not justify the unseaworthiness and conditions aboard this once-proud sailing ship. The replacement captained her to Darwin, where the oldest member of our crew, Mr. Chalker, at 80-some odd years, died. We didn't get to know Chalker well as he didn't really fit in. No fault of his own, except maybe the great age difference. Good show, old man, you showed us all up in the end. He was an old man with strong feelings of one last adventure in his life, and he really did it. Leo summed it up best. As we were shaking our heads in the negative about an 80-year-old being part of the crew, Leo piped up with, "Hey, listen, you guys. I got a lot of respect for that old guy. This is probably the only time in our lives that any of us will ever meet a guy whose balls are made out of brass. When he clanks them together they play *Stormy Weather* and lightning shoots out of his ass!"

Yankee sailed on and completed her last full circumnavigation, the last of six. Only one original crewmember was still on her when she threw her haws on a cleat back in Miami. Her name was Eileen Dickey. So good on you, Eileen. You turned out to have bigger balls than any of us! She deserves the respect of us all.

In 1963, *Yankee* set out once again to circumnavigate the globe. It was to be a hard luck cruise. She made it to the Galapagos Islands once again, and on the island of Floriana, a woman crewmember was tragically lost. I heard that Sadie Reiser was taken by a shark while wading in the sea. I later heard another story that she had walked inland alone and never came back. I believe the latter because in 1981, 18 years later, her bones were discovered on the island of Floriana.

Yankee sailed on and at Roratonga her engines broke down and with a typhoon on the way, she was abandoned by her crew and left to her own fate. The storm surge lifted *Yankee* and gently deposited her in one piece high on the reef. Hip hip hooray for Josh Slocum, probably the most famous solo sailor of all time, having been the first to circumnavigate by himself, and all that have followed and are following in the greatest of adventures. I did, and am a better person for doing so. *Yankee* sat high and dry, her brilliant white hull gleaming and her two masts standing proud and high, the lush green mountains of the most beautiful of South Sea islands in the background.

Yankee could not have found a better final resting place.

So long, *Yankee*

A Thing of Beauty

Rarotonga Island

Glossary of Sailing Terms

Beam: The widest part of the ship's hull.

Bear off: To turn the ship off the wind or turn to a different course.

Belay: To make a rope fast to a cleat or belaying pin. Also to stop the motion of an action.

Boom: A spar along the bottom of a fore- and aft-rigged sail that greatly improves control of the angle and shape of the sail.

Bow: Front of the ship.

Bowsprit: A pole (or spar) extending forward from the vessel's prow. It provides an anchor point for the forestay(s).

Brace line: A line that comes off each outer end of a yardarm and is used to move the yardarm back and forth to square the sail with the wind.

Buntline: A line attached to each lower corner of a square sail and used to trim the sail.

Clipper bow: The cutwater or stem at the very bow of a ship that dramatically slants forward at an angle. Derived from the clipper ship design.

Course sheet: A rope used to spread the fore course sail and open the sail to the following wind.

Dolphin striker: A steel stay line that is attached to the tip of the bowsprit and is bolted to the lower cutwater at the bow just above the surface of the water to stabilize the bowsprit.

Freen port: A small door placed along the side of the hull at deck level that opens from the water pressure of a boarding sea and lets the flooding water out and back into the sea.

Gaff-topsail: A small sail atop the mainsail top gaff that is used to streamline the top portion of a gaff mainsail.

Halyard: A rope used to raise a sail.

Jib sail: The most forward sail of a sailing vessel. *Yankee* had two jibs coming up two stays mounted on the bowsprit.

Lubber line: A thin wire under each yardarm for the sailor to stand on while working in the yards. Also a small pin on the outside of the compass rose to mark the course for reference to the helmsman.

Mainsail: The aft-most sail and usually the largest sail on a sailing vessel.

Mast: A tall post that rises vertically from the deck that the sails ride up and down on.

Pin rail: A plank of wood with holes to receive the belaying pins located on either side of the masts to tie off the working ropes for the sails.

Port: Looking forward from the stern, the left side of the ship. Also a little round window or an entranceway to go into the lower decks.

Reach: With the wind blowing across the deck, you are on a reach.

Ratlines: Small ropes tied between the mast stays so a sailor can climb up to the yards or to the mast top.

Scupper: Gutter that runs the length of the deck on each outer side that direct the water from a boarding sea to the freen ports.

Sheets: Ropes attached to the lower back end of sails used to change the angle of a sail for better efficiency.

Starboard: Looking forward from the stern, the right side of the ship.

Stay: Steel cable that stabilizes the masts.

Staysail: Sail that runs up and down the fore and aft steel mast stays.

Stern: The back end of a ship.

Tack: A point when sailing as close to the wind as you can get. Tacking is used to bring the bow through the wind and set up a tack on the opposite side of where you were.

Topping lift: A wire or group of wire lines used to stabilize the boom when the sails are not in use.

Vang line: A rope or wire attached to the peak of a top gaff used to trim the top of the sail.

Yardarm: A wooden pole that sits horizontally across the vertical mast that the top of the square sails are attached to.

Glossary of Diving Terms

Buoyancy compensator: A life vest device that fills with air from the tank on one's back. Used to keep oneself level at different depths. The air can be released or increased to compensate for different situations while submerged.

Contact zone: The distance at which visibility is impaired; can be an arm's length or one hundred feet away, depending on the situation.

Decompression limit: The time calculated to depart the bottom so as not to have to make a decompression stop.

Scuba: Self-contained underwater breathing apparatus. A tank filled with compressed air, usually at two thousand pounds per square inch. Invented by the famous diver, Jacques-Yves Cousteau, who first tested his design in 1943.

Three-stage regulator: An old-style regulator that is no longer used by most divers. To clear the mouthpiece one had to remove it from the mouth and hold it above one's head. Now there is a button to push that clears the mouthpiece.

Wet suit: In the old days, they were rubber suits that covered the entire body. They were very cumbersome but efficient at keeping one warm. Baby powder was used to put them on. Nowadays, most wet suits are made of foam neoprene, a synthetic rubber that contains small bubbles of nitrogen gas, or a blend of neoprene and rubber.

COCKPIT

Sixty-Five Years Flying Vintage Aircraft

Preface

This is the story of wind, clouds, luck, danger, humor, and adventure. This is the story of my life, how lucky I am.

If you don't want to hear the life problems—self-made or by the innocence of chance dealing with other people and/or your own kin—then maybe you should not read further.

If you don't want to enjoy the ol' country boy humor of a few of my great acquaintances, then this is not for you.

If you want to hear stories and feel the thrill of what it is like to fly fire-breathing, high horse power, propeller-driven fighters, bombers, and transports not in war but in peace, then continue.

If you wonder what it was like to wear helmet and goggles and be thrashed about by intense wind in an open cockpit bi-plane built in times long past, read on.

Or to know some of the characters called aviators that I have known, go for it.

Maybe what it's like to feel the stiffness of air surrounding your body in a prolonged freefall from 15,000 feet, your heart racing as you reach in for the ripcord, keep reading.

If you don't want to hear about close calls and touchy moments, then stop.

Yes, that was my life but mainly I write about my adventure so that my grandchildren will have documentation of what their ol' Grampa was all about, good or bad. I dedicate my book first to my grandchildren and then secondly to all the great people who helped make my life a collage of great, funny, serious, and adventurous times.

1

The Beginning: The End of the Golden Age, 1946 to 1954

Thumb on the starter switch, forefinger on the booster switch, and middle finger pushing the primer switch down, feeding fuel to No. 3 and in high boost. "No. 3's wet." "Select and turn No. 3." Thumb and forefinger squeeze together. The whole aircraft registers the jolt as No. 3's starter engages and out the co-pilot's cockpit window I watch the four Hamilton Standard propeller blades begin to move slowly in their 11-foot diameter pattern. I count aloud each blade as it goes through my focused field of vision: "1, 2, 3, 4, 5, 6, 7, 8, 9..." "Contact No. 3," and the engineer reaches up with his free hand and flips the No. 3 magneto switch to "both."

Instantly, there is an explosion and billows of white smoke pours out of the No. 3 PRT exhaust in the shape of a thunderhead, followed by staccato of random explosions and more thunderheads of smoke. Then, as the Wright 3350 Turbo Compound is starting to come to life, there is silence and I hear the descending crescendo whine as the turbine wheels in the PRTs and gearing inside the engine itself lose speed. The 3350 seems to take a breath, but not for long, as it belches a big orange fireball that just makes the leading edge of the wing only to disappear as instantly as its fiery life began. More random explosions of sound and more smoke comes blowing out and the 3350 comes to life. It does not quit again, and as the four Ham Standard blades grip the air, the stationary thunderheads of smoke are blown over and under the wing and form a thinner but bigger area of smoke. The engineer has moved the No. 3 mixture to the idle cutoff position to let the twin-rowed 18-cylinder radial engine breathe. The random staccato of explosions begins to smooth out as pistons, crankshafts, lifters, gears, valve stems, and PRT turbines begin to catch up with each other and get into smooth step. It's a mechanical symphony to my young ears, this galloping rhythm that only a big radial aircraft engine can deliver. Only then does the engineer go to "auto rich" on No. 3's mixture to feed the now living, breathing mammoth engine its constant drink of 145-octane purple fuel.

"Oil pressure is off the peg and in the green." "Hydraulics 1800 psi." I see a large puddle of oil blown onto the upper inboard wing route begin to stream back in rivulets on the top surface of the wing and know that everything is as it should be.

We go through the same procedures on Nos. 4, 2, and 1. Idle set at 800 rpm as I look out and see the huge circular discs of Nos. 3 and 4 doing their jobs. No longer eight prop blades but two discs gleaming in the sun. Our DC-7B is alive and at max gross weight of 128,000 pounds. We let the engines run as I read off the pre-taxi checklists, stopping only long enough to get an audible reply from the captain or engineer, depending on whoever is in control of whatever point on the list. "Check mixtures." "Auto rich." "Check." "Hydraulics." "1800 check." "Flight controls." "Free and easy." "Check." Brakes." "Set, check." "Oil pressure." "In the green, one, two, three, and four." "Checklist complete." "Taxi clearance, give me 1200 rpm taxi power."

The heavy bird slowly begins to move forward and is then brought to a stop again. "Brakes check." Again, we move forward and turn left, "Nose wheel steering check." We begin our taxi and receive our IFR clearance that I read back to clearance delivery. Delivery comes back, "Clearance correct. Contact ground 121.7." "Ground American League 816 Delta with you. Taxi for takeoff." "Roger, American League 816, taxi to 27 Left via taxi way Alpha. Hold short of 27L for runup." I repeat the instructions and we begin our long taxi to 27L.

I always enjoy taxiing a big aircraft. There is a certain rumble and movement in the cockpit, and looking out at the wing tip moving up and down, I can also see Nos. 3 and 4 cowling bobbing up and down as if nodding in the affirmative.

As we stop and begin our runup and checklist, I look out at my set of engines and note that the high humidity of the air has formed a ring of visible condensation around the tips of each disc. When the prop pitch is brought back for the prop check, I watch the perfectly symmetrical vapors change shape with changing angles of the prop blades and know that everything about those big Ham Standards are in perfect sync.

"Auto feather." "Checked." "Flaps to takeoff." "20° down." "Checklist complete." Captain gave the crew the brief, "This will be a normal max gross DC7B takeoff. V2 will be 127 knots. If we lose one between V1, 105 knots, and V2 at 127 knots, we will continue the takeoff "declare" and return to land on 27L. If we lose one before V1, 105 knots, we will abort the takeoff. Everybody agree?" "I agree," I said from the co-pilot's seat. "Ah Tower, American League 816 is ready to go." "Ah 816, you are cleared for takeoff runway heading." "Ah roger, 270°. Here we go."

Lined up on the runway and holding the brakes, the captain initiates the throttles forward and releases the brakes at 25 inches manifold pressure. "Maximum power," the captain says. "Max power," says the engineer, while he slowly and evenly brings up the four throttles while looking for four needles pointing at 238 BMEPS on four gauges, or 51 inches on another four manifold pressure gauges, whichever one hits first. When this occurs, the suggestion of immense power is transmitted throughout the airframe to the seats we are in, and we all know at the same time that Nos. 1, 2, 3, and 4 are pouring 14,000 horsepower to our churning propellers.

As we gain speed, the captain is steering, with a little wheel in his left hand, the DC7B straight down the runway at 50 knots. "50 knots, I got rudder control, transition," the captain says softly, as he let's go of the steering tiller, and goes to flight controls. At 105 knots I call, "V1," the nose wheel comes off the ground, and the mains come off shortly after that. I can feel the wings take the weight. "V2." "Gear up. METO power." "Gears coming up," as we feel *bump, bump, bump* as the gear takes the uplocks and the gear doors close shut. "Gear is up and locked. Pressure up. Standing by for flaps," I call out, and our heavy flying machine is now basically weightless.

"Contact departure. Squawk 0414 adios 816." "0414 adios 816." "Flaps up." "Flaps coming up," I repeat. "Climb power. Climb checklist." I read it, and settle back for our nonstop flight from Miami to LAX.

I was on another field, called "Meadows Field," in San Francisco. I watched as an open cockpit biplane—called a Stearman—taxied by. Both pilots had goggles, leather helmets, and white silk scarves flying in the breeze. I was shivering with excitement as I watched these two guys and thought, *that is so neat*. I was five-and-a-half years old. I knew at that moment that I was going to be a pilot and nothing was going to get in my way. I have never lost my wonder at the magic of flight.

My father had just bought a war surplus Cessna T-50/UC-78 Bamboo Bomber. She was big, had two Jacobs 275s, wooden fixed pitch props, sat on her tail, and was made of wood and fabric. She had a huge five-seat cabin, smelled fabulous inside, and was green with cream stripes. He hired an ex-B17 pilot to be his instructor. This tall, thin, handsome man, who flew fifty-some odd missions in Europe for the 8th Air Force, was a chain smoker and reeked of adventure. His name was Johnny Winters. I always saw him as a hero—he was the personification of a real pilot.

I went up in the old T-50 a lot, and I loved everything about her. I still remember the low rumbling sound of her two radial engines, the vibrations of her, and, most of all, the intoxicating smell of her very soul—gas, oil, wood, and leather.

My dad sometimes took business trips in the plane. When he realized that I was enchanted with this new world he often asked me to fly in the co-pilot's seat. Johnny told me that if I expected to fly with him, I had to know how to keep the aircraft straight and level, hold my altitude, and act as his co-pilot. I had to sit on my knees so I could see over the cockpit glare shield and see out the windshield. Johnny operated the rudder pedals as I flew the old Bomber trainer. He taught me how to use the controls, back up, forward down, left left, right right, and, before long, I could actually do my job well. He taught me to hold compass course and to spot ground features to help me know where we were at.

At five-and-a-half, I was done for, hooked. There was no turning back. Except for a one-year stint at sea, I have never wavered in my desire to fly and am just as in love with flight now at age 69 as I have always been. Since those days, I have flown 139 different types of aircraft. When people ask me what is my favorite, I tell them, "All of them."

I remember Meadows Field today as if I were standing alongside the runway itself, looking at the aircraft parked or taxiing out. It was 1947, and the field was crowded with T-6s, BT-13s, Stearman PT-17s, Navy N3Ns, PT-19s, PT-26s, Howard DGAs, Norsemans, and one guy even had a PBY. It was the norm, everybody flying surplus WWII aircraft. I was so proud of Dad's T-50 and to be a part of this fabulous flying world, I could not think of anything else—an addiction that lasts to this day.

Cessna T-50/UC-78 Bamboo Bomber

Ca. 1965, SNJ-4 and Waco RNF at Deland, Florida airshow

Good old days, two bipes lined up for formation takeoff, 1947

Good flying day with Dad, 1947

1951, I was a real airport kid and could con any pilot to take me up

Although the magic of those old aircraft is still with me, the world around me has changed, and I am not so sure for the better. The skills it took to fly those old timers has, for the most part, been forgotten in favor of having everything done for you. Nose wheels and GPS be damned, I am so happy that, even as young as I was, I participated in the golden age of aviation and have kept it alive throughout my life.

I remember the day one of my dad's friends bought a brand-new modern airplane called a Ryan Navion. It had a funny-looking tail and it sat on its nose atop a nose wheel. I got to fly in it, and came down thinking it was pretty cool, but probably a passing fad. I never imagined then that this aircraft was the beginning of the end for my wonderful round-engine world. I saw the day when most of the war-era birds sat forlornly rotting with weeds growing around them and canopies glazed and cracked. The wonderful roar and rumble of radial engines at takeoff power and the crack of prop blades breaking the sound barrier at takeoff pitch was slowly replaced by the buzzing sound of opposed engines that were now the rage. I sadly remember the day Meadows Field was closed so that it could be replaced by a baseball stadium.

We moved to Chicago around that time, and I remember the DC-4 flight we took. There was a gentleman seated next to us and I described to him what was going on throughout the takeoff roll. I could see from the look on his face that he was thinking, "How the hell does this ten-year-old kid know all this stuff about airplanes?" I charmed the good-looking stewardess into letting me go into the cockpit, and right off the bat the co-pilot and captain knew that I had been around aircraft. After a short boxing match of questions and answers, the captain asked if I would like to ride in the cockpit for the rest of the flight. He didn't have to twist my arm.

Shortly after I joined them, the co-pilot said he needed a break and asked if I would like to sit in his seat. It was a set up. The captain told me to put my hands on the yoke and then, "Let's see if you can fly her." I took over and, thanks to Johnny and a certain Bamboo Bomber, I was able to perform and he let me hand fly the DC-4 for a half-hour. He said he was impressed and that I was definitely a future flyer, and that it was time for me to go back to the jump seat. Hell, I felt proud of myself. He let me sit up in the jump seat for our landing at Chicago Midway Airport. When we shut down and got out of the cockpit, the captain had his hand on my shoulder. As Dad came up, the captain asked, "This your kid?" Dad said, "Yes," and the captain said, "He is a hell of a good pilot." The gentleman I had been sitting next to was standing behind Dad, his mouth agape. Reading his mind again, I could hear, "Who the hell is this kid?"

That's the way it was in those days. We really were a free society and I am deeply saddened to see what we have become today. I am also not happy at what aviation has become today. There was a time when a young aviator would have asked me, "What do you think I should do in aviation?" At that time, there was no question in my mind. "The major leagues are the airlines," was my standard answer. Not so today. It seems to me that the whole world is decaying and the future seems frightening. Sometimes I think that I am going to get off this world at just the right time. I seem to have been lucky with being in the right place at the right time all through my life.

We moved into a house in Kenilworth, Illinois, just north of Chicago. It was a culture shock to me but it wasn't long before I had friends. I was disappointed that when I would bring up airplanes, I would either get blank stares or one of my friends would start with making me and the others believe he knew more about the subject than I did. After a few broken lips and bloody noses I clammed up about aviation and tried to keep it to myself. One good thing about where we lived was that I was within walking distance to the Kenilworth Beach on the shores of Lake Michigan. We all spent the rest of summer swimming in the cold waters of the lake and hanging out at the beach, playing our boy games. I still could not get the thought of aviation out of my head and missed those magic days gone by at Meadows Field in San Francisco.

One day at the beach as I was horsing around in the water, I heard a familiar sound coming up the shoreline from Chicago. I looked, and there, right on the deck, coming at us at blinding speed and in close formation was a squadron of five P-51s, tip to tip and tight as hell. They screamed by us with the wonderful whistling sound of their 1,700 hp Merlins at high power setting. Right on the deck I could see each helmeted, goggled pilot, and even the oxygen hoses coming off each face were visible. My heart and soul were in the cockpit with those guys and I stared at them until they were out of sight.

I couldn't get that sight out of my mind and swore to myself—not knowing how or when—that somehow, someday, I was going to fly one of those sleek, fast flying machines.

Johnny came by for a visit after he re-enlisted in the then Army Air Corps. He got out of the cab and walked up our driveway, and, wow, did he look cool in his Army Air Corps uniform, which was topped off with a fifty-mission crush officer's cap. I knew this cap had seen it all from 1943 to 1949. Johnny stayed the night, and left the next morning to fly a C-54 to Tokyo. I never saw him again, and heard soon after that he had been badly hurt in a crash while shooting an approach into Tokyo. I still think of him to this day, and would love to know what happened to ole Johnny.

Summer turned to fall, and I was amazed to see what was happening to the green trees. Up until this time, this kid had never seen snow. I just figured the winters would be like San Francisco. In those days, everybody would just rake the fallen leaves into a pile and burn them. I loved the smell of burning leaves. To this day it is the essence of fall to me.

The day came when I had to return to school. Good old Sears Elementary School. It was a good school, and I liked all of my teachers except one. She was just meaner than a bagful of rattlesnakes. Obviously, we didn't get along, but the way I figured, she had to look at herself in the mirror everyday. I learned to play the trumpet, and one of the highlights of my day was when the whole school would gather together before the American flag and say the Pledge of Allegiance and then our band would play the Star

Spangled Banner. It was a great way to start the day and we all felt great love for our country. We also felt a deep respect for our president and, unlike today, we felt united in a great and honorable cause. I hope someday the people of this dying nation will wake up and put an end to the lunacy that is going on today.

Later in the fall, I noticed that there was a chill in the air that I had never noticed before in my life, and on a chilly morning we took a field trip to a very large and successful dairy farm. I was fascinated by the operation—the machines, the barns, the rows and rows of cows being milked. Best of all, it was way out in a rural area and I felt the freedom of being in the country very deeply. The best part of our trip was that we were under the final approach path to Midway Airport, either 13L or 13R.

Suddenly, I was way more interested in watching the landing gears dropping than some machine gently caressing the tits of some cow who was peacefully munching her hay. In spite of the barns, cows, and machinery, I was in the country like Meadows Field and my mind was in the cockpits of the DC-3s, Connies, DC-4s, DC-6s, and DC-7s overhead.

Our assignment was to write a report on our field trip. Mine went like this: We went to a farm. When we got out of the bus, I saw a barn. Just then a United DC-3 flew overhead and I watched the landing gear extend. I saw the cows. Then a DC-6 came over and it sounded like the props were out of sync. It was nice being at the farm because it was right under the approach path to Midway Airport.

Well, old Bag of Rattlesnakes was furious. She held me after class and very angrily told me that "We weren't there to watch airplanes," to which I innocently replied, "I was." She grabbed my cheek, pinching it very hard, and screamed that I would write on the blackboard fifty times, "I will not watch airplanes ever again." With tears pouring down my cheeks I took hold of her wrists and made her let go and then angrily told her, "I am going to watch airplanes and I am going to fly them also." She backed off and politely asked if I would rewrite the report and leave out the airplanes. I agreed to do so. I rewrote the report and gave it to her the next day. She got the last word, though, and put a big "F" on the report. She told me that she was going to talk to my parents and had them in the next day. Well, I don't know what Mom and Dad said, but from that day on, old Bag of Rattlesnakes acted as though I didn't exist and I never had any problems with her from then on. I suppose the big ugly bruise on my left cheek had something to do with it. She also changed the "F" to a "D."

Then it snowed. Snow. I never saw such a thing. I always walked to school and after four or five steps in knee-deep snow, I decided that I hated this cold, wet white stuff. Dad, why the hell did we move to this place? As we got further into winter and the snow got deeper, my feelings eased up immensely the first time I got on a sled and tore down a hill with my friends. Sears Elementary also had an ice skating program, and I learned to skate and joined the hockey team. Hell, except for the cold, this snow stuff wasn't so bad.

At Christmas that first year we all went to my grandparents' house for Christmas dinner. The smell of Christmas permeated the house and was punctuated by the big green cigar that Grampa used to smoke. Everybody was there—aunts, uncles, cousins, sister, Mom, Dad, Grandma, Grampa, and Grandma's helpers, Marie and Joe. Marie cooked the best apple pies I have ever eaten and she also became my best fishing partner during our summer visits to my grandparents' cabin on Lonestone Lake in the North Woods of Wisconsin. Times like these have given me the most wonderful deep memories that I still have to this day.

Winter faded slowly into spring, and I must say springtime on the shores of Lake Michigan is truly magical. School was dragging on and as the weather warmed up, I joined the baseball team and found a talent I never knew I had. I guess that my time in the air taught me to focus on fast-moving objects. The first time at batting practice, I literally nailed the ball, putting it way out of the park. Good ole Coach Tom always had his pockets bulging with bubble gum as a reward for doing well on his team. Tom said, "Hey, do you think you can do that again?" He pitched another and I got a hold of it again. Out of the next ten pitches, I put four out of the park, three long flies, two fouls, and one to the shortstop. Needless to say, my pockets started bulging with bubble gum, too, and whenever Tom needed a homer or a long ball, he put me in as a pinch hitter. Life was getting better.

We all went on another field trip later that spring. This time, it was right up my alley—Glenview Naval Air Station, now O'Hare International Airport. In those days, Glenview's ramps were wingtip to wingtip with F4U Corsairs, F8F Bearcats, AD Skyraiders, and the usual smattering of C-54s, KC-97 Tankers, and Lockheed Neptunes. The pearly gates were open, and I was in heaven again. We were escorted around by real navy pilots, all of whom had this aura of heroism in my young eyes.

They took us to an AD Skyraider and each of us were allowed a turn to sit in the cockpit. When it was my turn, I crawled in and instantly the magic and wonderful smell of the fighter's cockpit filled my nostrils. The instrument panel was no mystery to me as it was to the other kids. I felt at home again. My host said, "Pretty complicated, huh?" I pointed at each instrument and started naming them: altimeter, turn and bank, artificial horizon, DG, mag compass, G-meter, oil pressure, tachometer, manifold pressure, airspeed indicator, throttle, prop pitch, mixture, gear lever, tail wheel lock, rudder pedals, brakes, control stick, and, last but not least, gun trigger. I looked up and noticed on the commander's face the surprised look, mixed with an approving smile. He put his hand on my shoulder and said, "Kid, I need a good wing man. When are you planning on joining up?"

With that honest and from-the-heart statement, I knew I had just been accepted by this naval aviator, who knew that he was dealing with a future aviator. I felt so proud. Everybody on the ramp had heard the conversation and were standing silently and looking at us. I admit it was my moment of glory. Even Coach Tom was looking at me as if he was thinking, "Who the hell is this kid?"

My moment of glory was short-lived. As I was walking down the wing, I slipped and fell right on my ass in front of everybody. The ole Chief Pilot was not going to let me linger in this ego trip for long. The commander covered for me by saying, "He just thought he would dazzle everybody with his fancy footwork."

The next kid got his turn and promptly made a buffoon out of himself by picking up the relief tube and, thinking himself real smart, started talking into it like he knew this thing must be the radio mike. The commander and his fellow pilots were all gentlemen and tried to hide their smiles with their hands. When the kid got on the ground again, I, not being so gentlemanly, told him straight out that he was talking into the pilots' relief tube. "Whaz that?" he asked. I told him, "When the pilot has to pee in flight, thaz what he uze." The kid was horrified and promptly threw up. I am still begging for forgiveness for that, even though we all roared with laughter at the time.

The Navy was not through with us yet. They pulled out their new Cutlass jet fighter and put on a demonstration for us. I stood transfixed as, with ear-shattering noise, the fighter screamed down the runway and made a max performance climb until we could no longer see her. The pilot bent her over at the top, headed straight towards the earth, and pulled out just above the ground. The jet then made a low pass in front of us at blinding speed, pulled straight up, and did continuous rolls until out of sight. I stood, heart pounding, as that young naval aviator performed a graceful ballet of loops and rolls, gracefully maneuvering every motion with total control and precision. I felt so proud of our great country and the freedoms we all enjoyed in those days. I also felt deeply blessed to have the luck to be a part of this new and brave world given to us by two brothers way back in 1903.

Summer came, and our family made what was to be our annual pilgrimage to Grampa and Grandma's marvelous summer home, "Allynwood," on Lonestone Lake near Eagle River, Wisconsin. I remember most the silence and pine smell of the thick forest surrounding the gemstone lake. It was not unusual in those days to see huge herds of deer. To me, the whole area smacked of adventure. In the years to come, I would canoe many rivers in the North Woods of Wisconsin. It was here that Marie took me under her wing and taught me to fish. I had never dreamed of the adventurous world floating under the surface of that innocent-looking lake. There were perch, bluegills, bass of every type, walleyes, northern pike, and, king of them all—muskellunge, or muskies. I was introduced to muskies by the Queen of Muskie Fishing herself: Marie.

One still evening, I accompanied Marie on a muskie expedition. We had rowed to one of her favorite muskie spots and she was hooking up a "big muddog" lure to her line. She said in a whisper, "David, don't move, look over there." Sure enough, there was a slight swirl where she was pointing. Very coolly and precisely Marie smoothly cast the muddog lure out and just a little to the left of the swirl. I watched as the lure gracefully arched through the sky, heading precisely on target. The lure splashed into the water and Marie expertly began to reel it in, not giving the lure a chance to sit still in the water.

I could hear the little propeller slapping the water *tikity tikity tikity tikity boom!* Where the lure had been a half-second before, there was an immense explosion of whitewater. My heart stopped. I could not believe what I was seeing. *Ziiiiiiing!* went Marie's reel as the monster dove for the bottom. With the patience of Job, she let him run, sitting motionless, her eyes and mind focused on the battle about to begin.

Marie said, "David, he is going to make a jump." Another explosion of water and this time a tooth-filled jaw and madly shaking monster body came straight into the air and slammed back into the water. I was thinking, "There can't be fish like that in this peaceful little lake." We fought that Muskie for 48 minutes before we got him 56 inches and 48 pounds. We both admired his sleek body and ferocious mouth when he was lying worn out along the side of our boat. We gaffed him with a spring jaw gaff and lifted him high enough so we could administer the coup de grâce with a hammer. Marie said, "We got to dispatch him before we get him in the boat unless we both want to go swimming."

On another fishing trip, I caught a four-and-a-half pound crappie. This little lake was a real paradise and I had the great fortune to be taught fishing by the best fishermen in the North Woods—Marie and Joe.

We went every summer to Allynwood, and it was the highlight of my summers because it was such a pleasant place to be. Marie would cook fresh blueberry pancakes that were the best I have ever had, before or since. The only electricity we had was provided by a diesel generator from dark until 10:30 p.m. If we stayed up past that, we would break out the kerosene lanterns.

In the early spring before the ice melted, Joe and Marie would head north to Allynwood and cut ice blocks from Lonestone Lake and store them in the ice shed, which was covered over with sawdust. That ice would last the entire summer. Grandma had a 1918 Diamond T flatbed truck that Joe would have to hand-crank to get it started. It was the highlight of the day when Joe would haul the trash to the dump ten miles away. I went with him every day. He would talk to "Nellie" like she was a live thing. "Giddiup, Nellie, giddiup" as we started to roll. "Stay on the road, Nellie, stay on the road." We would get to the dump and it was "Whoa, Nellie, whoa." Every once in a while we would see a bear or two but they seemed harmless and never bothered us.

The respect for peace and quiet was very real at Allynwood. Grandma had a sign hanging on the front porch of the main log cabin. I used to read it a lot, and still smile when I think of it today. It said, "I got me two mongril dawgs. I got me a dble burrel shot gun what ain't loaded wif soffer pillers. Damn if I ain't gitten tired o all this hell raisen goin on here." Guns were strictly taboo anywhere on Grandma and Grampa's property.

I was in my own world up at Allynwood. My sister was always with us but to this day I don't know what she did to entertain herself. I know she loved it there and was, I am sure, in her own world also.

Joe came down with Parkinson's disease and, as bad as it got, he never wavered or lost his great sense of humor. He kept all of us in stitches most of the time. Allynwood stayed Allynwood until my grandparents died. I never returned, and eventually heard that a big developer moved in and progress took its unwanted toll on the wilderness lake of Lonestone. I hear there has not been a muskie caught since 1961. If you call that progress, you can have it. My two Norwegian friends, Marie and Joe, eventually passed away and if there is an afterlife, I know all I have to do to find them again is to get myself to a wilderness lake with muskies, sit down on the shore, and wait. Sooner or later, they will show up with heavy rods and reels and a few muddog lures.

Time passed and our family moved to Evanston, Illinois, a little further to the south and right on the shores of Lake Michigan. Dad seemed to be getting interested in aviation again. Of course, I didn't coax him. Much.

2

High School Kid With a Brand New Set of Wings, 1955 to 1959

"Tampa Center American League 816 level 11,000 feet. Squawking 0414 on the transponder, over St. Pete VOR:15 Hevin intersection:00 Mariana next." "American League 816 Tampa squawk ident." "Roger. Squawking ident 816." "Ah roger 816 radar contact cleared flight plan route." "816 roger." All four running smooth. BMEPs lined up across the board. Manifold pressure gauge needles lined up across the board. A pleasant rumble permeating our comfortable cockpit as 816 splits the air at 250 knots true. Ground speed a little slower, with a 10-knot headwind so 816's shadow is racing across the ground at 240 knots, or 280 mph. We always cruised American League's two DC-7Bs at a reduced cruise of 62 percent for maintenance reasons. Even at 62 percent and 250 knots, the old bird drank 415 gallons of purple every hour.

I didn't like Evanston much. I loved the lakeshore but Evanston seemed to lack the adventurous spirit I sought, and seemed deeply embedded in the depths of boredom. Everything I longed for seemed to be looked down upon. "Hey, Dad, what the hell did we move here for?" One good thing was that we lived under a departure route for eastbound airliners out of O'Hare International, and I never tired of looking up every time one would roar overhead.

Steam engines were still in use on the Northwestern Railroad, and were also a source of entertainment for me. I still think of that moaning wail of the steam whistles and the mighty explosions of the locomotives as they picked up speed. I used to hang out by the tracks and thrill to the sight, sound, and vibrating thunder of the ground itself as a highballing hotshot 1200 would roar by, engineer hanging out of the cab, waving and smiling at me as he went by. If he could have stopped, we probably would have been on a first name basis, we waved at each other so many times.

The Boring Years is what I call the time when I was between ten and fourteen years old. When I was thirteen, my dad made the mistake of sending me to summer school at the Culver Naval Academy. I was crushed, and had no intention of enjoying it or to even make an effort to learn anything.

I was in total rebellion and started smoking cigarettes while I was there. Of course I had to hide them because they were strictly taboo at the academy. One day I got caught by an upperclassman. He thought he could pull rank and told me to put my cigarette out in my hand. I just looked at him. He became agitated and said, "Hey, stupid, put your hand out like this," and then put his hand out, palm up. So I obliged him and squashed my cigarette out in his hand. As he pulled his hand back, I popped him right in the nose. On his knees, the upper classman didn't seem so tough anymore, with blood and tears running down his face. Later that night, two kid MPs came marching up to me and told me I was under arrest. When I refused to go with them, they looked at each other and one said to me, "Ah, come on, we'll catch hell if you don't." Apparently they had heard of my confrontation with the kid—who was much bigger than any of us—and just didn't want any trouble with me. I said, "Okay, let's go."

They walked with me to the sally port, where there were four regular army officers seated behind a long table. They looked very intimidating. They dismissed the MPs with all the salutes and military hoopla that went with it. I started to smile as they read the earth-shattering charges. "Wipe that grin off your face." "Do you think this is a laughing matter?" My answer, "Well, sort of, sir," brought them to a stop.

Three of the officers looked on the verge of rage, while the fourth, a colonel, held his hands out to calm the others. He said, "Son, I don't think the military is for you." I said, "You're right, sir. I hate it here. I got nothing against the military, but I would much rather be home with my friends." The old colonel must have been an understanding man since he took me into his office, removed his colonel's hat, and talked to me man to man. He convinced me to "play the game," take my punishment—110 times around the square in full pack—and go to class and formation while doing my best there. He also told me to report to Ensign Stafford who would give me sailing lessons. I will never forget that ole colonel. He turned out to be a good guy after all.

I did what he said and reported to the ensign, who taught me to sail this beautiful all wood gaff-headed catboat. He turned me loose. Every day I would spend my free time sailing this great old catboat, and have many good memories of the sailing I did with her. I wonder what the colonel would think if he knew that he had started a fire in my belly that I couldn't quench until I actually sailed on a square rigger around the world.

Days faded into days, and soon my time in stir came to an end. Though I was not fond of Culver, there were two things that it gave me that have lasted my entire life—sailing, and my lifetime friend, Bill McKinney, who I am in touch with to this day. Through the years I have found that no matter what the job or endeavor, and no matter what your feelings, positive or negative, in every situation I have always found something that has affected my life in a most positive way.

When I was fourteen and about to go to high school, I was at the YMCA swimming pool in Evanston, Illinois, splashing down from the high dive. From the time I hit the water until I surfaced, I became sick. That fast. I barely made it the seven blocks to my house. My mother took my temperature, which was 103.5. She called the doctor, who came to the house. After an ambulance ride to the hospital, it was determined that I had polio. Remember, I was fourteen and knew everything. This was a huge blow to me. Somehow, though, I survived it, and only realized years later how very lucky I was.

School started again, and I was a freshman. It was not long before I had a group of friends, one of whom was a kid named Scott Schmidt. He also had a burning interest in airplanes. We joined the Civil Air Patrol (CAP) as cadets. We had to go through weeks of military crap I had no interest in and finally got our chance to fly. Excited, I showed up at Palwaukee Airport and felt I was back where I belonged again. The CAP's airplane was a war surplus Stinson L-5, a high-wing, fabric-covered beauty with all the patchworks on wings, tail, and fuselage intact. The oil streaks were where they should be, her windscreen had the appropriate scratches. I was in love with the dilapidated old L-5, and when I crawled into the rear seat the wonderful smells of gas, oil, leather, wood, and fabric came flooding in, welcomed like a thirsty gulp of water.

We got started and taxied to runup, held brakes, did the runup. All okay. "You ready, kid?" yelled our CAP pilot. "Yeah," I replied, "Let's see if this old crate'll fly," to quote Johnny Winters. I saw the CAP pilot look in his mirror, wondering where I heard that one, but he never cracked a smile. "Keep your hands and feet off my controls 'til I tell ya." "Okay." The throttle was slowly pushed to full and I was taken aback by the noise in the cockpit of the old ship. She really had a hefty voice. We didn't roll far and then the magic began: the flight of a heavier-than-air flying machine. That moment and feeling is still with me to this day.

We climbed out at 70 indicated and soon leveled at 2,500 feet. After we were level, our air speed settled on 95 mph. "Okay, take her nice and gentle," hollered the pilot. I took the stick in my right hand and both feet on the rudder pedals. I held altitude and course perfectly. Nothing from up front. "Okay, now nice and slow start a 180 degree turn back to the airport." I saw his hand instinctively go for his stick, just in case. Everything Johnny taught me came flooding back. I initiated the turn and gently corrected back on the stick to prevent the nose from dropping. I noticed a raised eyebrow on the face in the mirror in the front cockpit as I leveled on recip heading and held altitude and heading. I put the nose on heading for Palwaukee's runways. "Okay, I got it." "You got it," and I shook the stick as Johnny taught me to do. I saw the look on his face, the same look I had seen before, as if thinking, "Who the hell *is* this kid?"

We made our approach and slowed to 60 over the fence flare, back on the stick, back, back, back. Squeak, squeal, as the mains touch the cement runway and the lighter-than-air machine magically turned herself into a heavier-than-air machine and slowed to a stop. We taxied back and shut down. I figured I did pretty good but the only thing I heard from the front cockpit was, "Careful getting out. Don't fall on your butt! Next!" Well, I was proud of myself anyway and hoped for the day I could squeak one on the ground as sweet as he did. I saw this pilot two years later as I was practicing solo touch-and-goes at Palwaukee in a 172 straight tail. I saw him watching as he stood alongside of the active, having just soloed a student. After about the third landing, I could see recognition on his weather-beaten face, and there it was again, "Who is this kid?"

My first year in high school passed like everyone else's did, fall to winter to spring to summer. Scott Schmidt and I continued with the CAP routine while they kept up the false promise that we would fly on the weekends, get checked out as backseat observers, and go on real search missions. The lieutenant in charge of our squadron maintained this screen until January of 1955, when I told him he was a "lying horse's ass, and on top of that you are filled up to your eyebrows with shit, and cement the rest of the way." That got me a Section 8 discharge and I was gratefully through with this do-nothing group of adults with nothing better to do than be in command of a bunch of hopeful kids. I am sure that in some areas of the country the CAP does a good job, but I have not been personally impressed with it.

My dad had become a successful businessman, and we lived comfortably. One of his business partners had a Ryan Navion and I became a bona fide pest until Jack finally took me along and, deciding I was pretty competent, let me do a lot of the straight and level flying from the right seat. I fell in love with that sweet flying machine called the Ryan Navion and, excuse the mistake, this one was not a Ryan but even earlier, built by North American. A lot of P-51 Mustang was built into the Navion—a low wing monoplane on tri-gear with a sliding canopy opening so you can step down into the cockpit and the big and comfortable cabin. She was powered by a Continental opposed six-cylinder 185 hp engine and had a controllable pitch propeller and could split the molecules at 128 mph indicated for a true of 150.

As Jack came up on the power, I marveled at how smoothly that 185 ran and as we gathered speed, Jack came back on the control wheel before we even had indication on the airspeed indicator. Jack brought the nose wheel two or three inches off the ground and kept it there throughout the takeoff roll until the mains left the ground and we could feel her wings take the load. Later I put a lot of hours in a North American B-25 bomber. The takeoff procedure was identical but the speeds were much higher. As we approached the departure end of the runway, Jack threw the landing gear lever to up using his forefinger to push aside the lock pin and his middle and two other fingers to physically raise the lever to the up position. I felt the landing gears thump into the up and locked position and watched the red "up and locked" light come on.

As I looked out the heavy airplane windshield I was gripped again by the magic. What a wonderful sight to see: the landscape receding and objects on the ground becoming miniaturized as in some toy set. The deep roar in the cockpit was music to my ears. As we leveled off, Jack said, "Here, you fly it." I put all my knowledge to work and kept constant altitude and course. After a while, Jack complimented me by saying, "I am going to take a nap. Let me know when we get to Clinton, Iowa." I think Jack recognized my ability to fly straight and level, staying on course. As we were scarfing down our $100 cheeseburgers at the Clinton Airport cafe, Jack and I talked at length about learning to fly. I hinted, well, maybe blatantly, at planting a bug in Dad's ear.

We got back in the Navion and I hand flew this new love back to DuPage Airport in Illinois. I was fifteen, and as we turned left downwind for Runway 28, I noticed two thin columns of black smoke rising up from the ground just to the south and east of our turn point for left base. I asked Jack what he thought it was. Jack said, "I don't know but it doesn't look good." We landed and right away noticed no line personnel anywhere nearby, in fact nobody was around. We went into the line office. Two people were there, and right away we knew by the long faces that something was terribly wrong. We found out that just prior to us arriving a J-3 Cub and Cessna 120 had a mid-air collision and both spun in, killing both pilots. Jeez, that was sobering. I went out to the ramp and looked at the two columns of smoke. Hell, I never even thought about getting killed in an airplane.

I made my mind up then and there that I would at all costs continue in my dream to become a flyer. That was my first lesson: aviation is truly heavenly most of the time, and that is occasionally interrupted by true tragedy. There is no in-between. I also noted that by the time I got home, I couldn't wait until the next time I could fly.

Ryan Navion. Photograph by Bill Harris.

Little did I know, later in life I would own a 225 hp Ryan Navion and had an engine failure right after takeoff. I had to make a landing in a soft field and crashed as gently as I could and the Navion proved its North American heritage by staying together and making a possible fatal crash into a survivable crash.

Jack took me up every once in a while, and I thoroughly enjoyed it every time. Jack also took me on a goose hunt outside of Benton, Illinois, a place that would become very familiar to me over the next few years. I shared a blind with Howard Hooker. Howard had become, and still is, remembered as one of my favorite characters. As he would have expressed my sentiments, "Erybody orta have a Howard." Howard was a WWII Navy enlisted and served on a carrier. Born and raised in the country in and around southern Illinois, he was a true country good ole boy and gentleman.

The day, and I mean the first day, we shared a goose blind, Howard wrapped me around his finger in the first five minutes we were together. He had a magnetic personality and a sense of humor I have never heard anywhere else. For example, I noticed a bunch of crows sitting in the tree in front of our blind. The day was sunny and the geese were way high in the sky. To quote Howard, "Well, looky there will ya? Them geese jest formed up with a B-29." Anyway, I made the statement that I had heard crows were real smart birds. That opened the door for a deep philosophical discussion on the subject of crows. Now ole Howard was a big guy with a pleasantly happy, lined face and would never be caught dead out of his coveralls and workman's boots. He made his living as an oil well "head roustabout." He never wore a hat but his dark hair parted dead in the middle and ended military perfect above his ears. Even in a wind, it always stayed neatly combed.

As we continued our conversation, I was convinced in my young mind that Howard was one smart guy, and he really was. The conversation swung around to "How do you make a crow talk?" By this time, I was deeply involved in this very interesting conversation and Howard hesitated just long enough for me to open my mouth. I thought I would show him that I knew something also, so I said, "Well, I know that you have to split their tongue to make them talk." Howard looked at me in a fatherly manner, and with a straight face said, "Well, son, why? Boy, ah thort erybody knew that the reason ya split a crow's tongue was so's he can lick both sides of his ass at the same time!" I hit the deck, laughing so hard I was doubled up. Howard just sat there grinning because he pulled one over on me.

The day dragged on and we might as well have left our guns at home. It never did get boring when in the company of this great man, despite of our lack of flying targets. Every day the horn sounded off at 4:00 p.m. and we had to unload our guns and call it quits for the day. At about 3:30 p.m. Howard said, "Get ready. Looky yonder." Sure enough, there were three geese, wings set and heading for a landing spot right in front of our blind. "Okay now, Dave, stay down til ah tell ya to get up and shoot." My heart pounding in my mouth, I checked the safety and snapped it off. "Git ready. Okay, take your limit." I sprung up and banged my head on the roof of the blind, which caused me to pull the trigger. The shotgun discharged straight up in the air where it was pointed with a ferocious "BOOM!" The recoil knocked me back down on the bench I had just departed and I just sat there feeling real stupid. I didn't want to look at Howard but I did. He was looking at me with this grin on his face. All the geese flew away and headed back to the sanctuary. Howard never even glanced at them, instead looking at me and saying, "Safety?" I said, "On." He still had the grin on his face and finally said, "Boy, yer like a bull. What you don't break ya shit on."

A couple of days later a storm front moved in and the clouds were right on the deck and so were the geese. By 8:30 a.m. both Howard and I had our limit of two geese each and so did Jack and Lester. It was a great day and a marvelous Thanksgiving feast in 1955.

I knew Howard as a hunting buddy for the next four years and always loved hearing about his experiences as a deckhand on a U.S. carrier, fighting the Japanese. I would sit spellbound for hours listening to his pleasant country-boy accented voice.

I don't mind hunting ducks for some reason but I never hunted geese again. Why? Well, that day in 1955 I gained a deep respect for the bird called a Canadian honker. I had knocked my first one down but did not kill it. I went out to get it when I noticed two more with their wings set, coming in to land next to the fallen goose. Hiding behind a bush, I saw my chance to fill out. I saw my goose looking at them and just at the right moment, he hollered out, "Brawk! Brawk!" Both geese aborted and headed back to the sanctuary. I was amazed. My goose saved their lives by giving away his position. I am convinced to this day that geese talk to each other. Then my goose looked at me and charged. I felt terrible to have to kill it. When I found out that they mate for life, I vowed never to hunt them again. Since then, I have seen squadrons of geese flying in perfect formation in between cloud layers at the same altitude that I was flying, hell, they are even instrument rated and qualify as brothers of the wind.

Howard and I got together many times after that and hunted quail, pheasant, and ducks. I would bring them home to Evanston and when Marie would cook them along with one of her famous apple pies, it was a meal to die for.

One lasting memory that I have of Howard was when I was visiting him and he was souping up his '38 Ford. I said, "Howard, do you think she will be fast?" "Fast? Why, she'll hoot and scoot over that hill like a mad goriler with a saw drawed across his ace!" People who like Americana love it when I talk about ole Howard and I will always fondly remember my friend.

In my sophomore year in high school I joined the football team. Not because I liked to play, but because the girls liked football jocks. During that season, one night while at dinner, Dad said that he and Jack had flown a Cessna 170. My ears shot up like a German Shepherd going on alert. "Well, what do you think?" I asked, eager for information. "Oh, I don't know." "Well, didn't you like it?" "Oh, it was okay." "How fast is it?" "Oh, pretty fast." He was not forthcoming with his answers, and I continued to interrogate him impatiently. "Did you go anywhere?" "Oh, we went to Milwaukee." "Damnit, Dad, How long did it take you to get there?" "Oh, no time at all." "Dad! Answer my damn questions, will you?" He looked at me with a twinkle in his eye and finally said, "Well, I guess you will just have to go out and fly it yourself to find out." *What? Did I hear that correctly?* "You heard me. You are going to take your first official flying lesson with Ed Casey on Saturday morning." This was on Monday, and it took what seemed like at least two years for Saturday to come around. In the meantime, my classroom studies turned into learning everything that could be read about Cessna 170 series aircraft.

Saturday broke clear and calm. In those days, Sky Harbor was way out in the country and the drive to it was in the country also. It took us forever to drive down Edens Expressway to Wheeling Road. It took another forever to drive the ten miles on Wheeling to the access road to Sky Harbor Airport. We drove to a large wooden hangar and got out of the car. I immediately noticed a beautiful, bright red 1928 Cessna A.W. hanging from the stress beams of the hangar. To this day I wonder whatever became of that marvelous piece of history.

Dad walked up to a shiny 1955 Cessna 172 and announced that it was ours. I was expecting a 170, but immediately fell head over heels with the most beautiful blue and silver straight-tail 172 in existence. I crawled in and, sure enough, all the smells were there, with the exception of wood. I caressed her yoke and panel and was in my own world once again. It was an awesome moment in my fifteen-year-old life. I tried out the rudder pedals and control limits and announced to Dad, "She fits me perfectly."

I asked, "How much did she cost?" He said with pride, "Brand new, from the factory, $4,800.00 including the whistle stop tuner com radio and an LF (low frequency) range nav radio."

LF range stations were still in use in those days. With four inbound and outbound legs to each station. Each leg had a yellow A leg · – dit dah and on the other side a blue or N leg – · Or dah dit leg. You had to wear earphones and constantly listen to the morse code beeps. · – · – – told you that you were on the left side of center line and then you knew that you had to correct right slightly until the · – · – faded gradually to a solid "be-e-e-e-e" and that told you that you were centerline inbound to the station. You would hold the correction until you started to faintly hear the – · – · – · that told you that you were in the blue side and then you would slightly correct left until you were in the solid be-e-e-e-e again. After a couple of corrections, you could hold a constant be-e-e-e-e and you knew then that you were inbound to the station. We called it "bracketing the course." As you passed over the station, everything would go silent—"the cone of silence." You would then take up the outbound heading to intercept the outbound leg. As you were outbound, you had to remember that the A and N quadrants reverse and then you had to navigate in reverse until you intercepted the next inbound leg to the next station.

With all that said, VHF (very high frequency), or VORs, were the new and coming way, using an instrument with a needle and an indicator "to" or "from" still oscillating in a yellow and blue painted arc on the upper face. Any bonehead could navigate without too much thought as to what you were doing. By 1958 I don't think there was a yellow and blue airway left anywhere in the United States.

Dad and I left our new bird and headed up a flight of stairs to the Blue Sky Cafe on an upper level of the wooden hangar. As we entered the dining area, I could not help but inhale the great smell of home-cooked food. The cafe was not five stars by any means, but just a room with tables, a bar-type credenza, and the cooking area open and just behind the bar—no liquor sold here. It was a real airport cafe, the kind of place people look for today but have little luck in finding. In those days, they were on every field, big or small. Gas was also only 21 cents a gallon in those days.

A very thin man of average height, with salt and pepper wavy hair combed straight back and thin face approached us. I could tell by the crow's feet and twinkle in his eyes that he was an aviator. "Ed, I would like to introduce you to my son, Dave." I looked him straight in the eye and gave him a firm handshake. Ed looked at me and said, "So you want to fly, David." From that first encounter, Ed always called me David, never "kid" or "son" and I liked that. I was taken aback by the high, scratchy voice but the words were fired at me with the focus and intensity of an expert marksman. I would come to love and respect that voice as its owner would flow through the complications of teaching me to fly with grace and ease. I told him that flying was the only thing I wanted to really learn how to do. "Well, then, we will have to see what we can do about that." Ed was not easy with a smile, but I could sense that my answer had pleased him.

We sat down and launched into a pre-lesson discussion with Ed presiding. I really wanted to impress him, not by showing off but to fly the best I could and use the skills I had learned from Johnny Winters. He went through a meticulous pre-flight and reminded me that after this first time I was expected to do the pre-flight myself, so "don't forget what I am showing you." We got strapped in and Ed went through the cockpit procedures and use of the controls, most of which I already knew but I said nothing. He talked me through the start-up, which was not very complicated, but he impressed upon me the use of "clear" and then waiting a few seconds to hear if a reply came back, and also to always expect to hear "not clear."

The next thing was to crack the throttle, switch the magnetos to "both," and pull the spring-loaded starting toggle and hold it until the engine caught, and then to let go. After a brief warm up, he told me to start taxiing the aircraft. This was my first time actually in control of a moving aircraft on the ground and I found it extremely simple to do. Of course, she was a nosewheel aircraft and, to this day, I feel people would be a lot better off if they would do their primary flight instruction in a tail-dragger or conventionally-geared aircraft. A tail-dragger will force you to learn finesse and coordination from the get-go, unlike a nose wheel aircraft. But at the time, so what, I was in heaven with our little silver and blue 172.

Ed showed me the runup procedures and then I made a 360-degree turn on the ground as Ed instructed me to look for traffic in the pattern. We lined up and Ed told me to follow him through on the takeoff because I would make the next one myself. The little bird accelerated at full throttle to about 60 mph and Ed helped her into the air with very slight movements of the controls. "Okay, David, you got it." I took the controls with a slight wiggle and repeated, "I got it," all part of the pre-takeoff instruction I had learned from Johnny. Ed nodded, and said, "Very good."

"Let's climb straight ahead after our clearing turn to 5,000 feet." He coaxed me through our 45-degree turn and then instructed me to hold 80 mph and climb to 5,000 feet. I held the climb steady and maintained heading. We leveled at 5,000 feet and Ed said, "Now follow me through. We are going to make a left 360-degree turn." We made a standard rate turn and when we got to heading, Ed retrimmed for straight and level flight. "Okay, David, let's see you do it." Ed, even though he didn't show it, was surprised to see me initiate the turn and at the same time trim slight nose up. I held altitude and "bump" hit our slipstream as we returned to heading. "Now give me one to the right," he said. As we completed our 360 to the right, I was a little low and did not quite hit our slipstream but was well within limits. Ed looked at me and said, "I think you have done this before." I tried not to show my pride and just said, "Yes, sir." "Good, we will do more later. Let's go ahead and advance to slow flight and stalls."

This was new territory for me but Johnny had, as it turned out, prepared me for this also and we did our ballet in the air without too much trouble. Ed admitted, "Normally, I do not get into this type of flying until the third or fourth lesson. You are doing very well." I felt a warm glow deep down. After more turns and slow flights, no flaps, full flaps, and everything in between, Ed said, "Let's go in and try a landing." I flew the pattern and Ed took over on short final with instructions for me to follow him through. We flared and—squeak—we were on the ground and slowing to a stop. "Taxi her in and let's have a post-flight talk."

We got out of the 172 and walked into the front office and into Ed's little office. Right away, I noticed a black-and-white photo of Ed Casey in helmet and goggles standing next to a Lockheed P-38 Lightning. "Is that you?" "Yup, flew P-38s against the Germans," and, without further comment, launched right into post-flight briefing. "Well, it's obvious you have had some time in an aeroplane. It shows. You're instructor did a good job of it—who is he?" I told Ed about Johnny Winters and the T-50 Bamboo Bomber and saw a slight rise in Ed's eyebrows when I told him I started learning when I was five-and-a-half years old. "Obviously Johnny worked the rudder pedals, and that shows too. I guess you were really and truly born into aviation," he said with a rare smile. I felt accepted and that the door to the aviation world had just opened to me.

"Tomorrow we are going to skip more air work and get you used to rudder work and do takeoffs and landings. I think you are ready for that. So remember our takeoff and landing because you are going to do all the work tomorrow. I've got to fly with your dad now so if you don't mind, give him a shout for me please." Trying to contain my excitement and not trip over myself on the way out, I said, "See ya tomorrow, Ed!" I got some money for the first of many of the best cheeseburgers and home fries in the world at the Blue Sky Cafe. I had to walk to the other end of the field to get to the wooden hangar and the cafe. I feel I could have cartwheeled the whole distance and about halfway there, I watched a 1938 Stinson SR9 Gullwing roar by, prop cavitating with a deafening wall of sound and immediately dissolve into the low rumble of the Lycoming R680 300hp radial engine that powered her. I stopped and listened to her rumble as it slowly abated and became inaudible. I remember thinking to myself that I am really going to be a part of this. I waited until Dad and Ed taxied out and took off and enjoyed the sight of our little silver and blue aircraft gracefully take to the air and fly out of sight. I couldn't wait for tomorrow.

1938 Stinson SR9

1931 Waco RNF

Somebody told me that tomorrow always comes. And this one was no exception—it came right on schedule. I pre-flighted with Ed looking over my shoulder. I must have done a good job because Ed never said a thing. We got strapped in and I got our C145 Continental engine primed, mixture full rich, throttle cracked, mags on both, and hollered, "Clear?" out my side window. I listened for about four seconds to give somebody a chance to respond in the negative. I see pilots who holler "Clear?" and immediately start their engines. I have on three different occasions, while flying bigger aircraft than a 172, caught a negative response and avoided a disaster because I hesitated the way Ed taught me to. To any pilots reading this: don't hit the starter right after calling "Clear?" Wait a few seconds, you might save a life and your own sanity.

I heard no response and pulled the starter tog, the prop made maybe one revolution and the engine fired and settled down to the only unexciting noise any opposed 6-cylinder engine can make but at least they are very smooth-running engines. We taxied out and did our runup: 1800 rpm, mags checked, carb heat out, drop in rpm, engine to idle, carb heat cold, controls, and flaps. I looked at Ed. "Okay, David, you ready?" "Not yet, Ed. I have to make a clearing turn and then I'm ready." No smile, but I could tell Ed was satisfied. After the 360-degree clearing turn, we taxied into position and Ed said, "Gently, smoothly, and slowly advance the throttle to full power. You have the takeoff." Ed also told me, "Never make a fast or thoughtless move in the cockpit. Always move slowly and with confidence that you know exactly what you are about to do. Even in an emergency." That is a piece of instruction that has stuck with me to this day and on more than one occasion has played a major role in saving my life.

As we started to roll and gain speed, I noticed the nose slowly began to move left of centerline. I also noticed Ed ready on the rudders, but I beat him to it and, remembering his instructions, slowly came in with right rudder and the little 172 responded instantly, giving me recognition and confidence in what my controls can do. I continued the takeoff dead center on the runway and at 60 mph slowly and gently came back on the control yoke. The little 172 responded by going airborne. I was again in familiar territory and kept her wings level and let her accelerate to 75 indicated, her best climb speed. I had no trouble turning crosswind or downwind and as we came abeam of the end of the runway, Ed said, "Pull on carb heat and close your throttle. Fly straight ahead and slow to 70 mph. When the approach end of the runway is at a 45 degree angle behind your trailing edge of the wing, make a left 90 degree turn to base leg." "Always clear yourself by looking around every quadrant and especially straight below you."

I was in new territory and being so close to the ground I felt I was all over the sky. Ed kept up the chatter, talking me through my first landing. As I turned to final approach, I felt I was too slow and too low. Ed said, "Use your power as you need it." I slowly came in with a little power and the little bird responded instantly, renewing my confidence for the moment. Somehow I managed to make a poor imitation of a final approach and as the runway boundary slipped below our aircraft, I did what every newcomer did, being basically afraid of the ground: I began flaring way too high. Ed gently put the palm of his hand on the control yoke and prevented me from coming back further on the controls. At the right moment, he released pressure and I arrived. If anybody were filming it would have at least rated XXX, it was such a terrible landing.

"Okay, let's bring her to a stop and taxi back for another one." My next four landings were not much better but seemed to be improving slightly. Ed told me on the fourth crash to "fly out of the pattern and let's do some more air work." We did, and he put me through a series of stalls and slow flight. When we returned I actually got the aircraft on the ground without scaring hell out of myself. We taxied in and shut down and retired to Ed's office for post brief. I was worn out and figured that Ed was probably going to tell me to quit while I was still alive. I was surprised when he did just the opposite, surgically dissecting our training flight. He then told me that next weekend we would start with air work and come back in for more takeoffs and landings.

It was Dad's turn since he was working on his private license. I stood alongside the runway and watched all the takeoffs and landings they made, and thought they looked pretty good.

On the way home, Dad said, "I just couldn't get those landings down today. I really messed them up." Shocked, I said, "They looked pretty good to me." He said, "They always look better from the outside." I thought that maybe I hadn't done as badly as I'd thought I had. It sure made me feel better about the whole deal.

The next weekend came around and after our initial air work, we entered the pattern. I noticed right off the bat that I felt much more comfortable and my landings started to smooth out as I had started learning where the bottom of my wheels were in relation to the ground. By Sunday I was making takeoffs and landings completely unassisted. At our post flight on Sunday Ed told me, "Well, David, your prior flight experience has put you well ahead of the game. Normally at four hours I would never consider saying this. If you were sixteen, and not fifteen, in the next hour I would get out and solo you. I would have no problem with that, but the C.A.A.—soon to be the FAA—has definite rules considering ages for solo. You must be sixteen. So anytime you fly, you must be accompanied by an instructor or somebody with a pilot's license." I told him that come December 21st, we could plan on it.

It was September and, in my mind, December 21, 1956 was a hundred years away. But I had a plan. I told Ed that I felt that the 172 was not much of a challenge and that on December 21st I would like to solo in a tailwheel aircraft. "Well, we got a couple of 170s for rent. I don't see why we can't check you out in time for solo. Work it out with your father." So I headed to the Blue Sky and devoured a great cheeseburger. I met Sylvia Roth there. She had short, dark hair, was about 110 pounds, and was wearing a leather jacket and Ray-Ban sunglasses. She not only looked the part, but was actually a great aviatrix. I introduced myself, and she said, "You're the new guy Ed has been talking about."

It felt great to be having lunch with some local pilots. One of the owners, Ed Tilger, was there. He was tall, thin, had reddish-brown hair, and was rarely seen without his pipe jammed in his mouth. Two transits were also there, both ex-military. The hangar talk between these pilots had me hanging onto every word, until Sylvia asked me what my plans were in regards to flying. I said that I wanted to fly commercially. "Not much money in that," she said. "Who cares?" I said flippantly, which elicited some chuckles and more conversation, this time including me. When I told them my plans for soloing, they all agreed that "once you learn to fly a taildragger, there is basically nothing you can't fly." I was excited and more determined than ever.

Dad eventually came in and joined us. He had also had a better day and was in a cheery mood. I was worried that I would hurt his feelings when I introduced my new plan. As we drove home, I just couldn't say anything about it. As we got onto Edens Expressway, he said, "Well, I think you ought to start learning to fly the 170 in November so you will be fresh when it comes time to solo." I sat there looking stupid with my mouth hanging open. How quickly I had forgotten his words to me a while back, "Do what makes you happy. Just two things: do it the best you can and make sure it is legal." Erybody orta have a dad like mine. I should have known that Dad would back anything we kids wanted to do as long as it fit into those two guidelines.

November was only three-quarters of a century away and, in the meantime, I had this brand-new shiny 172 to fly. It seemed the news was out about the new kid who used to fly a Bamboo Bomber. I don't know how that got out because I didn't say anything. Everybody wanted to try me and I had no problem finding qualified pilots to fly with me. The only problem was trying to get them to understand that I had been five-and-a-half years old when I first sat in an airplane and it was all I could do to keep the wings level. "Did you guys hear about the new kid who learned to fly when he was only three?" "Hey, did you guys know that the new kid was flying a B-17 with his dad who was a five-star general when he was only ten?" Come on, you guys, I can barely fly a 172 at age fifteen.

Soon November arrived and one bright, sunny Saturday morning Ed introduced me to the businesslike taildragger called a 170 Cessna. What a beauty. Pre-flight was about the same as a 172, with the exception of a tailwheel steering cable tension check. Start up was exactly the same and taxiing was nothing like a 172. The 170 had a mind of its own. Because it was a tailwheel aircraft, all the inherent stability of a nosewheel aircraft was gone. The 170's tail just decided it was going to go anywhere it damn well pleased and even had a wheel to do it on. Frustrated, I just could not taxi worth a damn. Ed constantly had to jab brakes, push rudder, and use the elevator and aileron to help this mustang behave herself. It became very clear in my mind what those other pilots meant when they talked about how flying anything else was easy after flying a taildragger.

Flying to Belen, NM in my 1949 Cessna 170. Photograph by Robert Anderson.

Cockpit of a 170. Very complicated to a brand new student.

We taxied into position and Ed reminded me to "hold back pressure on the elevator, lead in with a little right rudder, and be prepared to use your rudders quickly to prevent a bad situation." I applied power slowly and smoothly. The advice "Don't make any fast moves in the cockpit" became obsolete about one second after we started rolling. The little 170 got impatient to try the grass on the left side of the runway and headed for it. I came in with right rudder and then more right rudder and little 170 changed her mind and, faster than I could think, headed for the grass on the right side of the runway. That's when Ed took it. I lasted about three-and-a-half seconds and was amazed at how many different things a flying machine can do in that short period of time.

Ed instantly got control back and told me to stay on it. The boogie woogie started all over again. Ed had to take control several more times until we finally got airborne and I was back in a place I understood. My heart started to slow down, and Ed nonchalantly said, "Different, huh?" I thought if any of my new friends were standing along the runway describing the takeoff, their conversation would be something like this: "The new kid's got it." "Instructor." "New kid." "Instructor." "New kid." "Instructor." "He's safe now they're in the air."

Wow, how do you control this little monster? I wondered. The pattern procedures were the same as the 172 and turning final my heart rate abruptly went up and I was thinking, "Now we gotta get this slippery snake on the ground." Ed was a very calm instructor and passed the feeling on to all of his students. "Now flare just like in the 172 but keep your flare and as she slows, keep coming back," Ed instructed me. Well, it began alright but to every beginning there is an ending. I started the flare and before I flared more, *bam* mains, tailwheel *boing* we launched right back into the air again. "Power, David. Flare again, power off." And I managed to dribble the bird back onto the ground but Ed had to take her again. The remainder of the hour went like the first part and I was convinced that tailwheel aircraft were all designed by the devil himself.

With Ed's patience and calming nature I slowly began to learn finesse with the rudders and power when I needed it. Before long, things began to fall into place and I started to become more confident flying the 170. She was no longer a slippery snake or a monster but a very sweet flying machine. Once I learned her ways, she was easy to control. I also learned not to relax even for an instant because her devilish breeding would suddenly appear, grinning, as I fought to regain control. That little 170 opened the door for my love of old tailwheel aircraft that is still with me today.

It was getting close to December 21, 1956, and I was sure of my solo flight in a 170. Ed was there to meet me a few weeks ahead of time. He said, "I got some bad news for you." "What is it?" I asked, with trepidation. "The boss replaced the 170 with a 172 and a 182." "Does that mean what I think it means?" I asked. "Yup, you're going to solo in your 172." Disappointed, I thought at least I am going to solo. The day came, and it was a marvelous feeling to be by myself and in total command of a real aeroplane. I couldn't get enough of it and when I finally got down, Ed grasped my hand and even had a wide smile as he said, "Congratulations! You earned it. Hell, I thought I was going to have to get my shotgun out and shoot you down." It was a grand moment. Mom, Dad, my sister, and my new pilot friends were all there. My dream was coming true. I actually soloed in an aeroplane before I had a driver's license. That I got a couple of days later.

Now that I could drive myself to the airport, I took full advantage of this new freedom and flew every chance I got. I did T-and-Gs at every airport between Chicago, Kankakee, and Milwaukee. One day Ed collared me and told me he wanted me to start my dual cross-countries and he had made contact with pilot instructor "Bones" to fly the first one with me. Bones? What the hell kind of a name is that? "He wants you to flight plan for a round robin to Davenport, Iowa, and back. Be ready in one hour."

That's what I love about aviation: you never have to get bored for something to do. It always happens. I asked Sylvia if she had ever heard of a guy named Bones. "Everybody knows Bones, why?" she responded. "Well, he is going to give me my first dual cross-country." She gave out a hefty laugh and said, "You are a lucky guy. Bones taught the Wright brothers how to fly," then walked off, chuckling to herself. I couldn't wait.

So I flight planned the trip and made sure I had everything just right. I really wanted to make a good impression on Bones. Pretty soon this leather-faced guy wearing an oily, beat up golfers cap, leather jacket, and pant legs loosely tucked into rubber galoshes walked up and said, "You Dave?" "Yup, you Bones?" "Ya think ya learned anything since I had ya up in the L-5?" I didn't even think the CAP pilot knew I was there much less remember me years later. "I saw ya at Palwaukee a couple of weeks ago. Looked like ya were doin' fair." I later found out that that was a bigger compliment than Bones ever gave out.

I was soon on friendly terms with instructor pilot Bones, one of the neatest guys I have had the pleasure of knowing. Bones began his flying career in the 1920s, barnstorming in a JN4D Jenny. One of my favorite funny stories came from Bones as he was in the right seat of the same 172. I was struggling with navigating the old Cessna from Des Moines, Iowa, to the Sky Harbor Airport in Wheeling, Illinois.

"Here's my flight plan. Want to check it?" "What for?" he replied, "I know how to get there. You're the only one I'm worried about." I like ol' Bones right off. We strapped in and soon were level and cruising, indicating 115 mph I figured we would be about 1 hour and 15 minutes with a slight headwind. Bones hadn't said a word up to this point. "Ya think your gyro compass is right?" I double-checked with the magnetic compass and corrected. "I don't need to ask you again, hey?" "No, sir." How in hell did he know? A little while later, "Where are we?" "A little north of course." Bones didn't say a thing, just looked at me and I could tell he was thinking, Well, what the hell are ya gonna do about it? I corrected. A while later, "What's your tach say?" "2400." "What's 65 percent?" "2450." Again, the look. I corrected. In a little bit, "Ya got something against 5500?" I corrected back to 5500. Man, ol' Bones didn't miss a thing.

I saw Davenport and knew the location of the airport so I came back to 2200 rpm and started the descent. "Where we goin'?" "I got the field." "Looks like it to me, too." I flew over the field and checked the windsock and tetrahedron and it looked like 21 at Davenport Muni. I knew they had a great cafe and after we landed and were taxiing off the runway, I said, "You hungry?" "When you're eatin' you ain't flyin'. Let's taxi back and head for Sky Harbor." So that's what we did. I was hoping to re-flight plan over a juicy cheeseburger.

Being too young and inexperienced to just fly the recip course back to Sky Harbor, I took off worrying about our heading back to Sky Harbor. To make things worse, Bones fell asleep shortly after takeoff. About halfway home, I was totally lost. How the hell was I going to do this. So I put my most professional pilot hat on and figured I wasn't going to let Bones think I wasn't doing my job. As nonchalantly as I could, I said, "Hey, Bones, give me a fix, will ya?" Bones opened just one eye and looked at me for a few seconds and said, "What's wrong with the one you are already in?" and went back to sleep. The cagey old fox set me up. I had to start thinking on my own.

I figured that if I kept flying on our easterly heading, we couldn't miss Lake Michigan and then I would know where we were. As it turned out, things started looking familiar and, lo and behold, Sky Harbor came up right on the nose. I didn't wake Bones and squeaked it on in the cinders on Runway 010. Bones stretched and yawned and said, "You sure are a lucky young lad." He signed my logbook and departed as quietly as he had arrived. I was starving and the cheeseburger and fries tasted the best I could remember, all washed down with a bottle of Coke for 55 cents.

I felt I was a little less of a greenhorn now that I had flown a taildragger, soloed in a 172, and only got lost for a short time on my first cross-country. I flew with Bones a few more time and he never changed, never said much, so it must have been through mental telepathy that I expanded my knowledge while flying with this silent guy called Bones.

In January, 1957, Dad and I flew down to Benton, Illinois, on some business

Dad had to attend to. Dad had passed his instrument flight test with Sylvia Roth as his instructor. I think that Dad had picked this particular weekend to go because the weather forecast was IFR for the Chicago area beginning at 15:00 that afternoon. We flight planned to arrive at 16:30 just to make sure we would be in the weather in a single-engine aircraft.

In later years I developed an unbreakable rule that only when forced to will I fly night, IFR, or over water in a single-engine aircraft. But in those days, ignorance was bliss. As we took off from the grass strip at Benton, I noticed a high overcast that was the southern end of the front that was moving into Chicago. The little 172 engine was running smooth as we climbed slowly to 2,500 feet. By this time, 5849B was IFR-equipped and had all the bells and whistles 1957 had to offer in radios. The ol' whistle tuner probably went to a museum and it never worked anyway. Leveling at 2,500 Dad contacted Springfield radio and filed an IFR flight plan. A few minutes went by and Springfield contacted us with a clearance.

In those days, there were no FSS or transponders, and Victor airways were still in the future. Radar coverage was only around major cities. Dad announced, "N5849 Baker ready to copy." "Ah Cessna 5849 Baker, you are cleared to Palwaukee Airport from present position direct to Shelbyville ADF direct to Pontiac VOR, direct to Northbrook VOR. Expect VOR circling approach to Runway 28 Palwaukee. Expect radar vectors to Northbrook VOR at Joliet climb to and maintain 5,000 feet. Contact Chicago Center 120.4." As Dad read back the clearance, I tuned the ADF to SUZ and listened to the Morse code identifier. Faintly I heard ...S – · – – U – – · · Z. "Shelbyville identified on the ADF," I said. Dad centered the needle and continued the climb. I switched our com radio to our assigned frequency of 120.4. "Ah Chicago, this is Cessna 5849 Baker climbing out of 3,000 to level at 5,000 feet." "Ah Roger 49 Baker, continue climb flight plan route." And then, "49 Baker, there is no radar coverage your area. Expect radar coverage at Joliet." "49 Baker roger."

I watched the ground slowly slip by under our wings and enjoyed the feeling of just being there. I noticed long before we got to SUZ that the definition of the ground was beginning to become fuzzy. We were slowly entering the cloud base at 4,000 feet. Soon we were solid IFR and little 49 Baker seemed for all purposes to be standing completely still, no movement of any kind could be detected. Everything outside was solid grey, even the outer wing panels took on a blurry look. The ADF needle slowly rotated and pointed to 180 degrees south. We were over the station. "Ah Chicago, 49 Baker is over Shelbyville at :11 level 5000 Pontiac at :53 Northbrook next." "Ah roger 49 Baker. Palwaukee reporting 600 feet, one-quarter mile in snow." "Ah roger, keep us posted." "Chicago roger."

Dad bracketed the outbound course of 002 degrees and centered the station behind us on 002 degrees. This should put us on course for Pontiac VOR. I tuned in Pontiac 109.6 but we were still too far out. We had 46 minutes to go and I figured it would be another 25 or 30 minutes before we would make contact with the audible identifier. Feeling like we were standing still and being able to see only grey, it seemed to take forever for the time to go by. Soon I heard a faint · – – · · P – · N – T. "Pontiac identified on the VHF Nav."

Dad centered the needle and flew the course inbound. We determined that we had a pretty good crosswind from the southwest because we had to hold 348 degrees to hold our inbound of 002 degrees. "That ought to give us a tailwind," Dad said, "but Palwaukee is already below minimums." "What do you think we should do?" I asked. "We can always go into O'Hare," Dad said confidently. I always loved flying with Dad because he was so confident of what he was doing. In hindsight, this IFR flight just might have been a bit more than Dad had anticipated.

At 16:48 the VOR needle began to move, indicating we were over the VOR, so we were early and did have a tailwind. The indicator flag went from, to, to, from at :49, or 16:49. "Ah Chicago, 49 Baker over Pontiac, level 5,000. Northbrook at :44." It would be dark by then, and I hoped a little better weather. Alas, hoping has never worked and never will. The weather was getting worse. "49 Baker Chicago. Call us above Joliet ADF for radar identification. Palwaukee reporting 200 feet and zero visibility in heavy snow." "That's not good," Dad said to me. "Ah roger Chicago. How's O'Hare?" "O'Hare is reporting 300 feet and one mile." "Roger. 49 Baker is requesting clearance to O'Hare. Level 5,000." "49 Baker clearance." "Roger. Go ahead 49 Baker." "Cessna 5849 Baker you are cleared to O'Hare Airport. Present position direct Joliet. Contact O'Hare approach 128.4 over Joliet for radar vectors to ILS outer marker Runway 22 Left at O'Hare. Descend to and maintain 4,000 feet."

Dad read back our new clearance and I tuned in Joliet but we were still too far out. "Ah Chicago, 49 Baker is out of 5,000 for 4,000." "Ah roger, 49 Baker report level at 4,000." We reached 4,000 feet and Dad made the call. That's when I noticed movement outside our cockpit windshield. Snow. The thousands of flakes rushing at us looked really cool to me since we could see our speed in three dimensions.

We were over Joliet right on time and Dad tuned to 128.4. "O'Hare approach this is 5849 Baker with you over Joliet, level 4,000 feet." "EH roger 49 Baker. Make left 90 degree turn to 270 degrees for radar identification." "Left to 270 degrees. 49 Baker roger." About halfway through the turn, approach said, "EH 49 Baker, we have you in radar contact. Turn right heading 015 degrees for vectors to outer marker 22 Left. Expect clearance at the marker." "49 Baker to 015 degrees radar vectors to outer marker ILS 22 Left," Dad repeated. It was like two people doing a complicated dance as approach threw out many different headings and altitude changes, all leading to one tiny spot 1,200 feet above the ground called the outer marker Runway 22 Left at O'Hare International Airport. An amazing thing, especially in those past days of 1957.

"Outer marker inbound," Dad reports. "EH roger 49 Baker you are cleared for the approach. Contact tower 126.9." "126.9. Thanks for the help. 49 Baker." "Adios." "Ah O'Hare tower, Cessna 5849 Baker outer marker inbound." "5849 Baker you are number one for 22 Left. Cleared to land." I watched Dad focus on the slight control movements and power adjustments to keep the localizer and glide slope needles lined up and cross-haired as we descended in thick cloud and big snowflakes. The landing light literally blinded us when we turned it on and Dad instantly turned it off. "Call out when you see the runway." I could tell Dad was tense. I focused out the windscreen and called out, "500 to go . . . 400 to go . . . 300 to go." At 300 feet, I saw blurry approach lights begin to show and as Dad was just beginning to add power for a go-around, I hollered out, "I got the runway!" Dad looked up and chopped the power dead center on the numbers. I watched the big white numbers "22" pass beneath us and *squeak!* we were down.

I was very proud of my dad, the pilot, and hoped for the day I could do as well. Dad feigned wiping off sweat with the back of his hand and let out his *phewww* sound that I had heard so many times. "That was a bit more than I had hoped for," he said. "Good job, Dad." As we drove home that evening, I felt that great post hard flight glow for the first time. I would feel this many times in the future.

My high school friends were having a get together that evening and I got there late. A girl asked me where I had been, and I responded, probably with obvious pride, that we had just flown our 172 in from Southern Illinois. She gave me a look of disbelief, and asked, "In this kind of weather?" I said, "One hour ago we were shooting the ILS approach to Runway 22L at O'Hare." She looked at me again, and by her look I could tell she had made her judgment. She said curtly, "Only big airplanes land at O'Hare!" I couldn't enjoy the evening after that and considered my high school friends as young, immature, and uneducated. I longed to be sitting at a table at the Blue Sky Cafe, surrounded by my more interesting and mature pilot friends talking real flying, and not to be sitting around watching these kids trying to impress each other, painting great scenes of malarky pertaining to nothing in particular. That's when I noticed the prettiest of the girls looking at me in silence. I looked back, and she kissed me tenderly on the lips. She became my steady girlfriend for the next year-and-a-half. After graduation I never saw her again until our twenty-year reunion. She was still beautiful, but we never saw each other again after that.

Dad and I made many wonderful flights together in little 49B and every weekend I could be found at Sky Harbor. One thing Dad and I did a lot was to take off 49B at dusk and head for Midway Airport. The sight was awesome, with millions of lights etching the streets in whites, blues, reds, and yellows. The size and scope of the millions of inhabitants becomes crystal clear and is mind-blowing. We would climb to 3,000 feet above the ground and head right over the middle of Midway and circle. We would marvel at the tower controllers' ability to keep one after another large aircraft perfectly spaced and make the complicated traffic flow absolutely smoothly.

In those days, we didn't need a radio and there was no transponder. Radar was primitive, and as long as we stayed at 3,000 feet or above, we were perfectly legal. One night as we circled, Dad and I were watching a DC-7 lifting off. We said, simultaneously, "He's on fire." We were tuned to the tower frequency and heard the initial, very calm, emergency call, "Ah Midway, United 413 with a problem." "Yeah, we all see it. Looks like number four. You are cleared, any runway. Are you declaring an emergency?" "Affirmative." "Fire trucks are standing by." Dad and I saw a myriad of flashing red lights on the ground as the fire trucks and ambulances stood at ready. We also saw the trail of white-blue flame from number four slowly decrease and then disappear as the pros in that cockpit expertly handled the emergency that they were faced with. I wondered how the passengers were handling it.

"All aircraft on frequency immediately execute your missed approach procedures and contact your assigned frequencies. No need to acknowledge." Then, "Light aircraft circling, are you on frequency?" They knew we were there. "Affirmative." "Do not go below 3,000 feet and remain in 360-degree turns over centerfield. Do not acknowledge." As if by magic, the dozen or so inbound aircraft disappeared, probably sent to their alternate fields. This sure beats hell out of watching TV, I thought. We watched as all the flashing red lights formed up and headed for Runway 31 after 413 announced that they were going to attempt an emergency landing. We watched as 413 lined up on final and slowly closed with the threshold. Not a sound on the radio. On short final, a lone voice said clearly, "God be with you, 413." It was then that I realized the gravity of what was going on. 413 crossed the threshold and slowed to a stop and was immediately surrounded by hundreds of red flashing lights. They were down, stopped and safe.

"Light aircraft circling, do you need fuel?" "Ah 49 Baker negative." "Roger, 49 Baker. You can continue circling or depart. Your choice." "49 Baker. I think we will head back to Sky Harbor. And great work, tower." "Roger, thanks. But it was the guys in the cockpit of 413 that did all the work." We didn't say a thing most of the way back, then Dad looked at me and said, "Some show, eh?" "You can say that again!" Next morning, Dad proudly showed me the headlines: "United Airliner Makes Successful Emergency Landing at Midway." As I read the story, I felt very grateful to have been a witness to that miracle. My father and I had many more adventures together until his death in 1986.

When I was a senior, I played on the football team. I like playing but it couldn't even begin to compare with flying and every weekend I was again at the airfield. When a football game was scheduled, I would leave as soon as the game was over and I had showered before leaving to the airport.

In October of 1958, Dad decided that the company needed a fast twin for company business so he upgraded from the Cessna 172, which was IFR-equipped and had a Continental C-145 engine, to a Cessna 182, also IFR-equipped, but with a Continental IO-470. It was 240 hp that would cause her to split the molecules at a respectable 153 mph and 140 indicated. This was the machine I was to check out in and spent many wonderful hours in boring 150 mph holes in the sky over Illinois, Wisconsin, Indiana, and Iowa.

The company also bought a 1957 straight-tail, tuna tank Cessna 310—a beautiful light twin with tip tanks looking real cool out on the wingtips. She was powered by two Continental IO-470 engines that would pull her through the air at a fast true of 206 mph and 185 mph indicated (179 knots and 161 knots), burning 23 gallons per hour. That was hauling butt in 1958 and I loved that 310. Although I never formally checked out in this particular 310, I wound up with many hours in 310s during my flying career.

I graduated in 1959 and got a brand new 1959 Ford Falcon. I loaded up and planned to go out to California and get a job. I got to Great Bend, Kansas, and lucked into a job as a roustabout in the oil fields of the Arbuckle zone in Kansas and Oklahoma. It was hard, dirty work, but I made a whole $350 a month. That was pretty good for an eighteen-year-old. Heck, I rented a cabin at the Otis Motel, bought groceries, and still had pocket money left over. In January, I got a job at Kettleman Ridge and made my home in Bakersfield, California.

I rented an apartment with my new and lifelong friend Leo Devit for $45 each, which included a swimming pool. Leo and I were both interested in diving and long-distance sailing, which we both did. I traded the Falcon in on a hot MG 1500. Man, I loved that car. Leo and I taught ourselves to dive in Morro Bay. When we suited up, it would attract a small group of people who wanted to watch us. We would go in and complete our dive, resurfacing forty minutes later. There would be even more people when we got out, and some even asked for our autographs. That is how new diving was to the public in those days. We really were pioneers in the sport diving world.

Leo and I would go up to the Kern River, taking our diving equipment and a gold sifter that contained a trap filled with mercury, and spend the weekend working the bottom of the river for gold. We always came back with enough gold to buy our next week's supply of beer, which was usually all that occupied our icebox. I don't know how we didn't starve to death.

What a beginning to the adventurous life. Great Spirit, I thank you again.

3

Flight School in Ardmore, Oklahoma and The Little Yellow House, 1960 to 1963

"Tampa Center, this is American League 816 Hevin Intersection. :01 level one one thousand squawking 0414. Mariana Victor 521 at :35 Crestview next." "Ah roger 816 Tampa flight plan route." I was watching the morning sun reflecting off the sea and enjoying the waves lying in fairly straight lines slowly slipping beneath our Nos. 3 and 4 engines. Just a dark shadow could be seen close to the hubs of our four-bladed props turning in a blur at cruise. We were one minute late at Hevin Intersection and I adjusted our groundspeed to 238 knots. The captain looked over at me and said, "Hey, Dave, how about we swap seats and you take her in to LAX." No twisting of arms here, as flight engineer Bill Stevens maneuvered out of his seat and the captain and I switched places. I settled down in the left seat and took the controls, scanning the tach, BMEPs, manifold gauges, and checking that all needles centered above each other. All engine gauges in the green. Upper panels: every switch, gauge, lever are where they should be and the alcohol gauges are reading correctly.

I scan the flight panel: altimeter, 11,000; horizon, T&B, IVSI, gyros, and navigation gauges are doing what they are supposed to do, telling me that we are level at assigned altitude and dead center on Victor 521. I look out towards the left wing and look at Nos. 1 and 2 so gracefully designed, with eye-pleasing curves to the cowling, both props in perfect sync. I then look down the long, graceful wing and the endless sea beyond the tip and both giant Ham Standard props spinning invisibly as they pull us along at 250 knots. I notice normal oil seepage showing themselves as streaks along Zone 2 of each engine nacelle. It couldn't be a more beautiful day in this magical realm above the earth.

It was night, and Leo and I were driving down a two-lane road just south of Tijuana, Mexico. We were in my MG, top down, with all of our diving gear jammed in every conceivable nook and cranny of my tiny two-seater. We had left Bakersfield, California, heading for the Baja to do as much diving as we could in a week. I said, "Let's find a place to crash. I'm dead." We turned right down a small dirt road and onto a flat plain where the road ended. In an instant, we were both fast asleep. Before I opened my eyes, I was aware of bright sunshine but I couldn't resist keeping my eyes closed, it felt so good. Besides, the lapping sound of small ripples of water was so pleasing and reminded me of the times in the North Woods camping next to a lake. Wait a second, ripples? Lake?

I opened my eyes and was treated to a flat horizon and from that horizon right to the car was the Pacific Ocean. "Leo, Leo, wake up! We are about to get drowned!" Leo looked up and used his favorite term, no matter what the situation. "Hup a diddy. Can you start the engine?" "I'm trying. I'm trying." We had parked right on a tidal flat and the tide was coming in. Fortunately, it had barely made it to our hubcaps and I was able to get the engine running and figured if I backed straight back and didn't get bogged down in about 100 yards we would be back on our little dirt road and safe.

That's when we noticed three kids and an adult laughing their heads off about our situation. The adult, hands on knees, laughing, and obviously having the time of his life, and all three kids were lying on the ground too weak with uncontrollable laughter to stand up.

Well, we made it and our new friends came up to the car. "Como esta?" between laughs. "Muy bien, y tu?" Leo asked. "Bien, gracias," the man replied, then "Eh, señores, es carro, no barco," at which we all broke up and laughed until tears were running down our faces.

After introductions, Pancho said, "Vienen por mi casita, muy bueno comida para ustedes," an invite to his house for some breakfast of tortillas and coffee. So we followed Pancho and sons back to his little shack where abuelito, abuelita, mama, baby, three sisters, six dogs, twelve chickens, a burro, and a very skinny cow awaited us. Abuelito (Grandpa) could speak English. He urged us to have as many tortillas and as much coffee as we wanted, a combination that I love to this day. These people were so hospitable to us. Abuelito noticed our diving equipment and told us that his son was a diver and lived in Izcaeno at Bahia Sebastion. His name was Pablo Rivera. Leo and I thanked our new friends and headed south. Soon we were at a very small town on the coast and had no trouble finding Pablo. We gave him some items that Pancho had sent along with us and were instantly accepted as family. He couldn't do enough for us, including moving him and his wife out of their bedroom so we could use it. Leo and I declined, pulling out our hammocks.

The next day, Pablo took us in his thirteen-foot *barco* ten miles out into the open ocean to our dive site, Isla Navidad. He also had a compressor for us to fill our tanks from. His fees were US 50 cents for tortillas and coffee, ten dollars for the boat for one day, 25 cents for tank refills, and he threw in some fresh fruit for us to eat after our dive.

It turned out that Pablo was not only a superb host, but a skilled boatman as well. After a few minutes of being in his questionable craft, my worry turned to respect as I watched Pablo handle the boat masterfully. I relaxed and enjoyed the ride. About two hours later, we got to the dive site and powdered ourselves so we could put on our very modern (in those days) all-rubber wetsuits. We did a thorough equipment check, then dropped into the water. The initial cold of the 63 degree Japanese current invaded my wetsuit and, just as quickly, turned warm. The visibility was about 35 feet, not bad.

As we descended through 40 feet, we hit a thermocline where the temperature and visibility plummeted to 56 degrees and 5 feet respectively. We continued our descent and found bottom at 83 feet. Even though visibility had gone to hell, I could see that the bottom was littered with shells. Nice shells. Pretty shells. All uninhabited and ready for the picking.

As I was picking through some of them, I felt a definite swirl impact my back, as if from a fish tail, a large fish tail. I tried not to think about it. We had been down for 37 minutes and it was time to begin our ascent. Out of the murk a tail appeared, moving as in a power stroke. That's a shark's tail. That's a big shark's tail. That's a huge shark's tail, I said to myself. Leo never saw it. We got back to the dive boat safely, where I asked Pablo about what I had experienced. He said, "Si, that is why I never dive here. Eet ees the *casa por el grande tiburon blanco*." The home of the great white shark. Even in those days, divers knew of the great white's ferocity and reputation. I asked if there might be a better dive site around, and Pablo replied, "Oh yes, you no like the *tiburon*?" "Oh, we love them, but only when they are well-fed!"

One hour later we dropped the hook on the edge of a large kelp forest. Pablo handed out net bags and suited up himself. "You catch *pulpo* or *langosta*. I take the spear and catch the *grande pescado*." Octopus and lobster—that sounded more like it. We all dropped in together to a sea that was much warmer near the coast and found bottom at 45 feet. Visibility was much better at 40 feet than at the previous site.

The beauty of the kelp forest was a treat as rays of sunshine penetrated the depths through a constantly-waving liquid-looking forest of kelp. There were myriad small, busy fish spending their fish lives doing what fish do best. There were outcroppings of large boulders just about everywhere and in amongst them were the octopi and lobsters. We soon had our two bags filled. After we returned to Pablo's home, we turned our catch over to Pablo and he returned with a fistful of pesos. He wanted to give the money to us, but we insisted that he keep it. We loved diving and were not trying to make anything off of doing it.

We dove with Pablo several times after that, going to his favorite fishing spots where we filled our bags and he speared some very large fish. He made a small fortune with us helping him. He never charged us a dime for the boat, tank refills, or tortillas and coffee. The night before we left, Pablo's wife cooked a huge seafood meal and a bunch of their friends showed up with armloads of *cerveza fria*. We settled in to a night of beer drinking with our hosts and it is still a night I remember fondly.

As Leo and I made our way north, we both felt the warm glow of friendship with our neighbor to the south and knew if we returned we would be treated like brothers.

Leo and I continued our dive adventures all up and down the coast of California on the weekends. During the week I kept working on oil wells on the famous Kettleman Ridge on the southwestern part of the San Joaquin Valley. The work was hot and dirty, and my boss was a guy named Jr. Gates. Jr. was an army grunt on the front lines in Europe. He was pure country Americana and a great person to have known. He spun many yarns about what it was like to be a private grunt, have an M1 shoved into his arms, and be told to "go kill somebody." By 8:00 a.m., the temperature on the ridge where we were working was 110 degrees and one of my jobs was to keep our 25-gallon drinking canisters filled with ice and water. I liked that part of the job because it meant that I had to drive our work truck to town, refill, and get back to the job site, giving me a little respite from the pure hell and misery of mucking out pits, digging ditches, and carrying heavy pipes in 115-degree heat—all for a little over $300.00 a month.

One day Jr. told me that they needed a roughneck on a drilling rig near Woodward, California, that was going to break all records for deep holes drilled. The geologists had determined that a huge pocket of gas lay at 21,000 feet. So I was promoted to roughneck, at the impressive rate of $450 a month. On my first night as a roughneck, as I came on the rig a group of medics was bringing my predecessor down on a stretcher with his right arm gone. The tool pusher hollered at us, "Come on! We can't slow down now. Get your asses up here!" That was my first impression of how dangerous this job could be. Wow, what did I get myself into, I thought.

About two weeks into the job, the geologists determined that we were there and decided to frack the well. They dropped a charge of explosives down the hole and blew holes at the bottom of the drill pipe. We all had to vacate the rig and the results would not be known for several hours. At about 2:00 a.m. the big brass arrived at the site. The chief geologist opened the relief valve and an explosion of lasting sound roared out of the valve so loud you could not make yourself heard, even if you shouted at the top of your lungs. We had hit paydirt. It was a really great moment, with everyone slapping backs and smiling. We brought in the well and, to this day, it still supplies natural gas to the city of San Francisco.

Leo and I had a burning desire to sail a small sailing vessel around the world. We were both avid readers of works by Josh Slocum, Dwight Long, Alain Gerbault, and many other authors of stories about circumnavigating the globe in a small sailing vessel. It was a disease with a high fever, and we were both infected with it. We haunted harbor after harbor, looking at hundreds of boats. We had no money, but we were both silver-tongued devils and talked many an owner into allowing us to sail their boats. We sailed sloops, cutter, yawls, ketches, and on one occasion a schooner. We found one ketch that even today I feel would make the perfect long-distance cruiser. She was an Angelman ketch, very heavily constructed. Luff at the bow, low amidships, high at the stern, she was 38 feet long—42 feet including the bowsprit—with a 12 foot beam. All wood, large comfortable dry belowdecks, but, alas, all we could do was dream. Leo and I did eventually crew on a 210-ton hermaphrodite brigantine bound around the world and lived our dream. I got sick in the Solomon Islands and unhappily had to leave our ship in Australia and fly home for an operation. My long-distance sailing days had come to an end. Throughout my life, I owned and sailed three nice sea-going sailing vessels but never again made a really long-distance sail.

Looking out of the window just ahead of Nos. 3 and 4 engines on a United 707 on short final to Runway 22L at O'Hare International, about to end my long trek from Australia, I looked at the ground and at our shadow flying in formation with us. As we came across the fence, I watched the shadow of our landing gear actually appear to reach out and as it touched the ground, I felt us land. I was back in the magical world of flying.

In the meantime, though, I had a visit to the hospital. Turns out I was on a floor that was manned by young, pretty student nurses. I fell in love at every change of shift and then some. I convinced myself that these nurses were extraordinary and kind women. I even dated a few. It didn't take long to find out that if you push the wrong button, they could turn into the most unreasonable, vindictive monsters—in other words, they were as human as the rest of us. I hated having my bubble burst. So, I wasn't sailing, the dating scene wasn't working out so well, and finally it seemed as if there was only one choice left—flight school.

I showed up at American Flyers School for Airline Pilots in Ardmore, Oklahoma, in the spring of 1962. I looked at the line of aircraft and noticed that all trainers for taildraggers: J3 Cubs, C-140s, C-170s, C-180s, and a Lockheed L-12 for the multi-trainer. The airline end of American Flyers operated four DC-3s and four 749 Constellations. I was home again. This is the real McCoy. The owner and chief pilot was a short, balding gentleman named Reed Pigman, a man with a glorious history as a pilot in transport command in WWII. After the war, Reed started his current operation chartering to the military, and built from the ground up this great airline he was operating when I showed up. His philosophy was that only student pilots who initially train in tailwheel aircraft and are instructed by experienced veteran pilots become good pilots themselves. All my instructors were either fighter jocks, bomber jocks, or transport jocks, all of them with combat experience. I was about to get the best flight training anybody could hope to get.

I showed up the next morning at 8:00 a.m. and was assigned to Instructor Pilot Moe Turner. With no time wasted, he said, "Let's see what you can do. I get real pissed if you try to scare me." I like his attitude. We strapped into a two-seat C-140, started her up, and began to taxi for takeoff. I noticed that the 140 was a bit more squirrely than the 170 and remembered Ed Casey impressing upon me not to be in a hurry. We taxied into position and as I came in with power, Ed's gentle instruction came back to me in a flash. When the 140 started for the grass, I came in with gentle rudder and as all Cessna taildraggers do, she responded instantly and I corrected to hold the centerline dead center and made a good takeoff.

At about 40 feet, the engine quit. "What are you going to do?" "Land straight ahead." The engine came back to life. We climbed to 2,500 feet for some air work. The next 20 minutes was filled with standard turns interrupted by engine failures and me pointing out where we were going to land and our best glide speed. Moe worked our flight so that we were over a ridge on the Arbuckle Mountains. There went the engine, and there was no place to go. "Where are you going to go?" Moe asked. "I don't know," I replied. "Do something, damnit!" "All I can do is slow it up and hit going as slow as I can." "Where is the wind coming from?" "We took off on 35 North." We still had altitude and Moe said, "Fly to the north side of the ridge." Nothing but trees on that side, but I followed his instructions and crossed the ridge at about 400 feet. As we crossed, I felt a jolt going up. "You feel that?" "Yup." "Turn right, and parallel the ridge." To my surprise, we were in lift, rough but lift. Even with no power the little 140 was level at 70 indicated and I actually gained a little. "Where you gonna go?" "I think I can make that field at 11 o'clock." "Go for it."

When I got in position with enough altitude, I turned away from the ridge and started my final glide for a fairly large, treeless field. "Let's see if you make it." As we got closer, it became clear that I was going to make it. I looked at Moe and he said, "Get ready to land. This freaking engine really quit." Oh shit, I thought, and prepared to make my first real emergency landing. We floated over the end of the field and I started flaring, coming back on the yoke and just before we were to touch down, *roar!*, I had the engine back. Moe was looking at me with a shit-eating grin. He said, "Kid, don't ever give up and don't ever trust anybody. Most people are a bunch of fucking liars."

We flew back to the field and made one wheely and one three-pointer. We taxied in, got out of the airplane, and Moe said, "Well, I can see clearly that you have a little time so I am going to sign you off for solo flight. Go out and make four touch-n-gos and be back for ground school at 11:00 a.m." Moe walked away, then turned and said, "And don't bend my flying machine." "I'll do my best." Man, what a great first lesson. These guys are real serious flyers. I walked back to the 140 feeling great.

Our ground school instructor was a tall, thin, balding man named John. He seemed like somebody who could spend hours, days, or weeks immersed in a sea of monotony and love it—perfectly suited to his job. He had been in the USAF as a ground school instructor, and had also spent time as a master navigator aboard a B-36. Ground school was interlaced with John's narratives and most incredibly dull and boring U.S. Army Air Corps technical films on carburetors, fuel pumps, electrical, props, oil systems, landing gears, engines, and control surfaces. When these films finished, we were actually looking forward to John's discussions of what we had just slept through, I mean watched.

On one occasion, the film started with the same dull, low, toneless lead-in music with USAAC emblazoned across the U.S. eagle and then faded into the title, "The Operation and Working Features of the Aircraft Hydraulic Pump." As it faded out and the feature faded in, it became instantly obvious that some wise guy had spliced in an 8mm porn film with the star-studded stick of the stag films doing his thing in a very close-up shot. Of course, we all laughed and figured that John would pull the plug any second. Instead, he let it run full-length, and when it was over turned on the lights and, with no change in expression, said, "Well, this film is not exactly what I had in mind, but it does demonstrate the workings of exactly what the function is of a working hydraulic pump," at which point we all lost it. Even John was smiling and from that day on, we saw him as a man with a sense of humor and all looked forward to attending ground school. John turned out to be a damned good instructor who was always willing to help when we needed it. I wonder to this day if he didn't put that film in on purpose.

Our flight training went on as scheduled and we came to the solo cross-country portion. We each had to make a six-hour cross-country flight on our own. Otis Parker was the chief instructor for the flight school. He was short, in his late forties, and had a face like a bloodhound—two sad-looking eyes above two oversized jowls that would shake like a hound dog's ears every time he moved his head. We called him "Hound Dog." Otis also had a great and uncanny sense of humor, probably one of the funniest guys I have ever met. Lamar Ford, Wild Willie, Hank Peterson, Jim Boden, and I were scheduled to do our cross-countries the next day. As we were flight planning, Lamar said, "Damn, this is bullshit. Why don't we all meet up at Autry Lake and go fishing? If we all flight plan in a different location, get out of sight of the field, then swing around and land on the road next to the lake, we can spend the day fishing and when the time is right, take off and return to the field and nobody will be any the wiser." We all agreed it was a great idea, so when the time to take off came, we all made our takeoffs and separated in five different directions. My direction was northeast as I was heading for Newton, Kansas, as my first stop on my three-point legs. It was also on the exact course to the lake and about ten minutes later I was on final for the dirt road. I was real proud of my perfect three-pointer and began getting my fishing gear out.

Before long, we were all on the ground and enjoying a day of fishing. We were catching bass one after the other. About an hour later, with full stringers, we were discussing our upcoming beer party and fish fry. Uh-oh. "I hear a 140. Listen." Sure enough, a 140 was heading our way. We were thinking, alright, another one to join the party. The little 140 turned final and rounded out for a graceful three-pointer, taxied up, and shut down. The door opened and out hopped Hound Dog. Our smiles quickly disappeared. "Howdy, boys." "Howdy," we all responded. "Boys, I could smell those bass back in Ardmore. Sure are going to taste good along with some ice cold beer at my beer bust and fish fry I'm gonna throw for the boss and the instructors. Shore do thank ya. Oh, by the way, you're gonna get in late tonight and I got ya scheduled for night flight at 4 a.m. So when ya get in tonight, ya better go right to bed and I will tell ya tomorrow how the fish tasted." "How the hell did you find us?" I asked. "They don't call me Hound Dog for nothin'! Have a good trip, guys."

And with that, Otis crawled into his 140, and with our fish and fishing gear taxied to the road, poured the coal to her, and took off, performing a crop duster turn and then proceeded to flat hat us all. We saw him laughing his ass off as he went by.

We all completed our cross-countries and returned to the field at around 9:00 p.m. Sure enough, there was a rip-roaring party going on at Reed's barracks. When we got back to our rooms, our fishing gear was neatly laid out on our beds, each with a handwritten note, "Don't forget: off the ground at 4:00 a.m. Love, Hound Dog." How can you dislike a guy like that? I still think fondly of Otis "Hound Dog" Parker.

Our flight training went on with cross-countries, night time, instrument basic flight, and precision flying. I went to Oklahoma City and took my 8-hour commercial pilot written test. I figured I knew the questions and answers all right but came away not feeling so hot about it. Our marvelous FAA brothers claim to this day that there are no trick questions on the written test, but I have always thought differently about that. There are two questions where the feds have calculated the most common mistakes that people will make and included among the list of choices one that would be chosen if those mistakes were made, and that would ultimately be the wrong answer. I was careful to double- and triple-check my calculations, but I was still doubtful about the results. I was elated to get my results back: 94 percent correct. I had passed the exam.

I continued flight training with Moe. He continued failing engines on every flight. I got really good at potential forced landings and would reap the benefits of Moe's training more than once in my future flying career. Thanks, Moe, you saved my life a few times.

There was one student of Moe's who was angry at Moe for constantly cutting his engine and said, "I'll show that sumbitch." He took the key out of the 140 he was assigned to and had it duplicated at a key shop. The next day, he and Moe departed for their lesson.

I was on the line when JJ Hamilton came hurrying up to me and said excitedly, "Moe and his student are down in a wheat field. Come drive out there with me." "Are they okay?" I asked. "I don't know." We jumped in JJ's pickup and took off in a cloud of dust. It wasn't hard to find them. By the time we got there, flashing red lights of police and ambulance were already there. My heart slowed down when I saw the little 140 sitting upright and no apparent damage. Moe and a chagrined-looking student pilot were standing by a police car, giving the report to the police about what happened.

When Moe and the student came over to us, Moe said to the student, "Well, dumbass, you wanna tell 'em or should I?" It turned out that the student pilot had made the spare key as part of the surprise he had in store for Moe. He replaced the original key into the magneto key slot and went to bed anticipating their flight the next day. Moe and his student made a normal takeoff and climb to the practice area and in the middle of the turn, Moe pulled the mixture and waited to see what the student was going to do. In a rage, the student said, "Fuck you, Moe," and turned off the magneto and pulled out the key, opened his side window, and threw the key out. He turned and looked at Moe and said, "Well, what do you think of that?" Good old Moe, never changing his facial expression, said calmly, "Hope ya got a good field picked."

As they passed through 1,000 feet, the student was smiling as he reached into his pocket to retrieve the spare key. Moe knew instantly when the student's smile changed to a look of fear that he had forgotten to bring the spare key. The student looked at Moe wide-eyed. Moe said, "It's your airplane. Don't fuck it up." The student didn't and all ended well. "The kid was going to teach me a lesson," Moe said, starting to giggle. "You should have seen the look on his face." We all, including the student, got a good laugh out of it.

Written passed, Moe signed me off for my flight test in Perry, Oklahoma. "Hand your paperwork to Harry Elian, the designee out of the Perry FSS. He's gonna give you the ride." He continued, "Oh, go check out the 150, N7390F. Go fly it around for a couple of hours and read the A/C flight manual. That's the one you are going to get your ride in." I looked at him incredulously and said, "What? A goddamned nosewheel airplane?" Was this some kind of cosmic joke? I got cheated out of soloing in a taildragger, and now had to do my commercial ride in a nosewheel plane. "Oh," Moe said, "grab a chute and practice some spin recoveries." Spins were required on the commercial check ride in those days. "What for? I'll never get out of the son of a bitch if I had to anyway." "Wanna bet?" he asked, with that wise-ass grin of his.

So I took the 150 out and tried to get it into a spin. I kicked in full left rudder and the little bird enters a spin to the left, just as pretty as a picture. I held the stick all the way back but the second I released pressure on the rudder pedal, she came right back to level flight and mushed wings level. I had to admire the engineers at Cessna. They built an aircraft for rank beginners that force the pilot to have to work very hard to get her into a spin and keep her there. I climbed back up and did an eight-turn spin with the same results. When I turned loose of the controls, little "Mickey Mouse" instantly recovered and automatically sought a straight and level flight altitude with no coaxing from me. I climbed back up and put her into another spin and after four turns, I unlatched the door and to my surprise, the door opened to its limits, allowing me plenty of room to get out.

I landed her and Moe was on the ramp, waiting to ask me, "so, what do you think? You still wanna bet?" "Nope." He seemed satisfied that I had done what he expected me to do.

Next morning I blasted off for my plodding flight to Perry. I landed on Runway 35 and taxied up to the flight service station and shut down. I opened the door and saw a gentleman with bushy grey hair and accompanying eyebrows. He never looked up from his paperwork. "Bring your log and paperwork?" "Yes, sir. Name's Dave Allyn." "Yeah, I know," he replied, still not looking up. He completed his paperwork, then looked at me for the first time. He had sparkling, deep blue, friendly eyes through the massive amount of hair and eyebrows. He stuck out his big bear claw of a hand and said, "Everyone calls me 'Hair.'"

The oral lasted about an hour, and I didn't falter on any one of his questions. "The wind is out of the north at 5 knots, ceiling is at 500 feet but to the south you can see sunshine so you file a special VFR to depart southbound, knowing you have to scud run for a short while and stay below 500 feet. Can you do it?" "No problem. But I would have to make a nonstandard right turn out to the east." "Why?" "To avoid the 1,000-foot tower that is sticking up into the cloud base situated to the west of the field."

"Let's go fly," Hair said, finally satisfied with my answers. The flight test turned out to be a cakewalk and in about 45 minutes, Hair told me to return to the field and "gimme a touch-and-go." I squeaked on the landing and came in with power for the go portion. As I became airborne, Hair pulled the mixture to idle cutoff and the engine quit cold. I landed straight ahead. As Hair went rich on the mixture and I got the engine back, he motioned to go idle and instructed me to taxi back in. As I shut down, I looked at him and asked if we were done. "Nope," as I think, shit, where did I screw up? "Go get your chute, we didn't do spins."

I crawled back in, my chute strapped on, and notice that Hair was standing next to my door and doesn't have a chute on. "Are you going without a chute?" I asked him. He said, "Goin', are you nuts? Ya'll gotta be crazy to go up in a flying machine that's about to do something that dangerous. Nope, sonny, I'll jes stand here and watch." I chuckled throughout my solo aerobatic demo flight and was still smiling when a happy-faced Hair handed me my signed, sealed, and delivered temporary Commercial Airman's Pilot Certificate. He clapped me on the shoulder with his great paw and drawled, "Boy, ya done good." I thought to myself, Johnny Winters, wherever you are, I made it. I took a giant step.

We had a big beer bust that night. This time all the instructors were there to welcome me into the brotherhood. It was one of many of the happiest and proudest moments of my life.

Instrument flight training was conducted at the airline school based at Meacham Field, Fort Worth, Texas. I packed up what little belongings I had and jammed it all into my MG Elva race car I had recently purchased. Pedal to the metal, I tore south on I-65 with high spirits and looking forward to instrument training. Feeling good and smug, that's when I noticed the flashing red lights in my rearview mirror. Shit. I pulled over and got out my license. This guy could have been in the movies—cowboy hat, dark glasses, unsmiling face, sharply creased uniform, the whole nine yards. "License." I handed it to him. "I got you doing 95 in a 70 mph zone." "Yeah, it's kind of hard to keep your speed down in this kind of car." "You got two choices: pay the ticket or go to jail. You got two more choices: learn to drive that kind of car slower or get rid of it." "Yes, sir." Jeez, what a grouch.

I took the ticket and was on my way. I held my speed down for a while, but before long I was tearing down the highway at 95 again. Gosh, it was great being young and dumb with a fresh commercial pilot's license in my pocket. That was when I saw the flashing reds again. Shit. One ticket in Oklahoma and one in Texas. In those days, they didn't have computers so no one was the wiser, but each ticket cost me 35 dollars, a total of 70 dollars. In those days, that was a bunch of money.

When I arrived later that day, I found an apartment near Meacham Field and showed up at the flight school office the next morning at 8:00 a.m. There were six of us and we started ground school right then. I buddied up with Lamar Crawford, one of my fellow students from Ardmore, a big guy with the funniest laugh that went along with his great southern Alabama accent and great sense of humor. Our ground school instructor was Jim Andrickson, a captain on DC-3s and professional airline pilot who was a great guy. My instructor was L. J. "Lonnie" Edwards, also a captain on 749 Constellations. We were under the wings, so to speak, of real professionals. In charge of the link trainer, also known as the "sweat box," was the airline chief pilot Judd Fowler and did he know how to make us sweat.

I was assigned to Beech Bonanza N5497D, a 1947 version of the Bonanza. We went to ground school, flew the sweat box, and trained under the hood in the air. In the beginning, I didn't think anybody could possibly keep wing level, navigate, hold course, take clearances, tune radios, talk constantly to approach center, tower, trim, hold patterns, shoot precision approaches, shoot ADF non-precision, keep constant attention to altitude, do power management, scan all instruments, read maps—all this while flying blind under the hood. Lonnie kept saying, "It will come. Keep trying."

Then one day, as if by magic, it all fell into place and became as natural as flying on a clear day. I could suddenly picture in my mind exactly what was going on and exactly what to do. My approaches started to work out exactly as they were supposed to and monitoring all of the gauges and controls became second nature. After hours of studying the A.I.M. (Airmans Information Manual) and learning all the rules and regulations of instrument flight, weather, flight procedures, and radio phraseology, I was ready for the 8-hour written test.

I took the test and, like the commercial written test, felt I may not have passed. Again, my fear turned to elation when my telegram came. "Instrument written passed." 94 percent again. Okay. All I needed to do now was pass my flight test and I felt confident about that. Judd Fowler was my designee and met me on the field the next morning. The check flight went okay and Judd handed me my temporary Commercial, SEL, and Instrument Pilot's Certificate. I could now actually get paid to fly. But right now I had to get my multi-engine rating. The school offered two aircraft to get that rating in: a 1957 Cessna 310 or a 1938 Lockheed 12A. It was a slam dunk. Round engines forever, naturally.

N19919 sat gleaming in the sunshine on the ramp at Ardmore. She was the most beautiful of aircraft I have known. Jim Andrickson was to be the designee and L. J. Edwards my multi instructor. 919 was bare aluminum with the red lightning stripe down the fuselage—just like when she came out of the Burbank factory in 1938. Her beautiful lines, rounded wingtips, elliptical vertical fins only on Lockheeds, long graceful fuselage, artistically designed engine cowls snugly fitted around her Pratt & Whitney 985 engines, she would more than quench the thirst of anyone who has a passion for graceful perfection in a flying machine. I was about to get to know her intimately. She would set the pace for my desire to fly as many of those period flying machines as I could get my hands on.

Lonnie handed me the flight manual and performance charts and said, "You got tonight. I want you to know this manual and charts inside out by 8:00 a.m. tomorrow and be prepared to answer my questions." I strapped myself into the left seat and soaked up the wonderful odors of a 1938 Lockheed and familiarized myself with her businesslike cockpit. After that, I spent the rest of the day until midnight poring over the seemingly tons of information given to me by Lonnie. She would be the first real professional's airplane that I had ever flown. I was as near to heaven as I could get. That night, one of my fellow students asked, "Are you really going to get your multi in that old Lockheed?" His tone of voice indicated to me that he had no soul. "Yup," I replied. "You know that bird is a mankiller, dontcha?" "Yup. You scared of it?" He didn't answer, and I walked off, wondering where in hell some people get their information.

1938 Lockheed 12A Electra Junior

1938 Lockeed 12-A

Vertical fin

Next morning at 8:00 a.m. sharp, Lonnie and I sat down and went over weights, dimensions, speeds, fuel dump, feathering procedures, VMC, V1, and V2 (yeah, in those days we used real procedures, not painted lines on an airspeed indicator), and all checklist items. Lonnie said, "Stall full flaps?" "57 mph." "Stall no flaps." "72 mph." "VMC." "78 mph." V1 V2." "The same, 98 indicated." "Emergency fuel dump procedure." "160 indicated. Switch to non-dumpable tank, fly straight ahead, dump, when done, get on the ground as quickly as possible." "First 10 degree flaps, what airspeed?" "First 10 degree, 160 indicated, ailerons droop also with first 10." "Engine zone 2 fire." "Mixture, throttle, prop, feather button, select, and fire CO_2 bottle into zone 2 of affected engine." "Let's go fly."

I strapped into the left seat, Lonnie was in the right. I primed and started No. 1 first, No. 2 second, watching the smoke dissipate and enjoying the galloping music of the two 985s. I think about the comment my fellow student had made about this plane being a mankiller. I convince myself that anything this beautiful has got to fly beautifully. As we taxied out, I enjoyed the heavy aircraft feel. I was also surprised at her stability while taxiing. A little throttle here, a little throttle there, a little brake here, a little brake there, and when taxiing straight ahead, just throw on the tail wheel lock and relax. So far, she was proving to be a controllable, gentle sweetheart.

I finished the runup and taxied into position on 35 at Ardmore. Lonnie looked at me and said, "What's takeoff manifold?" "We got 12-1 blowers max manifold 41 inches." "I will tap the back of your hands at 41 inches. It's your aircraft." I slowly brought both throttles forward and was pleased by immediate rudder control as we began the takeoff roll. When I reached 41 inches manifold pressure, Lonnie tapped my hand and as the Ham Standard prop tips broke the speed of sound—called cavitating—I was taken aback by the screaming howl penetrating my very being. V2 98 mph indicated and I eased gently back on the yoke and never felt 919 leave the ground. Gear up, METO (maximum except takeoff) power 39" 2,000 rpm. The howl of take off changed to a low rumble that was pleasing to the ear. 30" 2,000 rpm and we settled into a 900 fpm climb at 125 indicated. I was overjoyed at what a sweet flying machine Lockheed had produced in 1938.

We climbed up to 8,000 feet in the practice area and did a thorough familiarization: turns, stalls, single engine, VMC demo, single engine go-arounds at altitude—soon to be right after takeoff and close to the ground. Then we came back for my first landing, holding V2 on final. I crossed the fence at about 90 mph and eased back on the yoke. For the first time, I was treated not to the squeak of light plane tires touching but to the *erk erk* of a heavy airplane's tires kissing the pavement and letting all inside and outside know that a real flying machine has just landed. We taxied in and shut down. Lonnie gave me the post flight and scheduled our next flight for the afternoon. As I was walking out of the flight office, I ran into the fellow who warned me about the Lockheed being a mankiller. I asked if he had ever had any time in a 12A and when he said no, I advised him that he "should learn to differentiate between truth and pure bullshit," trying to help the kid out a little.

Ten hours later I was ready for my check ride with my check ride pilot, Jim Andrikson. I passed with no problem. Jim handed me my temporary Commercial Instrument ASEL (Airplane Single Engine Land) and AMEL (Airplane Multi Engine Land). I now had a commercial pilot, instrument pilot, ASMEL rating, and was a full-fledged commercial pilot. Jim was a great instructor and a great pilot. He was also the chief pilot for the airline and about three weeks after he gave me my multi engine check ride, he was involved in a very unfortunate incident.

As captain of a DC-3 on a military airlift contract, Jim realized shortly after takeoff that he and his co-pilot had failed to remove the elevator external locks and he had no elevator control. Jim, thinking fast, decided to use the elevator trim tab control. He began trimming to control the vertical axis of the aircraft. He had to remember that to get the nose up, you had to trim down and vice versa. Jim, with nineteen people on board, turned final at Meachum Runway 16, set the power and opposite trim so the old DC-3 was descending at 200 fpm at 100 indicated airspeed. All passengers were braced for a crash when Jim crossed the threshold and started easing back on the power. The DC-3 at the last minute dropped out of the sky and hit so hard that the impact drove both landing gears up through the wings and the solid old bird slid harmlessly to a stop 2,000 feet down the runway, nobody hurt.

A hard fact is that most DC-3s carry a broomstick device in the aft compartment just for this scenario. You can take this broomstick and stick it through an opening and unlatch the elevator lock bungee and use the stick to push the lock out and away from the elevator, then let it fall harmlessly away in the slip stream. Neither Jim or his co-pilot thought of using it and sadly the lack of a good pre-flight and neglecting to remember cost these two good men their careers.

I got my first paying flying job with Ed Ritchey Flying Service on Meacham Field. My first job was to fly three members of the board of the First National Bank of Fort Worth in a straight-tail tuna tank Cessna 310 from Fort Worth to Sweetwater, Texas, and return the next day. We all loaded and took off, the three passengers having total confidence in their dashing and hot pilot, who had all of 300 hours of experience.

There are two things I don't like about the early C-310. One, she has a very stiff landing gear that makes for squirrely takeoffs and stiff hard landings. There is a way to make softer landings but it required some violent manipulating of backpressure on the control column and I never used it with passengers on board. The second thing is that while on straight and level flight off auto pilot, the old girl just loves to wander on all three axes. You have to fly the old buzzard constantly. I love the 185 knots she will give you and leaned out, she sips green gas at 23 gallons per hour. She has a very comfortable cabin and low noise level. Even with her faults, she is a typically well-built Cessna aircraft.

The flight from Meacham to Avenger Field at Sweetwater was accomplished in clear, smooth air with a 10-knot headwind and a fast ground speed of 175 knots. I overflew Avenger and set up left downwind on Runway 4. 10 degree flaps and gear down, base to one-half flaps, final full flaps and 110 indicated, across the threshold carrying slight power flare, *squeak, squeak, bump, bump,* and we were down with a good and smooth landing. My passengers were happy and still joking so I guess I did okay on my first paid flight as a professional commercial pilot.

After shut down, we headed over to the Holiday Inn and secured our rooms for the night. I stayed good, according to professional procedures. In other words, I had dinner and then went to bed.

The next morning, I looked out the window. Shit, we were socked in. The front I knew was coming had sped up during the night and arrived ahead of schedule. I called Eddie and the old grouch jumped all over me for talking too much. "Eddie, goddamnit! I'm calling you from my room—it's just you and me. We got a weather problem and 6760T is not certified IFR. What in hell should I do?" "We are clear here. Scud run, damnit!" he shouted and hung up.

Scud run. Everything I have been taught not to do. Well, I guess I better learn fast. By the time we got to the field, the ceiling had lifted to about 400 or 500 feet and visibility looked to be maybe one mile. I checked out our route carefully for towers or other obstructions and filed a special VFR. Checking the weather, I found I should be out from under the front about three-quarters of the way to Fort Worth. I informed my passengers that we would be flying low for the first part of the flight but the weather was clear at Meacham.

"Well, then, why don't we go up through the clouds?" asked one of them. "Icing level is low and we don't want to fly in those conditions. We do this all the time," I responded, not quite truthfully. My passengers started smiling and joking and said, "Okay, let's go." We loaded up and took off, leveling at 300 feet, and am horrified at the low visibility. At first, I felt we were moving at way too high a rate of speed judging by the speed at which the ground was moving by beneath us. I never really got used to it and remained on edge. As we got to the leading edge of the front, visibility got worse and if we had one-half mile, I would be surprised, but I could see a brightness in the mist ahead and suddenly we broke out into bright sunshine. I climbed to 3,000 feet and soon we were on final to 16 at Meacham. We shut down in front of Ritchey Air and got out.

The three bank executives came over and begin patting me on the back and telling Eddie that I am one great pilot, that I really know what I am doing, and that they would fly with me anytime. I concealed my surprise. Ignorance really is bliss. Eddie paid me $38.66 for that trip, not bad for 1963.

We walked into the flight office and Eddie introduced me to a man who is a cop in Chicago and had just bought an old primary trainer, WWII vintage, and needed a good tailwheel pilot to go to Davis, Oklahoma, and ferry his new pride and joy, a Fairchild PT-26, back to Fort Worth for relicensing and painting and then deliver it to Palwaukee Airport in Wheeling, Illinois. I was overjoyed and we both agreed on $400.00, delivered to Palwaukee, all expenses paid.

Before leaving, I checked in with Judd Fowler at the airlines flight office and told him I would be back in a couple of days and wanted to sign up for a type rating in one of the Douglas DC3s the airline owned. "Okay, Dave, see you then."

I was to leave for Davis that afternoon so I hitched a ride in a 140 Cessna. You gotta know that I didn't have the foggiest idea of what a Fairchild PT-26 was or the nasty reputation the Ranger 200 hp inverted engine had but who cared. She was WWII vintage, sat on her tail, had tandem cockpits covered by a birdcage canopy, and was made of wood and fabric. Right up my alley.

Standing with one hand on her wingtip and admiring her lovely lines painted all primer grey, I asked the ex-owner how long she had been sitting in the grass. He said, "All spring." I had procured a ferry permit from Fort Worth G.A.D.O. before I left and figured I would have enough daylight to make it back to Meacham that day. I looked her over with what my 300 hours of experience told me was a thorough inspection. Ha ha ha. I noticed the front instrument panel was missing some instruments but I had needle, beetle, airspeed, altimeter, tachometer, and oil pressure. That is all I need. I went over the flight manual and, finding nothing strange, determine that she is as straightforward as can be.

I followed the ex-owner's instructions on starting procedures. Quite different from what I was used to. I crawled into the front cockpit, turned the mag switch to left mag, cracked the throttle, crawled back out, unlocked the external primer, primed six shots, jammed the starting crank handle into the receptor provided, hollered clear and began to crank. The prop began to turn as I cranked and after one revolution, the old Ranger fired and came to life with a belch of grey-white smoke and a pleasing deep rumble as the inverted Ranger settled into a smooth idle.

I crawled in, stowed the crank handle, and strapped in. As I taxied back and forth, I was impressed by the docile handling qualities of this old Fairchild. The runup was normal and I got an excellent mag check, so I lined up and gently and slowly advanced the throttle to the stops. The old eagle sounded off with a deep ear-pleasing roar as she began to gallop down the runway gaining speed steadily. As she lifted off the ground gracefully, the ease of control put me right at ease. What a lovely flying craft, I thought, feeling right at home.

My homey feeling was not to last long. As we climbed through 500 feet, my attention became fixed on one of the empty instrument holes as the first hairy leg of eight reached out and fixed on the outside of the instrument panel, pulling the rest of the repulsive body out. It was the nastiest-looking spider of them all—the tarantula. And full-grown to boot. Shit, I hate spiders. I made a quick crop duster turn and to hell with landing procedures. I just want back down and out of this flying house of horrors as quickly as possible. Throttle off, over the fence, full stall, mixture and switches off, and before ol' 75463 came to a complete stop, I jumped off the trailing edge of the wing and went head-over-ass in the dirt as the plane slowed to a stop on her own. The ex-owner came running up with a concerned look and yelled, "You okay? What in hell happened?" "I'll tell you what in hell happened. My fucking co-pilot is a tarantula!" A moment later, we were laying on the ground with tears rolling down our cheeks. We got hold of the local exterminator, who came out and covered 463 with a tent and pumped a cloud of poisonous gas into it. We had to leave her covered overnight, so the ex-owner and the exterminator invited me to a steak fry and beer drinking wingding that night. We had a great time.

The next morning we pulled the tent off and let 463 air out while we went into Davis for breakfast. After looking into and cleaning out each inspection hole, we were amazed at how much debris came out of wings, tail, and fuselage. Mostly rat and mouse nests, common insects, and, even scarier than the tarantula, was a black widow's nest on the main spar, just under my seat. It was a good lesson and I never picked up an old ferry that had been sitting for a while without spending at least a day inspecting completely my charge for the ferry flight.

Satisfied and ready for the afternoon flight, I strapped in and repeated my previous takeoff, this time without the panicked landing of the day before. This time, I continued the climb to 4,500 feet southwest bound for Fort Worth and to also clear the Arbuckle Mountains just north of Ardmore, Oklahoma. I always wondered why the Oklahomans called them mountains when to me they were really big hills. They were big enough though. One night as Captain Reed Pigman was shooting an ADF approach into Ardmore with 99 U.S. GIs on board a Lockheed Electra, he flew into one of the hills. As the Electra slammed into the hill, a small section on the right side of the fuselage broke loose and with seats and passengers still attached slid to a stop. The nine or ten bewildered passengers unstrapped and walked away unharmed while 90 of their fellow passengers and crew perished.

I think Ernie Gann hit it on the head with his famous book, *Fate is the Hunter*, leveled out, ol' 463 was just as stable as can be, indicating 101 mph or 112 mph true and 1,800 rpm. She was drinking 14 gallons of red every hour and that gave me a little over an hour's reserve when we got to Meacham. I had called the tower earlier and gave them an ETA in a PT-26 with no radio. "No sweat, just circle over the field above pattern altitude and we will shoot you a light." Sure enough, as I circled over the field, I got a green light from the tower and, according to the tetrahedron, I fell into left downwind for Runway 6, shot the pattern, and as I crossed the fence, chopped the power. At this point, the engine crackled a few backfires and I three-pointed ol' 463 with just a bit of a squeal and no jolt. Smooth landing on mains and tailwheel simultaneously. "Shit, I love it. Oorah!" I taxied over to Ritchey's and shut down. The new owner and Eddie were standing there and grinning like a couple of school kids.

None of the other guys I was in flight school with had ever flown anything like this and I felt shit hot inside. I told myself that I am going to continue this type of flying and not get stuck in the light airplane rut that so many of my colleagues did just to build time so they could get on with the major airlines, another area I wanted to avoid. I would soon discover Corrosion Corner in Miami and it was perfect, but more on that later.

Eddie was going to relicense ol' 463 and have her painted, so the new owner headed to Chicago where I would deliver her in about a month. That gave me plenty of time to get my DC-3 type.

I walked into Judd Fowler's office next morning and let him know I was back and ready to start. Judd was one of my favorite instructors and was a very experienced heavy-aircraft pilot. He was also a nice guy. He said, "Okay, be here tomorrow morning. We have a seven-day ground school before we get into the aircraft. It'll be $1,200 for the rating. Pay some now or as we go." Ya hear that, all you modern guys? $1,200 would get you typed in one of the most famous and sought-after aircraft ever. Probably costs $25,000 or $30,000 today.

I walked out to the ramp where Douglas DC-3 N1911 sat in all her glory. She looked so perfect and businesslike. This is the aircraft that made the airlines and, as Ike Eisenhower said, "The C-47 did more to win the war than any other machine built." The "3" is so good that a large number of them still operate in the world today. When test pilot Tex Johnston gave his speech about the newly-tested Boeing 707 in front of all the officers of Boeing, Generals, Admirals, and dignitaries from around the world he ended up by looking at them all and saying, "Above all, when the 707 is dead and buried, it will be a DC-3 that flies over its grave." And he was right. I climbed into the cockpit of 111, as usual enjoying the odors that come with her. I made myself familiar with her businesslike cockpit that was jammed with switches, levers, and instruments. I felt very excited that I was going to get to know intimately this royal queen of the skies. I was at the apex of my flight training—I was about to become a DC-3 pilot.

Queen of the Skies, a 1940 Douglas DC-3

I had a hard time sleeping that night but was rarin' to go the next morning as I showed up with six others—all Arabs—for ground school. I made two good friends and wonder today if they survived the backward belligerence of their own brothers. I sincerely hope so.

We were issued a DC-3 flight manual—a very thick manual—and in seven days we went from cover to cover. By the end of the seven days, we could draw a schematic of the electrical, hydraulic, fuel, and oil systems from memory. We could recite dimensions, weights, turning radius, speeds, power settings, emergency procedures, and V speeds by heart. The big day came for flight training. I strapped into the left seat, Judd in the right. First off Judd said to me, "We need to make a 360-degree turn on the ramp. How much room do we have to have?" "57 feet, 6 inches." "Wing span?" " 95.0." "Prop diameter?" "11.6 Ham Standard full feathering 3-bladed." "Length?" "64 feet, 5.5 inches." "What's the first power reduction after takeoff?" "METO at 120 indicated." "Cowl flaps at METO?" "Open." "Engines?" "P&W 1830-90D 1,250 hp at max 42 inches and 2,500 rpm." "Max gross?" "28,500 pounds." "Max landing weight?" "18,500." "V1 V2." "98 mph indicated." "Explain why V1 V2 are the same." "Because this aircraft cannot be operated off a runway that you cannot abort and stop before the runway ends between VMC and V1 V2. At V2 we can lose No. 1, the critical engine, and continue to fly and climb out safely." "Okay. Pre-start checklist. Let's fly this mutha."

Always a true pleasure for me to start any radial and these being the biggest for me so far made it even more exciting. As the 1830 started, I watched the clouds of white smoke curl over and in front of the whirling Ham Standard then curl back into the prop and get sucked back and blown behind the prop and wing. Coupled with the galloping 1830, I felt so lucky to be sitting where I was at that moment. Pre-taxi checklist complete, I eased the throttles up to 1,200 rpm to get the "3" to start moving.

As 111 started to move, I retarded the throttles and brought her to a stop with the brakes. ""Pre-taxi checklist complete. Taxi check next." Judd started the taxi checklist last item "Contact Ground." "Ah flyers 19111 Meacham ground flyers ramp, taxi for takeoff." "Roger, flyers 111 taxi Runway 16 wind 160 degrees 8 knots altimeter 30.10." "Ah roger, 111 taxi 16, 30.10 on the altimeter," I repeated. Great, we got 8 knots of wind right down the runway. That's good. Taxiing the DC-3 using slight break, differential power, and rudder proved to be no different than the Lockheed, only everything responded much more slowly and I had to stay ahead of the aircraft and anticipate what was coming next before it happened.

I taxied out to the runup pad and swung the big bird around and into the wind. "Runup check list." "Controls." "Free and easy." "Throttles." "1,800." "Props." I pulled the prop controls all the way back and the props respond. "Props check." "Feather." I tap each feather button and let the props come back 200 rpm. "Feathering check." "Mixtures." "Auto rich." "Mags." "No. 1 both left right, No. 2 both left right check." "Cowl flaps." "Open." "Flaps." I moved the flap lever down. "Flaps indicate down, flaps up. Hydraulic pressure up 1,200." "Throttles." "800 rpm." "Controls." "Free and easy."

199

"Trim." "Takeoff, aileron trim set, rudder 2 right check." "Pre-takeoff crew brief." "This will be a normal Douglas DC-3 takeoff. If we lose one before V1 V2, we will abort the takeoff. If we lose one at V1 V2, we will continue. Co-pilot read checklist, clean the aircraft up, talk on the radio. I will fly the aircraft and return for a single-engine landing." Judd said, "Checklist complete. You ready?" "I am ready."

Before I called the tower, I looked out my window and see a Beech 18 taxiing by and realize how high we sat in 111's cockpit. The 18 was the same size aircraft as the L12 and it looked like a toy from where we sat. "Ah Meacham tower, flyers 111 ready to go." The 18 was on the roll. "Roger, 111, taxi into position and hold." "Position and hold 111, roger." Turning onto the numbers and straight down the runway, Judd said, "Takeoff check tailwheel." "Locked, gyro compass." "160 degrees check." "Flyers 111, you are cleared for takeoff. Make a left downwind departure when speed and altitude permit." "Ah roger, 111 rolling left downwind."

As I slowly increased our throttles, my heart rate increased also. Both 1830s increased to a low and powerful rumble as we reached max power. I was pleasantly surprised by the perfect control I had on the rudder and kept 111 straight down the runway until Judd called, "V2." I came back gently on the control column and 111 came off the ground with all the grace and beauty all DC-3s have at that magic moment. "Gear up." "In transition." "Gear is up and locked. Pressure 1,200." "120 indicated METO power." As I came back to METO, the cockpit noise also decreased and we both could talk in normal tones. At 500 feet, I started our left turn and was surprised at the heavy control pressures I encountered and the slow response. I cranked in left on the yoke and it was a full second before anything happened. She was really an honest flying machine. I was delighted.

"Climb power, climb check list." I called, "Power." "Set." "Cowl slaps." "Trail." We climbed out at 120 indicated at 1,000 feet a minute. We were light. Judd grabbed the controls and dipped a wing to the right. "My house. I thought I would wave to the wife." I looked out my window at the city in miniature below the No. 1 cowl, silver prop hub, and silvery shadow of the 11-foot, 6-inch Ham Standard at climb power pulling 2,000 rpm. Shit. I was actually in control of a legendary queen of the sky—a DC-3.

We spent two hours doing turns, cruising at 145 indicated, truing at 173 mph and 100 gallons an hour, slow flight, steep turns, approach to stall clean and dirty, single engine flight and just generally getting comfortable in 111. Soon we were on short final for 16 and cleared to land. I came across the fence and started to flare when we hit and did we hit—*kawham!* I flared way too low and heard all the dishes fall out of the galley and crash in the aisle. Coming in with power as we bounced back into the air, I recovered and dribbled 111 on the ground for a terrible landing. That's when I noticed Judd grinning from ear to ear. "She is a little taller than you thought, eh? Don't worry, we all do it."

We taxied in shut down, doing our post-flight in the cockpit. I looked at Judd and said, "Today I flew a dream. In spite of that shit landing, I am happy as hell." He replied, "Let's call it a day. Tomorrow we will do single engine work and takeoffs and landings before we start shooting IFR approaches under the hood. Sometime during our training I am going to show you something about the 3 only one time." I headed off the field wondering what Judd had in mind.

Our flight training continued and shortly I was making smooth landings—some we couldn't even feel her touch the ground. She was truly a pilot's dream to fly. Twelve hours into our training, I felt ready for the check ride. Judd felt so also, "But we need one more hour 'cause I want to demonstrate to you how dangerous the ol' 3 can really be." I couldn't imagine what he was talking about and couldn't wait to find out.

The next morning, we saddled up, taxied out, and I made the takeoff like I knew what I was doing. "V1. Damnit. There goes No. 1." "Gear up, feather No. 1, maintain max power No. 2," I hollered. "Gears coming up. Here, Davey, you got No. 1 back." Judd would not let me relax, keeping me on my toes constantly. What a great instructor.

"Head for the practice area and climb to 10,000 feet." "We are going high today," I noted. "You'll see why." I leveled 111 at 10,000 feet and went to cruise. "Slow her up and give me full flaps and gear down." We dirtied her up and I maintained 98 indicated. "Now power off and give me a full stall." This was definitely different from how we normally approached stalls—never went to full stall. As 111 slowed down, I felt the shacking burble as the wings began to lose lift. At 65 indicated the ol' 3 broke and dropped through straight ahead. "Recover." Control column forward and 111 began flying again. I held her nose down until we had sufficient airspeed and gently brought her back to level flight with a loss of close to 2,000 feet. "You don't want to do that close to the ground," Judd said. "Climb back to 10,000 feet."

I complied and leveled off at assigned altitude. "This time, bring her to a stall and bury that yoke in your belly and hold it there. Don't let either wing drop more than 75 degrees before you begin recovery." Holy smokestacks! WE were about to do a spin entry in a DC-3. With my heart in my throat, I took her through the stall and at the break I buried the yoke, holding back with all my might. She was shaking severely and suddenly and violently broke left as I watched the horizon begin to go inverted. I came forward and full right aileron and rudder. 111 began to recover as I saw nothing but ground in our cockpit windshield. 111 started to pick up speed and I neutralized all controls. As the speed built, I began recovery and came in with power back to straight and level with a loss of close to 4,000 feet.

"Man, that was something," I said. "If you ever spin a 3, make sure you got altitude but, as you can see, she will recover if you don't let it go too far," Judd said. "Climb back to 10,000. We got one more." I leveled at 10,000 and Judd asked, "What would be the worst—besides fire—you could expect to happen to you?" Slam dunk. "A multiple engine failure," I replied, as Judd retarded both throttles to 11 inches manifold pressure to simulate both engines feathered. "Give me best glide and pick a field, a big one." You gotta be kidding. "Hold 120 indicated. Leave the gear in the well until you got it made."

N111 was coming out of the sky at a pretty good rate but not that bad, maybe 1,500 to 1,800 feet a minute. There was lots of empty space where we were and I had a big, flat-looking field at 12 o'clock, just about where I expected to make contact with the ground. As we approached the field, it became obvious that my timing was correct. "Leave the gear in the well, and at 200 feet let's go around." I initiated the go-around, confident in my own mind that we would have made it. "Would you have put the gear down?" Judd asked. "I would have dropped the gear and gone to full flaps and full stalled her onto the ground." "Good answer. Let's go back to the field. Check ride tomorrow morning, 7:00 a.m." All right, I thought to myself.

I met my designee, a grumpy guy named DeWitt—my middle name, but I was convinced not the nice guy I am. I was not about to let him get the best of me and figured he was probably testing my threshold as part of the flight test. I turned out to be right. The check ride went off well and when it was over, ol' Grumpy's demeanor completely changed. Smiling for the first time, he handed me my temporary Commercial Instrument ASMEL DC-3 type certificate.

"Don't let it go to your head," Ritchey growled. "Okay, ya old fart. How's the 26 doing?" "We will have the annual done at the end of the week and then she will go to the paint shop. Probably two weeks. I'll call you." "Okay, I am going to head for Ardmore. Call me there."

Eddie, being the nice guy he really is under all that exterior grouch, put out his hand. As I grasped it, he smiled and said, "Congratulations on that 3 type. That's great."

I stopped by Judd's office to say good-bye and thank you. I asked Judd, "Why do you consider the maneuvers we did in 111 so dangerous? She seemed to respond quite well to every extreme maneuver that we did." Judd looked at me with a big smile and said, "Lad, now you know why she is known as the Queen of the Skies." Great answer. She sure is.

I dove in the ol' Elva and headed for Ardmore at VNE but made it this time with no tickets. I met up with all my friendly cohorts and the beer bust began. Everybody had graduated and a few had jobs, mostly light plane instructors. I was not envious. Before we started drinking, one of the guys said, "Ol' Jimmy Hawks got a job flying a Comanche 250 for the labs at Los Alamos." "Hey, that's great," I said. "Not so great—he got killed yesterday." In shock, I asked, "No shit. What happened?"

It turned out Jimmy had to fly two technicians to Albuquerque, basically a 30-minute hop from Los Alamos. The weather was stinking and nobody will ever know why Jimmy didn't file IFR and go. Instead, he elected to scud run. As he was about to round the bend in the Jemez Mountains, it closed in on him and apparently he decided to make a 180 and go back but he turned the wrong way and flew right into the side of a mountain.

We all toasted Jimmy with our first drink. The next day we got news that Elvis Jones, who had helped me pass my commercial written, had taken a job crop-dusting and flew into some telephone wires after a pass in his 450 hp Stearman and exploded in a ball of flames. The attrition rate was sobering. That was three good guys since I had started. It's the name of the game.

I was in the cockpit of an aircraft about to have an engine failure. All of a sudden, there was thick black oil covering my cockpit windscreen and the engine was dead. I looked to the left off the red wingtip and saw a dirt road. I banked left and continued the turn until I was lined up on the road. As I got lower I noticed a little yellow house with a bay window facing the road just to the right of where I expected to touch down. I thought, Good, at least there is somebody around in case I ball it up. I looked back up just in time to see the wires I was going to fly into.

I woke up in a sweat and, breathing hard, justified the nightmare by convincing myself that Elvis Jones and his tragic death was the catalyst for my nightmare. I ate breakfast and headed for the line office where there was a call waiting for me. It was Eddie. "Dave, we are ready for you. When can you get here?" "There's a DC-3 heading that way at noon. I'm sure I can hitch a ride. I'll see ya about 1:30 today." "Great. See ya then."

I talked to JJ and he said, "No sweat. Just load on and go." "Thanks, JJ." "Oh, by the way, it's Curly who is flying." I went back to the lunch hall where I had seen Curly earlier. Good ol' cigar-chomping Curly Ransom, a short, paunchy, strongly-built guy with a knot of very curly hair perched on top of his round head and a face that has a perpetual look of "yeah, I am a wise guy. You wanna make sompin' out of it?" You couldn't be around Curly for ten minutes without bustin' a gut about the way he tells a story. I had always liked him. "Hey, Curly, how's it?" "Damn, ya open the corral door and any mule can get in here! How's it, Davey?" "Guess I'm riding to Meacham with you today." "Riding, my ass. Co-pilot. Just don't do anything stupid or I gotta kill ya." The good humor did not end until we shut down at Meacham and parted company.

Lamar was standing on the ramp and asked if he could ride back seat to Ardmore. I said, "Sure. Ardmore will make a good stop to check the ol' buzzard out." We both head over to Ritchey Air. "Hiya, Eddie. How's the 26 doing?" "We are about to pull her out of the hangar. Why don't we step into my office and we'll go over the logs and papers." Everything was in order and signed off by the AI (Aircraft Inspector). "How long you figure it'll take ya?" I tell Eddie, "Ardmore tonight, probably Joliet tomorrow, and early the next morning Palwaukee. Probably eight to nine flying hours." "You taking your time?" "I always add an extra day for weather and winds." "Shit, the weather goes down you can always scud run." "He ain't paying me enough," I said with a grin. I walked out the door and freeze as I saw the PT-26 newly painted bright red. I instantly flashed back on the dream and instantly shoved it back in its drawer and scolded myself. Damnit, it's just a stupid dream.

The date was February 4, 1963. I looked at Lamar and told him in "Duke" fashion, "Saddle up. Let's go to Ardmore." I did an especially intense pre-flight and checked basically everything. Satisfied, I hollered at Lamar in the back cockpit, "Brakes!" "Brakes locked." I primed three strokes and locked in the primer. I jammed the crank handle into the receptor and hollered, "Brakes, left mag, and contact." I heard Lamar shout back, "Brakes, left mag, and contact!" I began to crank and the prop also begins to move, maybe one-half blade and the old Ranger 200 hp engine explodes into life and settles. They sure do start easy. I climbed up the wing and into the front cockpit and strapped in.

"Ah Meacham ground Fairchild 75463 Ritchey taxi VFR Ardmore," I announced on the new Nova Tech radio just installed. First class. I can talk to somebody, I think. "Roger, 463. Taxi 16, winds 140 degrees, 10 knots, altimeter 30.54." "463 rog." I adjusted the altimeter to read 30.54 in the Kollsman window and checked the gauge to make sure it was reading field elevation 710 feet checked. I took my time checking mags. I wanted engine temps to read normal before takeoff and decided to make a right downwind departure over 17 just in case. I guess I was still spooked by that dream. I looked out over both wings as I did the control check and felt a little weird as those red wings matched exactly the wings in my dream. Knock it off, I scolded myself. I went to tower 118.3. "Ah 463 is ready. Right downwind, please." "Roger. 463 cleared for takeoff. Right downwind approved."

I taxied into position and slowly advanced the throttle to the stops, the throaty growl of the Ranger filling the cockpit as 463 began to gallop down the runway, gathering speed smartly. Final check. Oil pressure, temps all in the green. Gently coming back on the stick, I performed my magic I still love so dearly and soared smoothly into the late afternoon sky over Fort Worth. Canopy closed and 500 feet I began a silky smooth turn to the right and steady up on right downwind for 16. Everything in the green, airspeed 85 indicated, VSI 700 fpm, needle and beetle centered, and engine smooth as silk. Nothing to do but relax and soak up the freedom of flight.

Like a huge cinema screen I watched the lovely landscape slowly drift by beneath our beautiful 1940s magic carpet called a Fairchild PT-26. As we flew north over the prairie so gold in the afternoon sunlight, I noticed several big columns of white smoke as the wheat farmers were burning off last summer's fields. The sun shining on them made the smoke columns stand out brightly and cast long shadows on the golden ground. The scene was surreal as everywhere I looked there were these columns of smoke and long, thin shadows on the ground. I was at total peace.

There was a four-lane highway being constructed that I was following and a small town coming up on our left. I cross checked the chart and identified the town as Thakerville, Oklahoma. I listened to the steady healthy roaring hum of the Ranger *hmmmmm cough mmm cough cough mmmmm cough bang!* The prop froze straight up and black oil covered my windscreen. I had no time to think of anything but getting this bird on the ground in one piece. I looked off my left red wingtip and there was the still-not-completed four-lane I-65. Dead into the wind, I went to best glide 85 indicated and began a left base for the highway. Turning final I had lots of highway in front of me. I noticed the highway is compacted dirt. As we got to about 100 feet, I noticed a yellow house with a bay window facing my landing zone. This ain't no dream, as I quickly looked up and forward and saw no wires. At 30 feet I began my flare and gently touched down on all three and rolled to a stop.

"Nice job," from the back cockpit. I unbuckled and stood up, thinking the dream wasn't exactly right: there were no wires. Lamar jumped out and started pumping my hand, grinning from ear to ear. "Good flying, Davey, you put this bird under that telephone wire just perfect. I thought we were going to eat it." "Wire?" I looked back and, sure enough, there was a telephone wire strung between two poles that I flew under and never noticed. "The Great Spirit's in the neighborhood," I muttered. "Huh?" "Oh, nothing. Shit, that was an exciting ride, eh Lamar." "You can say that again."

Just then an old beat-up pickup truck rolled to a stop and a big guy in coveralls stepped out, walked up to 463, and said in a deep Oklahoma country accent, "Boy, don't you know this ain't no aeroport?" "Yeah, I know, but we lost our engine and had to make an emergency landing," I said with a touch of pride. "No, ya didn't. That motor is steil on the front o your aeroeoplane jest plain as day."

I heard Lamar start to giggle and it took everything I had to keep from bursting out. Desperately trying to control myself, but with a smile I said, "What I meant to say is that our engine quit running." "Doggone, I thort it were funny seeing that prop standing up and down like at." That did it. Lamar and I broke up and I tried to let this country gentleman know that we weren't trying to be insulting. I stuck out my hand and as he took it in his huge hand, I introduced myself, "Hi, I'm Dave and my knees is still a shaking," at which point this giant of a man, with his big workingman's face and unkempt blond hair, broke into a big grin and said, "Howdy. They call me 'Punkin.'" Introductions over, ol' Punkin, with all the grace of the society he knew best, said, "Spect y'all need a phone. Maw's got some beens on and would love to meet you fellers."

We jumped into Punkin's truck and made the short ride to the little yellow house with the bay window. Turned out it was his. Also, turned out that Maw—and that's what she preferred to be called—not only had beans but roast beef, potatoes, corn, vegetables, and pie for dessert. "That was a feast," I said. "Ya jes never know who might drop in on ya," said Punkin.

After a few phone calls we got one of our mechs to agree to come down and pick us up. About two hours later, after a great evening of talking, looking at photo albums, and lots of laughing, we bid goodnight to our two new friends, Maw and Punkin, and climbed aboard Jr.'s pickup. Punkin said, "Don't worry about yer flyin' machine. I'll take good care o' her."

The next morning the police officer and new owner of 463 had made arrangements for a flatbed and two mechanics and we headed south for Thakerville. Cops in Chicago must make pretty good money, I thought to myself as we headed south. We pulled the wings and set 463 on the flatbed and brought her to a maintenance shop located on the field at Ardmore late that afternoon. The owner of the shop met us and said that a brand new 200 was on the way and he figured I would be able to deliver her to Palwaukee Airport in about two weeks. I headed back to Fort Worth and built up my reserves by flying some more charters for Ritchey in the 310 and also for Robinson Flying Service in a sick 160 Apache.

The end of the adventures with beautiful 463 is that I successfully delivered her to her new owner and he learned to fly in that ol' piece of history. The sad part is that on her next annual inspection, they found dry rot in the center section and she was cut up and burned. The best part of my time with her is that I found out that the spirit is on my side and I will never forget Maw, Punkin, and their marvelous little yellow house.

4

Four-Engine Flying Boat in Tahiti—A Trip Back in Time and North Atlantic in January with One Caged C-46, 1963 to 1964

"Tampa 816 with you level one one thousand squawking 0414 over Mariana at :35, Victor 198 Crestview :56 Semmes next." "Roger 816 Tampa flight plan route." "816 roger." "816 Tampa contact Jacksonville 134.3." "Adios Tampa." Chuck switched our coms to 134.3. "Ah Jacksonville. 816 is with you level one one thousand squawking 0414." "Roger 816. Radar contact flight plan route." "816 roger." Well, at least there is no clearance change but I bet we get one soon, I thought to myself. I knew we had weather over New Orleans and another system was moving into Los Angeles. I could see the high clouds in front of us and that would be the leading edge of the front still a ways off. I was not worried about the system over New Orleans. We would penetrate the front and fly right on through it. LAX, when we checked weather, was forecasting fog, rain, one-half mile, and 200 feet at our time of arrival and I was sure we would get the ILS on the long runway 25L when we got there.

The DC-7B's cowl flaps are operated by four knobs located on the upper engineer's panel and when activated, they respond with a series of audible clicks so the engineer, Bill Stevens, can cross check the cowl flap position on each engine by the number of clicks he hears. Takeoff, all four open. *Click click click.* Climb, one-half open. *Click click.* Cruise, cowls closed. *Click.* I had a bad habit of holding my ball point in my hand, on my lap usually, and clicking the pen when I was thinking about something and that is what I was doing at that moment. *Click click click click click click.* I noticed Bill focus his attention on the cowl flap knobs and reach up and touch each one to make sure they were all in the same position he had put them in. I quit clicking my pen. I thought, I will screw with Bill's mind a little. I put the pen in my shirt pocket and a little while later, when Bill was scanning the ignition analyzer, I pulled my pen out and *click click*, he immediately focused again on the cowl knobs and had a slightly concerned look on his face. I put the pen away and feigned an interest in the charts on my lap. Chuck noticed what I was doing and looked at me with his slight, devilish grin but said nothing.

Sitting 18 feet above Fa'a'a (pronounced *fah-ah-ah*) Lagoon in Tahiti in the cockpit of a Short Sandringham four-engine flying boat, Captain Blackburn called for Nos. 3 and 4 to go to runup, rpm 1,800 as the big flying boat began a lazy 360 turn on the lagoon— the normal runup procedure for a multi-engine seaplane is to just let her go around in big circles as you check mags, props, feathering, and all the other items listed on the check list. "Nos. 3 and 4 complete." "Idle Nos. 3 and 4 1,800 on Nos. 1 and 2," as the 60,000-pound flying boat stops its left turn and slowly began one to the right. This boat had a 112-foot, 9.5-inch wingspan and these maneuvers are done in the middle of the lagoon way away from shore. I looked out at Nos. 3 and 4 and just outboard to the wing-mounted pontoon and watched our movement through the crystal-clear, blue waters of Fa'a'a Lagoon. How the hell can I be so lucky? I wondered to myself.

Short Sandringham sitting on the blue lagoon at Fa'a'a, Tahiti. (Wikipedia)

This was real history—Boeing 303s, Sikorskys, and the great age when PanAm flew the world in giant seaplanes. I thought of Eddie Musick, exploring routes in the Pacific for PanAm. He took off from Pago Pago, Samoa, in an S-42, a four-engine flying boat and was never seen again. He radioed that he was dumping fuel, a dangerous procedure in that plane, and he and the crew died in a tremendous explosion that was seen from far away. His name remains a legend to this day. I felt that I was reliving the past, sitting in this four-engine seaplane about to take off from a South Pacific paradise and fly to another South Pacific paradise, the first stop on our daily route to service three islands.

I was short final to land on Runway 21 at Palwaukee Airport. I floated across the Fox River and the highway, canopy open on the old PT-26, and flared as the threshold stripes passed beneath me. *Urk urk*, I could sure make smooth, soft landings in this old eagle, I thought as we rolled to a stop and turned off to taxi to tie down. The new owner was standing there to meet me. Naturally, he was all smiles. We shook hands and retired to the C.A.V.U. Room Restaurant and Bar. In the bar, ol' Fritz, the German barkeep, had a sign that was always lit up. On one side it said, "This bar is VFR" and on the other "This bar is IFR." Being 10:00 in the morning, the VFR side was showing and I was right on schedule. We retired to the restaurant for a coke and to hand the new owner his papers.

I left the airport to drive to my folks' home with a scheme in mind to talk my father into footing me a ticket on a steamer to go spend some time in Papeete, Tahiti, the paradise that I fell in love with when I sailed there in 1961. Of course, my dad didn't refuse me and a week later I was on the deck of the Matson liner *Mariposa* (known to my Tahitian friends as "Merry Pussy") watching the chaos her giant screws were making on the calm waters of San Francisco Bay as we slipped through the bay, headed for the Golden Gate and a ten-day journey to Tahiti.

One day out of 'Frisco (excuse me, Mom, San Francisco, as you would have corrected me) an announcement came over the speaker, "Are there any passengers with a shellback certificate? If so, please report to the purser's office." Well, I happened to have one of those, having crossed the equator in the 210-ton hermaphrodite brigantine square-rigger *Yankee*. Our certificates were way different than the vanilla drab card given to stinkpot sailors. Because we crossed in a real sailing ship, ours were traditional—hand-printed on a piece of parchment, signed by the captain, and sealed with a piece of marlin and tar, real sailing ship tar. I was proud of that certificate and I happened to have it with me.

I went to the chief purser's office and showed it to him and saw his expression change as he realized what he was holding. Shit, I love getting my ego blown way up. He turned to his assistant and said, "Looks like we have our King Neptune for the ceremony." Then he looked at me and asked if he could take my certificate to Captain Jarvis because he loved sailing ships. "Sure, go ahead." I walked around the deck and watched all the people drinking, playing shuffleboard, chasing women, and, of course, the regulars sitting drunk at the bar at 10:00 in the morning. I don't think I like being a mere passenger, I thought to myself. I felt completely out of place. I missed the brotherhood of my seamen and airmen friends and there was certainly none of that amongst my fellow passengers.

I saw the chief purser head my way with my shellback certificate in his hand. "Mr. Allyn," shit, I wish he would call me anything—Davey, Bilge, Tiny, Dave, anything but Mr. Allyn—"the captain would like to meet you and have dinner in his cabin at 6:30 p.m. tonight." "18:30, five bells, I will be there with bells on," I said, smiling. It's amazing to me what certain little keys will open certain little doors.

I showed up right on time and was introduced to Captain Jarvis, a big man with neatly-combed grey hair and a lined, tan face that only a seaman with many years on deck could age to. Deep, blue eyes, firm handshake, and looked very smart in his dress white uniform. He apologized that he could not drink but offered me one. I declined. He started right off by saying, "That's some certificate you have there. Not many of them around these days." "Yes, sir, I am very proud of that one." I noticed a light Nordic accent when he spoke and he later confirmed he was born and raised in Oslo, Norway.

There was a knock on the door and the first officer and first engineer joined us for a marvelous evening of conversation, mostly about ships and airplanes. Right down my alley and, as it turned out, theirs too. Somewhere in our conversation they all sensed my uneasiness with my fellow passengers and completely understood my feelings. It seemed I had been accepted as a brother of the sea even though I was but a lowly A.B.S., but it didn't matter. After all, I was an A.B.S. on a real sailing ship and had the papers to prove it. The engineer asked me if I had any interest in a tour of the engine room. I said, "You bet I do." Captain Jarvis said, "Tomorrow, you take Dave on his tour and," then to me, "after lunch why don't you spend some time on the bridge?" I was overwhelmed and happy that tomorrow was all planned.

Descending into a hot, white, loud, and chaotic-looking engine room, I was amazed that anybody could possibly understand the tons and tons of huge machinery, all running in unison and with one common mission: to transmit massive amounts of power to two big shafts on the end of which were attached two gigantic three-bladed propellers, each weighing in tons themselves. All of this moved the graceful ship through the seas at a measly 10 tons of fuel a day and produced 24 knots at economy cruise. I was equally amazed that anybody could keep track of the miles of conduit containing even more miles of electrical wiring, not to mention the miles of pipes of every size, bending around here, up, and down in every direction, all doing their individual jobs. here were the thousands of levers, knobs, valves, and emergency equipment in red, located everywhere I looked. It was truly an engineering masterpiece to my untrained eye.

Then there was the human factor: the wipers keeping the massive area wiped clean, the oilers keeping things lubricated, the firemen keeping track of temps in the machinery, the electrical mates keeping track of the electrical system and the first, second, and third engineers overlooking all positions and everything that had to do with this giant power-generating factory.

I thanked the engineer as I departed and had lunch, my head spinning with all I had just seen. I looked around the dining hall and wondered if anybody had even a clue as to what it took to allow them to be enjoying their peace and quiet on this beautiful liner. But they probably don't really care as long as they are comfortable. If I had chosen the sea instead of the air, it would be tankers and freighters for sure.

After lunch, the chief purser looked me up and escorted me to the bridge deck. Unlike the roar of the engine room, the bridge was quiet and very orderly, extremely clean with brass polished, and as businesslike as the cockpit of a large aircraft. I expected to see a large helm and was surprised to see a small helm wheel that seemed completely inadequate for such a large ship. Both telegraphs set on either side of the helm set at "Ahead," you could ring in another setting called "Flank Ahead" and I wondered how much faster this giant ship would go at that setting. The helmsman was standing in place but not actually steering as the *Mariposa* was on the "Iron Mike" (autopilot).

The officer of the watch in this case, the 12 to 4, was the first officer who I had dinner with last night. He explained the workings of the bridge and told me that if I wanted I could spend some time on either wing of the bridge. I knew that even though this huge ship was only moving at 24 knots, the focus of the crew on watch was just as intense as the crew on watch in the cockpit of an aircraft cruising at ten times this speed so I kept silent so as not to interrupt their concentration. I spent the next two hours enjoying the view from the open portion of the bridge wing of this giant liner as she powerfully plowed her way through the blue Pacific and I loved every second of it, not to mention that I was learning a great deal about the operations of a large ship while at sea.

The day came for the crossing of the line. The ship's horn sounded at 11:00 a.m.

and I performed my duties as King Neptune. The ceremonies were designed to pamper the paying guest and was about as far removed from a real shellback ceremony as could be. These polliwogs didn't even rate polliwog status so much as the honor of shellback status. But I guess the Matson Company had to play the game to keep profits up. I only hope I didn't displease our king of the seas who also holds the only key to Davey Jones' locker. There have been a few times since when I was sailing my small boats that I wondered if King Neptune was getting even with me by throwing a few violent storms my way and making my life miserable. At any rate, these phony and pretend shellbacks were too high on their rum swizzles and margaritas to really give a damn. Just remember, King Neptune, that I am a true and loyal shellback and in a moment of weakness, I was forced and ordered by the captain himself to perform this blasphemous duty. Next time I am at sea, I beg your forgiveness and mercy.

As we approached the Papeete channel the skipper came down and wished me good luck in Tahiti. I bid farewell to the good Captain Jarvis and his good crew aboard the M/V *Mariposa*. We docked and cleared and I went ashore and stopped in to see who was at Quinn's. Sure enough, Vaima, Angel, Tani, and best of all, Black Black and Suzy No Pants, were all there and it was if I had never left. Remi Vili Vela ran up and gave me a big hug and we all had wet eyes for a little while. The party began again right where it left off two years before.

I checked into the same grass hut Leo and I had spent so much time in when we were there as crew on the brigantine *Yankee*. Things had not changed as yet in Tahiti but were about to. The international airport was finished and Air France was just beginning to fly into Tahiti and bring my paradise out of the 19th century and into the complicated and freedom-killing work of the 20th century. I was sad about that but before that happened I was focused on meeting the crew of that beautiful Short Sandringham four-engine flying boat floating so peacefully and serenely on Fa'a'a's blue waters. I was in luck.

Captain Blackburn and his wife showed up at the Bel Air, where I was staying, for dinner that night. I couldn't believe my luck. It didn't take long before we were talking airplanes and flying. Captain Blackburn had an amazing past, being a command pilot on the Shorts Sunderland patrol bombers for the Royal Navy during WWII. He had been in flying boats ever since. We became friends over the next several days and, as it turned out, his co-pilot, a French gentleman, was becoming rock-happy with Tahiti and was desperate to leave. He asked me if I had any interest in flying as co-pilot until he could get another co-pilot who had to be either native or of French origin. He said, "I can't legally pay you but I could work out something temporary so we can keep operating."

I tried not to drool all over myself as I agreed. I don't know what Captain Blackburn did but he must have had some pull, as we had the blessings of the local officials. The next morning I was in the company launch and heading for the flying boat. The night before, Chris and his wife had me over for dinner and ground school on my duties as first officer aboard the Shorts.

I climbed aboard the boat through the forward-loading door. To the left was the entrance for the cramped compartment where the boat boy sat during operations. As far as I could tell, his job was to secure us to the buoy float and unsecure us when we left. He also cleaned the passenger compartments. All passenger compartments were partitioned off into comfortable rooms with three seats facing each other. I remember we could carry twenty-one passengers in six compartments.

The boat also had an upper level behind the trailing edge of the high wing in her glory days. She had a dining area and cooking galley so you could enjoy home-cooked meals, probably cooked by a Cordon Bleu chef. Just in from the entrance door was a ladder that led into the cockpit. The cockpit itself was massive. I climbed the ladder and strapped in the Bermuda-class flying boat. I was familiar with the P&W R-1830s this ship was equipped with giving her 4,800 hp on takeoff at max gross of 65,000 pounds. Her range was extensive at around 3,500 miles at cruise of around 155 mph and 200 gallons per hour that would make for a long trip. I always wondered what the 900 hp Pegasus Bristol-powered Shorts must have been like to fly. Probably pretty doggy in comparison. We never worried about gross weights and were always light.

As Nos. 3 and 4 idled back and Nos. 1 and 2 throttled up the big boat slowly changed from a left circle and into a right circle as we ran up Nos. 1 and 2. It seemed strange to be moving perfectly smoothly with no bumping, swaying, or bouncing so familiar to a land plane. As we finished our runup and throttled back, I could hear the cockadoodledoo below us of our caged animal passengers laid neatly and secured down the aisle. Roosters and chickens going to Raiatea, probably for the stew pot.

As Chris lined up into the wind, we reviewed the emergency checklist as pre-flight brief. Lined up, Chris initiated the throttles and as he advanced to the deep-throated roar of maximum power, the big boat began to gather speed. There was no splashing or volumes of spray over the cockpit as I have seen on other seaplanes. Her huge size prevented that. I could feel her hull smoothly slicing ever faster through the surface of the lagoon. She flew onto the step smoothly with no dramatic rising of the nose and as our indicated airspeed jumped to 75 mph, we knew we were on the step. I looked out at Nos. 3 and 4 churning steadily at max power and looked just aft and saw the displacement spray peeling away from our hull at tremendous speed. I glanced at our pontoon and noticed a thin trail of vaporizing water coming off the bottom aft of the float, looking more like a trail of smoke than water.

I called V2 at 98 indicated. I could feel the *whoosh* of the hull riding on top of the water and knew instantly that we were in the air when I could no longer feel the *whoosh*. This really was seat-of-the-pants flying. We settled down to 120 in the climb and climbed just above the small scattered Qs (cumulonimbus clouds) that are always there leveling at 2,500 just above the Qs. Cruise power set, and 135 mph indicated, I calculated we were truing at 143 mph and probably burning 160 gallons an hour at this reduced cruise setting. As the puffy Qs drifted slowly by beneath us, I watched the steep high cliffs of Moorea drifting by even more slowly on our port side, the mountain peaks far above us at our low cruising altitude.

I saw Pao Pao inlet come into view and reminisced about the wonderful time we had at Leeteg's mansion and the great evening at the One Chicken Inn. I still couldn't believe I was flying a four-engine flying boat amongst some of the most beautiful Polynesian islands in the South Pacific. The roar and vibrations of the Shorts cockpit does not let me sink from reality for long as Chris told me to take the controls. I knew that she would be heavy from my experience flying the DC-3. But this baby was even heavier even with the oversize control yoke made big for this very reason so you can overpower her massive wings.

I soon had the feel and her stability in flight because of her high wing configuration was unmatched in any large aircraft I have flown since except the Stinson tri-motor and maybe the B-25. Forty-five minutes after departure from Fa'a'a, we were in a long descent on final for the lagoon at Uturoa on the island of Raiatea. I called off airspeed as Chris flew the old Shorts at no more than 200 feet per minute rate of sink. I admired his smooth technique and his self-confidence. He was a real pro as a flying boat captain.

At 200 feet per minute, the flying boat was in perfect position to make contact with the surface of the water. The trick was to put the old seagull down exactly where you wanted to. Chris certainly knew how to pull off that trick. As we were exactly over the touchdown point I heard *whoo-oo-oosh* as the keel made contact with the blue and turquoise waters of the lagoon. Easing off the power on all four engines the continuous *whoosh* became less intense as the hull settled into the water and we became a slow-moving boat. Shutting down Nos. 1 and 4 engines, Chris expertly turned into the wind and sailed right up to our docking buoy and shut down Nos. 2 and 3. As the boat came to a stop within boathook reach of our mooring line, Manu, our docking crew, reached out and secured us to the buoy and we read the shutdown and securing checklists.

There were several launches standing by just in case we had a problem but mainly to ferry passengers, roosters, and crew to shore. I volunteered to help Manu out and stay on board while Chris went ashore to do some business. Our layover was 1 hour, 30 minutes. Departure at 10:15. I spent the time getting to know F-DBIP intimately and there is no better way to get to know her than to help clean her up for our next group. She was truly a magnificent aircraft, totally different than any aircraft I had been around up until then.

It was very difficult to get used to being in an aircraft and hearing the gentle lap of small waves against her hull and looking out and being surrounded by water. At 10:15 a.m. sharp we started our first engine and soon we were making lazy 360-degree turns in both directions while we did our runup. Turning into the wind and slowly coming to maximum takeoff power, the old seagull made with the magic once again for our short 35-minute hop to Bora Bora. We leveled off at 1,500 feet over the neighbor island of Tahaa and could already see the magmatic peaks of Otemanu Mountain at Bora Bora. I looked down on the serene beauty of Tahaa slipping by beneath us. The heart stopping beauty of her vivid blue and turquoise waters of the lagoon and eye-piercing white beaches surrounding the high green island set in motion by this magic flying boat. This was really where it was at and something I had been dreaming and hoping for my whole life.

Thirty-five minutes later we were on the long and graceful final glide for another magnificent and smooth water landing at Faanui Bay, Bora Bora. This was long before Bora Bora became a tourist mecca and was still being serviced by either Copra schooners or Short Bermuda flying boat. As we sailed up to the buoy, I was struck with *deja vu*. The last time I saw the panorama that I was looking at was as an able-bodied seaman aboard the brigantine *Yankee*. Our stay would be two hours with a scheduled departure at 12:50 p.m. for Rangiroa, a flat, true South Seas atoll. This time I went ashore with Chris and met up with quite a few past acquaintances, much to Chris's surprise, as I had told him nothing about my past experiences. When I labored through a few brief native conversations with some old friends, Chris shot me this look of "Who in hell is this guy?"

We had a great lunch and I clued Chris in as to my past experiences in this part of the world and it opened up a new level of friendship with my captain. At 12:50 No. 3 was turning and after a few blades the radial puffed her smoke and worked up to a gallop after a few coughs and hesitations. Soon we were on the step and shortly we broke surface and were in the air—a feat that all through history the experts and intelligence of humanity claimed to be an impossible feat. Well, I was a witness this time, and it was definitely not impossible.

Climbing out we set a course for the atoll of Rangiroa, a bit north of east and one hour's flying time. We'd had 21 passengers from Raiatea to Bora Bora and now had only two on this leg of the trip, but lots of freight and our usual animal friends—the royal roosters of Polynesia singing to us all the way. I have always considered atolls beautiful—so awe-inspiring from the air—but boring after a few days. We didn't go to Rangiroa much, only when the company could make money on the freight, passengers being few and far between. Another condition that would cancel a trip to Rangiroa was wind and wave conditions in the lagoon. Rangiroa has the largest lagoon in all of French Polynesia and in any wind conditions can produce a wave fetch that the flying boat could not handle safely.

Today was perfect as far as wind conditions were concerned. The atoll of Rangiroa came into view one hour after leaving Bora Bora. The huge blue lagoon was ringed by large and small low island atolls, each with a ridge of bright green palm tree forest in the middle. Ringing both sides of the beaches was the contrasting brilliant turquoise waters of shallows fading into the bright blue of the deeper waters of the lagoon and Pacific Ocean, an immense treat to the eyes of the beholder—mainly, me. We circled our landing site and set up final approach to land between the passes of Avatoru and Tiputa. Avatoru, the grass hut village was still basically in the 19th century. Rangiroa was still a dream island to those of us with an adventurous spirit and incurable romanticism guiding our lives.

Chris put the old seagull down in another feather-light and silky-smooth landing right up to our mooring buoy. Many boats and people swarmed aboard and began offloading the supplies while the cockpit crew stayed on station for a speedy departure for Tahiti so as not to tempt Mother Nature and her grounding winds and waves. Unloaded, we started engines and taxied out and split the waters of the blue lagoon of Rangiroa leaving our wake disappearing into nothingness as we became airborne. Climbing out on a WSW heading and leveling at 1,500 feet, we split the molecules at 153 mph for Fa'a'a Lagoon, Tahiti.

Looking out at our wing pontoon slung under the wing and outboard of Nos. 3 and 4 engines to the endless horizon of the South Pacific slipping serenely by beneath us, I thought of my first four-engine seaplane flight. Wow, I could spend a lot of hours doing this. I wondered if there was a chance that I could become a regular paid pilot for the company. This turned out to be an impossibility. Be it national pride or whatever, the odds were stacked against me. I made several more flights with Chris in his magic boat that actually flew and remember fondly every second of my time as co-pilot of the magnificent Short Brothers Bermuda-class flying boat called the Sandringham. I am very pleased to know that the very boat I co-piloted is today still on display at the "Musea de l'Air" in Paris, France. It wasn't long before a new French co-pilot was trained and replaced me, making everything legal and above-board again, as it should be.

I don't count the Shorts as an aircraft amongst my 139 other types that I flew as pilot in command because I never made a takeoff or landing myself in the aircraft.

My replacement co-pilot and notice from the draft board came just in time as I was learning very acutely what "rock happy" meant. As beautiful a paradise as the island of Tahiti is, I was feeling very confined and sick and tired of seeing the same beauty day in and day out. Another dull day in Paradise, I would say to myself upon awakening in the morning. I was ready to leave and did so as to arrive in Chicago in time to check in with the draft board. First, I checked in with a friend who was flying helicopters as a warrant officer in the army. He told me that I would qualify with a high school diploma coupled with my flying experience. He gave me an address and some names and told me that when I passed the induction physical to take the papers to this address and look up a certain officer and they would most certainly let me sign up for helicopter training and that the Army was building up their fleet of choppers. This was before our involvement in Vietnam so the Army knew something the rest of us didn't.

I showed up at the recruitment center and filled out the paperwork and proceeded to have my physical. I remember that some of the pictures and questions were really dumb. For example, a picture of a screwdriver: "Do you know what this is?" and so on. I was even more determined not to go in as a grunt.

I was standing on a ramp on an airport in Texas, waiting to take my first lesson in a Bell 47 helicopter for my chopper rating. One of the other pilots had the first lesson and I was observing the operation as I was next in line. They got started and did the runup and as they started to lift off, a sudden gust of wind hit them. Before the instructor could react it moved the 47 back and the tail rotor just barely ticked the fence. *R-r-r-ring!* I saw small pieces of the rotor fly in every direction and the chopper began spinning in circles

215

before my eyes. As the cockpit spun by, all I could see were four huge eyes and I knew right then that instructor and student were just passengers participating in a very wild carnival ride. I heard the chopper's engine cut and the "cuckoo" bird tilted just enough to clip a rotor blade on the ground.

Now this insane excuse for a flying machine didn't crash like a normal airplane does. It just began to eat itself up piece by piece, culminating in a pile of smoking wreckage. Thank the Spirit it did not catch on fire. Disregarding my own safety, I dove on the pile of junk and helped the two very shaken pilots out and away from this self-destructing pile of garbage that was a few seconds ago a weird-looking flying machine.

Still shaking, the instructor told me that I would have to wait until tomorrow for my lesson. "Just leave it in the hangar. I don't think I need the rating that bad," I said. I got hold of the student and invited him for a birthday drink at a local bar. I was buying. After I told him what it looked like from my perspective, and as we started through the door of a local drinking establishment, we both began to laugh uncontrollably and the bartender booted us out because he thought we had already had too much to drink. And here I was passing my physical with the distinct possibility of being forced to fly one of these machines. As it turned out, it was at the beginning of the Vietnam War.

At this point, I got on the scales and weighed in at 222 pounds. The person keeping and marking the paperwork put three Rs down. When I asked what that meant, he told me that I was one pound overweight and that the army could not accept me and that I would be reclassified 1Y. If I could lose that one pound in a month, I could get in. I tried to hide my joy, but don't think I did a very good job of it as I practically jumped up and clicked my heels together on the way out. Let's see: lose one pound and I could get in the army. I knew the exact solution for this problem as I entered the ice cream store and downed two hot fudge sundaes. I did leave off the cherry since I needed to lose one pound.

I was also overjoyed to be able to put aside the prospect of flying helicopters and not think about it again. Sorry, all you chopper lovers and pilots. Years later, I did get checked out in a Bell 47 and do agree that they are very versatile ships but my feelings for them have not changed.

So, what now? I jumped into the Elva and four speeding tickets later arrived at the seaplane school at Lake Worth in Texas. I was going to get a single-engine seaplane rating and then move on to the Grumman Widgeon, powered by two beautiful Lycoming R680 300 hp radial engines, to get my multi-engine seaplane rating. But it never happened. We started seaplane training in a Lake Amphibian Skimmer and I really got to like that little bird, she flew on and off the waters of Lake Worth so smoothly and gracefully. Our landing procedures were identical to the big Shorts, holding 200 feet a minute descent until touchdown and the little Skimmer would smoothly *whoosh* onto the water just like her big sister. We practiced docking, sailing, and engine out landing procedures and after ten hours, my instructor declared me ready for my check ride in the morning.

I went back to my apartment in Fort Worth and just as I walked in, the phone rang.

It was Wilhelm, a German pilot who was getting his ATR (airline transport rating) and who was employed at Flo Air, an international ferry company on contract with Beechcraft. He was ferrying aircraft all over the world. I had told him that, if possible, I would love to make a crossing as a co-pilot. "Hi, Dave, this is Wilhelm. Hey, you still want to make a crossing?" "Damned straight!" "I just talked to the chief pilot and he approved a co-pilot to fly a Beech Queenair 65 across the Atlantic. You gotta be in Wichita before morning." "I'll be there."

Jeez, this is great, I thought. I called the seaplane school and cancelled indefinitely my check ride— I never did get my seaplane rating, but have the pleasure of knowing I have real time in a Shorts brothers four-engine flying boat—grabbed my passport, packed, and one speeding ticket later was at Amon Carter Field. I think I gotta get rid of that Elva. I got on an old Braniff red-eye DC-3 direct to Wichita (Yeah, Braniff was still flying DC-3s in those days). That's when I learned that ferrying aircraft around the world involved more delays than actual flying.

I was put up in the Holiday Inn and soon met the chief pilot, a Humphrey Bogart look-alike, right down to short, strong stature, stone face, and hairlines. Doug Hinton, who became a lifelong friend and diving buddy, welcomed me with a cold beer and word that we were delayed two days from the factory before we could get Beech 65 D-ILGD, already with German markings. Two days later, Wilhelm and I flew D-ILGD the short distance to Newton, Kansas, for tank installation so we could make it across the Atlantic. The tanking consisted of three 55-gallon tanks set in the main cabin and an electric pump to be able to refuel our wing tanks as we burned the fuel from them. The interior of the corporate twin was neatly packed and stowed on top of the tanks, giving the pilots no way out in the event of a ditching so the windshield was designed to be able to be kicked out, if need be. I thought, yeah, right.

Biplanes: windy, uncomfortable, squirrely, slow, beautiful, graceful and wonderful flying birds

Doug Hinton, fellow adventurer

Harry Oliver, all-around good guy

I liked Doug right off and spent a lifetime with his great jokes and many hours of laughter, not to mention flying and diving together. I have known his daughter, Kira, since birth and her daughter calls me Uncle Dave to this day. Doug's wife, Uta, is also with us on our diving adventures and is a trusted dive buddy. Another great result of not being afraid to speak up and say to a stranger, "Any chance of joining up on a crossing?"

I noticed by a hangar at Newton a burned-out wreckage that resembled a Sky Master. I asked what happened. It turned out that a Pan Am 707 captain decided he wanted to ferry across the Atlantic and took a job flying a Cessna 337 to Europe on his solo checkout. He flared the little 337 at the same height he would have in a B707—way too high. To everybody's horror, he held the flare and stalled the Cessna, which hit the runway on her nose, rupturing the fuel tanks and exploding on impact. An avoidable situation caused by improper check out and I am sure a bit of overconfidence, resulting in a needless fatal accident. A sobering thought as the mechanics finished our tanking and Wilhelm and I flight planned our non-stop flight to Boston Logan Field—an eight-hour flight that gave us the opportunity to check all of our equipment before hopping the pond.

We loaded our tanks to capacity, 160 gallons in the ferry tanks and I believe we had another 240 gallons in the wing tanks for a total of 400 gallons at 38 gph. That gave us 10:30 minutes of fuel at 165 knots or 190 mph. We had a range of almost 1,830 nautical miles or 2,065 statute miles. Plenty of range to make it from Gander, Newfoundland, to Santa Maria in the Azore Islands, our furthest over water portion of the flight, 1,300 miles. So we were pat on the fuel.

Having time in a 65 before, I could certainly tell we were heavy by the power it took just to get us moving. We took the two Lycoming IGSO-480 flat opposed engines up to 1,700 rpm just to get us moving. In fact, we were 25 percent over gross, legal on a ferry permit, which meant that for the first few hours over the ocean, if we lost an engine, we had no alternative but to ditch as the 65 wouldn't stay in the air at that weight. We were alternate IFR, legal going into Boston Logan and if we lost an engine on this leg, no sweat because there were plenty of places to go. Not so over the Atlantic.

We did our runup and everything looked good. We lined up on the runway and Wilhelm initiated the power. I tapped the back of his hand as the manifold pressure needle reached 44 inches of manifold pressure and the cockpit became filled with the powerful medium-pitch roar as the IGSO-480s reached maximum power. The newborn bird just kicked out of the Beech factory nest began to move sluggishly at first then gathered speed smartly and at 110 indicated I put up two fingers to indicate V2 had been reached and we simultaneously took flight, gear coming up, METO power and clean her up quickly to climb power and 140 indicated. Flaps up, and the 65, in spite of her weight, climbed out at a comfortable rate. If a failure is to occur, it usually does within the first 25 hours out of the factory—a comfortable thought as 40 percent of our flight would be in the danger zone.

Both Lycomings sounded healthy and strong and all the gauges read in the green. Slight right turn out contact Wichita departure. "Ah Wichita, departure Beech Delta-India-Lima-George-Delta. Just off Newton in a right turn squawking 1,200. Request IFR Logan International." "You going non-stop?" "Affirmative." "What type of Beech are you?" "Beech Queenair, model 65." Long pause. "Final destination?" "Bremen, Germany." Longer pause. "International ferry, you had me going there for a minute." "Yeah, I think we got enough fuel." "Ah roger Lima-George-Delta. Clearance." It was a long one and after I read back I sat back to navigate and enjoy the flight.

I figured en route time to be 8:30 minutes and we would arrive at Logan about 8:00 p.m. that night. We had an average ground speed of 175 knots and true of 165 knots with the power pulled back to 60 percent long-range cruise and that gave us a 10 knots tailwind average. We departed Newton at 10:00 a.m. or 12:00 noon, Logan time. That gave us probably four to five hours of daylight and three to four-and-a-half hours of dark as it was December and Boston Logan was reporting ground temps of only 12 degrees and blowing to 20 knots. I checked Gander, Newfoundland, temps and they were 17 degrees below zero.

I always enjoy watching the ground drift by beneath us. Even though this route is not the most exciting country in the world, I still enjoyed my perch looking down on the geography of the land and complete layouts of towns, villages, and cities as we soared high above this panorama, always moving and changing. Light was beginning to fade as we came on to the Mississippi River. Always a milestone on any flight, west or east. I enjoy looking down on this famous waterway and industrial lifeline for our country.

I wonder what the Mississippi must have been like before the stem to stern traffic of the modern day barge streams all the way up and down the river. I have seen just about every section of the Mississippi during my flying career and from St. Louis south is the only section of the river that comes even close to what she must have been like.

Darkness has come not far from the river and the magic of night flight came on full blast. Out west in the desert areas, lighted towns are few and far between with bright starlit skies and pitch blackness on the ground, interrupted once in a while by a light here and another there. Each one an isolated ranch house, one of the reasons I love the west and southwestern part of our country. Not so east of the Mississippi, with lighted towns and cities everywhere you look. To me they look like lighted jewels and are in their own way very beautiful.

I have never forgotten what my father once said as we were making a night flight so many years ago. We were flying over a small town all lit up with strings of lighted roads and cars heading in scattered directions from the town. As we followed the strings of light they all headed to another lighted area or town in the distance. He said, "If you could x-ray a human body and light up the cancer in the body, I wonder if it would look just like that." Maybe we humans are the earth's cancer that will eventually kill it all. Sure hope Dad's idea is only that. I prefer to think that things are just naturally the way they are supposed to be and peace and understanding are born from chaos.

"Ah Delta-India-Lima-George-Delta. Logan approach, turn right heading 140 degrees for radar vectors to Runway 32 Logan." "Lima-George-Delta 140 degrees on the heading." "Ah roger squawk 1244 and ident." "That's 1244 and here's the ident." "Roger Lima-George. Radar contact continue 140 degrees." "140 degrees roger." "Left 125 degrees for Lima George." "125 degrees Lima George." "Further left 320 degrees you are on 3 ½-mile final Runway 32 Logan. Contact Logan tower 128.8." "128.8 adios approach. Thanks for the vectors." "See ya." "Logan tower D-India-Lima-George-Delta 3 ½-mile final 32 full stop." "Roger. George-Delta cleared full stop runway 32."

Gear down, airspeed 120, flaps full, power off, engine exhaust crackling, as the engines come to idle, threshold lights slip by below us and the tires sound off as they make contact with the cold asphalt of Runway 32 at Logan International Airport, located outside of Boston, Massachusetts. "Turn right next turnoff and hold short of taxiway. Contact ground 121.9." "George Delta hold short contact ground .9." "George Delta is going to the Beech dealer on the field." "Ah roger George Delta. Taxi as requested." We taxied in and shut down.

On further inspection, we found, true to the 25-hour rule, that we had a starter motor seal gone on our No. 2 engine (right) and a pretty good oil leak. The FBO had a new starter motor and supplied us with a mechanic. Doug had arrived one hour before us and was at the Logan Hotel waiting for us. Wilhelm told me to stay with the aircraft and meet them when the job was done. "You are just a co-pilot," he added. What the hell is that all about? I wondered. It was not to be the last belligerent comment I was to receive from my so-called friend.

I waited in the pilot's lounge until 11:00 p.m. for our mechanic to get started and he planned to change out the starter in the cold of night on the ramp. I decided to give him a hand since he didn't seem too happy about the situation himself. It took us two hours and I don't think I have ever been so cold before or since as I was that night on the ramp at Logan. We finished up at 1:30 a.m. and as I was just getting warmed up, in walked Doug and Wilhelm. "Hiya, Dave. We got a good window into Gander. We gotta be in the air by 2:00 a.m. and that oughta put us in Gander by 6:30." The sun doesn't come up in Gander until 9:00 a.m. in December so it would be a night flight all the way and I probably wouldn't get to see Newfoundland on this trip. Welcome to the world of ferrying aircraft.

Wilhelm and Doug flight planned and checked weather while I went out and pre-flighted both airplanes. They showed up on the ramp and Doug said, "Severe clear all the way to Gander." We only fueled the wings and reserve tanks and that gave us IFR plus range. We would be passing over Nova Scotia, again in the dark, but what the hell. This flight was going to Gander, Newfoundland, and that suited me fine. It was going to be a whole different ball game from the balmy tropics where I had been flying just a few months before.

We strapped in and clearance delivery shot us a clearance, which I read back and went to 121.9 ground control. They sent us to Runway 33 with 10 gusting to 25 knots straight down the runway. That was going to give us a headwind and a crosswind for our flight to Gander, about 030 degrees on the gyro compass. I switched to tower frequency 128.8. "Ah tower Delta-India-Lima-George-Delta we are ready." "Ah roger. George Delta cleared for takeoff, right turn after takeoff on course. Contact departure on 133.0." "133.0, here we go."

Takeoff was normal and after gear up and climb power, we started a slight right turn to settle on 030 degrees. "Departure Delta-India-Lima-George-Delta is with you 133.0. Just off of 33 left in a right turn squawking 1010." "Ah roger George Delta, radar contact report reaching niner thousand." "Call you level niner thousand." I sat back and enjoyed the lights of Boston slipping by below us. A little further and we were over a black void called the North Atlantic Ocean south of Nova Scotia. I hadn't seen Wilhelm switch to our auxiliary tanks but what the hell. I was just a co-pilot and why in hell should the captain of the Queenair keep his lowly co-pilot informed as to what the hell is going on in his cockpit. Besides, I was tired as hell from lack of sleep but I wasn't about to fall asleep, especially in front of my skipper.

I was fighting to stay awake and nodding when both engines quit. The fight to stay awake was over and I won. I reacted by reaching up to the glareshield as Wilhelm hit the boost pumps and switched tanks. Instantly both engines roared back to life. That is no way to treat two geared engines brand new from the factory but what the hell. They just had to get us across the Atlantic and then it was the new owner's problem. That's when I realized I was getting my ass chewed. Wilhelm the Conquerer was in a raging tirade.

In an uncontrolled and loud voice, becoming thicker with his German accent as the tirade went on, he said, "Vat in der hoilen you tink you is doink. You gonna take over," etc. etc. etc. I just looked at him with a controlled smile on my face that pissed him off even more. "Vat you tink you vas gonna do?" he screamed. "I was reaching for the checklist in case you needed it, cappy," I said in a calm voice. "Vell you just keep you hands to youself yah?" "Aye aye, sir," I said in a low voice. "Vats dis aye und aye?" "Oh, just agreeing with you." "Ya, okay den." Just like Berlin, the battle ended and peace was restored to our cozy, friendly cockpit. Wilhelm had told me how he was in the Hitler youth and had fought in the streets of Berlin in 1945 and that he "killed lots of 'ahmy' soldatens." I guess he is still pissed off that he and his country got their silly asses kicked by the "inferior ahmy" forces. The battle in the skies over Nova Scotia came to an end and things settled down to the routine cockpit duties of flying an airplane to Gander, Newfoundland.

As the north end of Nova Scotia slipped by, we were again in the black void of the sea between Nova Scotia and Newfoundland. "George Delta," I heard Doug say over the radio. "This is George Oscar. I just had the left windscreen crack and I am flying from the right seat. Am in contact with Gander approach and getting vectors to Gander. See you on the ground." The 25-hour gremlins were alive and well.

"Ah Gander approach, this is Delta-India-Lima-George-Delta 25 south of Gander inbound, level niner thousand, squawking 1010." "Rogah, Lima George. Descend and maintain 4,000." "Outa niner for four, Lima George." "Report reaching 4,000 Lima-George." "Call you at 4,000. Have you been in contact with Delta-India-Lima-George-Oscar?" "Affirmative. He is aboot to touch down now." No question we are definitely in Canada. "George Delta has the airport." "George Delta descend to 1,500 and contact Gander tower on 118.1." "George Delta 1,500 and 18.1. See ya." "Ah Gander, this is Delta-India-Lima-George-Delta, 8 south airport in sight. Full stop." "Rogah George Delta. Call left downwind runway 21 altimeter 29.98, wind 220 degrees 10 knots." "Left downwind 21, George Delta."

And then—this was a first for me—"Caution George Delta, caution. Wolves have been seen on 21, use caution." "Ah Gander, how is George Oscar doing?" "Rogah. He is tied down at Gander Aviation and safe." "That's good news. We are left downwind now." "You are cleared to land runway 21, wind steady 220 degrees at 10 knots." "Cleared full stop. George Delta." "Think you can handle it, Willy?" Uh-oh. No sense of humor from the left seat, just a watch-your-ass look from Wilhelm.

Three greens, full flaps, threshold lights slipped by as Wilhelm made a glass-smooth landing. "I knew you could do it. Nice landing." Still no smile. Oh well, I tried. The honeymoon was definitely over. "Turn right next taxiway. Contact ground 121.9. Clearing." ".9 clearing George Delta." As we turned off, standing right next to the taxiway, sure enough, looking right at us, stood a majestic and handsome wolf. What a great welcome to Gander, I thought. I kept my thoughts to myself. I don't know if he saw our welcoming committee and if he did, I don't know if he cared.

"Gander ground, George Delta is with you point 9, goin' to Gander Aviation." "Cleared Gander Aviation, George Delta." As we taxied by Doug's aircraft, I could see the crack high-lighted by the light that George Oscar was parked under. The crack went from middle top across the entire windscreen, all the way to the lower left corner. Doug was damn lucky that the windscreen did not give way. That could have proved fatal. Even had the windscreen given way after Doug had changed seats, I don't know whether or not he could have kept the Queenair in the air or not. The wind chill in the cockpit would probably have been down around 60 or 70 below and even though Doug, through years of experience, kept dressed warmly and the heat off, he probably couldn't have lasted very long in that low temperature and hurricane-force wind blasting through the cockpit. When I brought all this up to him, Doug, not known for showing emotion, coldly looked up at the crack and muttered, "Damned gremlins," and headed for the warmth of the line shack. We called for rooms at the airport hotel and Doug said for Wilhelm and me to meet him in the restaurant by 9:00 a.m. for a brief and to decide how to carry on.

It was getting light as I sat down to a hot cup of coffee along with Wilhelm, who had said nothing to me since his mental glitch. To give him credit, he had not seen a pillow in 27 hours and I justified his mood by that and kept my own mouth shut as well. Doug showed up a few minutes later and told us that Gander Aviation was going to stuff ol' George Oscar in the hangar until the new windscreen arrived from Wichita, and that he and Wilhelm would take George Delta across the pond and deliver her. Then Doug would come back and pick up George Oscar. He continued, "Sorry, ol' chap. I guess you are bumped." I jokingly said, "Aw hell, the old kaiser here wouldn't mind a vacation here in balmy Gander. Why don't you let him stay and take me as co-pilot?" Doug responded with a puff of smoke and slight chuckle that I would get to know through the years since.

The daggers were coming hot and heavy from Kaiser Willy. "That went over like a fart in a diver's helmet," I said. Doug started to laugh and it seemed that even Wilhelm began to relax. "If you want to wait around for a few days, you can come across with me. We can't pay for the room." "You don't have to twist my arm. I will be here. And I'll wash dishes if I have to." The deal was done and we all dove into a great Gander breakfast, complete with reindeer sausage.

I decided to walk out on the ramp and see what was to be seen, feeling lucky that I was still on as co-pilot for the trip across, this time with Doug. I looked out past the approach end of 21 and there were two bright landing lights attached to a Curtiss C-46 Commando on short final. I watched as this beauty flared too low and *er-r-rk boomph* back up for No. 2 *er-r-rk* smoke coming out from under the right main wheel as the pilot got on the right brake a bit heavy to prevent a possible ground loop to the left. *Er-rr-r-r-rk!* Smoke coming out from under the left main this time as the pilot corrected the overcorrection to the right, the tail smacking the ground and a little bounce as if reprimanding the pilot for such a shitty landing.

I stood and watched the beautiful Commando taxi in and dwelled upon the luscious thunder of four-thousand wild horses galloping in front of me in the form of

Pratt & Whitney R-2800s. I listened to the cut as both big black painted Curtiss electric props slowed to a stop. Just before stopping No. 1 sipped a little residual fuel and made one last throaty gasp and then slowed to a stop. The only sound was the crackling and tinking sound of a freshly shut down radial engine. N355 Whiskey was an old warhorse that probably scraped rubber on just about every runway in the world and a lot nobody had ever heard of.

I walked past the trailing edge of the left wing in time to see the big cargo door swing open and a tall, balding man hook the ladder in place and start down with a handful of red "Remove Before Flight" flags. Just as he was getting to the last rung, he slipped and if I had not been standing where I was, he would have had a nasty fall. "Thanks," he said, and wow, did he smell like a whiskey brewery. "You the pilot?" I asked. "No, jusht the firsht offisher." I thought, Mister, you're a damned disgrace to the good name of aviation. Just then, a short wiry guy, hair chopped short, face like a road map, and a raspy commanding voice, hollered, "Ya didn't break yer fuckin' neck, didja?" "Not this time," said the firsht offisher. "You the captain?" I asked. "Aw, shit, don't get worked up. I land like that all the time." "Where you coming from?" "Picked the old snake up in Dominican Republic, heading for Germany. You ferryin'?" "Yeah, but I got bumped. Won't be leavin' for a week or so." "Got any heavy time?" "Typed in a three." "That so!" I could tell he was sober and a bit pissed.

Turns out his name was Jimmy Carlin, a renowned pilot out of Corrosion Corner at Miami International. Jimmy and I would cross paths in the future a few times until he bought the farm in a ratty, near-dead "Connie" just after takeoff. "Name's Jimmy. Let me tend to my co-pilot," he said, as he rolled his eyes and with a confident sailor's swagger headed towards his charge. Jimmy was another guy who would have you laughing within a few minutes of meeting him.

I went to my room and laid down. I dropped off for about an hour and a half when I heard somebody rapping on the door. It was Doug. "Dave, you know that guy flying that old 46—Jimmy?" "Yeah." "He wants to see you." I had a great feeling. This might be my lucky day as I splashed cold water on my face and joined Doug. We met Jimmy in the restaurant and sat down. "You Dave." "Been called that all my life." "I got me a bitch of a problem." I think I know where this is going. "Say you are typed in a three?" "That's right." "I got to take my co-pilot with us but if I give him a couple bottles of hooch, he would be happy to ride jump. How about you fly the right seat with me?" I tried not to drool all over myself as I accepted. "Takeoff at 2:00 p.m. Let's go to weather and flight plan."

Shit, don't these guys ever sleep? I think to myself. Jimmy handed me some performance data sheets and said, "Here, bone up on these and we will flight plan at reduced power for 175 mph." As I breezed through the data sheets it became clear to me why the army was desperate for the C-46 to replace the C-47 and have Curtiss build over 3,000 aircraft by the end of the war. Empty weight at 30,000 pounds and max all up at 48,000 pounds gave her a load capacity of 18,000 pounds, more than twice the weight of a 3 (C-47). With a 1,400 gallon fuel capacity in three tanks per wing, she was long-legged for sure. That's 8,400 pounds of fuel so this hauler could carry 10,600 pounds useful load at 175 mph. she could float her cargo for 2,100 miles. Now for 1943 that's a war-winning combination. With extra fuel in the cabin, she could ferry across any ocean with a ferry range in excess of 3,200 miles.

She had a pair of 2800-51 radials and at 2,700 rpm and 52 inches of manifold pressure she was pushing 4,000 horses on takeoff. Being that she had a wingspan of 108 feet and length of 76.3 feet and weighed in at 48,000 pounds, she was twice the size of a Gooney (DC-3). She also held the distinction of being the largest twin-engine airplane in our inventory at that time. Shit, I say to myself, I can't wait to get to know this gorgeous flying machine.

The only cargo we had on board was one R2800-51 spare engine and even with full tanks we were still light, with plenty of range to make Santa Maria Island and even make it to the Portuguese coast in an emergency. By the time I had our weight and balance and flight plan ready for Jimmy, I had quite a stack of papers. I heard laughter coming from the flight service office and as I walked in Jimmy was leaning on one elbow and the three weather personnel were wiping their eyes and still laughing. I was already enjoying the change of personalities.

"What you got there, boy?" "I got our weight and balance, CG charts, manifest, and flight plan, sir." Jimmy, with acted-out surprise and big eyes, "*Sir?* Shit I love green co-pilots." He scrunched up his face and said, "Aw, he'll get to know me better by the time we get to Santa Maria. What in hell we going to do with all them papers? Ah, I know, toilet paper, right?" More laughter. "Well, I guess we need to file our flight plan anyway. What in hell for, Santa Maria's that way," pointing to the southeast. After a good joke session, Jimmy said, "Well, it's about time to tempt fate. Less go."

Strapped into the right seat of the C-46's roomy cockpit, Jimmy reverted to professional cockpit etiquette and called for the pre-start checklist. Our first officer was happy and strapped into the jump seat, caressing his booze. How in hell could he trade all this glory for that crap, I couldn't figure out. Checklist complete, I reached up and hit boost, primer, and starter toggles, pushing the starter toggle after shouting "Clear!." The starter motor impacted with a thud and the big Curtiss electric propeller jerked to life and started to turn. I counted off ten blades, "Contact No. 2," as Jimmy switched to "Both" on the No. 2 magneto switch.

Unlike the Wright engines, the P&Ws need not be flooded before contact and with my forefinger and middle finger pull both togs back to my thumb. Almost instantly, I heard a *cough* and *chug* and the prop began to gain rpm as the cockpit came to life with the vibrating, galloping symphony of an R2800 coming to life once again. Wisps of white exhaust smoke found their way into the cockpit and once again I breathe in deeply the starting exhaust odor only a radial engine can deliver to your senses.

Idle cut off on the mixture to let the big 2000 hp engine breathe, release starter and boost tog, stand by to tickle the primer and No. 2 begins to gallop steadily, rich on the mixture. Boost pumps to low and release all toggles. The engine is running at 800 rpm smoothly. Same procedure on No. 1, only I handled the boost pumps throttle and mixture controls as Jimmy handled the toggles and counted blades. With both 2800s running smoothly, we just sat for at least ten minutes to build up a little heat in both engines. I called ground "Ah Gander ground, Curtiss November 355 Whiskey on the ramp. IFR Santa Maria international." "Rogah 355 Whiskey Gander ground. Are you ready to copy?" "355 Whiskey is ready to copy." "Rogah Curtiss November 355 Whiskey you are cleared to the Santa Maria airport. Standard 5 degree meridian reports until 40 degrees west by 43 degrees north by consolan fix then direct Santa Maria. Climb to and maintain niner thousand after takeoff. Contact Gander departure on 128.5. Expect high frequency channel 610 for Gander Oceanic Centre squawk 1410." I read back, "Clearance correct contact Gander tower 118.1 when ready." Okay, I thought, we are legally cleared to fly across the Atlantic Ocean. That's cool.

"You buy the drinks at Santa Maria and you can have the takeoff," said Jimmy. "Done deal." "Any problems, I got it right back." "Gladly." "Okay, let's get taxi clearance." We were cleared to Runway 31 with a slight crosswind from the right. I found taxiing the big 46 not much different from the 3, only heavier on the feel and brakes a little more sensitive. I also noticed that the old bird had a stiffer gear leg than the 3. Where the 3 would softly canter as you taxied, the 46 was like a trot, probably making her squirrely on landings.

I taxied her to the runup pad and set the brakes for runup: props, check, feather pumps, check, mags, check, throttles back, hydraulic pressures, check, controls free and easy. "Let's close the cowls for takeoff but monitor the cylinder head temps and be prepared to go to trail if need be. V2 110 mph," the captain said. "You ready, lad?" "I'm ready," I said back. "Les make like a bird and get the flock outta here." "Takeoff flaps set, hydraulic pressures steady 1,500 pounds." "Ah Gander 355 Whiskey. We're ready." "Rogah 355 Whiskey. Taxi into position and hold runway 31." "Position and hold 355 Whiskey," I repeated. I brought Nos. 1 and 2 up to 1,600 rpm and the Commando began to move. I kicked in right rudder and a slight touch right brake retarding No. 2 at the same time and coming back in with a little power as the old workhorse pointed her distinctive greenhoused nose toward the numbers of 31 and let her taxi on her own to the numbers. Then I retarded No. 1 and slightly up on No. 2 with a touch of left brake and at the exact moment our butts were directly over the numbers and we were pointed straight down the runway, I braked the old buzzard to a squealing stop. "November 355 Whiskey after takeoff make a right turn on course. Cleared for takeoff." "Right turn on course. Here we go," Jimmy growled to the tower.

"Landing lights, on, transponder, on, fuel boost high." I felt my heart beating. As I initiated the throttles forward, I heard both Curtiss electric props hunting for the correct rpm as the two 2800s increased in power. I instantly had rudder control and found the now galloping C-46 a delight on the controls. The props were still hunting as I slowly came up to takeoff power. At first, I heard a *r-row-w r-row-w* and as I gained power, the pitch got closer and closer until at 52 inches and 2,700 rpm I could not hear the difference and the heavy roar of engines and props equalized to a steady deep howl. Her tail started up at about 70 mph and was level by 85.

At 110 mph Jimmy held up two fingers, V2, and with slight back pressure on the yoke the rumbling coming from the mainwheel tires went silent and we were no longer a ground lover but were in the air with the grace of the exquisitely designed Curtiss, wings giving the big ship the magic of weightlessness.

"Gear up METO power," I hollered at Jimmy as he performed his duties. "Gear is up and locked. Pressures up." "Climb power VSI is up steady, flaps up, climb checklist." "Let her drift up to 140 indicated for climb," Jimmy said as he read the climb checklist to me. As we climbed through 500 feet, I initiated a slight right turn and was impressed by the heavy but very smooth control pressures of the 46. "November 355 Whiskey contact departure 128.5 and have a good trip." "128.5 see ya and thanks."

I was very pleased with myself and totally in love with this great flying aircraft when Jimmy cut in and said, "Tuck it back in your pants. Not bad for a greenhorn." Great compliment from an old eagle as I broke into a big grin. As we approached the coast, we also broke into bright sunshine and for the first time I could see how rugged the ground features are in Newfoundland. Absolutely no place to go if you needed to. Nothing but broken rocks and deep canyons running all the way to the sea with not even a beach as the cold blue north Atlantic unleashed her giant rollers to dramatically explode against solid rock cliff walls. The sight sent a shudder through me. I thought about "The Lone Eagle," Charles Lindbergh, as he plodded along at 80 mph indicated in his Ryan Brougham high-wing aircraft with a Wright J-6-5 270 hp radial, the only engine he had. He did it in April but the end result of an engine failure, whether over land or sea, would probably be the same. He obviously had a strong and above-average will. His cockpit had open side windows and was drafty and cold but even though we didn't have the draft, our cockpit was probably colder than his due to the time of year. It was December 21, my birthday, and what a great present being co-pilot on a trans-Atlantic flight in a C-46. It don't get any better.

Our cockpit temperature was by the gauge 21 degrees below zero. Jimmy said, "Let's try our Janitrol heater and see if it works." As he hit the igniter switch there was a loud *pop!* and a two-foot flame roared out of the orifice. "Shit!" Jimmy shut down our only source of heat. "It's colder than a nun's buns in this cockpit," Jimmy complained. I agreed as we slipped through the frigid air over the blue North Atlantic Ocean. I looked down on the deep blue sea but it did not look friendly as did the deep blue sea of the South Pacific. Also, knowing that if we have to go down and ditch, if we survived the ditching but got wet we had a total of four minutes, and if we managed to get into an open life raft without getting wet, we probably had twenty minutes. And if we managed to get into a covered raft, our survival time would significantly increase by four or five hours. That would maybe be enough time to get rescued by a Coast Guard ship or aircraft, provided somebody heard our mayday call of distress.

Curtiss C-46 N355W gave us a thrilling adventure over the cold North Atlantic in December 1963. Photograph by Werner Fischdick.

I was thinking about all of this as the sunny day was transforming itself into the fading light just before dark. "Let's switch to the rear tanks and burn off some aft weight." "Okay. Fuel boost on high," I said. The fuel selectors being on my side, I asked, "Ready?" "Do it." I switched to our rear tanks and the engines ran steadily for a short time, then No. 2 began to backfire and was followed almost instantly by No. 1 backfiring. "Go back to the front tanks now!" Jimmy shouted. I switched back in record time. No. 2 backfired then quit. I checked the boost pumps and they read high. No. 1 backfired then settled down to a steady and normal healthy roar. "Keep No. 2 turning. Try everything!" Jimmy shouted. Idle cutoff, throttle full forward, throttle closed, auto rich, fuel boost low, fuel boost high, mixture moved slowly through its limits, mags, L, R, Both, off, back to on. Nothing.

"Feather the sumbitch. Call Oceanic and declare a pan." Doing my best to sound calm, "Gander Oceanic this is Curtiss November 355 Whiskey. Position 360 miles southeast estimate 47 degrees west 46 degrees north. Declaring pan, pan, pan. Repeat pan, pan, pan. Over." The voice had a definite urgent note, "Ah rogah 55 Whiskey. What's the nature of your problem?" "We have feathered No. 2 and are in a 180 degree turn to return to Gander." "Rogah 55 Whiskey. The Coast Guard has been notified and have dispatched a cutter and have an albatross standing by." "55 Whiskey. Roger." "We will need fuel information." "Roger. Stand by. We will get back to you."

It was half-dozen to one whether we went to St. John or Gander so we decided to go to Gander. What the hell was I thinking about, being over these seas on one engine? All of a sudden I was not so smug. "We got 285 gallons left in the center tank and about 65 in the front tanks." Jimmy said to me, "I am not so sure I want to cross feed in case we suck up whatever caused these engines to hiccup. When they fueled us at Gander they got through fueling both forwards and both centers and had to get a different truck to fill the rears. I got a feeling we got bad fuel in those tanks. Work out our fuel burn distance and speed." "I'm on it, Skipper." A few minutes later, "Looks like we are slowed to 90 mph across the ground and we got 356 miles to go. We got 90 gallons in the leading edge tank without cross feed and we still got 285 in the center. It looks like we are burning 96 gallons per hour and have 3:56 to go. Think we can trim out the extra weight in the right wing as we go?" "I don't know if we have to use all the trim. We will have to take a chance on going to cross feed."

I called Gander and gave them the information plus cargo and landing weight on arrival and fuel remaining. "Ah rogah. 5 Whiskey you are cleared present position direct Gander runway your choice." "5 Whiskey roger." "And 5 Whiskey, Coast Guard albatross is on the roll and expect intercept with you in about one and one-half hours." "Thanks Gander. That's a good boost to our morale. When we have the albatross over us I think we will try to cross feed and hope it's a clean transfer."

We decided to keep feeding off the center left tank for weight and balance purposes but in the last 20 minutes I was having to lift the left wing and that is not good for our indicated as it was causing just enough drag to slow us down even more. "We can't keep doing this, Jimmy. It's just gonna get worse the more we burn," I said. "Yup. Think we might have to make a critical decision and I think we need to make it now." In the meantime, the only indication that the first officer had any worries was that he seemed to be sipping a little more often.

"Give Gander a call and tell them what we are doing and a position, just in case." "Ah Gander this is 5 Whiskey. We are going to try cross feeding off the right tank. We are not sure if it will work or not. Our position is 306 miles southeast level at niner thousand." "Rogah 5 Whiskey. As soon as you know, call us." "Will do." "Fuel boost high, it's as good a day as any, go to cross feed center tank." Gee thanks, Jimmy, as I turn to cross feed. "Pressure is up fuel selector to off on the left." I turned the left selector but was ready in an instant to go back on. No. 1 does not even cough and keeps running normally. "Fuel boost off," said Jimmy, as I go to low and then off. A great relief settled in our cockpit. We now had over 600 gallons and as long as No. 1 keeps running we had Gander made. We continued trimming by burning from one side to the next.

"355 Whiskey. This is Gander, you still with us?" "Roger Gander. We are okay and running fine on No. 1. We would like to descend and see if we can get out of these strong headwinds." "Rogah 5 Whiskey. Any altitude. We were getting a little worried here." "Sorry about that. I owe you a beer." "That will be a great pleasure." As we droned on through the cold of the Arctic black night, I continued to work my E6B computer wheel, constantly updating myself on our progress, still feeling a bit insecure on one engine over an unsurvivable cold and unforgiving sea. If we even survived a night ditching in reported seven-foot seas, we probably would surrender to hypothermia before anybody could get to us. I monitored the engine gauges more than I normally would but all that would do would be to announce our demise and there would be nothing to do but fly a glide until impact. Jimmy had taken the aircraft shortly after going to cross feed and was flying the bird when the radio came to life.

"355 Whiskey. This is Coast Guard Rescue. Flash your landing lights." As we did, "5 Whiskey we have you in sight. What's your altitude?" "Ah roger Rescue. We are level at 3,000 feet." We turned off the cockpit lights. I got him one o'clock high as I saw his lights on steady. "What is your indicated 5 Whiskey?" "We are indicating 125 mph." "We will fall into a loose formation on your right side." Misery loves company but we were too aware of the fact that there was probably nothing he could do to help if we did lose No. 1.

Time seemed to be moving slowly as we crept towards Gander and I kept looking out our right wing at our guiding angel for reassurance. We were both very thankful to have a VFR clear night and not be complicating things by having to fly through clouds with the assurance of icing problems to boot. Right on schedule, I picked up the rotating beacon in the distance at Gander International Airport and reported it in sight. "Ah 355 Whiskey cleared to land any runway. Wind 300 degrees 10 gusting to 20. Do you need the trucks standing by?" I looked at Jimmy and he shakes his head "no". "Ah negative Gander, but we will probably need a tow in and we are straight in for Runway 31, 3 miles out." "Cleared to land and there is a ramp vehicle with tow bar standing by to assist." "5 Whiskey this is Rescue. Sure glad when it turns out like this. See ya." "Thanks for the help, Rescue." "Just part of the job."

Jimmy set up for a slight left crosswind, a little left wing low and a touch of right rudder as the approach lights slipped below us. "Full flaps." As I came down all the way on the flap handle and just as they reached full down limit, Jimmy flared and the left main tire painted itself on the asphalt as if Jimmy knows what he is doing, followed by the right main and we dropped the tail and slowed to a stop. "Help's coming, 5 Whiskey. Nice job."

Help came and soon we were towed onto the FBO's ramp. I noticed that Doug's Queenair was still on the ramp and Doug was on the ramp watching as I climbed down the ladder. Doug had the slight grin he was famous for just before assaulting you with a smart comment. As I ducked for cover, sure enough "Jesus, Dave, you could fuck up a two-car funeral. What in hell happened?" I told him the facts and invited my friend for a drink at the bar. "No, we were just getting ready to go when we got the news that you guys were in trouble so we delayed until you got here." "Where's the kaiser?" "He's in the airplane." "Just like him." "Yeah, well we're off. See you on the other side," Doug said with a chuckle.

Before Jimmy and I headed for the bar and then to our rooms for the first full night's rest in three days, I went out on the ramp to see Doug and Wilhelm off. Willy was back to being human again. After some jokes and laughter and well-wishing, I watched them taxi out and listened to the old queen's deep and hefty growl on takeoff and stood and listened and watched as Doug turned right on course for Santa Maria. As her noise and lights faded into the night, I hollered out, "Keep the greasy side down and good luck you guys!"

Jimmy said, "We need to go to D.O.T. paperwork. Might take a while." "Where is the first ocifer?" "Sent him to the bar with enough money to keep him occupied. You don't know nothing about him, right?" "Who?" Jimmy smiled and we headed for the tower. The paperwork didn't take very long since we never really declared an emergency and soon Jimmy and I were nursing a few drinks at the Gander Airport bar and post-flighting. The first officer was nowhere to be seen. Just as well, I thought.

The company that fueled us had the aircraft towed to a heated hangar. They assured us they would make it right and they really did. They drained and steam-cleaned the rear tanks and confirmed it was tainted fuel, flushed the system, and ran up both engines after topping off the fuel tanks at no charge to us. I got nothing but respect for that kind of honesty. Seems to me the lower 48 could do some soul-searching compared to our northern friends.

I went to bed that night and, instead of thinking, Whew, that was close, I thought out the whole flight and felt, Yeah, that was shit hot, I love this flying game. I went to sleep that night feeling very proud to have been a part of a very professional job well done under trying circumstances.

The next morning I headed for the chow hall and ran into the first officer, who was already seven sheets to the wind. Jesus, this guy doesn't give it a break. "Say, kid, would you mind riding co-pilot again. I could use a break." I thought, sure, you effin' lush. But instead, I snapped my fingers and, looking chagrined, I said, "Aw shit, oh alright. Hell, somebody's gotta do it. I guess I will." I think the first caught on as he grinned and said, "Thanks, kid." He will never know how happy he just made me.

After chow, Jimmy and I headed for the maintenance hangar and talked to the AI (aircraft inspector) in charge. He showed us the tainted gas and his sign-off in 46's logbook. Jimmy put on a humble act as he said, "Phew. For a minute there I thought you guys had it in for us!" After a few jokes and laughter, we headed for weather and got a briefing. We would hit a front with moisture about halfway to Santa Maria, with freezing levels at 4,000 feet. Jimmy decided for a 1:00 p.m. launch. As the departure time approached, I looked out the window of the chow hall and saw snow beginning to come down. We gathered up the first officer, who had rounded up a couple more bottles for the trip, and strapped in.

After a good runup and clearance, we lined up, Jimmy flying, and at max power gracefully left Earth once again. "Gear up, METO power," as I performed my co-pilot's duties. The gear wasn't even in the well when we entered the solid grey interior of the cloud deck. "Climb power, climb check," hollered Jimmy. This completed, we broke out in between layers and Jimmy leveled at 5,000 feet, which put us skimming through the tops of the lower cloud layer. I love this kind of flying since you get a real feeling of speed as you blast through wisps of clouds rising from the main cloud deck.

"Hey, Jimmy. This is the position where we had our problem." Jimmy quickly put both hands out, palms down, and said, "Shhh. Let that dog sleep." I called Gander Oceanic and gave them the 5-degree meridian report, level 5,000, heading 125 degrees. I looked out past the windscreen and noticed a dark area of what looked like solid clouds but I was not sure because daylight was fading fast and the cockpit temps were also on the decline, thanks to our errant Janitrol heater. The cockpit temperature was somewhere minus zero, the first officer was completely zonked out and obviously oblivious to the cold. He wasn't a bad guy. Mostly I felt sorry for him and sincerely wished he would make it through this alcohol front he was immersed in. I did hear years later that he did make it with the help of AA and I sincerely hope that the rumor was true.

Jimmy turned on all of our lights and brightened up the cockpit. Being as how we were the only ones out here, it really didn't make much difference. We couldn't see anything outside anyway. I figured our speed over the water at 195 mph with a 25-knot tailwind. Remember, this was before knots were the standard and our airspeed indicator was in mph. I had cut my teeth as a sailor and knowing we were going to contact the U.S. Coast Guard weather and navigation ship *India*, which was permanently stationed in this portion of the North Atlantic, I translated into knots just to maintain my sailor's etiquette.

We were over the water at 170 knots. We started to hear the ticking of ice crystals on our windscreen and Jimmy turned off the inside lights and turned on our ice lights, illuminating the leading edges of our wings. Through the dense grey of the clouds we were now flying in I could see the thousands of strings of snow and ice crystals streaming over our wings at blinding speed. Sure enough, our leading edges were bright white with building rime ice. Our only protection was inflatable rubber boots, and Jimmy said, "We will let it build a little before we inflate." We kept the ice lights on and a few minutes later *bhumph bhumph bhumph bhumph* as ice was being slung off our props and banging noisily against our hull. Ice plates. "Okay, let's cycle one time through," Jimmy said as he activated the air to the boots. I watched as the build-up of rime split and instantly disappeared over our wings as the boots retracted to the deflate position. Jimmy stopped the cycle to let the ice build up again before restarting the inflate cycle. If you don't do this procedure, the ice will concave and leave an air space between deflate and inflate and the boots become useless and then you are at the mercy of the elements. Soon the ice will build up and you will completely lose all lift on the wings, the end result of which is obvious.

Jimmy had handed the flying portion to me shortly after takeoff and as we droned on through the weather, I noticed that my right foot, which was on the rudder pedal, felt numb. I grabbed the flashlight and, sure enough, my whole foot was covered in snow that had come in through some tiny crack in the fuselage. I asked Jimmy to take over as I needed to go aft and use the relief tube by the cargo door. "I got it," as Jimmy wiggled the control wheel to show me he had the airplane. I also wanted to get circulation started again in my frozen foot. As I opened the crew door and entered the dark, cavernous cargo area, I thought, Man, it's even colder back here than the cockpit. I found the relief tube and relieved myself, not thinking about the 20 below temperature in the cargo area.

Then I noticed that I was frozen to the relief tube. What the hell was I supposed to do now? I took a deep breath and with a quick pull freed myself, albeit in instant pain. I hobbled back to the cockpit and Jimmy, noticing the grimace on my face, with no sympathy whatsoever grinned and said, "What's a matter? Get your pecker froze in the relief tube?" Ha ha ha. "You must have been there before, sumbitch," I retorted. "Naw, in these conditions we jes let her fly at the crack in the bottom of the door." Ha ha ha. "I'll think about that next time." Ol' Jimmy loves a good joke. I strapped back into the co-pilot's seat, filing the incident away in my memory banks.

In the next hour, things began to improve as we slowly broke out into clear skies. The temperature started to rise in the cockpit as we flew southeast towards the Azores, a group of islands off of Portugal. Jimmy told me to tune in the consolan station in Ireland and then the one in Spain and get a position. Well, consolan is now a thing of the past. As I recall, I got Ireland clear and then had to count the dots and dashes and it should have added up to 60 plus or minus 4 or 8 or something like that. Then for cross check I tuned in the one in Spain and counted the dots and dashes and added them up, then went to the chart and saw where the numbers cross on the chart and, bingo, that's where we were.

I added up everything and told Jimmy, "I got our position." "Well?" "I got us right over Kingston, Jamaica." "Goddamnit, Dave, you could fuck up a one-sided conversation with yourself. Here, you got it. Let me try." About ten minutes later I looked at Jimmy's perplexed face. "Well?" "Aw, shutup." "Bullshit, Jimmy, where are we?" "By my calculations we might oughta contact Chicago Center." After the laughter calmed down, Jimmy continued, "Screw this modern shit. We will do it the old-fashioned way. What's your ETA at the fix to call check ship India." "I figure we oughta be there in 25 minutes," I respond. "Good, give the ship a call in 25 minutes and tell them 43 degrees north 40 degrees west."

That's the way it was in those days. Pilots would revert to seat-of-the-pants navigation when all else failed and it usually worked out fine about 90 percent of the time. In time, I learned Jimmy never knew where he was most of the time but he had an uncanny knack of hitting his destination right on the money every time. Twenty-five minutes later, I make the call, "India, this is Curtiss November 355 Whiskey, meridian 40 degrees west 43 degrees north with you, level 5,000 inbound Santa Maria." "Howdy, 5 Whiskey been expecting you cleared direct whenever you figure out where it's at." "Ah we will find it. How you guys doing?" "Bored."

I sure didn't expect this sort of laid back conversation but these guys had probably been floating around in one spot for 30 days or more. Jimmy keyed his mike, "Hey, you guys, hear any good ones lately?" "Yeah. You hear about Little Red Riding Hood walking down the trail on her way to Grandma's house?" "No." "Well, the wolf jumps out of the forest and said, 'Hiya, little Red Riding Hood. I'm gonna eat you.' Little Red Riding Hood gives the wolf a bored look and said, 'Eat eat eat. Doesn't anybody fuck anymore?'" Jimmy countered with another and we all swapped jokes back and forth for the next hour.

Check ships were a real necessity back then and had a great record of rescues. One story I heard was when an air force transport—I believe it was a DC-6—got into a situation where they had to ditch next to a weather ship. The Coast Guard ship laid a patch of oily foam on the surface to knock down the waves and stationed two rescue launches on either side and when the aircraft stopped after the successful ditching, they sped up to the crew door. As the story goes, the crew stepped into the rescue boat without even getting wet, then they backed off and watched the "6" sink.

After about an hour of the most incredible radio conversation I have ever participated in before or since, we bid farewell to the great Coast Guard crew of weather ship *India*. We were at that point far enough south that the warm southern climate was beginning to overpower the arctic cold. As things began to warm up, the moisture inside the Commando began to condense and we started to get occasional drops of rain. I went back into the fuselage cargo bay and it was soaking wet—ceiling, floors, engine, all of it. It was almost like a light rain falling, once in a while kerplunking on my face as I inspected our engine to make sure her boomer straps were still tight and holding the big R-2800 firmly in her cradle.

Strapping back into the co-pilot's seat and resuming control, I wondered if there were any other aircraft in this part of the world when I heard through my earphones somebody key his mike *click*. I keyed mine *click*, then heard *click click*. I responded *click click*, then came *click click click* and I went *click click click*. Then nothing until *click*. "Smart ass." Jimmy was grinning and I said, "Well I guess we are not alone." I never did find out who it was but thought about the phrase "two ships passing in the night." As for the weather ships, they too are a thing of the past, being victims of satellite navigation and long-distance communication systems. They are admittedly amazing replacements but certainly have taken all the fun and camaraderie out of the picture.

Five-and-a-half hours after our departure from Gander, I saw lights on the horizon and called out, "Lights 11 o'clock low." Jimmy said, nonchalantly, "Yup. Oughta be Flores Island." I checked our chart and, sure enough, the island of Flores was right where it should be and right on time. The old eagle has done it again, we are dead center on course. "We oughta be abeam Faial in 45 minutes," I said. Jimmy told me to contact Santa Maria Oceanic and tell them we were picking up Flores ADF. I figured in about 55 minutes with another 220 miles to go to Santa Maria or 1:05 minutes flying time from Pico Island and called Santa Maria Oceanic and gave them the information. I added, "Santa Maria ADIZ at 11:51." "D-r-royer three five weesky contact Lages Air Force Base on 125.6." "Ah Lages approach three five Whiskey is with you, level at 5,000 you got a squawk for us?" "Roger five Whiskey, squawk 0330 and ident." "0330 and here is your ident." "Roger three five Whiskey radar contact 10 northeast of Flores. We got your penetration time of 11:51." "Ah roger three five Whiskey." "And three five Whiskey, we got two F-100s making a practice intercept on you. One is at 6 o'clock and will pass beneath you and another making a pursuit curve behind you and will pass your 3 o'clock in a steep left turn." "Ah we're looking three five Whiskey."

Just as I finished the response, I saw the lit afterburner of the first F-100 scorching by and out in front of us, pulling up and disappearing in the night sky. At that moment, I got nav lights at 3 o'clock, indicating an aircraft in a steep left turn going by us at blinding speed—F-100 number two. "Ah Flores you can tell those guys they can paint a C-46 under the cockpit rail," I said. "Roger." "Hey C-46 this is Cracker One flight of two. How about we come in close for a look see?" "Yeah, come on in, we will put a suit and tie on for the occasion." "Roger. Number one is coming up on your left and Number two is coming up on your right." "Ah roger, Cracker, we will kick up our indicated to 190 mph indicated." "That'll help." "Here we come, you oughta see us at 8 o'clock and 4 o'clock." "Gotcha. You always fly at that high of nose attitude." "Only when we are trying to fly at the mindless speed of a C-46. That sure is a nice-looking piece of history. Have a good trip and thanks." "Thank you guys. You're doing all the work. See ya."

That was shit hot. Man, I love this flying game, I thought as I re-contacted Santa Maria Oceanic. I tuned in Santa Maria VOR on 113.7 and was surprised to pick up such a strong signal this far out. "35 Whiskey, Oceanic calling. Keep a lookout while passing Faial and Pico, we have a light aircraft missing and overdue." "5 Whiskey rog. We are on the lookout. What was his last position?" "D-r-royer, he call passing Flores. It is a light single-engine Mooney coming from Gander." My heart sped up a bit and I looked at Jimmy. "That's the kid we were talking to before we left Gander, ain't it?" "Yeah, it sure was. Hope he is okay."

The kid, as Jimmy put it, is the son of a famous aircraft manufacturer and is also a special breed of international delivery pilots—a renowned and respected young pilot in his prime. One day he took off from Gander again in a Mooney single-engine aircraft, flying the northern route to England, stopping at Reykjavik, Iceland, to refuel. He never made it. As he was passing over the iceberg lane south of Cape Race, his engine quit. Thinking fast and staying focused, he glided to a big flat-topped iceberg and successfully affected a gear-up landing on top of the berg. He made several mayday emergency calls and rescue had his position fixed. Then the weather closed in and rescue could not launch a helicopter for three days. In the meantime, he waited for the weather to clear. No food or shelter, listening to the creaking and popping of the iceberg and fearing that the berg would crack apart or, worse yet, turn turtle as they do sooner or later. Finally, after three fearsome days, a helicopter made it to him. His first words upon entering the warmth of the chopper were, "Shit. The owner had got to be pissed. Get my ass to Kef quick so I can pick up another bird and get it delivered."

I think, This tough guy has got to be okay, and I focus harder hoping to see a flare. We flew on through much warmer night air with Pico slowly slipping by our left wing. I kept searching the black surface of the Atlantic in high hopes of seeing a flare that would indicate our comrade is okay. Nothing.

The lights of Santa Maria appeared dead ahead and I identified the airport rotating beacon. Jimmy said, "Well, I screwed up the landing in Gander and would love to just sit back and watch you fuck this one up." "Any bets?" I asked, confidently. "Yup. You screw it up, you buy the drinks. If you don't, I buy." "Deal."

On short final I got the ol' kiwi tamed. I got pegged 120 slowing to 110 over the fence, full flaps carrying just a touch of power as I began to flare. *Wham!* We hit way before I was ready. "Goddamnit!" as I came in with a touch of power. She settled *wham!* Back up again. "Stiff-legged sumbitch," as we hit and bounced again. This time the ol' buzzard was out of jokes and through flying. I felt her tail wheel slam and bounce a couple of times, getting the last laugh. Jimmy, grinning from ear to ear, "Well, at least you're current, lad. Ha ha ha." I still felt great as we shut down and the three of us unhitched and enjoyed the good feeling of standing up and walking aft to the cargo door. We also enjoyed a new sound: silence.

As we checked in to D.O.T. flight ops, my pleasure at the thought of what we had just done was short-lived as we were told that our fellow aviator's aircraft had been found embedded just below a ridge on Faial Island. Nobody will ever know what really happened but will be certain and clear that nobody has any guarantee, no matter how experienced or how really good you are.

That night at the bar, Jimmy and I drank brandy and black coffee to our friend gone west. I thought the Spirit has got to have a special place and great duties prepared for a brave guy like that. Jimmy and I joined our first officer and drank ourselves silly before turning in.

5

Chicago White Sox, DC-7B and Air Caicos DC-4M Northstar, 1964 to 1966

"Ah Jacksonville, American League 816 with you. 134.3 0414 on the squawk. Level one one thousand over Crestview at :57, Victor 198 Semmes at :18, Picayune next." "Roger 816 flight plan route." "816 roger." I turned the A-12 auto-pilot knob to intercept 263 degrees outbound Victor 198 over Crestview and the DC-7B responded by gently dipping her left wing as I set 263 degrees on the OBS (omni bearing selector). As the needle centered, I snapped the navi switch to "On" and 816 navigated on her own.

Chuck worked his E6B wheel and said, "We are slowed to 235 knots (272 mph)," and gave me a subtle smile as I pulled my ballpoint pen out and gave it a few clicks. Bill was right on the ball as he checked our cowl flap knobs and sat back in his seat, staring at the overhead, trying desperately to figure out what was behind the clicking he was hearing. Chuck held his hand up to his mouth and looked out his window to conceal his widening grin from Bill. I was looking sternly at our gauges as if not noticing Bill's concern.

"Ah 816 contact Houston Center on 127.0." "Roger 127.0 Houston, so long." "Houston Center American League 816 is with you 127.0. Level one one thousand squawk 0414." "Roger 816 clearance." I knew it was coming. "816 ready to copy." "You are cleared V552 Picayune V70 Baton Rouge flight plan route. Maintain one one thousand." Chuck read back and checked the charts. I looked out my windscreen and saw more definition to the clouds in the front we would be penetrating in a little while.

Well, that wasn't so bad. They just moved us a little north of the Moissant Terminal control area and that made good sense. "Chuck, looks like we will be going on the gauges here in about 20 or so minutes." "Looking at the radar that looks about right, Dave," Chuck replied. We were already passing over some scattered Qs that are associated with the front we are heading for, they are definitely pre-frontal. From the looks of the high anvils, this front was jammed with imbedded thunderstorms and may be rough. Our radar will not reach out that far but a quick call to flight service confirms our fears.

As we approached the front, our radar can contour the worst of them and between center and our own radar we should be able to vector around most of the bad stuff. I was not too worried about it. We wanted to make the passage through the front as smooth as possible as we had a $12 million baseball team on board called the Chicago White Sox, on their way to play the Los Angeles Angels. The Angels were owned by a great aviator and movie star by the name of Gene Autry, who by tradition had invited all flight crew members to his house in Thousand Oaks for dinner and a famous Gene Autry beer bust. We didn't want our team to get shook up. No matter how great a guy Gene is, we still wanted our team to win.

Holy crud, I thought, the goddamned French Foreign Legion has been marching through my mouth as I woke up feeling like hell. A good shower, tooth brushing, and a double Alka-Seltzer would go a long ways to cure my temporary illness. Man, we tied one on last night, I said to myself. After the preliminaries, I headed for the chow hall and was surprised to run into a pissed-off Jimmy. "Fuckin' windstorm last night busted up our rudder and trim tab, damnit." "I'll go out with you," I said and we both headed out to the ramp. The 46 still looked pretty as a picture sitting at her tie-down and didn't look damaged at all. As we got closer, I could see the rudder looked just a little cockeyed and I couldn't figure out the oblong square piece of metal jutting out at 90 degrees to the trailing edge of the Commando's rounded rudder. That's when I realized that it was the trim tab moving freely in the wind. "Shit, we ain't going nowhere," I said. "Don't look like it," Jimmy hissed.

Jimmy got hold of the Miami-based headquarters and they had the parts we would need. They would be shipped as quickly as possible. "Looks like we will be here at least a week. I could think of better places to be stuck," he said. I thought, Well, maybe so, but I have never been here before and I planned on exploring the whole island. I spent the rest of the day rounding up a car for the next morning and showed up at the saloon for another brandy and coffee. After a couple of drinks I asked Jimmy if he flew during the war. He began to tell me his story and it was good.

Jimmy went to Army Air Corps flight training and graduated a 2nd Lieutenant Officer and was told to pick his choice of duties he would like to have. He picked number one, fighters; number two, fighter attack; and number three, bombers. He was given transports so off to transport school for Lt. Carlin. He checked out in C-47s and was shipped out to North Africa somewhere around 1942. Jimmy flew C-47s into and out of some very hot areas and on one mission he got shot down. His skill in the 47 saved his life as he put his crippled C-47 down on the front lines of a hot zone. He and his co-pilot, with bullets flying all around them from both sides, ran for their lives towards the American lines, diving into a foxhole and hugging the ground. A few minutes later a battle-tough sergeant jumped in with them carrying two M-1 rifles and handed them each one. Jimmy said, "Hey, wait a minute. We are both officers and need to get back to our base." "The ol' sarge growled, "I don't give a shit if yer both generals, you are in the infantry now so get ta shootin' sumbitches."

Jimmy spent the next three weeks fighting for his life with nothing more than an M-1 30.06 as his weapon. When the fighting was over, Jimmy was sent back to his transport group and resumed his piloting duties. He flew the hump in C-46s and C-82s, a cargo version of the B-24. Jimmy told me that when the war ended and they were all getting discharged, he took a fresh co-pilot, a young guy, who had never had a woman before to a pleasure house and got him hooked up with one of the ladies. She asked the young guy what he wanted and, bewildered, he said, "I ain't never done this before." She became very concerned and said, "I know just the thing for you. I will take you around the world." The young co-pilot brightened right up and blurted out, "Hey, great, I already been over the hump in a C-82," at which everybody hit the deck howling with laughter, including his lady.

The next morning I ran into the first officer, who was surprisingly sober. He asked if he could go along for the island drive. I wondered if that was a good idea and then figured what the hell and said, "Sure." He tried to assure me that he would not drink but I put an end to that BS and told him to bring whatever he needed. "You're a good guy, Dave," he said, and added, "I got a real problem that way and I hope someday I can stop." "I hope so too, in the meantime, let's go see what the island of Santa Maria is all about," I answered as we loaded up and started to drive. Turns out that Bill, that was his name, was a pretty good guy after all, and never—even after beaucoup drinks—got the least bit obnoxious, and we both had a great time of it. I actually gained some respect for Bill and I won't use the term "first ocifer" anymore.

As Bill and I toured the island, I was amazed at how used up this volcanic island was. Unlike the fresh natural islands of the Pacific, this, like all islands in the Azores, had been farmed for many centuries. Through the years family acreage has been split and divided so many times that most plots are little more than an acre.

As we stood on the ridge overlooking what once was a caldera, we could see it was now only half a caldera as the whole eastern half had split off and slid into the sea, causing a tidal wave of unimaginable height that slammed into Europe and Africa, changing coastlines into what they are today. Further to the south in the Canary Islands this process is still at work and will happen again sometime in the future.

The remaining half of the caldera is a large half-moon-shaped verdant green steep cliff area leading to a very large and gently sloping plain rich with the small farm plots. As I looked at the thousand or so not-so-square plots in varying colors of green, it became clear to me why First World War German camouflage on the upper surfaces of the fighters' wings looked just like what I was seeing at that moment. This was confirmed later when I flew over these same type of farm fields all over Europe—so different from our huge farms and ranches here in the United States.

Bill and I returned to the hotel late in the afternoon and I watched him navigate with difficulty—with many course changes—the path to his room. I genuinely felt for him, but he seemed to have had a good time.

Jimmy met me and asked if I had any interest in seeing a movie. "Sure, let's go." We hiked into town and had no difficulty finding the one and only theatre in town. The theatre was nothing like we are used to but was instead just another whitewashed Portuguese structure like all the rest. Everybody was heading for the building that was showing the one-day-a-week event—a movie. No cokes, no popcorn, no candy, but we all had a bottle of either brandy or wine to enjoy as we struggled through the most boring black-and-white, German- and French-subtitled, Portuguese language movie I have ever seen in my life. Jimmy woke me up 30 minutes after the movie started and said, "There is no written description for this crap. Les go ta the bar." It was a great idea and we spent the rest of the evening playing penny poker with a couple of other ferrying types and made a good evening of it.

As we stood on the windy ramp there was a chill in the air and about a 1,700 foot overcast. I was looking at the tail damage to 355W and noticed that the fix would be simple, just a matter of replacing a few parts and a small patch on the trailing edge of the rudder and we would be back in business within a few hours of starting the work.

Suddenly, I heard the crash siren in the tower go off and the roar of fire trucks pulling out of their emergency hangars, and then watched them race to the side of the active runway. I walked around the tail of the Commando and looked out to the final approach course. Way in the distance I could see a small speck. I could identify the bird as having four engines, but it was far enough away that I could not quite recognize the type of heavy transport she was. I saw the landing lights come on and, as the aircraft got closer, I recognized her as an Air Force C-124—a giant in her day, with a double-deck fuselage and powered by four P&W R4360, four-rowed 36-cylinder 5,000 hp engines. She was a member of the workhorses of ours and many other countries' militaries. She carried tanks, trucks, general cargo, and soldiers anywhere in the world they were needed.

As the old condor got in closer, I could see that she had not one, but two, feathered engines: Nos. 3 and 4 were standing at attention. Wow, I thought, two out on one side. She must be a bear on the controls. Actually, I found out later that you can trim out all of the pressure with rudder trim, but at the time I thought the crew flying this giant must be supermen.

I watched as she gracefully crossed the threshold and flared for a perfect landing, leaving in her wake two small clouds of smoke where her mains first kissed the runway. As she taxied by, I filled my ears with the herd of horses galloping out of the exhaust system of the most powerful radial engine ever used on a production piston-driven aircraft, and it was a full symphony to my aviation-oriented mind.

She squealed and squalled to a stop and shut down Nos. 1 and 2. I watched as the enlisted crew scurried down a ladder, each hand carrying the equipment they needed to secure the 124. No drunks here. These guys were professional and seriously trained airmen in USAF uniforms and they were to be admired. A major who looked to be in his mid-forties was next out, and I put my hand out and said, "Nice job, Major." He said, "Thanks. I ride side-saddle." Hmmm, he is the engineer, I thought. Then a light colonel came up and I said the same to him. "Thanks, I'm a right-seater." Hmmm, a co-pilot. I figured the next guy out would probably sport a star at least, I thought as a lieutenant about my age came down the ladder. The colonel said, "He is the pilot in command." I concealed my surprise as I shook hands with him and congratulated him on a great job. "You a flyer?" "Yeah, I am the light colonel on that C-46." We all got a belly laugh and then I showed them over to flight ops so the crew could make arrangements for repairs from Lages.

"Well, I guess you guys are here for a while." "Yeah, we probably won't get outta here 'til about six tonight." "Six?" I couldn't believe my ears. Within the next hour, we got two more 124s on final and as they opened the front loading doors, out came two trucks, each with a 4360, a crane, tool trucks, and a large team of mechanics. I watched spellbound as they proceeded to change out both bad engines and had the old buzzard buttoned back up and ready to go by, not 6:00 p.m., but 4:30 p.m. Hey, man that's our Force at their best. I was impressed as I drank in the hefty rumbling roar as the morning-sick C-124 tore down the runway and into the air, totally healed and healthy again. Of course, the crew couldn't talk about their mission and I didn't ask. What a great feeling it must be to have that kind of support in contrast to our wait for our puny little parts that were lost in transit somewhere on the planet earth. Miami was desperately trying to find them as we waited at Lages.

Next morning after breakfast, I walked out to the grounded Commando and just as I arrived, I looked out the approach end of the runway. Lo and behold, there was a Queenair on short final. As the little bird turned off, I saw plainly written on her fuselage the ID letters "D-ILGD." Doug is flying that bird, I thought. As he taxied in and shut down, he put both hands up in a "What the hell?" gesture and I shrugged my shoulders. Doug greeted me and said, "I thought you guys would be in Germany by now. What's up?" I explained our situation and Doug told me, "I am going to top off and head for Lisbon in an hour. You comin'?" "Yeah, let me tell Jimmy what's up and see if he is comfortable finishing the trip with Bill." I saw Jimmy and he said, "No problem. Let me give you our number 'cause I got a feeling we will be looking for a co-pilot." Great, I thought. I liked the prospect of flying for a freighter outfit and felt excited about finishing the trip with Doug in D-ILGD.

I packed up and raced to the ramp just as the fueling crew finished. "We are severe clear all the way to Lisbon," Doug said as we strapped in and ran the pre-start checklist. As we made a left turn out over the sparkling blue North Atlantic Ocean, I could see the eastern point of Sao Miguel Island moving serenely by our left wingtip. Immersed in the loud roar of our IGSO 480 opposed engines and a warm sun shining on my lap, I felt completely at peace, enjoying the millions of shining diamonds dancing in a wide shaft on the blue sea below us.

We were in bright sunshine all the way and five hours later, we were on short final for Lisboa International. Across the threshold Doug greased her on in the expert manner I was to see him do many times in the future. We shut down, did our post-flight, and gave our fuel order for an early morning departure for Bremen, Germany.

"Let's head for the Ritz and get checked in. I will show you around town," Doug said. The Lisbon Ritz is just exactly what its name implies. On a scale of one to ten, the ritzy Ritz scores a 25, right down to the marble bathrooms and crew of Cordon Bleu chefs. Doug and I headed for town where he, being well-known in any town he has visited, took me to a little bar in a building that was probably 800 or 900 years old. As we walked through the door, a balding, aged man with his bartender's apron covering his hefty belly, threw out his arms and with a genuine smile called out, "Ahhh, Dooglas, ol' a fren!" The delight was mutual as Doug and "Pepe" exchanged hugs and then Doug introduced me. I also got the warm greeting.

"Shust a one a minute," Pepe said, holding his forefinger up high so everybody would notice. "Watch this," Doug said out of the corner of his mouth to me. Pepe disappeared into a back room and then returned with an old bottle wrapped in some sort of silver cover. "This is a brandy especial for Doogy," Pepe said. "Eet a eez one hunred an a feefty year a old an a especial for a my fren a Doogy." Pepe put three brandy snifters down and poured a good amount of this incredibly smooth 150-year-old brandy into our snifters. The friendly atmosphere got friendlier and soon I was part of the family. It was a great beginning in a super city called Lisbon.

Doug bid adieu 'til next time and we headed for the end of the block where an elevator would take us up to the next level of the same street. I thought it strange and asked Doug why they designed a street in such a manner. "They didn't. At one time, that street was at the same level as this street. One day there was a terrific earthquake and the street we are on now dropped. Since there were no cars in those days, they solved the problem by putting a lift here and they still use it to this day." We got on the lift and, shaking my head and smiling, I thought, Amazing animals, us humans.

As we got off the lift and immediately to the left was one of the world's greatest seafood restaurants called "La Quinta." All the tables were set so you could look down on iced shelves brimming with myriad fresh fish, crabs, and shellfish. All you had to do was point at whatever you wanted and voila, you were served a seafood dinner unmatched anywhere in the world. Unbeknownst to me at that moment, these iced fish trays would be the catalyst for one of those incredible funny stories that last a lifetime.

Doug and I were both enjoying our feast and carrying on a great conversation, he spinning yarns about his fighter pilot days flying for the RCAF in a "Voodoo" fighter. He told me about a night mission in which a young pilot was flying in a Harvard trainer (North American trainer T-6 Texan). "It was a black night and he was flying low over a straight stretch of railroad track when he spotted the single light of a train heading right at him. So he dropped down to about level with the train and turned on one of his landing lights, making sure it was dead center between the tracks. As we screamed over the top of the train, he noticed huge amounts of sparks pouring out from under each one of the cars as the engineers were frantically applying emergency braking, just knowing that they were about to die. I think the railroad authorities are still looking for that guy for that little piece of vandalism."

Of course, that story started the joke telling, which went non-stop for the next hour or so. I was in the middle of telling one of my jokes that needs to be told while using a pantomime skit with my hands. As I was getting to the punch line, there was a horrendous crash behind me. I turned and there, in the middle of the iced fish bin, was a woman on her back, both arms and legs flailing away and her body covered with ice and fish. We all raced to her aid and asked what happened.

As it turned out, she was so fascinated with my pantomime that as she watched me, she was backing up slowly but did not notice that she was approaching the railing above the fish display. She backed into the railing and over the top and landed in the fish and ice on her back. Of course, everything that happens is my fault and this was no exception.

Doug and I left La Quinta, trying to keep straight faces and we actually made it about a block before we looked at each other and let go our pent-up laughter, which took the better part of the day to quench.

Still breaking up in sporadic laughter, we hiked around the old fortress that dominates the skyline and looks down on the whole city of Lisbon. The fort has been built on top of ruins of other forts dating back several centuries and is named after King John VI in 1822. We had a great walking tour of Lisbon and returned to our luxurious rooms at about midnight.

"Dave, Dave, get up," I heard through the fog of sleep. It was Doug. "Come on, we're going to Germany." I looked at the clock. 3:00 a.m. "Geez, don't you guys ever sleep?" Doug replied through his laughter, "Get your lazy ass up. We gotta beat a front into Bremen." At least he gave me ten minutes for a shower and to brush my teeth. We jumped into a taxi cab, in which the driver proceeded to break Barney Oldfield's record in the dark of night. No headlights on our cab, nor on any of the other vehicles out at that time of morning. Jesus, talk about scary.

After pre-flight and filing our flight plan, I climbed over the ferry tanks and strapped into the right seat. "Gears coming up." The hefty roar of takeoff power subsided and was replaced by the even, smooth and pleasing sound of climb power as the Beech 65 steadied up on climb and 135 mph indicated airspeed. Doug was using the radio and doing the talking as he knew most of the controllers and can even fill in the blanks in their own language if need be. I was basically just handling charts and enjoying the ride. "Goddamnit. I left the damn flashlight in the aft cabin. How about crawling back there and retrieving it for me?" Doug asked. So I unbuckled and wormed my way back and find it easily as Doug left it: turned on. I handed it to Doug and thought, Hey, there is a nice flat spot on the top of the ferry tanks think I will crawl up on top and catch up on a few Zs. I got situated and fell right to sleep. Even asleep, my brain was registering the steady roar of our engines and through the fog I heard the roar on the left side stop, start, stop, and again. As Doug tells it, he never saw anybody uncouple off the top of the tanks dive through the narrow cockpit door and strap into a seat as fast as I did.

"C-46 got ya a little spooked?" Doug asked me with a big grin. "Sumbitch," I retorted. "Just wanted you to see the Pyrenees Mountains in the moonlight." But the real meaning was not lost on me: No sleeping while on watch. And Doug was right, I should have known better. The meaning was crystal clear as we passed over the Pyrenees in total darkness with no moon.

The morning began bright red and orange as we droned over a steady layer of clouds over France headed for Germany. I couldn't but think that not that many years ago these same skies were filled with B-17s, Spitfires, P-51s, Me 109s, FW-190s, and P-47s all mixed up in life and death dogfights over these same clouds and in the same beautiful sky I was looking at. I tried to imagine what that must have been like with all the white vapor trails and few trails that weren't white but black, trailing from a bright fire ball that pointed to the few who would not survive that morning. As I was thinking about this I drifted off to sleep. I was instantly back as our cockpit was assaulted by this shrieking roar. "Just thought I would see if you could open our little ice window in flight," Doug said, looking at me with his Bogart grin. Okay, okay, I won't fall asleep again. I was tired and with nothing to do, I found it very difficult to stay awake but managed to anyway.

As we approached our destination the clouds had risen and we were in the soup—a grey soup with no definition whatsoever, nothing for reference to indicate we were even moving. I knew we were splitting the grey molecules at a steady 178 mph. We were given a decent clearance by a controller with a strong German accent. We started to descend and set up for an ILS approach to our destination airport at Bremen, Germany. I watch Doug and his stone cold face as he intercepted the outer marker, went to climb pitch setting, dropped the gear and 15 degree flaps, and then proceeded to dead center the localizer bar and the glide slope bar and hold a totally perfect crosshair as we descend through the murk. Man, ol' Doug is a cool-headed pilot.

I focused on the windscreen, looking for definition that is always there as you approach break out from the clouds. 300 feet, 250 feet, man, this is low, I think, as I saw the first dark definition race by and at 200 feet we broke out and there, dead in front of us, were the approach lights racing us to the runway threshold. Doug dropped full flaps, went all the way forward with the prop pitch, and eased off on the power, flared, and squeaked the old bird dead on the numbers. "Nice, Doug," I said. "Beginner's luck," ol' Doug replies. "Turn r-r-right next taxivay und contact gr-round vun two vun point seven." "Point seven," Doug responded to the German controller.

As we stopped on the diagonal, Doug told the ground controller he needed to hold for a minute to dig out his taxi chart. It's a setup. "Vats ze matter you haf never been to B-r-r-remen before George Delta?" the controller replied arrogantly. Doug didn't hesitate, "Yeah, once in 1944 but we didn't stop." I could hear the laughter in the background as the arrogant controller keyed his mike, "Ach du liber velcome home Doogy." We both laughed as we were cleared to taxi as requested. I think I am going to like this place called Germany.

We landed at Bremen on December 31 at 10:00 a.m. Doug drove me into town and billeted me at the Intercontinental Hotel, not as nice as the Ritz but very comfortable. After a nice lunch with Doug and his wife, Uta, and their baby, Kira, I laid down. I figured on catching up on some needed Zs and passed right out. *Knock knock* I heard through the fog. *Knock knock.* Yup, it was really happening as I went from fog to reality and bleary-eyed looked at my watch. Wow. A whole 30 minutes, this must be some kind of record. I opened the door to Doug, Wilhelm, and Uta. "C'mon, Dave. We're goin' to Heintsez Kellar, we got you a date." "Are you shittin' me?" "C'mon ya ol' stick-in-the-mud. It's New Year's!" "Aw, all right." Oh, to be young again. I don't know how I did it but I had a great time of it anyway.

As midnight came and 1963 turned into 1964 and we were all of the correct attitude by that time. As the clock struck twelve o'clock Kaiser Willy produced a pistol and proceeded to empty the clip into the wall, thinking he was a regular riot. Everybody was so loaded nobody even flinched. After the smoke cleared, I said, "Kaisher Willy, yer a fuckin' idiot!" Everybody broke up and the party really commenced to light up. I wound up with some dish that must have been really impressed with me. We fell into bed at 5:00 in the morning and I zonked out until the next afternoon. She was gone and to this day, I have no idea who she was.

It was during this time in Germany that I met my future wife. She came to Sarasota, Florida, when I was flying for the Chicago White Sox. We were married in Sarasota and then got divorced the same way we got married—no lawyers, in front of a judge—fifteen years later and left our children completely out of it.

I spent five or six days in Bremen before I got hold of Jimmy. Jimmy told me to meet him at the *bahnhof*, or railroad station, in Frankfurt. I got off the train and there he was. We loaded up the car and headed for the cargo depot at the Frankfurt am main *flughafen*, or airport, where I saw 355 Whiskey being loaded for a trip. He introduced me to Captain Beck, who proceeded to give me an interview in the third degree. He was not impressed with my low time—only 460 hours at that point—and the fact that I did not have an ATR (airline transport rating). He was impressed with my DC-3 type rating and a good word from Jimmy. My lack of time and ATR had killed any chance at Flow Air, the ferry company that Doug worked for, and did the same here. "Sorry, Dave. Your low time won't fly with the insurance types. Can't do anything for you now but go build time and get your ATR and I would be glad to have you aboard."

I thanked the chief pilot for his time and assured him that I would do what he said and check in with him some time in the future. I was disappointed but not discouraged. After all, with only 460 hours I was typed in a DC-3 and flew a C-46 as co-pilot across the Atlantic. There was not much competition with other pilots my age and my level.

Chris Hartnebrig looked me up in Frankfurt. He was a Dutchman that I had gone to flight school with and who could speak eight languages fluently. He was also one of the heirs to the Bohls liquor fortune. Chris and I hung out in Frankfurt for a few days and then went back to Bremen. He had decided he wanted to be a delivery pilot and wanted to meet Doug. Chris made a hit, and in one month was given the job of ferrying two 180 hp twin Bonanzas to Bremen from the factory in Wichita.

I figured I had better get started building time and booked a red-eye Pan Am 707 flight to New York and then to Chicago for a meeting with William G. "Buck" Buckingham, who basically got me into aviation and had told me that the Artnell Company owner of the Chicago White Sox and big in the oil business was planning to purchase two Douglas DC-7Bs from Eastern Air Lines and start hauling American League teams around. Buck and I had become good friends and he opened the door for me. He hired me as a co-pilot on one of the company's Queenair 65s. Gee, co-pilot on a Queenair. I guess I should have been a little depressed but I wasn't. It was a front for me to gain some good experience for three months and then join as a member of our DC-7B crew and report for first officer training at Eastern on Miami International. Resisting the urge to jump up and click my heels together as I walked off, I thought, You lucky sumbitch and $960 a month. Not too bad in those days.

Gain experience, I did. No limit on flying time, and fly we did. Toledo, Akron, New York City, Detroit, Chadrin, Nebraska, Sarasota, Miami, St. Louis, and Dallas, not to mention all the puddle jumps inside Illinois and Wisconsin. In the three months I flew the Queenair, I picked up another 375 hours and an additional 70 hours as part-time co on a DC-3 and L-18 Lodestar owned by a big construction company in Chicago. Shit, I was never home in my rented apartment but, tiring as it was, I gained beaucoup experience and a little respect as a commercial pilot, plus an additional 445 hours in my log book for a total of 905 hours, one Atlantic crossing, and heavy time to boot by the time I reported for training on the DC-7B. During my flying duties on the Queenair, I flew a lot of left seat time, thanks to my friend Buck and when we didn't have passengers on board he let me take her out solo.

Wm. G. "Buck" Buckingham, Chief Pilot American League Air

Brand new co-pilot for Chicago White Sox

Ring, ring, the phone was ringing. I looked at the clock. 5:00 a.m. "Hello." "Dave, it's Buck. We got a paper run to Cadillac, Michigan. Bunch of files they need at United Seating. Takeoff 6:30, then you gotta wait all day and load the same files after work and bring them back. There are no passengers so you go solo, capito?" "Yeah, okay, Buck. I'm on my way." Jeez, sittin' around all day at the tiny airport at Cadillac sounds like a blast. This damn corporate flying sucks. It is so typical to fly one or two hours and sit around on the ground for six or eight, twiddling your thumbs.

United Seating was one of Artnell's companies and the name says it all: they make driver's seats for trucks. That also put them under the thumb of then alive and well Jimmy Hoffa's union. I have never strapped into a cockpit seat more comfortable than these union-controlled truck seats, all thought put into the design for comfort for the tender asses of the truck drivers. Maybe the old joke about the pilot sitting in a bar as some guy goes over and puts a dime in an IQ machine and pushes a few buttons and the card pops out and reads, "Congratulations. Your IQ is 98. What trucking outfit do you drive for?" The pilot says, "Well, if he can do that, let's just see how I fare." So he does the same thing and his card says, "Hey, dumbshit. You got an IQ of 42. What airline do you fly for?" Must be true. In any event, it was a United Seating executive we had flown to Detroit that asked me if I would like to come with him and meet the big cheese: Jimmy Hoffa himself.

I went with him and actually met Hoffa but the best part was that I also got to meet—and will never forget our one-and-a-half hour conversation—the "Brown Bomber," Joe Louis himself. He was an educated gentleman who could talk about any subject you wanted to talk about. You can say what you want about Hoffa, but when Joe got crossways with the IRS and wound up broke, it was Jimmy Hoffa who came to his aid. Joe Louis was probably the only real gentleman to hold the heavyweight title for as long as he did.

Mags, check. Prop, check. Controls, free and easy. I advanced the throttles and Queenair N846Q's cockpit resounds with the healthy, hefty roar of her IGSO 480 engines bellowing at 44 inches of manifold pressure. Gear up. The cockpit roar subsided a bit as I came back to climb power and headed northeast for Cadillac. I got a hefty tailwind of 30 knots as I passed over the shoreline of Lake Michigan on a course that would just about take me up the length of this long, narrow Great Lake. It was one of those rare, super-clear days with 150-mile visibility—a treat in this part of the country.

It was late September and chilly. The lake below me looked more like the ocean, with long, evenly separated rollers, the tops of each one sparkling like diamonds in the morning sunshine to give Lake Michigan the appearance of blue surface with long, straight lines of sparkling diamonds laid down by some supreme artist. Hey, Spirit, are you around here somewhere? I asked as I enjoyed to the fullest my privileged perch 7,000 feet above this masterpiece.

Later that evening, on the flight home, I thought the Great Spirit must have been riding co-pilot when I needed all the help I could get. Full flaps, ease off the power, and I managed to squeak the landing on the numbers 25, then taxi in and shut down. As Buck said, "You gotta wait all day," and that's what I did. To make matters worse, they didn't quit work until 6 o'clock and we loaded ol' 846 up and I put the gear in the well at 7:10 p.m. I like flying at night so what the hell. We were under a thin overcast with a full moon shining through the overcast and reflecting on the surface of the lake, again causing the magic of shimmering diamonds but this time produced by bright moonlight. The whole surface of the lake was covered by massive areas of dancing diamonds interspersed with black voids. I sat spellbound by the scene as we sped smoothly through the night air for Palwaukee Airport, north of Chicago.

I looked down to check a chart and when I looked up, I gasped aloud as I looked into the night sky. But it wasn't there. Instead, I was looking at black and diamonds where the sky should have been. I was instantly disoriented and dizzy as I shouted out loud, "Shit, we are upside down!" My first impulse was to roll the Queenair back over and recover but before I could act, my co-pilot forced me to bury my head in the cockpit instrument panel and focus on my gauges. Thanks, Spirit. All gauges were reading normal, no papers or pencils were flying off the right seat. We were straight and level. So, what the hell? I looked back up and there it still was. I watched and snapped on the auto-pilot for backup while I watched, fascinated at this incredible optical illusion that damned near ended my flying career. The scene faded out and then reappeared and faded and came back again. I got it. The moon was shining through the thin clouds and reflecting off the surface of the lake. As we flew under the clouds there were thicker spots in the clouds that were just the right thickness to act like mirrors and cause this phenomenon. It was probably a very isolated situation as within several minutes it ceased and I have never seen it again.

The next day I told Buck about it but I didn't think it really registered so I just shut up about it. About two weeks after our DC-7B training started, Buck came up to me, obviously very excited, holding a newspaper and telling me, "Jesus, Dave, Eastern just dropped a 7B in the ocean, just offshore of New York last night. Here, read this."

As I read, I got goose bumps. It seems a DC-7B was in a right turn over the ocean under a thin overcast when suddenly the aircraft rolled over and plunged into the sea. Another flight in the same area reported a strange phenomenon to the FAA that it appeared that the ocean surface was reflecting off the bottom of the clouds and that the flight crew became disoriented for a few seconds until they could confirm by their instruments that they were flying straight and level. The FAA stated that there might be a connection with this phenomenon and the unfortunate loss of the other aircraft. That night I looked up and, sure enough, the moon was full.

We flew the old Queenair day and night and provided speedy service to out-of-the-way places not served by airline service and usually had our corporate execs home in time for dinner. I got along pretty well with most of the execs. They were generally a good group of people, with the exception of a few, but for those types on board we usually found some rough air or a nice thunderstorm to fly through and that would usually humble the big mouths, that is until they were safe on the ground.

On one solo night flight I was solid IFR and as we were approaching the shoreline of Lake Michigan, center handed me off to Chicago approach 128.45. "Ah Chicago approach, Queenair 846Q is with you, level 6,000 squawking 1254." "Queenair 46Q approach, clearance." "Ready to copy." "Ah roger 46Q, descend to and maintain 4,000 feet direct to White Fish intersection and hold non-standard right turns, expect approach clearance at 19.45." I read back. Shit, I didn't expect that. I set up White Fish on the VORs and thought to myself, Now all I gotta do is figure out how to get into the holding pattern. My weakest point on the gauges up until then were holding patterns and my inexperience was about to catch up with me. Talk about getting humbled.

Let me see, parallel entry, teardrop, or direct. Shit, I can't figure it out. I can always request radar vectors into the hold and let everybody know that there is a real greenhorn amongst them. Better than a violation on my record. Just as I was about to press the mike button and make the request, the old Spirit jumped in and saved my ass as I broke out of the clouds and into a beautiful clear night sky. The whole shoreline of sparkling lights lay before me and way in the distance I could see the rotating beacon on the field at Palwaukee Airport. I didn't hesitate and, grinning, called approach, making sure to put on my best "Smiling Jack" professional demeanor. "Ah approach 46Q, I got the field in sight. Cancelling IFR." "Squawk 1200. See ya 46Q." Did I hear "lucky this time, youngun" in that controller's voice or just my own guilt feelings?

I made a normal VFR approach to Runway 6 and lined up on final, gear down, flaps down, off on the power, and flare way too high I drop the old buzzard in from 20 feet and make an awful landing. Okay, okay, Spirit, just keeping me straight, eh, I thought to myself.

I spent the first two days at Miami International hiking around Corrosion Corner, the most fascinating aircraft boneyard in the world. Every type of transport imaginable was to be seen rotting away in this yard. There was even a Boeing Stratoliner sitting so proud and beautiful, a modern four-engine pressurized 250 mph masterpiece in her heyday, way back in the 1930s. DC-3, 4, 6, 7, Connies, C-46s, C-80s, Corsairs, Northrop three-engine very rare transports, and even a stainless steel twin-engine transport built by North American and the only one of its kind anywhere. Just south of this spot were the maintenance facilities for all the Central American and South American cargo outfits, all hauling anything and everything to anywhere. The boneyard had many C-46 Commandos, all with the names in Spanish emblazoned on the fuselage and all with just about every Central and South American country's identification letters on their tails. Almost all had melted aluminum skin underneath and behind No. 1 or No. 2 engines. Not exactly an A+ for the maintenance department, to say the least.

One day as I was watching a "Ranza" C-46, not long into the takeoff roll I saw ribbons of white smoke peeling away from the left main landing gear wheel as the pilots heavily braked to a stop. One of the pilots scurried down the portable ladder and ran to the wheel, now on fire, with a fire bottle and a sledgehammer. He quickly put it out with the CO2 bottle. I figured the fire trucks were on the way but I heard no sirens. I stood in amazement as the pilot began beating the wheel with his sledgehammer, throwing the fire extinguisher off to the side of the runway. He tore back to the ladder, scurried up, slammed the big cargo door closed and completed their takeoff. My mouth was open in amazement as they disappeared on a southerly heading until out of sight. Good ol' Corrosion Corner. I still love that part of Miami International.

On another occasion, when a completely unmarked C-46 Commando taxied into position for takeoff, suddenly the peace was shattered by the wail of many sirens and out of nowhere 20 or 25 police cars surrounded the 46 with guns drawn. They entered the Commando and reappeared with both pilots cuffed and roared off to some jail somewhere, leaving the C-46 on the runway looking very forlorn. Pretty soon, a tug hooked on to her and with police escort slowly towed her back to where she came from. I found out later the old "Pterodactyl" was loaded to the gills with machine guns and ammo headed for some revolution in progress in any one of our neighbors to the south.

Standing around and observing Corrosion Corner was like watching a Hollywood adventure movie that continued on day and night. Little did I know then that in a few years I would be directly involved with the Corner, only it was with a very legal and upstanding company called Air Caicos 510, flying the wonder DC-4 of them all. The DC-4M Northstar was equipped with four Merlin Rolls Royce P-51 engines. They are not in actuality the same engine that was in the 51, being a light bank Merlin Rolls Royce that would produce 1,610 hp at 68 inches manifold pressure on takeoff. The difference was that the Merlins we used on the Northstar were the heavy bank version of the same engine. At 71.5 inches they would produce 1,740 hp for a total of 6,960 hp on takeoff. Most P-51 owners eventually converted to the heavy bank for obvious reasons.

The whole crew reported to the Eastern Airline Ground School facility to begin our two-week intensive ground school on the Douglas DC-7B. The manual itself weighed in at 22 pounds and was probably 400 pages of size, weights, hydraulics, electrical, controls, fuel, fire protection, performance charts, weight and balance, CG charts, emergency procedures, power settings, and much more. At first glance, it seemed impossible to learn all of this in only two weeks but we had probably the best ground school instructor in the business, Ed Russell. He was an old hand on the DC-7B and a senior captain with Eastern.

We attended ground school classes for six hours every day and at the end of our sessions I was actually dreaming about systems pertaining to the DC-7B. A large section of the manual was on the Wright R3350—a massive 3,350 cubic inch radial turbo compound engine producing 3,250 hp at maximum takeoff. That gave the old eagle a total of 13,000 ponies on takeoff. The Ham Standard four-bladed propellers were a masterpiece of precision engineering and six hours were spent just studying the feathering, reverse, and cruise gearing that made this huge fan work. We had to draw by memory the impossibly complicated electrical schematics for the entire aircraft, and once you did it, it made perfect sense.

The emergency procedures were long and complicated, nothing wasted and every one of the numerous procedures may mean the difference between life and death in an emergency situation. This was definitely the major leagues, and I loved it.

Ed Russell, ace DC-7B flight instructor

Buck Buckingham and L. J. Edwards

Yours truly standing under the nose of our training bird

After class, I would wander around and check out the huge warehouse and hangars that belonged to Eastern. There were many of these facilities on Eastern's area of operations. Each huge building had to be somewhere in the vicinity of tens of thousands of square feet and was stocked full of engines, props, tooling, jet engines, and spare parts in unimaginable quantities just to keep this major airline operating. I would never have believed that in the next two generations Eddie Rickenbacher's great airline would be in ruins and totally bankrupt. Such a historical company with such a heartrending and sad ending.

We passed our ground school and advanced to the simulator portion of our training for another two intensive weeks. As you walk into the simulator you literally walk into the operational cockpit of a DC-7B. The simulator was fixed and, unlike the modern $35 Million virtual sims the airlines use today, this old Neanderthal did not move but you could simulate every possible scenario known in those days. The control pressures were identical to the actual DC-7B and during our training we built fires, engine outs, every conceivable situation was thrown at us and we became good on the gauges. I was awakened at 2:00 a.m. and told to head for the sim room, where I spent two bleary hours having engine fires, two engine go-arounds, gear problems, and dealing with just about everything else imaginable. When we were through, Dick Silvas, the sim instructor, said, "Well, it is 5 a.m. See you at 7 and we will finish this session." It seems everybody does this scenario, and for good reason. There have been quite a few times in my flying that I was tired and didn't really want to go but had to, so why not make it part of our training. One thing was for sure: those American League teams would be flown through the sky by highly trained professional flight crews. After two weeks and 46 hours in the simulator, we were ready for the last phase—actual flight in the aircraft called the DC-7B.

The actual simulator

Our DC-7 before paint job

My first takeoff in the seven was pretty much as I thought it would be: lots of power, lots of speed, and very heavy on the controls. My first landing was not as I thought it would be: the term "crash and go" came into perfect focus for me as I slammed the old brute onto 9L at Miami. I heard later that the Earthquake Center in California registered a minor earthquake epicentered just west of Miami, in the location of Miami International at the moment I made that God-awful landing. As time went on, between instruction and learned finesse, I began to make fair, then good, and once in a while I literally painted this beautiful flying machine onto the numbers. One secret was on short final to trim nose up so I was pushing fairly hard on the yoke and then as you hit the flare point, just release the forward pressure and help her set up just a little bit and the ol' buzzard would squeak almost every time.

We did lots of engine out approaches, V1 cuts, two engine approaches, and go-arounds, all under the hood and blind flying by the gauges. In those days, it was a regulation that you must make a gear up, flaps up, or clean full stall. I couldn't imagine doing that with this heavy aircraft but here I sat at 10,000 feet, using all my strength to wrestle the yoke back into my belly at 135 knots. I could feel the buffet transmitted to my hands through the yoke. As the speed decreased the buffet increased and as the airspeed needle ticked 128 knots, she broke. Big airplane, big moment, big stall, and did she drop. I must say that the old eagle was totally controllable and after a few thousand feet, we were flying again.

You would wonder with all that effort and warning buffet how the hell does a professional crew wind up stalling and crashing, usually right after takeoff? Simple. At 128,000 pounds, the clean stall speed is 128 knots indicated, but with 10 degree flaps, the stall comes at a much lower indicated, about 105 knots. V2 comes at 124 knots. Captain gives the first "Gear up." The first officer grabs the flap handle by accident and pulls up the flaps instead and all of a sudden you are short 4 knots of being able to stay in the air. To correct the problem, the gear lever handle sits in a vertical position while the flap lever handle sits in a horizontal position, so you can supposedly feel the difference. But it still happens. The answer? Simply *look* at whatever you are about to activate before doing so. Thanks, Buck, you taught me that one. We practiced day and night approaches, touch and goes, instrument procedures—almost always with one engine in simulated shutdown and feathered. I swear I have more three-engine DC-7 time than most Ford tri-motor pilots had in their whole career.

We had one member of the flight crew that just could not grasp the concepts of flying heavy four-engine aircraft. He had flown light aircraft all of his life, and was just plain not ready for the complexities involved in heavy transport flying. In any event, we were all ready for our rides with FAA heavy transport inspectors. Our problem flyer was not, so the decision was made to hold off on my type ride to give him more time. I was righteously steamed and made it known to the chief pilot, Buck. No matter what I argued, even "Do the American League teams really deserve a non-type rated member of the flight crew?" To no avail and as it turned out, our problem pilot, after using up all of my time, was dismissed after all. I was signed off as a non-typed DC-6 and DC-7 co-pilot just to make it legal. I was promised a type rating at a later date but, true to the nature of humanity, it never happened. To this day, I have no type in two aircraft I was trained in and should hold a type rating in. But I foxed 'em.

My lifelong and best friend P. C. "Chuck" Meister, a captain for American League, always gave me left seat time, as did Tex Cobble. No so with Dusty Burke. He held on to his left seat throne as if it were made of gold. It was alright, though, because I loved my own throne, the right seat, just as much as the left.

The time came when all type rides were complete and we all as crewmembers flight planned to Fort Worth, Meacham, then to LAX for refit of the passenger cabin to all first-class seating and repaint from "Eastern" to "Chicago White Sox" paint scheme.

Just out of the paint shop

American League 816D, Chicago White Sox personal aircraft

Understandably, I, along with the other first officers, were consigned to the passenger cabin—as passengers—for the trip to the west coast, while our captains increased their skills, flying 816D to LAX. My turn as co-pilot came soon enough, and after our refit, I was assigned permanent co-pilot on 816D. Occasionally I flew 813D, a DC-7B that at one time had a very hard landing and flew 3 degrees cocked to the right in straight and level flight. But she was 9 knots faster than any other DC-7, go figure.

Our first flight out of LAX was to Denver, Colorado, United simulator school for crew coordination sim time. We had another captain on this flight and I will just call

Brand new co-pilot in a brand new uniform

him LJE. There was conflict with him and the rest of the crew from the start. It was not long before we realized our new captain must have had a little "Bligh" blood in him as his arrogant and controlling nature soon became apparent. We were directed to be in Denver that evening so I was surprised to see that my flight plan had been changed for a stop in Midland, Texas. "What the hell, LJE?" In his heavy Texas accent followed as usual by his nasal snickering, he said, "They got good ribs at the Red Apple BBQ joint in Midland. Thought we would stop fer lunch. *Schnuck schnuck schnuck*." "But Cap, the weather is calling for freezing rain and low ceilings at Midland and CAVU at Denver, not to mention the extra 1,200 gallons of fuel it will add to our flight if we make that dog leg, sir." "Ahm, the captain and you will do as I say. *Schnuck schnuck*." "Okay, Cappy. Guess the engineer and I will get to pre-flighting." Engineer Bill Stevens asked, "What's up?" "Guess we are having ribs for lunch in Midland, Texas," I answered. "Shit, I don't even like ribs," retorted Bill, obviously displeased with the captain's decision.

To fly into severe weather conditions when we did not have to. Takeoff and flight were normal until about 30 minutes out of Midland. In the clouds and picking up ice that we instantly controlled with our heated wings, we were "cleared for the approach ILS runway 7. Caution, runway 7 is reporting ice on the entire surface. Use extreme caution." I looked at LJE and said, "Are you sure? We can head for Denver now." LJE looked at me with his command look. "Goddamnit, Captain, that runway is only 5,000 feet long, short for us on a good day. This is nuts." LJE looked at me and snickered, "In range checklist." I looked at Bill and he looked down and shook his head. I think, Okay, you sumbitch. We better be good. We shot the approach and at exactly 200 feet, I saw the threshold lights and called, "Runway in sight. Break out."

We touched down on the numbers, I grabbed the controls and went full forward as LJE called for the reverse gate bar. Bill pulled the gate bar all the way back, which allows you to handle all throttles in reverse movement. Bill said, "No. 1 brown light, No. 3 brown light, No. 2 brown light." The brown lights—actually amber—indicate propellers are in reverse pitch and ready to power up in reverse but No. 4 hesitated for maybe two seconds and, in that short time, the 7 cocks about 30 degrees to the runway and in that time we as flight crew were transformed into passengers, with the aircraft sliding uncontrollably on the ice of Runway 7. The Spirit was riding with us and the old buzzard slid straight down the runway and came to a stop about 400 feet from the end. We all let our bated breath out at that time and I looked at ol' Bligh. "You ready for the post landing checklist?" I felt like adding a well-deserved "You stupid sumbitch" but thought better of it.

Well, we ate our ribs and when we returned our beautiful DC-7 was completely iced and we were stuck for the night. LJE wanted us to stay and help with de-icing while he got a hotel room. I can't remember which one of us told Skipper to "kiss my ass," maybe it was both of us. In any event, we arrived in Denver at 9:00 a.m. the next day, tired, but had to report to the sim room in 30 minutes for an all-day session. Thanks, Captain Bligh.

Our crew coordination training was very intensive with very complicated procedures and an instructor who was an expert at pitting the crew against each other. An example was Chuck in the left seat, me right, and shooting an ILS approach with No. 3 and No. 4 caged. Remember Santa Maria and the C-124? I had the ol' sim trimmed out perfect and was shooting a perfect approach when I noticed I kept having to increase forward pressure on the yoke and, unbeknownst to me, Chuck was moving the trim wheel with his knee, trying to mess up my approach on orders from the instructor. I focused on flying the simulator and made a perfect approach. When the instructor showed me the trace chart you could not tell what was the printed schematic pre-drawn on the chart and the just drawn trace of my two-engine approach.

We passed our last obstacle with flying colors and left knowing in our own minds that we were a very highly trained professional flight crew declared competent to fly twelve million dollar ball teams from city to city anywhere in the world if need be. As for

Captain Bligh in the spring and our first trip of the season, he landed in Indianapolis and, thinking himself some kind of privileged and untouchable sky god because he was flying a major league ball team around and against directions from the tower, parked N813D on an active taxiway that shut down one of the runways. His last transmission to the tower was, "This is where we are going to stay. You'll just have to figure out how to get around us." Then he went to his hotel where he was met by the police and, disregarding the reputation of the ball team he was flying, began to argue with the police.

Not until he was threatened with jail did he gather up his crew and go out to the field and move 813D to its designated parking spot. The FAA was not so lenient and filed twelve violations on him and the company. Next day he was fired, *schnuck schnuck schnuck*. To a man, we were all relieved that this nut was gone. Chuck and I were having a beer together the night he got canned. Chuck chuckled, and I looked at him questioningly. He said, "You know, old LJ is the only bird I have ever met that can find a great nest and turn right around and shit in it." We both got a good laugh out of that statement.

We flew several American League baseball teams to and from the cities they were playing in and had many famous names on our passenger rosters. Mostly, the players kept to themselves but there were quite a few that were genuinely friendly and happy to see us and share in a good joke or two. Then there were the prima donnas who would have nothing to do with anybody and they mostly had big names in their profession. One prima donna, an announcer who made it big but boy, was he stuck on himself, was never a pleasure to be around.

On the other hand, the announcer for the Chicago White Sox, the one and only Jack Brickhouse, was one of the nicest and funniest gentleman I think I have ever met. He was always ready with a funny story and sharing experiences with anybody. Bill Veeck was still active and I got to know him fairly well. He also was a stand-up gentleman who was always friendly and engaging in any subject. I have two stories about Bill that will last me my life. Bill got his leg shot off as a young marine, I believe at Tarawa. He mastered the use of a wooden leg and if you didn't know he had a prosthesis, you would never guess when you saw him walking. He was a heavy smoker and when he would show up at a cocktail party, he would purposefully sit where there were no ashtrays and light up. Pretty soon, an alert host or hostess would walk over and offer Bill the ashtray. Bill would wave off the ashtray and reach down and pull up his pant leg and there, to the surprise of the host, would be a personalized ashtray built into his wooden leg. It always broke the ice and got the party going.

The funniest story about Bill—I was sitting in the air-conditioned press box at the time—was about the game where he made an announcement on the scoreboard PA. "Ladies and gentlemen, husbands and wives, I want to announce that today, here at Cominsky Park, is a special day. On the strikes all husbands will kiss their wives and all wives will kiss their husbands on the balls." It took just a couple seconds for it to sink in, but when it did, 40,000 fans went berserk, not to mention the bedlam in the press box.

Bill claimed it was an honest mistake and a slip of the tongue, but knowing Bill Veeck, I don't think so.

We watched many games, always in air-conditioned comfort, eating free food and drinking free beer. We met great people while watching our passengers play professional baseball. It all sounds very romantic and exciting—it was anything but. A typical trip was, say, Chicago to Detroit. We would flight plan, pre-flight, cater, do the paperwork, and load the team for a Friday 5:00 p.m. departure and land 42 minutes later in Detroit. We could go to the games free if we wanted, and did when we were not touring or working on the 7.

The DC-7—being a natural trouble-producing flying machine, as all aircraft are—kept us sweating and cursing constantly. We all felt an obligation to keep her in A+ condition for the safety of our both beloved and hated passengers. We had a lot of problems with the Wright engines, mostly PRT (power recovery turbines). They would microscopically crack and it would kick off our fire-warning bell and under part 121, it was a mandatory shutdown. Almost all shutdowns occurred when we were deadheading between games and had no passengers on board. All but two were these damn cracks and in one season we had thirteen shutdowns—one on the ground and twelve in the air.

We only had one in the air when the team was on board, and it was a doozy in a left turn out of Lambert St. Louis at 1:00 a.m. and pitch black. We had just leveled the old buzzard, heading for Chicago, when *ka boomph!* the sky brightened up and the fire-warning bell shattered the peace. All three of us hollered at once, "Number three!" Chuck gave the command, "Feather number three. Combat the fire." As we went to idle cutoff on number three mixture, the fire went out but we went ahead and pulled the No. 3 Zone 2 and Zone 3 isolation levers just in case. Checklist read No. 3 secured, we were cleared back to Lambert, any runway and fire trucks standing by.

"Dave, go back and calm the team." I put on my cap and, in my best nonchalant act, entered the first cabin. I noticed one of our star pitchers, hands firmly grasping his armrests, staring straight ahead with a wide-eyed stare that showed fear. I addressed him by name and asked, "Are you alright?" He then looked at me and I could see that he was slightly shaking. "When are we going to crash?" he asked me. I sat down next to him and, as calmly as possible, said, "You don't think I would be sitting here talking to you if we really had a serious problem, do you?" He said, "But we are on fire!"

I then realized that he had not looked out the window since the fire had first broken out. I explained to him that a part broke loose from the engine that he was sitting near and raw gas was pouring on the hot exhaust pipe, which caused the fire. I explained further that we had shut off the engine, which put out the fire, and were returning for a normal landing back to Lambert on our remaining three engines. It seemed to calm him down some and I excused myself to check on the rest of the team. All of the other players were shook up but seemed to be handling it fairly well. I got on the P.A. and gave the standard calming speech, "No problem. This DC-7 flies just as well on three as it does on four. We are returning to Lambert for a normal landing." Then, thinking that a little humor was in order, I added, "All this means is that the best team in the league—you guys—simply have to win the pennant so we can pay for that goddamn engine!"

It worked. The majority turned and looked at me with big smiles and quite a few raised thumbs. I stayed with them to answer any questions they might have. We made a normal landing and within two hours had them all loaded on our other DC-7 and on their way home. I just hoped and prayed that they had no more problems, and they didn't.

That incident confirmed my feelings that the DC-7 just might not have been the best airplane to use for the transport of highly professional ball teams because of its nasty reputation for engine problems. There didn't seem to be any repercussions and the team that was with us that night seemed to appreciate our ability to handle an emergency in such a professional manner and were always happy when they found out we were to be the crew on their flight.

We had another problem just after takeoff from Atlanta, where we were known as the "Lopez Leaper" in honor of the team's manager, Al Lopez, one of the finest gentlemen I have ever had the pleasure of knowing. On the flight we had on board the business people from Vantress Farms who were going to a convention in Miami. As we were putting the gear in the well, the old buzzard yawed mightily to the right. Chuck hollered out, "Number four!" Bill Stevens hollered, "Lost a jug, confirmed number four!" "Feather No. 4, feathering checklist."

I read the checklist and after we got everything secured, I called the tower. "American League 816. We just shut down No. 4. Request priority landing clearance." "Ah roger 816. You declaring an emergency." I looked at Chuck and he said, "Negative." "Negative Atlanta, but we would like to have priority back to 20L left-hand pattern." "Ah roger, Lopez Leaper cleared to land 20 left, wind 190 degrees 5 knots." "Lopez Leaper, ah roger, cleared to land 20 left." "Equipment will be standing by." "Leaper 816 cleared to land." "And, Leaper, how much fuel on board and souls?" "Ah roger, we got 2,500 gallons, 15,300 pounds and 57 souls."

We set up for our three engine approach and on short final we heard, "Atlanta tower, Eastern 652 outer marker inbound visual number two behind 816. We are also running on three but there is no problem." I looked at Chuck and he looked at me with his grin and said, "What do ya bet it's a 727?" "Yeah, that's probably what that smart ass is flying." Of course, the 727 only has three engines.

Everything was under control as we floated over the threshold and smoked the numbers in a smooth three-engine landing. "Gate bar reverse 2 and 3 only, 25 inches," ordered Chuck. "Nos. 2 and 3 brown lights, 25 inches trimmed," replied Bill. "Ah 816, second taxiway Foxtrot, hold short of Alpha." "Foxtrot short of Alpha," I replied. As we turned off, I looked at the approach end and, sure enough, here came 652 and was a confirmed 727. As he landed, I keyed the mike, "Nice landing, wiseguy." In a theatrical, over-acting voice, "Ah roger, it takes a real man to handle three orifices at the same time." Atlanta tower broke in, "Awright, you guys, when the tea party is over, 816 left on Alpha. Taxi as requested. Wise guy, left Foxtrot, hold short Alpha."

We could hear everybody in the background laughing in the Atlanta tower. Rarely, and I mean rarely, does the radio talk go from deadly serious to occasionally hilarious, and this was one of those moments that stays with you for the rest of your life.

On the not-so-funny side of this occasion, we had one of our passengers totally freak out and panic when he saw our No. 4 propeller come to a stop as we feathered it. He jumped out of his seat and ran screaming down the aisle and into a washroom, locking himself in. It took paramedics almost thirty minutes to calm him down and get him to come out. As it turned out, he had lost his daughter in a crash one year earlier and the plane she was in was a DC-7B. We really felt for the poor man and spent some time talking to him.

We were last in line behind five other carriers on 135.2 La Guardia clearance delivery, all of us waiting our turn to receive our flight IFR clearances. The FAA clearance delivery controller was strictly business with a deep monotone voice and shooting out our clearances in a precise and rapid manner. "TWA 351 clearance." "351 ready to copy." "TWA 351 you are cleared to the Denver Stapleton Airport via SID1, left turn after takeoff to heading 265 degrees to cross 360-degrees radial of the Poughkeepsie VOR at no higher than 3,000 feet then climb to and maintain 5,000 feet until Allyn intersection. Expect higher at Allyn, flight plan route squawk 1431 departure frequency 127.05." TWA read back just as efficiently as received. "Roger, TWA 351 contact tower when ready 118.7." That was probably the least complicated clearance to be issued. Clearances were delivered and read back to all five of us, then there was a silence in our headsets. Somebody keyed their mike and "Ah bullshit" was heard by all, including our business-like controller, who took it hook, line, and sinker, demanding, "Aircraft using foul language identify yourself immediately." Big mistake, as TWA 351 very coolly responded, "TWA 351 negative on the bullshit." "United 5 negative on the bullshit." "Allegheny 27 negative on the bullshit." "United 17 negative on the bullshit." "American League negative on the bullshit." There were lots of wide grins in the cockpits that night as silence reined at clearance delivery. After a long pause, "Awright, you guys go to tower. See ya." Like I said, there are precious moments in this profession that are locked in the old computer for life.

Again at La Guardia, six of us lined up for takeoff on Runway 4 and most of us in the middle of our runups. We were a combination of DC-7s, Connies, and Convaires, a good crosswind causing our prop washes to burble across the approach end of Runway 4. We were all crowded together and all late because of a bomb scare earlier that closed down the airport. I noticed an American DC-6 on final and just after I returned to the checklist, Bill Stevens, our ace flight engineer, hollered out, "Jesus Christ! Look at American!" The urgency in his voice made Captain Dusty and me immediately look up. We were met with a scene of horror as we were looking at the belly of the American DC-6 in a forty-five degree bank and his left wing seemed inches from the runway. "Shit, he's going in!" I hollered.

He had been caught in the intense burble from our prop washes and in a nose high attitude and steep left bank. I didn't think there was any chance for a safe recovery. The engineer, not waiting for orders, probably said, "Screw this shit," and jammed all four throttle to the firewall. All four of those great P&W 2800s came to life at the same time and with full right aileron the big bird sluggishly righted herself and literally staggered back into the air, much to the great relief of us all. The Spirit was definitely riding the cockpit of that American DC-6.

Bomb scares were not limited to airports or major carriers. All it takes is one pissed off and insane fan to cause the heart rates in the cockpit to raise. Coming out of St. Paul, Minnesota, and just after hand-off to center, we were just getting settled in and relaxing. "Ah American League 816, return to the field immediately." That ain't Hoyle, I thought as Dusty and I looked at each other with raised eyebrows. "Left turn radar vector please." "We will vector you to final. Turn left 255 degrees and cleared to 2,000 feet." "What's going on, center?" I asked. "Telephone call. Someone says you got a bomb on board." "Just the news I was hoping to hear. Let's not dilly-dally around. Quick as we can, sir."

Fear comes in different forms, sometimes sudden and is over with so quickly that the worst part is thinking about it afterwards. Then there is the building fear when something goes wrong and you have a long while before you can land and be safe again, as in a C-46 on one engine over the North Atlantic with 600 miles to go. This type of fear continues to constantly nag you and you have to keep putting the tiger back in its cage. It plays on your imagination and, if not controlled, can cause serious errors in judgment, affecting the solution to the problem and compounding the situation until there is no solution left, sometimes leading to headlines in the world's newspapers. This type of fear we were all faced with at that moment, and it was brought on by some human being who was either insane or wanted some attention.

In any event, we really had to keep our shit together even though there was a 98 percent chance that it was some idiot playing a prank. It's the two percent of this scenario that caused 100 percent of the fear. We decided that we would shoot a straight in on Runway 22, even though we would have a 6-knot tailwind on landing. The reason was not to overfly our departure route just in case the two percent of the problem was somewhere out there with a remote detonator, waiting to see if we would return.

As it turned out, it was just some sicko's prank that caused this huge disruption of the air traffic system and expense of operations all the way around, not to mention the loss of peace of mind for our professional and confident ball player athletes. Maybe that sicko slipped on a bar of soap exiting the shower and cracked his stupid skull. Maybe, eh Spirit?

Good ol' Dusty was one of our captains who could fly the aircraft just fine. He flew B-52s in the Air Force and transports for the brass out of Andrews. Col. Dusty had a well-rounded career and was basically a nice guy. He was tall with short, cropped grey hair, with a face—and I don't mean this derogatorily—that closely resembled Curly of the Three Stooges. He also had an abrasive personality, that was just good ol' Dusty. He was also accident prone. One day he started out the crew door just behind the engine analyzer and as he stepped onto the ladder, he slipped and fell about 12 feet to the ground and broke his wrist. We immediately went to his aid and rushed him to the local ER where they set and casted his wrist. There was nothing funny about that incident, but the funny part came later when his unintentional abrasiveness was the catalyst for Chuck and I to laugh for many years to come.

We flew a major league football team to Kansas City and as we were unloading our football heroes out of the main cabin exit, the coaches had decided not to wait but to follow the crew's exit down the ladder at the crew door, the same exit Dusty had his one-way flight out of. Now you gotta remember: these coaches are all ex-pro players and no sissies but genuine tuff guys. Dusty, still in his cast, saw them exiting and brusquely walked over to a couple of these giants. Not thinking what he was about to say, he raised his arm with the cast in the face of one of the coaches and said, "You see this?" I am sure Dusty was going to explain why he didn't think it was safe for them to use the crew exit, but before he could say anything the coach, being naturally spring-loaded, was just getting ready to clobber ol' Dusty. I dove in between the two of them and calmed the irate coach down.

As we walked away, Chuck and I desperately trying to hold back our laughter, I said, "Jesus, Dusty, why don't you pick on somebody your own size?" With a perplexed look on his face he responded, "Well, I didn't mean anything by it." "I know, Dusty, I know."

On another occasion, Dusty slipped off the wing and dislocated his shoulder. It got to where when someone would holler, "Dusty run!" we would stop work and get ready to take ol' Dusty to the doc's office. He came walking around No. 4's propellers one day without his hard hat on—hardhat being a requirement—and put a 7-inch gash in the top of his head. Freddy Ottenbergh came running up to me and said, "Goddamnit! We got another Dusty run. Go help him, I'll get the car." I went into the hangar and there sat Dusty, chin in his hand and blood running down his face, and now wearing his hard hat. Concealing my impulse to laugh, I said, "C'mon Dusty, ol' bubba, let's go get ya sewed up." "Shit, Dave, their gonna fire me if I keep this up." "Aw shit, Dusty, it ain't yer fault if they give ya a cheap hard hat to wear."

They didn't fire Dusty, but there was one flight that caused a certain amount of concern. It was night. I was riding jump, Chuck co, Bill engineer, and Dusty captain. We were going into Washington National and had the Chi Sox on board. We were being vectored to the river approach. "Ah American League 816, turn right heading 030 degrees for vectors for the Potomac River approach." "Right 030 degrees 816 roger," as Dusty started left heading for Andrews just off left wing. I don't know whether it was a brain bubble mixed with old habits. Chuck shouted, "Dusty, you're heading for Andrews. Turn right 030 degrees!" Dusty responded by cranking in hard right aileron and coming back on the yoke. The old 7 responded instantly by slowing down and as the airspeed paid off to a dangerous level, Chuck hollered, "I got it!" He immediately came in with

METO power and we staggered back to a safe flying speed. Dusty was definitely shook up and I am sure he did a lot of soul searching afterwards.

Dusty stuck around for about six more months and met up with a 22-year-old stewardess, ran off with her and got married. Dusty was 60. He lasted about 5 years and we all heard that he died suddenly of a heart attack. We all took bets that Dusty went west with a big smile on his face.

We had a star first baseman named Pete Ward. We put the old 7 on the numbers "01" at Kansas City Wheeler Downtown Airport. I didn't like Wheeler because the field was surrounded by buildings and you had to drop it in over rooftops and take off over buildings—no place to have an emergency. After a hard landing we taxied in and shut down. The Sox were, of course, billeted at Kansas City's finest hotel and, for privacy reasons, the flight crew usually stayed at a fine hotel somewhere else. In this case, we were on the other side of town. We always limited our drinking, except on one occasion when we joined up with the team for a wild birthday party for star catcher Smoky Burgess. We were invited to join and, yes, we let it all hang out. Where we stayed there was a restaurant—with great steaks and baked potatoes—that was the fuselage of an old 1049 Constellation and it was a natural place for all of us DC-7 crew to eat our dinner.

Kansas City, as in all cities in the Midwest, at this time of the year was invaded by swarms of sand flies. They don't bite or sting but because of their mega numbers are a maddening nuisance, and they were out in the billions that night. As we were walking down the sidewalk, Chuck was trailing behind and started to call to us to wait up. As he opened his mouth and took a breath he inhaled a whole mouthful of the little pests. I saw Chuck dash for the curb and upchuck his whole dinner in the gutter. At that precise moment here came Pete Ward who quickly walked by us, staring straight ahead. I have always wondered what our star player was thinking about our star captain puking his guts out in this sleazy part of town. Okay, Pete, if you are still around and happen to read this, now you know. Chuck and I have been laughing about that little incident ever since.

The owners decided that it was time to introduce the American public to the game of soccer and tried to develop a major league team called the Chicago Mustangs. How in hell do people get in such a powerful position and then manage to do such dumb things? When we flew our ball teams to their games we were inundated by thousands of fans. When we flew our soccer teams in, it was like a ghost town, even when we brought famous soccer names to help promote the teams. This all amounted to not thousands of lost dollars, but millions. One of the higher-ups, another genius, decided that to make the Mustangs look good, he would transfer millions in losses to the aviation department, which resulted in a major black eye for the steadily developing American Leagues Air Lines and we all saw the writing on the wall. It read, "Screw you."

Standing on the ramp at Miami, preparing for my last trip as first officer of DC-7B 816D, I watched a Canadair DC-4M Northstar howl down the runway, all four Merlin engines screaming at 71.9 inches of manifold pressure and turning heads all over Miami

International. She sounded like a squadron of P-51 Mustangs taking off in formation. I was excited to watch her perform as, thanks to my father's co-signature on a bank loan, and along with David Lindsey, had just closed a deal with the Canadian RCAF to purchase six of these beautiful birds. I was about to become very familiar with the Star and begin a new chapter in my life.

6

Northstar, Central, South America and Dolphin Aviation, 1966 to 1972

"Houston 816 over Semmes at :18, Picayune at 47, Baton Rouge next, level one one thousand, squawking 0414." "Ah roger American League 816, radar contact flight plant route." "816 roger." "Still 235 knots'" I said to Chuck. "Probably slow down some after we get through that front with a more northerly wind." "I am sure of it," I said. Chuck planted his face into the opening of a long cone affair attached to the actual radar scope. It does not allow outside light to interfere with the round screen itself and Chuck could look directly at the yellow-green glowing screen with shadows of brighter blobs and darker blobs that mean nothing to the untrained eye. But to a trained observer, such as Chuck and myself, every sweep of the thin bright yellow line slowly moving back and forth across the screen makes sense. For a couple of seconds the line brightens up and then darkens the seemingly meaningless blobs and brings forth a crystal-clear meaning as to what exactly is going on inside the massive white and grey wall that is directly in front of us.

Using this device, nowadays considered ancient technology, we could navigate through this fearsome-looking mass with ease and avoid the bright blobs in favor of the darker blob, which would eliminate the shit-kicking we would get by blundering into the lighter blobs. Crew coordination in a professional cockpit such as ours is crucial. When one pilot is scanning the radar, the other pilot and engineer are on watch, four eyes scanning outside and inside the cockpit, never letting up on the scanning. This procedure remains in effect even when in the solid grey surroundings of thick clouds, at which time the focus of the two is switched to scanning the instruments.

"Ah Houston, 816 level one one thousand 0414 on the squawk. Over Picayune at 47, Baton Rouge at 08, Alexandria next." "816 roger, flight plan route." I turned the OBS to 262 degrees and old 816 responded slightly, centering the needle to indicate centerline on airway victor 70 outbound from Picayune VOR. "And Houston, we are coming up on a solid wall of clouds and are printing some pretty sizable cells. We might have to deviate once in a while." "You all also known as the Lopez Leaper?" came back in a deeply put-on southern accent. "Ah roger, that's us." "Is the big chief on board?" "Yes, sir, that is affirmative."

We were all smiling at this totally non-regulation radio talk coming from Houston Center. "Well, tan mah hide, yo wish is my command. We sho don't wanna shake up those mighty Chicaga White Sox." I laughed and replied, "We is humbly appreciative of that, suh." Back to normal, "Just let me know what you need 816." "Will do." We all got a chuckle out of a small break in the serious world of aircraft to center communication and I would think a few other cockpit crews who were on the same frequency were smiling also. I decided not to mess with Bill's mind as things were about to get deadly serious.

As I watched the ground rush effect of the white and grey mass of convex and concave surface of the wall in total anarchy began to rush at us and all the convex and concave features were increasing in size at an impossibly fast rate. *Phump!* We were in and everything was grey, even our secure and cozy cockpit darkened and seems to drop a few degrees in temperature. I looked up and made sure the fasten seatbelt sign was on.

I was on the wing of 816D fueling while at our maintenance base in Sarasota, Florida, when this big guy in dirty trousers, Hawaiian aloha shirt opened at the bottom and exposing a rather large beer belly, big jowled face, blue eyes, and a sandy blond clump of unkempt hair perched on top of his huge head. "Heyya, I'm Doc Smith," as I grasped his huge hand in a firm handshake. "Dave, Dave Allyn, first officer on this corrosion palace." We settled into a hilarious conversation and I decided this guy was okay. A lot of mechanics go by the name of "Doc" and it is usually a fascinating story of how they accomplished some miraculously impossible feat to get an old wounded buzzard back in the air again. So I asked Doc how he got the nickname.

"Oh, I got the degree at the University of Chicago. Put myself through medical school barnstorming biplanes in the twenties." After I picked my jaw up off the surface of the wing I said, "You're a real doc!" "Guess so." Turns out he was not only a "real" doc, but a heart surgeon to boot, and in the field of medical research. He was not like any famous doctor any of us would think of. First, he was a flyer. Second, he owned a hot North American A-36 Apache divebomber. Ol' Doc had one day a week to himself. He would come to the field and fly his bomber and then retire to the bar and drink shanty-gaffs and tell flying stories and great jokes until I would load him up in his great old car and take him home to sleep it off. The next six days he would save lives in the pressure cooker of a very busy surgery room. Doc would become one of my best friends. He had an airline pilot buddy named "Herman the German Wilhelmy," who also was a true character. When the three of us got together, the world became a hilarious and fun place to live.

April 1, 1968. Eastern flight 60 from Miami and continuing on to Chicago landed at Sarasota and had an hour-and-a-half layover. It was a Lockheed L188 Electra Senior with a 480 mph cruise 4-engine turboprop, an in-between aircraft that was very successful as an interim aircraft between recips and jets. Doc and I always met Herman the German, the captain on flight 60, for breakfast. After breakfast Herman said, "You guys come on out and see us off. I am going to pull an April Fool's joke on our passengers." "This oughta be rich," I said to Doc. And it was.

Standing at the gate, all the passengers loaded, the stewardesses, flight engineer, and co-pilot were waiting for Captain Herman to show up. Herman walked out of the terminal, a small pillow stuck under the back portion of his uniform jacket, making him look like the Hunchback of Notre Dame. But that wasn't all. He was also wearing a long green tie that hung well below his waist and, to top it off, he had small, round, dark glasses on and carried a red-and-white striped cane. He tapped his way out to the aircraft, banged each side of the boarding ramp, and tapped his way up and into the forward loading door. All the while there were serious-looking faces peering out all of the passenger windows and it was dead silent in that aircraft. Herman disappeared into the aircraft and then we heard his voice calling out to the stunned passengers as he peeled off his costume. "April Fool's, folks!"

Sid "Doc" Smith with his North American A-36 Apache divebomber

Everybody started laughing, cheering, and clapping. I saw Herman take his seat and look at us with his big devilish smile and his thumb sticking straight up in the aviator's salute. Both Doc and I, laughing our guts out, returned the salute with both hands.

We lived in a friendly, happy, and honest America in those days and America was respected the world over. Many business deals were done on a handshake without the aid of some greedy lawyer working under a maze of ridiculous rules, regulations, and loopholes imposed on us by a government seemingly gone insane. The lawyers, with their knowledge of these foolish regs, will work out an impossible agreement for you and they seem to be the only one who benefits from it and to hell with honesty and reason. The dumbing down of our education system has allowed stupidity and greed to take hold and gain undeserved power. The result of this is that today we live in a world of hate, bickering, dishonesty, and everybody is at each other's throats, nobody knowing what the future holds, if anything. The counter culture was just beginning and at the time we all thought it was just a passing fad.

Doc and I watched Herman and his magic flying machine gracefully take to the air and then we spent the rest of the day with smiles on our faces. Just try that today. More than one tiny-minded jerk would find a way to be insulted and whine and cry their way to cause a very funny April Fool's joke into something it was not. Then some whiner in politics would come up with an uncalled-for rule based on this jerk's feelings and squash the sense of humor we all used to have when people were people and not self-centered sensitive twerps that we seem to have become.

During this time, I met another lifetime friend, an 8th Air Force fighter pilot ace and vice president of Trans Florida, Jerry Tyler. He had a short, firm body, thinning hair, friendly face, and when he smiled, crow's feet that extended to his ears. He was the personification of what a hot fighter pilot should look like and he had the track record to prove it. Our meeting was the result of a violent tragedy that happened at the airport in Sarasota.

I was standing on the ramp in front of Trans Florida, a company that rebuilt P-51s for private use and were doing a very successful business of it. Jerry was also their chief pilot. On this day they had just completed the refurbishment of a two-seat TF51D, which a pilot—not Jerry, thank God—named Bill, and a mechanic were taxiing out for a test flight. I watched them take off in the screaming howl only a Mustang can make at full throttle. After becoming airborne, the pilot began a right turn off the departure end of 22. He climbed over us out of a 270 degree climbing turn and as he passed over us, I heard a series of loud reports coming from the Merlin engine. Then, as if in a horror movie, the whole aircraft erupted in a ball of fire. The wind against the fireball elongated it to look like a comet or meteorite passing through the atmosphere, trailing dense black smoke.

As the burning P-51 started its final plunge, I saw a body depart the aircraft as a terribly burned Bill successfully bailed out with a thin streak of white trailing off his back and blossoming into an opened parachute. In horror, we watched as a second figure stood up in the back cockpit and immediately activated his chute, which became entangled with the vertical fin and jerked the hapless mechanic out and drug him behind the Mustang. He and the P-51 went straight down and slammed into the ground with a sickening sound and the aircraft and mechanic disappeared in a large ball of orange fire that slowly dissipated into a sickening black mushroom ball of smoke rising slowly skyward as I stood in disbelief at what I had just seen.

Bill survived but was severely burned on 100 percent of his face and hands and had to wear a mask to hide the ugly scars and burned-off lips, nose, and ears. In time, the plastic surgeons were actually able to rebuild Bill's face and hands. The last time I saw him I could hardly tell he had been so awfully burned. Bill, being the tough guy that he was, tucked the awful experience into his memory banks and used the power of the human mind that the great Spirit has given us all and completed an aircraft engineering degree at MIT. Bill lived a long and successful life as an aircraft engineer.

Jerry Tyler and I became friends as a result of this awful crash. I used to hang out at Trans Florida and help Jerry pre-flight the P-51s he was about to fly. One day Jerry said, "Goddamnit, Dave. Get your ass in that TF and I will check you out in a 51." He didn't have to twist my arm very hard. As I strapped into the tight cockpit of the world's hottest and greatest prop-driven fighter, I was impressed with the ease and simplicity of the layout of all controls. Rudder, elevator, and aileron trim knobs positioned within easy reach of your left hand as were flaps, gear lever, and throttle stick between your legs, feet on adjustable rudder pedals, canopy release and controls for your right hand and the all-familiar instrument panel where it should be. Nothing weird or unusual and I felt right at home.

Jerry Tyler in the 51, I am left seat in the Star

Clunk as the starter motor engaged the massive twelve-cylinder Merlin engine and the big four-bladed prop began to slowly rotate. Fuel boost on high and tickle the primer mags to both and, unlike the big radials with their displays of smoke and fireballs and buildup to the galloping sound, the Merlin fired off and right into the businesslike staccato of a powerful and massive v-12 engine. No buildup or hesitation, a precise work of genius in engineering perfection. The 51, with her wide gear, was literally a dream to taxi, not to mention she had a steerable tailwheel but if you needed to turn her tight, you pushed forward on the stick and it would unlock her tailwheel and she would literally turn inside of herself.

After runup, we lined up on Runway 32. I have heard many horror stories about uncontrollable torque factors on takeoff, all unfounded and probably spoken by wannabes rather than experience. As I came up on the power to 47 inches m.p., the only thing that was intimidating about the 51 was the incredible bellowing roar in the cockpit and I quickly built up speed for a much-needed rudder efficiency. When I advanced the throttle to 69.5 inches or full throttle—and, yeah, the torque is strong but never uncontrollable—it seemed that the hot little fighter leapt into the air before I drove the throttle all the way home. If I thought she was loud at 47 inches, she went to a screaming bellow at 69.5. She literally clawed her way skyward in a heart-beating rate of climb and

The P-51 Jerry Tyler checked me out in. It took all 1,650 hp to get this lardbutt off the ground.

175 knots indicated. Wow, was I in love at first sight. All I had to do was think about turning and she seemed to read my mind.

We climbed to 10,000 feet and leveled out coming back to 65 percent cruise. She settled down on 275 knots indicated and 68 gallons per hour. 316 mph indicated she was truing at 375 mph and costing, in those days, 24 cents a mile, cheaper than a Beech Bonanza. I took her through some aerobatics and her roll rate was astounding, causing the earth to rotate 360-degrees every three seconds. She was scary at first in a full stall, but once I got used to it she was just a spoiled brat when I denied her the wind she needed to fly. We came back in and on short final, gear in the green, full flaps, and 115 knots indicated, I wheeled her on in soul-pleasing smooth landing.

Next day, we did nothing but touch-and-goes until I felt comfortable in any kind of takeoff and landing scenario. I was hooked. I had to own me one of these fighter flying machines. If you could fly one of these fighters every day, you would never have the need for a psychiatrist. So, on Jerry's advice, I went out and bought the next best thing.

Now hear this: I went and paid a whole $3,500 for a low-time North American SNJ-4 fighter trainer. Okay, quit drooling all over my carpet. I kept and loved that beautiful flying bird for 35 years before succumbing to a $150,000 cash offer and I still shed a tear or two for ever letting her go.

Air ballet or psychiatrist's couch? My SNJ4.

Instructing a new guy from the back

Yup, I used to be young once

Jerry told me that Trans Florida was going to become Cavalier Aircraft and go into the arms business, supplying Central and South America's air forces with active P-51 fighters. The owner, David Lindsey, wanted me to come to his office at the Sarasota Herald Tribune—also his—and discuss a possible partnership in buying six RCAF DC-4M Northstars for $19,000 apiece, all in flying condition, to support his new operation by flying parts to the Caribbean, Central and South America. On the return trips we would fly produce supplied by United Fruit South America. I was excited. Hell, you could buy these birds for 19 and never set foot in one and sell each one for 120,000 on the market in those days. I had to do it.

I didn't have the money, but dear old Dad did. He co-signed the loan for four of these birds with the condition that I had to sell at least one of them as quickly as possible to pay off the loan and I did. I was way wrong thinking I was going to get $120,000—I got $150,000 for CFUOY. After paying back the $76,000 and keeping $74,000, I was in tall cotton. When the time came to ferry from Trenton, Canada, all six, one at a time, to Sarasota, I was handed the job. Since I was one of the owners, I flew left seat on all six. My instructor pilot was Buddy McNair and since I had DC-7 time, I found this masterpiece of a flying machine a total delight to fly. Buddy was a great guy to fly with. He became our chief pilot of operations.

I handed in my resignation to American League to be effective after one more trip to LAX. I flew the old 7 quite a few more times as a favor to my pals, and finally the dumbshittedness of the company's financial wizards finally caught up with them and American League Air Lines was forced to close its doors. 816D was sold to a cosmetics giant who used her for several years until CEO and owner killed himself in a P-51, of all things. I don't know what happened to her after that. I flew first officer with Chuck on 813D's last flight to Atlanta, where she was scrapped. A sad ending for such a one-time proud airliner, not to mention the really great people put on the street by the stupid antics of those few in charge.

I hopped a Trans Canada flight from Tampa to Toronto, Canada, to spend the next two weeks dealing with the Canadian DOT or FAA. It wasn't easy. I kept running up against arrogant officials who seemed bent on hindering rather than helping. Putting my hands in my pockets and counting to ten, we finally got the reams of paperwork completed and were cleared to take our prizes home from Trenton AFB where all six were parked.

The base was great, and we were treated like royalty. We had the run of the base and all the help we needed. The officer's club was wide open to us and we were accepted as though we were squadron members.

One night as we were all drinking our fill and the BS was about knee-deep, a squadron leader walked in. One of the pilots, way over the limit and really tying one on, managed to upset the squadron leader, who then ordered the out-of-control leftenant to leave and sober up. The loaded leftenant put his overcoat and hat on backwards, staggered over to the squadron leader, and stuck his finger in the leader's ear. "I bet yu shought I wash leavin dincha." At first the leader stood up and I thought we were about to have to break up a fight, but he stopped and said, "You got discharged today?" "Yup." "Well, why in hell didn't you say so? Drinks on the house." The joke was on the squadron leader and he took it real well. By the time the evening was over, both leader and leftenant were arm-in-arm, staggering across the ramp and babbling complete nonsense. Great evening, thanks to the Trenton Transport Base officer's club.

Buddy led me through the Northstar flight manual for two days before we took No. 1 south. CF-UXB. As I strapped into the left seat and Buddy into the right co-pilot seat, I was really anxious to get to know this long-range RCAF transport. We entered the DC4M the same way we did the C-46: up a ladder through the cavernous cargo doors and into the large and long cargo compartment. No pretty Interior covering here, just row after row of aluminum fuselage ribs forming her round fuselage, bare emergency lights in place above the emergency exits, conduit wiring running in place the length of the interior neatly exposed, fire extinguishers in regulation areas ready for instant use.

The cargo floor was a heavy-looking green painted wood in three sections—left, center, and right—running the length of the cabin, each one with tie-down points every so many feet. This cabin certainly was not designed to ease the fears of a group of leery passengers. She was pure business with no soundproofing anywhere. Fold-down benches ran the length of the cabin and I felt pity for the troops forced to ride sideways, jammed next to each other, for hours in the unheated, extremely loud cabin of the Canadair DC-4M Northstar. Nonetheless, she was a beauty, a well-mannered lady of the air.

As I entered the crew door, there was no question that she was designed for long-distance flights as there was an enclosed head with a washbasin, honey bucket toilet, and mirror. Just ahead of the head were upper and lower bunks for long-distance crew rest areas, and on the right side the crew door for exiting or entering the aircraft.

Hanging from the ceiling and next to the forward bulkhead was a coiled rope with a T-bar attached to the lower end of the coil for emergency exit if need be. This area also had first aid kits and cockpit fire extinguishers attached to the bulkhead.

Moving forward and on the left was the radio operator's station. Riding sidesaddle, he had a massive stack of every kind of radio available with a mind-bending amount of knobs, switches, wires, plugins, morse code keys, and ancient tube-type radios all stacked in perfect order. To the right were two comfortable seats for spare crewmembers. Just forward was the actual flight deck with its own mind-bending number of switches, levers, knobs, instruments—all round—not only on the panel in front of the pilots' seats but scattered in tight confusion on the three panels situated over the cockpit windshields.

To the novice, it would appear to be mass confusion but to Buddy and me it was a more-than-familiar place. We could throw switches, pull levers, work throttles, mixture, prop controls, feathering buttons, or anything we needed to touch blindfolded and I kid you not that was part of our test on many more than one aircraft. Buddy pulled it on me and I passed. Satisfied to let me fly PIC—pilot in command—Buddy started reading the pre-flight checklist and I answered each query. Starting No. 3,4,2, 1 in sequence, just like the 7 or any four-engine Douglas aircraft as the designers put a generator only on the No. 3 position, there was also a generator on No. 2 so we did have a backup.

It was hard to get used to the 12-cylinder staccato of the Merlin engines as they were brought to life. It looked like a Douglas cockpit, but it sure didn't sound like a Douglas but rather a flight of four Spitfires or P-51s getting started for a mission. Our Merlin engines differed slightly from the light-bank Merlins used on the 51-D fighters in that these were heavy-bank engines and could pull 73 inches of manifold pressure and produce another 140 hp rather than the 68 inches of the lighter-bank ones.

We carried 3,800 gallons of gas, and at a fuel burn of 263 gallons per hour, we were out of gas at 14 hours and 45 minutes, and 2,890 miles at 200 knots our cruise at 65 percent power or 230 mph for 3323.5 miles. Not bad for 1938 technology. No wonder the DC-4 is still in use in some parts of the world even today. Obviously we never fly to fuel exhaustion but even with reserve of one hour and 45 minutes, she was and still is a contender for international cargo hauling, not to mention the fact she can take off and land fully loaded on short dirt strips in the jungle, tundra, or wilderness anywhere in the world where it would be suicide for most jets to try.

I felt mighty good sitting in the command seat on such a historic ship, even though she was equipped with four strange type engines idling in perfect sync. I learned to love those Merlins and actually felt more confidence in the Merlin than I did for either P&W or Wright radials. She taxied like any other Doug and the runup only slightly different from the P&W-powered DC-4.

The RCAF gave us special for No. 1 for takeoff in front of 10 transports on a mission. Those guys bent over backward for us for sure. After being cleared into position and hold, I taxied the bird onto the runway at Trenton Royal Canadian Air Force Base and stopped her on the overrun, her nose pointed straight down the 9,000-foot runway.

We set 900 rpm on all four tachometers. I felt ready, surrounded by the chatter and uneven vibrations of the four Merlins playing their mechanical music while we waited for takeoff clearance from the tower. "Ah Charlie Foxtrot Uncle Xray Baker, you are cleared for takeoff. Right clearing turn after takeoff, as soon as speed and altitude permit." "Xray Baker is rolling, right, after takeoff, roger."

The last item on the takeoff checklist is to close all cockpit windows which was okay by me, as it was January and 19 degrees Fahrenheit in Toronto that day. I grabbed my cockpit side window lever as did Buddy on his side and we shoved them forward. Buddy's did what it was supposed to do and seated itself in properly, but mine started to seat and then imitated a freshly cut-down redwood tree and slowly began to fall inward, winding up off the tracks and in my lap. I picked up the heavy window, frame and all, looked at Buddy's shocked face, and all I could think of saying was, "Shee-it." Buddy, thinking fast as usual, said, "I guess we are flying a convertible Northstar. Les get the flock outta here." I quickly stowed the errant window on the engineer's seat and grabbed a handful of throttles.

Without another thought about the O.A.T.—outside air temperature—being at a balmy 19 degrees, I started to slowly advance the throttles to their stops where the engine wastegates stabilized all four at 73.9 inches max power. No hunting for manifold pressure readings to prevent overboost as on the P&Ws and Wrights—a real time-saving design. The noise level in the Star's cockpit went from low chatter to her mind-numbing bellowing howl as all four Merlins let the world know a Northstar is on the roll, requiring all crew members to wear tight-fitting muff type earphones so that all communication was through an intercom system.

The old eagle was accelerating much faster than the 7 I was used to and before I was ready, I heard Buddy's mechanical voice, "50 knots." "I got rudder control, transitioning to flight controls," as I let go of the small nose wheel steering wheel and grasped the yoke. "V1." I started gently coming back on the yoke, checking the airspeed indicator and as the nose lifted gently off the ground and the airspeed ticked 110 knots, "V2," the old girl gently and gracefully transitioned into her element. We were in the air at V2, and could safely fly her back to the runway in the event of an engine failure.

She didn't feel much different on the controls from the 7, maybe a touch lighter as the airspeed tapped 145 mph and I started a smooth turn to the right to clear the takeoff path for the departing wing of transports behind us. I steadied up on a course that had us over the frigid-looking grey waters of Lake Erie, climbing at an impressive 1,500 feet per minute and 165 knots indicated.

Speaking of frigid, that blast of 19-degree wind coming through the gaping hole that was supposed to be a closed window certainly was an uninvited guest. Buddy was reading my mind, probably because he was freezing his ass off and was already putting the window back on the track and reattaching the activating bar. Soon we had the window closed and seated. Our freezing cockpit soon gave way to the heating system built into the cockpit by Canadair especially for Arctic and Antarctic operations.

Douglas built the perfect aircraft in the DC-4, Canadair perfected the DC-4 when they made her a Canadair DC-4M Northstar. The feathering system on the Doug was standard on all Ham Standard props:

1. Retard the throttle
2. Mixture idle cutoff
3. Retard the prop
4. Push and hold the feathering button
5. Shut off the fuel
6. Close the cowl flaps.

Six time-consuming steps to shut down and secure one engine in an emergency can seem like an eternity when your life depends on it. On the Star if you lose an engine just activate the feathering button and all six steps are done automatically. Just keep flying the wounded goose and when everything is stabilized, you can worry about cleanup and checklist later. I can't say enough for the thought that was put into our lovely flying machine by the engineers at Canadair. She definitely was the best DC-4 ever, not to mention the increase of 35 mph and same fuel burn by using the sleek v-12 Merlin engines. All you pencil-neck mathematicians out there, do the math and you can see why we could come in with a load and line our pockets with more gold than you could with the round engine 4.

Our route was a straight line basically on a south-southwest heading, dead reckoning all the way, using WAC VFR charts, and our VORs strictly for fixing our position on the WAC chart. We had 1,100 miles to go from takeoff at Trenton Air Base, situated on the outskirts of Toronto. We only carried seven hours of fuel and our ETA for the trip was five-and-a-half hours. This gave us one-and-a-half hour reserve so we were light and our true airspeed was slightly high. We throttled back to 60 percent and this added another hour to our reserve at 200 knots. We would overfly New York, Pennsylvania, West Virginia, Kentucky, Tennessee, North Carolina, Georgia, and half the length of Florida.

We picked up flight following from New York Center so that we were in radar contact all the way and could receive positions on other aircraft in our vicinity for safety. We were on a ferry permit so we couldn't go IFR or at night but the weather along our route of flight was forecast to be severe clear all the way and as soon as we crossed Lake Erie, we flew out from under the overcast and into bright sunshine and it stayed that way all the way. We had no restricted areas and no high mountains so I picked 4,500 as our cruising altitude, low enough to really enjoy the diverse scenery drifting slowly by beneath our silver wings.

I settled back and hand flew the 4M all the way. She trimmed out and was so stable I basically flew her with the trim wheel and very slight rudder pressures to bring up a wing or nudge her back on course, very slight movements on the trim to raise or lower her nose and keep her in perfect flight position and on the step constantly in the smooth air we were immersed in.

Me clowning for the camera in the DC-4M Northstar cockpit, Buddy in the right seat

Even Rolls-Royce engines fail, the Merlin, No. 4, feathered

Buddy McNair

The steady loud roar of her four Merlins filled the cockpit with a powerful reassurance. Any change in tone, however slight, or flicker of an engine instrument needle would instantly put captain and first officer on red alert which would not end until we discovered and corrected the problem or were satisfied it was atmospherics and not a gremlin working his evil ways.

"Ah Charlie Foxtrot Xray Baker, New York Center traffic 12 o'clock, 3 miles level 5,500 opposite direction, light twin." "Ah roger New York, we have contact, a twin Beech looks like," as I watched the Beech pass 1,000 feet above us at what looked like an impossible speed at over 400 mph closing speed. "Ah roger, Uncle Xray Baker confirm type as a DC-4?" "Affirmative." "Ah you pulling extra power we got you at 210 knots." This controller is a sharp guy, I thought to myself. "No, we're pulling 60 percent actually slowed down a tad." This really threw him for a loop because he was showing us splitting molecules a full 35 knots faster than any DC-4 or C-54 he has ever controlled. He also knew there was no wind to speak of at our altitude.

After a long silence, he called back with a smile in his voice, "You guys got a flight of four P-51s pushing you along?" "You got it, all four in perfect sync." "A Northstar. This is a first for me. You sure got a standard 4 beat for speed." "Fuel burn is the same also." "Heck of a deal." We got that type of chatter from most of the controllers along our route.

As we soared over the Northeastern countryside, we watched the wooded fields, straight roads, small towns, big town, rivers, lakes, and cities slip below our cockpit. I was in love with this superb flying machine. She responded instantly to any input of her flight controls, unlike the DC-7. The old 7 would take 1.5 seconds from input to action and basically had little feel to her because of her weight. Not so the Star. She was heavy on the controls but all three axis' responses were instant and you could really feel her.

I don't know why they even bothered to put an A-12 auto-pilot in her as in smooth air she was a delight to hand fly. Of course, in rough air you had to manipulate the controls to keep her from wandering, as in any airplane and in rough air nobody in their right mind would do anything else but hand fly any aircraft as an auto-pilot would literally beat pilots and aircraft to death so the only time we would engage the auto-pilot was in smooth air.

As we flew south-southwest the OAT steadily warmed and we had the heat turned off by the time the Georgia-Florida state line slipped below us at 200 knots. Even though you can't actually see a state line, the changes in topography and plant life can let you know when you have entered a different state.

We passed over Tampa Bay with St. Pete to the right and Tampa MacDill AFB to our left. Descending to 1,500 feet, I tuned in Sarasota Tower on 120.1, "Sarasota, Charlie Foxtrot Uncle Xray Baker is with you, 1,500 feet, north over Manatee inbound for a full stop." "Roger Xray Baker, state type." "Ah roger DC-4M Northstar." "Hey, Dave, welcome back, cleared straight in Runway 4, wind zero, call 3 mile final, altimeter 29.97." Ron Billib, an ace tower controller at Sarasota and friend I still see today was on duty that day and I recognized his voice right away. I signaled to Buddy with the microphone in my hand and said, "Ah roger Xray Baker, straight in to 4, call you 3 miles final." "Xray Baker, roger."

"Hey Ronola, wait 'til you see this hotrod we're flyin'!" "Yeah, Dave, you got an audience just waitin' to see you." I loved the ease and friendliness of those days. I throttled back and called for 20 inches trimmed across the board. We had made a cruise descent and were indicating 220 knots and, being the clean bird she is, it took some time for the airspeed to bleed off. At 175 knots I called for the in-range checklist and in-range flaps set to 20 degrees. Checklist completed, the old eagle was down to 160 knots and I called gear down and 30 degrees on the flaps. The Star slowed to 125 indicated and Buddy called the 3-mile fix, "Roger, Xray Baker cleared to land for full stop."

No VASI in those days or approach lights on 04. You had to put the runway between your legs and fly power, needle and beetle, and airspeed. Final check complete. "Full flaps and 15 inches across the board trimmed." Buddy was concentrating on the procedures I was using and seemed to be pleased at what he was seeing. On the 7, you never landed power off but held 11 inches manifold pressure right to touchdown. I trimmed nose high so I was putting heavy forward pressure on the yoke.

Just short of the threshold, Buddy cut the power and as I heard firecracker popping of all four Merlins, I thought, Shit, we are going to fall out of the sky. But the Star didn't flinch and we glided across the threshold like a Piper Cub. I released pressure on the yoke and slightly helped her to set up and she literally painted herself on to the numbers 04 without even a squeak from her tires. I gently let the nose down and took the nose steering tiller as Buddy went full forward on the yoke.

I guess I had that shit-eating grin as Buddy said, "Not quite like the 7, eh?" "Wow, I guess not. I thought we were going to cream it when you pulled power on short final. I am in love with this great flyer." "Same with a full load. She will never let you down." "A real lady," I agreed. As we taxied off the active and turned towards Cavalier, there stood the whole staff and crew on the tarmac. Ron was right, we really did have an audience. Everybody was happy to see the first aircraft arrive. After shutdown and welcoming banter with everybody, I went home and ran the flight over and over in my head. How lucky I felt to be doing a job that you did not have to leave at the office, but could bring home and enjoy the memories as much as the actual flying. It has been that way throughout my life and I am so thankful for the many great memories.

By July we had all of the aircraft home with no problems. CF UXB got an interior lift. The radio station was removed, the cockpit heavily soundproofed, and six first-class passenger seats installed in the crew area. She also got an all-white paint job and later a blue stripe was added along with "Air Caicos" emblazoned on her upper fuselage just above the passenger windows amidships.

David Lindsey, the owner and CEO of Cavalier Aircraft and Air Caicos had made a deal with the Canadian Embassy in Havana, Cuba, to supply the embassy on a weekly basis. Part of the deal was that the aircraft must be Canadian-registered and be flown only by Canadian pilots. This, of course, was due to our embargo against Cuba. No problem, all you politicos, we got the bird and we got the Canadian birdmen. Thank you, Fidel. Just keep the checks comin' to our company based in the good ol' USA. One of our secretaries thought Castro was very sexy-looking when he was eating a banana. Ha ha ha, Lizzy, you got a great sense of humor.

Air Caicos at its peak

Anyway, these negotiations prompted a trip to Washington, D.C., with the company lawyers to finalize the contracts with the Canadian contacts based in D.C. Dave Lindsey volunteered UXB to take them up, drop them off, and then we would deadhead home. I thought this would be an expensive trip but then Dave was very proud of his accomplishments so I figured he deserved some bragging rights and I got the right seat so I was happy also.

We blasted off from Sarasota on a non-stop IFR flight plan to D.C. The weather was stinking in D.C. with 200 feet and one-quarter mile as Washington approach 124.7 vectored us to the outer marker 36. I called the outer marker and Washington National Tower cleared us to land as Buddy called, "Gear down, 24 inches across the board, and approach flaps." The ILS crosshairs centered and stayed glued all the way through the approach as did our airspeed, nailed at 125 mph. The surrounding grey began to darken at 300 feet and at 250 feet, the bottom of the overcast and fascia streamed by our cockpit windows. As we broke out, I called, "Break out, I got the runway." "Full flaps," Buddy said, as I dropped full flaps, and Buddy came all the way off the power. The Merlins lit off their crackling string of firecrackers through the exhaust ports and Buddy painted her on dead center on the big white numbers of 36 at Washington National.

We taxied to Omni Aviation and shut down. We unloaded our passengers, who I believe were ready to get out, even with the extra soundproofing the Star had a very loud cockpit. They were going to conduct their business and spend a few days. Buddy and I refueled for Sarasota. Clearance delivery 128.25 shot us our clearance and handed us off to ground 121.7 who stacked us in between two brand new shiny B-727s, both American. As we taxied out, the chatter began.

"Can you see anything through that cloud of corrosion dust comin' from that Wright flyer in front of us?" Smartass! "No, but I think I saw Wilbur and Orville in the cockpit." Smartass! Buddy continued taxiing with a slight grin on his face. "Hey, ground, did you notice if they had to hand prop that thing to get it started?" Smartass! Even the tower personnel were enjoying it as we could hear the giggling in the background when they keyed their mike to talk. We were free in those days and it was fun.

"Uncle Xray Baker cleared position and hold." "Ah roger, position and hold 18, Uncle Xray Baker." On the crew brief, Buddy said, "Gimme 30 degrees on the flaps. This will be a max per takeoff at 10 above VMC, get the gear as soon as you can, after takeoff." I broke into a big grin as it sunk in what Buddy was about to do.

I know the Star will really perform as light as she is, and I figured with only 200 feet to reach the cloud base and disappear into it, this oughta look pretty impressive. I also knew that everybody was watching.

"Uncle Xray Baker cleared for takeoff. Maintain runway heading." "Xray Baker, runway heading, we're rolling." "Max power," Buddy said, and I slowly brought the throttles to the stops. Buddy was holding the brakes, the Star shuddering and straining to be turned loose. Buddy released the brakes and the Star's nose rose up. As she felt her freedom, she stepped out smartly and in a very short time I called out "VMC." Buddy hauled the yoke almost to his belly and the Star responded by lifting her nose high and then leapt off the ground and climbed like a homesick angel and into the stealth protection of the thick cloud base.

"Holy cow, did you see that?" we heard in our headsets. "Was that really a DC-4?" came another astonished exclamation. What they didn't know was that we reached 350 feet before airspeed started to pay off and Buddy was now gently and gingerly nursing her nose down and building up lost airspeed while not losing altitude so as not to pop out of the overcast and expose our false scheme to those who were watching below. We won the race.

"Ah Xray Baker contact departure 124.7, he who laughs last." I could hear the laughter in the background as I confirmed the transmission. Even the serious tones of a departure controller took a slight break as departure crackled into my earphones, "Xray Baker radar contact. Turn left on course, climb to and maintain niner thousand and nice show, even though we know the truth." "Ah roger, left on course to niner for Xray Baker and we won't tell if you don't." "Xray Baker affirmed." Buddy and I grinned the whole way back to Sarasota and still smile about it today.

Operations began with a trip to supply a hotel in the Caicos Islands and brought back a load of frozen lobsters. We took off on an IFR flight plan, destination Nassau for a customs stop. As we taxied to customs, we were met by a sharp-looking customs official, his white uniform and cap standing out brightly against his native black skin.

"Good morning and welcome to Nassau, gentlemons." In those days, we always carried a bottle of scotch in the flight case next to our customs papers. "Papers, please." As we opened the case, he reached in and smiled a huge smile and, lifting out the bottle, said, "Das me favorite. Jus sign here and you gentlemons have a good day." We shook hands and as we strapped back in, we grabbed a quick pop-up to Caicos Island. I understand you can still do the same thing today, only a bottle of scotch doesn't do it anymore, now all they accept is cash. We stayed low at 2,000 feet and in the warm tropical air above the indigo blue seas of the Atlantic, I filled the artistic side of my brain as the islands of Eluethera, Cat I, Long Island, Crooked I, and Great Inagua slipped by. Although different from the atolls of the familiar South Pacific, they were just as beautiful from the air.

Caicos Island appeared dead ahead and right on time. The islands are representative of all the islands located in the windward and leeward group of Bahama Islands, but are, or were, a West Indies protectorate, being low coral uplifts and desert in nature. On all the islands there are huge coral boulders that were unexplained until recently. We now know that centuries ago one whole side of an island in the Canaries collapsed into the sea and sent a mega-tsunami, some say over 1,000 feet high, racing west across the Atlantic. When it reached these islands it ripped the existing reefs up and deposited huge sections of them onto the islands. The geological history of the earth is a fascinating subject to me. When I hear of these events, I try to imagine what something that awesome must have looked like when it actually happened.

As we approached Grand Caicos, I dropped down to 200 feet and circled the village of Bambarra to let them know we had arrived. As I circled the island, I called for climb power and watched the oceanic waves and the turquoise shallows with the island itself in the background race by my left wing and Nos. 1 and 2 engines at 200 knots indicated (234 mph) and rolled out on a long final for the 5,000-foot coral runway. I began a gentle descent so as to cross the threshold at no higher than 50 feet and 215 knots (249 mph). As we tore down the runway in this four-engine transport buzz job, I thought I saw a man standing on the side of the runway. At the departure end, I came back gently on the yoke and began a graceful pull-out and left 180 degree turn to put us on a left downwind and 1,500 feet at 124 knots. Gear down, 20 degree flaps, checklist complete, base, final, full flaps, easing back on the yoke, and a gentle touchdown on the end of the coral strip.

"Do you see him?" Buddy shouted through my headset. "Shit, we are committed," I said back. My man had grown long ears and two extra legs and a tail and called himself a wild jackass and was now standing on the runway. I watched him disappear under No. 1 and waited to feel the impact with our No. 1 propeller tip but he must have been standing a tad out of the way and as we both breathed a sigh of relief, I braked the Star to a stop and turned 180 degrees to see a terrified jackass in full gallop, seeming to be outrunning Man o' War for safer ground. "Welcome to Caicos Island," I said to Buddy's smiling face.

As we shut down a pickup truck drove up carrying our unloading crew. Buddy and I hung out in the shade of a wing and in about thirty minutes, we were unloaded and strapping in for the short flight over to Grand Turk Island and Cockburn town where we were to attend an early afternoon lunch at the Governor General's home to welcome us for bringing air service to Caicos Islands.

After takeoff and a slight left turn for Grand Turk, I noticed several excellent dive spots and, since we were on a schedule for Caicos and would spend the night on many occasions, I vowed to bring my dive gear with me from now on. We landed on a well-kept asphalt strip at Cockburn and were escorted to the Governor's mansion.

The Governor was a gentleman from England and a charming host. We ate an all-native meal: conch, lobster, jerked pork, and a host of seafood dishes. Later that afternoon, we flew back to Caicos and smoked off the strip again, Buddy captain this time. We saw no more jackasses, but we made low passes a procedure on all unimproved strips we landed on after that trip.

We were put up at the only hotel on Caicos for the night and the next morning we supervised the loading of frozen lobsters to be delivered to Miami by noon. How do you keep frozen lobsters frozen in an unpressured aircraft in the tropics? The answer is simple, you use a Northstar, climb to 25,000 and put on oxygen masks and in high blow and sea level pressure you cruise at 220 knots and burn 263 gallons an hour and land in Miami a full hour before a standard DC-4 gets there, lobsters rock-solid frozen. Hey all you DC-4 operators, quit drooling on my rug, damnit!

After clearing customs, we taxied over to, yeah, you guessed it, my old stomping grounds, Corrosion Corner, where we unloaded and taxied out for takeoff to Sarasota with a whopping profitable check in our pocket.

I tuned in Sarasota Tower 120.1, 35 miles out and was just about to give an inbound position report when I heard Ron clear a Piper Comanche. "65 Papa you are cleared to land runway 04. Wind calm, altimeter 29.94." "Roger 65 Papa cleared to land 04," came the reply. I made my call and got my reply, then Ron again, "Comanche 65 Papa it appears your landing gear is still up." No reply. "65 Papa your gear is still up." No reply. Ron never changed his tone, "65 Papa cancel your landing clearance. Go around, your gear is still up." No reply. "65 Papa go around, go around, repeat go around." The next transmission told the story, "Cessna 56 Yankee, go around."

We flew over the field and, sure enough, sitting cockeyed to the runway sat a Comanche with distinctive skid marks behind her. Later I asked Ron what the hell happened. Ron looked down with a smile and shook his head. "The pilot said that he couldn't hear the tower because there was a loud horn going off in the cockpit." I looked at Ron in disbelief and said, "That's scary, we got to share the same air with a dumb bastard like that." "Yeah," as we both got a good laugh out of it.

We flew P-51 support parts to our contractors in Chile, San Salvador, Guatemala, Honduras, and Dominican Republic. On the other half of the island that the Dominican Republic is on is Haiti, at that time run by a brutal dictator who called himself "Papa

Doc" Duvalier. Cavalier supplied P-51 fighters to Dominican Republic, which had been run now by the benevolent and elected Presidente Balageur. Air Caicos supplied the parts and brought general cargo home. By supplying P-51s to Dominican Republic, the country was able to maintain military control and thwart any attempts to cause trouble by Papa Doc, who only had a handful of T-6s, no match for the P-51. Even though piloting a transport of parts to a friendly island nation like Dominican Republic, my part was but a tiny pinch on the ass of the Duvalier family and a tiny help in the eventual overthrow of its brutal dictatorship.

Cavalier also supplied the air forces of Honduras and San Salvador with P-51s to guard their nations against Nicaragua, which was equipped with the formidable F-4U Corsairs. The 51 was a better fighter than the F4U and should have kept the balance of power with San Salvador and Honduras. Against the advice of his engineering staff, the head Generalissimo demanded that the P-51s be equipped with wingtip tanks to give them an extremely long range. This made the great P-51 an inferior fighter to the F4U, and the F4U Corsairs had a field day. One young pilot flying for Salvador, using extreme skill and bravery, shot down five Corsairs and became the leading ace of the war, albeit on the losing side. A few days after the conflict ended, a certain generalissimo, after a long, non-stop flight in an unmarked P-51 with tip tanks, landed safely in Texas and claimed asylum.

The airport at La Paz, Bolivia, sits at 12,000 feet and is the highest airport in the world. The DC-4M Northstar shines at La Paz: all four Merlins produce sea level performance, giving the Star perfect performance at this altitude. When the standard DC-4 would be grounded on a hot day, the Star would be flying. In 1973 the presidential palace was stormed by a revolutionary army and I understand that a squadron of P-51s were involved in the action, most certainly supplied by Cavalier. The end result was Bolivia's demise and retreat into the depths of a manmade hell. Thousands disappeared and many more murdered outright.

Bolivia was no paradise when we were active in that part of the world and even then was fraught with extreme poverty. It was a place that you were happy to leave in spite of the awe-inspiring beauty of the land itself. We had a mechanic with us that couldn't get used to the altitude and complained bitterly that he "couldn't get it up and even if I did when the moment came, poof powder." After regaining our composure, we forever more knew him as the "Powder Puff Kid." Even in a harsh depressing atmosphere we always managed to come away with a smile.

Dick was a wealthy gentleman and had a great record of flying hot aircraft. He was almost identical in stature to Jerry Tyler, weighing in at about 150 pounds, blond, well-kept hair, square jaw, and cleft in his chin to give him that movie-star look. Dick was looking for a fast personal transport to use on his many business trips. He was very qualified in both hot flying machines and skills of instrument flight. The nice thing about the 51 is that you could climb above most weather systems and make most of your flight in VFR conditions on top and also use the jet stream when eastbound and that gave you a 460 mph flying machine.

Dick had Cavalier build up a Cavalier P-51 for his own personal use. Dick's bird had everything you could possibly want in a fully-equipped IFR-certified flying machine. He used the aircraft for exactly what he wanted it for and used Cavalier as his maintenance base. It was always a great pleasure to see the amiable and friendly Dick when he came in for maintenance in his beloved Cavalier P-51.

About a year later we made another weekly trip to Caicos Island and had a layover for two days so I brought my diving equipment along. I dropped below the surface alone (you didn't read that, did you, NAUI and PADI divers. Hey, it's not my fault there were no divers to buddy up with in Caicos in those days) into the blue and crystal-clear waters of the sheltered lagoon at Caicos. As I descended to 50 feet, my maximum depth when forced to dive alone, I was soon diving with lots of huge barracuda and I mean *lots*. Everywhere I looked there were these six- to seven-foot long blue-striped, silver-bodied fish with big round staring eyes and mouthfuls of sharp teeth. It took a little while to relax, but, as usual, they were totally benign and I enjoyed a 1:15 dive with my not totally trustworthy friends.

I made another dive later that day to 30 feet on a beautiful and untouched reef and felt the familiar joy of living on a foreign planet for a couple of hours. Next day I hung out with Buddy and a couple of friends who rode down with us. We mostly played nickel poker under the swaying palms at the hotel (aw, don't get jealous, somebody has to do it). As we pre-flighted for our trip home, I ate a great lobster sandwich, and as we turned final for Runway 22 at Sarasota, I wasn't feeling too good. That night I was kept awake by the worst headache I have ever had before or since. Those damned lobster were getting even. As it turned out, though, the sawbones figured it wasn't the lobster but the mayonnaise they were prepared in. I felt fine in the morning and checked in at the office to find Jerry sitting at his desk with his head in his hands, obviously very upset.

"What's up, Jer?" "We just got news that Dick just went in." "Bad?" "Hit the ground vertical at compressibility." "Jesus," I whispered," what happened?" "Dug a 20-foot crater, not enough left to figure it out." Wow. Compressibility is around 550 mph. "Any witnesses?" "Yeah, several, and they all say the same thing." It seemed that the witnesses looked up when they heard an unearthly wailing howl and saw Dick's P-51 in a vertical dive at tremendous speed, then saw it impact the ground. ATC had Dick level at 27,000 feet and when they tried to contact him, they heard nothing back, and shortly after that Dick disappeared off the radar scopes. It was about a year later when the report from C.A.B. came back and pointed the finger at a failure in the oxygen equipment and oxygen starvation as the cause. We were all blown away by Dick tripping over the invisible feet of fate. Fate was going to play a big role at Air Caicos also.

In between flights with Air Caicos, I flew the SNJ every chance I could Jerry taught me aerobatics and close formation flying, usually hooked up with a P-51. Jerry's expert instruction and skill in WWII fighters was priceless and he handed it out to me as a friend. I will never forget him and use his teachings any time I fly an aerobatic flight, even today. One of the stunts Jerry taught me with the warning, "Never do this with anybody but me." We would hook up wingtip to wingtip and begin a gentle dive to indicated 170 mph and off the 51's right wingtip and my SNJ-4's left wingtip and Jerry instructing in the back cockpit of my SNJ-4 until I had the maneuver perfected. AT 170 indicated I would ease back on the stick and as the nose came up I would start a left roll so as to be perfectly inverted over the straight and level P-51, then continuing the roll to recover wingtip to wingtip, only this time my right tip to the 51's left wingtip.

The first few times were sloppy but with time I got it down to perfection and with Jerry in the 51 and me in the SNJ-4 spent many hours doing our aerial ballets with each other and getting into dogfights, rolling, diving, looping, and generally enjoying the wonders of flight to the max. Of course, Jerry in a 51 had the advantage and I was dead meat every time. Except once.

I caught Jerry screaming out of a cloud in a 30 percent pursuit curve doing at least 450 mph just before he was in firing range and position on my tail (or six o'clock). I snapped the SNJ over on her back and as the earth's horizon perfectly above and inverted I sucked back on the stick to vertical. As the windscreen filled with Florida's green countryside, I continued back pressure and began a recovery at about level and 215 indicated. I cranked in a vertical right turn and pulling heavy Gs, I pivoted and there in my windscreen was Jerry's 51 still in a vertical left turn and in perfect position for a kill. I keyed my mike "Tacka tacka tacka." I heard Jerry's voice crackling in my headset, "Good show, good show, Dave. Let's go on in, I owe you a beer." I tucked in on Jer's tail and we made a perfect in trail formation landing and as we hopped out of our cockpits, Jerry grasped my hand in a tight handshake and, grinning, said, "Nice piece of work." What a compliment from a real, live fighter ace, it is stored in my memory as one of many great flights I have had. We retired to the airport lounge and ran into Doc, who was already well into his shanty-gaffs, and friendship, booze, and jokes continued well into the evening.

Another memorable—though not so pleasant—flight occurred shortly after my victorious dogfight with Jerry. I strapped into the SNJ-4 with my always present parachute strapped on to me for an aerobatic flight we called "a visit to the psychiatrist couch." I primed, cracked the throttle, idle cutoff on the mixture, held the inertia starter switch up, and listened to the ascending whine of the flywheel. At the right pitch of the whining spinning wheel I engaged the starter switch. The prop came alive as the whine began its descending crescendo and *ca chug a de ca chu* the P&W 1340 belched white smoke and flame and began its galloping sound I still love so much. I let her breathe for a few seconds before going to full rich on the mixture. After warmup, I taxied to the active and lined up. I gave the old eagle the throttle and left the enslaving gravity of Earth, gear up, 30 inches and 2,000 rpm indicating 125 mph. We began our climb and right turn, crossing over the bay and shoreline to the blue waters of the Gulf of Mexico and leveling at 10,000 feet, still holding climb power and indicating 148 mph. I dropped the nose and at indicated 210 I sucked back and looking out at my left wingtip, watched the earth's horizon rotate gracefully to vertical, inverted, vertical, and level again in a perfect loop. My soul was filled to the brim with the great delight of the adventure of aerobatic flight as I watched the horizon rotate 360-degrees to the right as I performed a barrel roll to the left and followed another to the right, watching the earth's horizon reverse and gracefully rotate 360-degrees to the left. Back to straight and level, I pushed over into shallow dive and regained my 210 indicated. I came back on the stick to vertical, straight up flight and centered the stick going straight up. The old flyer ain't gonna last long before losing all airspeed and stalling. I checked my left wingtip to make sure we were vertical before kicking rudder in just before stall to perform a hammerhead turn. I hesitated too long and with no warning felt the old buzzard start a tailslide.

"Oh shit!" I hollered as the stick was ripped out of my hand and slammed forward against the stops. I hung on my shoulder straps as the out-of-control bird violently settled on her back and began an inverted flat spin. I rotated the stick and full left and right rudder, to no avail. The controls had no feel in my hands. Shit, this old pterodactyl has a mind of her own with no brain to give her any common sense, I was thinking as I desperately tried to regain control. We were coming out of the air at a pretty good clip. My mind was racing and trying every trick I knew as I was faced with the sobering thought of having to bail out. I figured I would carry it down to 2,500 feet, snap off a mayday call with position, and leave her with the worry that once I opened would the SNJ-4 come down on top of me in my parachute.

I had no time to be scared and the adrenaline was in afterburner. I distinctly remember hearing Jerry's calm voice in my head, "Dave, if you ever need power when pulling negative Gs, just reach down and wobble up fuel pressure with the hand pump." I reached down and pumped like hell and *roarr-rrr!* The engine caught and the sudden torque snapped the SNJ-4 just enough for a wing to grab air and snap her into a normal spin, full forward stick and right rudder. I hesitated long enough to gain airspeed so as not to secondary into another spin, I didn't have the room. I gently pulled her nose up and regained straight and level flight at 1,500 feet above the surface of the Gulf.

Shook up and heart racing, I headed back to the field and full stalled her on the numbers. I taxied in and shut down then just sat there, still strapped in for at least 15 minutes before I got out and walked shakily back to the flight office where I drank beaucoup cups of water. It took a couple of days to sort out what had just happened and to completely calm down and get back to normal. The Spirit was on my wing that day.

Bob Hoover was a client of Cavalier Aircraft. He was of average height, slender, had a kind face, and thinning hair that was usually covered by a Panama hat. If you didn't know Bob, he would probably come across as a schoolteacher. That is, until you read his resumé: Test pilot US Army Air Corps. Job: Test flew all captured enemy aircraft through the Korean War, all new American and enemy jets; Backup Pilot for Chuck Yaeger; Chief Test Pilot North American; several hundred types logged in Pilot Log Book; and, at the time, Airshow Demonstration Pilot, P-51 Shrike Commander, or just about anything you got that can fly.

When anybody tells me that they are an expert, I usually consider them for being an expert at foolishness. Not so with people of Bob Hoover's caliber, which are few and far between. Bob is an honest-to-goodness Real Live Expert. It was always a pleasure when Bob Hoover, first class demo pilot and true gentleman, would come around.

One day I was talking to Bob about my SNJ-4 and he told me, "Son, stay away from snap maneuvers in T-6s or SNJs. Even North American cannot tell you why this aircraft will rarely not recover from a spin or snap maneuver." The voice came from universal knowledge of flight and I never spun or snapped in an SNJ or T-6 again.

Fate was to play two more roles in the operations of Air Caicos. The first one was when the worldwide moratorium on the operation of supersonic fighters for Central and South America was lifted. The end result was that WWII fighter aircraft technology became obsolete almost overnight and the P-51 market dried up. As our southbound trips became fewer and fewer, Jerry and I could see the writing on the wall.

One day as I was sitting in Jerry's office, he said, "Dave, you ever think of starting an FBO operation?" An FBO—fixed base operation—deals with light aircraft and general aviation pilots, the majority of which are private pilot sport fliers. "Quite frankly, the thought really bores hell out of me," I replied. "You got any better ideas?" he asked. "Nope, what's your plan?" "Maybe we can go into a joint operation with Cavalier and lock up this field." "Let me think about it."

The more I thought about it, the more I began to like it. Jerry and I spent the next few weeks drawing up a business plan and a proposal to show to the principals at Cavalier. We brought our plan to the directors and it seemed at first that there was interest until one of the directors became very agitated and in a raised voice began accusing Jerry and me of being traitors and disloyal to Cavalier. I was speechless. Shit, it's just an idea, I thought to myself.

Next day Jerry called me and said, "I just go fired and I guess they don't need your services at Air Caicos either." "What the hell?" I asked in disbelief. "Screw them. We'll take it to the city and get our approval and do it anyway. To hell with Cavalier." "You got the money?" "I did pretty good with that DC-4 operation and as backup I know my dad would love to get involved. It's a sure thing, partner." "Great. When do we get started?" "Yesterday," was my answer. I was not overly thrilled with the prospect of starting and running an FBO, but when I found out that my trusted friend was in fact the one who was putting the pressure on the ungreased dowel he was trying to shove up our butts, it gave me reason to focus on the reverse maneuver.

Getting approval, although we both knew they couldn't refuse us, was a test of endurance and temper control. Dealing with the city "officials"—ha ha—took us a year, but we got it. When the news hit downtown, I swear I could see a bright glow and smoke coming from a certain office building downtown. So be it. Jerry, Dad, and I were in business. Buddy took the reins at Air Caicos and began hauling general cargo throughout the Caribbean and remained a good friend. I was very happy for him and wished him the best.

We named our new business Dolphin Aviation, Inc. and began construction straight away. Construction complete, we opened our doors and began the business of supporting the general aviation crowd and, as I had feared, I was bored to death. The flare for heavy transports and hot aircraft was forever entrenched in me. There was only one thing to do: continue my adventurous life. I had the money, and old fighters and biplanes were cheap in those days. So I started collecting.

We always had a radio on and tuned to the tower during our 24-hour operation. About 10:00 a.m. I heard Buddy in CF UXB, the only aircraft operating at Air Caicos, call in for landing instructions. Since CF UXB was my love at one time, I sat back and listened to the radio. "Tower, Uncle Xray Baker we got a problem." I sat up and listened intently. "Roger, UXB, what is the nature of your problem?" Ron radioed back. "Ah we have a left main landing gear that won't come down. We are going to fly out over the Gulf and see if we can get it down and locked. Stand by." "Roger, UXB, we will divert traffic to stay clear of you. Are you declaring an emergency, UXB?" "Not yet, but stand by."

This was serious. I grabbed my camera and made a dash for the ramp. As I got to the ramp I heard the powerful roar of the Merlins and snapped a shot as Buddy came over the runway in a low pass. Sure enough, the left main was up and locked. After a half-hour I heard, "UXB Sarasota Tower, we are declaring an emergency and are going to attempt a gear-up landing in the grass on the right side of Runway 32 past the intersection of 4-22." After giving fuel and cargo information to the tower, "Ah Uncle Xray Baker, you are cleared for a gear-up landing in the grass on the right side of Runway 32 past the intersection of 4-22. Fire trucks and ambulances are standing by and we all wish you best of luck and a safe landing." "Amen and good luck, Buddy and crew," I said out loud.

I watched as Buddy made a long final, all three landing gears up and locked. I noticed the entrance door had been jettisoned as Buddy made a perfect flat approach and just before touchdown I heard the unmistakable crackling noise of Merlins being shut down. Flown by a real expert, UXB barely skimmed the grass and gently settled on her belly in a perfect gear-up landing, trailing a line of dust as she gently came to a stop. The only damage was bent props and I gave a sigh of relief.

UXB never flew again after that and Air Caicos was through as an air freight company. It was a sad ending to a great idea. The funny part was the fact that she had a load of frozen lobsters and the wise FAA would not allow UXB to be jacked up to remove her cargo. They didn't show up for the inspection for two days and we got the last laugh as we watched the government inspector retching at the more-than-rotten odor emanating from this once-proud princess of the skies.

The last landing for CF UXB. What's this? No left main?

Final all up, CF UXB

Gorgeous gear-up landing of CF UXB

7

Ferrying Bipes, Bombers, and Fighters and Jumping Out of Perfectly Good Airplanes, 1968 to 1972

"American League 816, Houston clearance." I knew it was coming. They were sending us to the north, probably for reason of traffic. "Ah Houston, we are ready to copy, 816." "Roger, you are now cleared Baton Rouge Victor 70, Lafayette Victor 20, Lake Charles Victor 306, Daisetta Victor 306 to Navasota. Flight plan route, maintain one one thousand, squawk 0414." Chuck read back and returned to his radar watch. I was hand flying 816 in the dense grey of the interior of the front we were flying through.

I took a quick look at Nos. 1 and 2. No. 1 was slightly blurry in the dense clouds and the wingtip was almost out of sight. The scene looked serious—as it certainly is anytime you are on solid instruments. I quickly went back to my instrument scan and focused entirely on flying 816. Bill was concentrating on engine gauges and running a complete scan on the analyzer scope. I thought to myself, Bill is a hell of a flight engineer, and I felt secure with him as part of our crew. Bill was the second-most important man in the cockpit, even though he was the second officer below me as first officer. Nonetheless, he could save our asses in an emergency.

I heard Chuck's voice on the radio, "Houston, this is 816, we got a big cell at 12 o'clock. We need 30 degree left deviation." "Ah roger, 816, Houston. Turn left heading 232 degrees. Let me know if you need more." I made a slight left turn and steadied up on our new course of 232 degrees. Chuck said, "I think this will work fine, Dave," never looking up from his shield. I felt a series of jolts as we hit some mild turbulence from the cell we were now flying south of. Nothing major. "We are over Baton Rouge, Chuck, right on time at 08. We are still 242 knots." I heard Chuck make the position report to Houston, estimating Lafayette at :17 and turned 816 to our outbound course of 239 degrees to intercept victor 70.

"We are clear of that cell, Dave, and it looks like we should be out of the worst of it just past Lafayette." "Houston, 816, level one one thousand, squawking 0414 over Lafayette at :17, Lake Charles at :32, Daisetta next." "Ah roger, 816 flight plan route." I noticed a lighter cast to the clouds themselves and they become visible as they start tearing by our cockpit, in and out at close to 300 mph and *poof!* we were in bright sunshine. I reengaged our auto-pilot and clicked my ballpoint pen as we all started to relax.

I heard an audible, "Damnit," from Bill as he focused on our cowl flap controls again. The sunshine and smooth air felt good and, as we figured, our D.M.E. (distance measuring equipment) was indicating that we had picked up a headwind. I have always been able to concentrate on the demanding issues of flying an airplane and thinking of something completely unrelated at the same time. As we flew in the now sunny and smooth air, I started thinking of a very funny incident that happened at the Roosevelt Hotel in New York.

We were all in our uniforms and standing outside the entrance door, waiting for our ride to LaGuardia. A plump, middle-aged woman with a stern look on her face came brusquely walking up to me. In a demanding voice, she said, "Boy, take my luggage to the cab. I am in a hurry." I touched my cap with my finger, said, "Yes, m'am," picked up her luggage, and stowed it in the luggage compartment of the Checker cab. She looked at me and said, "Here you are, young man," and handed me two bucks. I wheeled around and, with a beaming face, held up my bucks, totally enjoying the reaction of laughter from all my cohorts.

I must have been grinning to myself because when I looked at Chuck, he had a slight grin and questioning look on his face. "Just thinking of my days as a bellhop at the Roosevelt in New York," I replied. Chuck put his hand up to his face and started laughing. We could hear Bill's snorting laugh echoing through the cockpit. He said, "Yeah, you earned your wages that day." We never let ourselves get too relaxed, but for short periods the cockpit can become a very funny place.

Outbound from Sarasota to Harlingen, Texas, for the annual airshow and convention of the Confederate Air Force. I was piloting a brand new 1968 Cessna 310—a good little airplane that is fast and economical. I still am not too keen on light modern aircraft, having heavy iron running through my blood, but I do enjoy being in the cockpit no matter what I am flying.

Dolphin Aviation was doing great with flight school, maintenance radio shop, and 24-hour line service. But I missed the excitement of flying serious iron. So when the opportunity to get typed in a Boeing B-17 presented itself, I was packed and on my way yesterday. Next morning, I checked out our new 310 and was splitting wind at 210 mph for Harlingen. Landing at the C.A.F. headquarters and taxiing in, I was awestruck by the WWII iron that was tied down on the ramp and in the hangars—P-51s, P-47s, P-38s, B-26s, T-6s, B-25s, A-20s, C-82s, A-26s, Me-109s, HE-111s, and on the ramp in front of me was "The Texas Raider," a gorgeous Boeing B-17G. I had a date with her and intended to become very familiar with her every quirk.

The B-17, a heavy bomber that ensured our victory over the Fuhrer's gang, has four Wright 1820s, developing 1,250 hp at takeoff for a total of 5,000 hp at maximum takeoff power. Max power came at 2,600 rpm and 45 inches manifold pressure at sea level. The military operated the 17 at 65,000 pounds; fully loaded she could carry an 8,000 pound bomb load. We operated her at a few thousand pounds below the military's weight. She was designed by a group of Boeing engineers who kept in mind that very inexperienced young pilots would be flying the 17 and so she was created with that in mind.

I recognized the thoughtfully simple design features of the cockpit as I strapped in. For instance, her throttle quadrant was like nothing I had flown before. She had four throttles, of course, but her Nos. 1 and 2 were two vertical levers that formed two right-angle handgrips, one below the other. Nos. 3 and 4 were the same, only the right-angle grips pointed to the left to mirror Nos. 1 and 2, which pointed to the right. The genius of this configuration was that the extra right-angle grips set below the actual throttles allowed the pilot operating the throttles for takeoff to merely put his hand around the lower two grips and start forward, which would bring all four throttles up to max power automatically. All manifold pressures were controlled by superchargers and waste gates on demand with throttle position and prop pitch. It was a thoughtful device that took that much more task loading off a 500-hour pilot in command mind.

The remainder of the cockpit was just as well thought out, with little simplifications that probably helped to save the lives of many young flight crews forced by war to fly a complicated aircraft way before they were experienced enough to do so. I can't imagine what it must have been like for those young flight crews. I have nothing but admiration for them all.

Engines started, checklists complete, I lined up on Runway 35 Left—an 8,300-foot runway at Harlingen, Texas. I placed my right palm on the lower grips and began to slowly push forward. Sure enough, all four throttles in perfect unison started to move forward. The low rumbling roar of four Wright 1820-97s began to fill the cockpit and as the roar and vibration increased in intensity, I reached the stops and check the tachometers. 2,600 rpm, manifold pressure 45 inches, airspeed 60 mph, and the tail was becoming light so I helped it out just a touch and we transitioned to the tail-up wheel position and gained airspeed smartly.

I was pleased with her almost complete rudder control practically from the beginning of the takeoff roll. V2 comes at 98 mph, and I gently eased back on the control column. As I heard and felt the rumble from our main wheels disappear, the magic began and this heavier-than-air, huge machine transformed herself into a giant silver, weightless and graceful flying machine. Yeah, I am a romantic and I don't intend to change.

I looked out at Nos. 1 and 2 and was thrilled at the sight I had seen in so much war footage of B-17s. Instead of looking back at the front of an engine, I was looking directly to my left at the soft, rounded shape of Nos. 1 and 2 cowls, the silver round hubs spinning, and the dark shadows of our three-bladed Ham Standard propellers betraying their otherwise invisibility, and in the background the fertile ground of Texas was drifting by as our airspeed built up.

"Gear up, METO power," I commanded. "Gear is in the well and locked, METO power established," came the reply a moment later. "Climb power, climb checklist," I commanded again. We were climbing out at 130 indicated and just about 1,000 feet a minute as we were light today. We climbed to 6,000 and leveled out. I felt for the step and our airspeed steadied up on 147 indicated about 175 mph true, 200 gallons an hour on fuel consumption. The control pressure and response were big airplane heavy and slow, as most all of the older types are.

We maneuvered, stalled, and engine outage for about an hour and started to head back for the field when all of a sudden I got an Me-109—actually a Spanish Casa-built 109 with a Merlin engine—peeling off in a steep climbing turn and right on his tail was a beautiful P-51D, hot after him. I felt I should have helmet, goggles, and oxygen mask on instead of my ball cap. The more than realistic play turned into a twisting, turning, mock dogfight between the two fighters and right in front of us. I was thrilled just watching from the inside of the cockpit of a real B-17.

Gear down, full flaps, and 98 indicated, just short of the threshold I chopped all four and felt the controls as I eased back on the control yoke and the old eagle set up for a smooth touchdown on all three—a gentle three-pointer. I found her gentle on the rudders and only had to lightly tap brakes as she lost wind effect on her big rudder. I was in love with my new mate, the Boeing B-17 flying fortress. No wonder inexperienced and young pilots still talk about the B-17's great flying qualities. We went back out for one more closed pattern flight, then taxied in and shut down for the day.

That night, after muchas cervezas and great flying talk, I was awarded my C.A.F. wings by none other than Madame Chiang herself. She gave a great talk and I was deeply impressed. One of the pilots—the one we all watched doing mock combat who was flying the P-51—had gone to town with friends for BBQ. I heard later that he had gotten a mild dose of food poisoning and had to report into the emergency room for treatment.

The next day we went out early and did closed pattern work in preparation for our VFR type rating rides. We came back and had a quick lunch and returned for our oral exams by our designee, Dick Disney. I had it down pat as we were queried on weights, speeds, engines, and specs. "Okay, you guys, let's go fly her," Dick said.

As we were preparing the pre-flight I watched the 109 and the P-51 make a formation takeoff. As the pair howled by us I really felt in the mood. They immediately started tangling tails in a climbing left turn. We watched, fascinated, as a second P-51 joined the fracas. The first P-51 was in a steep climbing left turn with the 109 on his tail, then the other 51 came out of nowhere made a perfect high-speed gun run on the 109. If it were war, it would have been another Hun bites the dust from the P-51's gun. But it was all show. I watched as the lead P-51 in a tight left turn climbed through about 1,500 feet and I thought, he is getting too slow for that tight a turn, and as I thought that, I saw him high-speed stall over the top, half-roll and then the 51 pointed her nose straight at the ground. I said in disbelief, "Shit, he hasn't got enough room!."

I heard the engine and wind noise increase in pitch and watched, feeling sick, as he closed with the ground and disappeared behind a row of trees. *Wumph!* and a ball of orange fire marbled in black smoke rose slowly from behind the row of trees. I've been here before and I still can't believe what I have just seen.

That ended the flying for the day and threw a wet blanket on the rest of our activities. I never did get my type ride and still wonder to this day how much the food poisoning of the night before counted for the tragedy we all witnessed that day.

Ready for type ride B-17 Texas Raider

Just after this picture was taken, Tom Kachinsky flew his P-51 straight into the ground

A rare P-63

As I was getting ready to leave, I watched an FM-2 Wildcat come in and land. Since it is one of my favorite Second World War fighters. I hung around to meet the pilot-owner.

The Wildcat, although inferior to the A6M Japanese Zero, used the tactic of hit-and-run and were able to hold off the Japanese Air Force until we could produce a fighter that could turn inside, outclimb, and outdive the little Zero. Grumman produced the F6F Hellcat that could do just that. At that point, the Japanese started losing the air war in the Pacific. Hit-and-run for the Wildcat was a matter of diving from altitude, pick your target, hit him, and keep right on going. The old Wildcat—as you nose the fighter toward the ground—would pick up airspeed pretty fast and then stop at about 270 knots indicated. This was just enough to continue the dive, level out, and still have enough speed to outdistance the Zero.

Then, Lt. Thatch and Butch O'Hare came up with an amazing sucker punch called the "Thatch Weave." One would be bait and sucker in an unsuspecting Jap fighter and then whoever was high would dive and trap the Jap in between the two. No matter which way he turned, dove, or climbed, he had one of the two F4F Wildcats on his tail.

Keith Mackey taxied his Wildcat in and the short stacks on the Wright R1820 radial give her a sound more like a horse galloping on a sheet of steel, making a delightfully raucous sound.

Keith climbed out of the Cat's cockpit, and we introduced ourselves. I found him to be a delightful guy with a great sense of humor. He was also a Captain for National Airlines.

"Keith, you got a fighter I would kill to own," I said to him. "How 'bout I sell it to you instead?" "No shit?" I asked, startled. "How much you want for her?" "Well, I just closed a deal on a P-51 and I need to get rid of the Cat. Oh, I 'spect $25K would do it."

I was stunned. Hell, this bird would be worth a half-mil someday. I was wrong. The last time I heard, 76Delta sold a few years ago for $800,000. "Let me make a phone call and I will get the cash," I said. Hell, I wasn't going to argue price. "I'll get the logs. She's real low time. You are gonna like it," he said.

And I did, with only 350 hours on the airframe and 80 hour majored 1820 for a horse. I couldn't be happier. By 10:00 a.m. I was the proud owner of one of the coolest fighters ever built.

"Hey, Jerry, jump on the line and fly out to Harlingen, Texas, and fly this piddly little 310 home so I can fly my new chariot home." Chuckling, Jerry said, "What in hell'd you do now, Dave?" "Just get your sorry ass out here. You're gonna love it."

I went through the manual and at 4:00 p.m., figuring I got P-51 time, I got SNJ time, I got PT-26 time, I got PT-17 time, so that's everything those young fighter jocks had so what the hell, I am going to fly this eagle.

I strapped into her very roomy cockpit and felt right at home. All the levers, switches, throttles, instruments, and gear levers were right where they were supposed to be. Did I say gear levers? Not quite. It was there alright, but it was a crank that took 31 full turns to raise the gear and 28 to lower the gear, all attached to a pair of bicycle chains that would raise and lower her short coupled landing gear.

My Grumman FM-2 Wildcat N2876D

I was a wee bit concerned about her short-coupled gear and figured her to be a bit squirrely on the ground. I shouldn't have worried—she was a delight and with her mid-wing she was no problem, even in a crosswind.

After a few bars of mechanical symphony at start, and a short warmup, I taxied out to the active, did my runup, and lined up on 35 Left. With heart rate high, I slowly fed in power and, unlike the low quiet rumbling roar of the B-17, the Cat's cockpit literally screamed with a mighty blasting roar. A little right rudder and she responded instantly and honestly and after a very short run, leapt off the ground and climbed out like a homesick angel. I unlocked the gear switch and began to crank. I am sure Keith and the other pilots got a charge out of my dance as I was cranking . The Cat responded in kind by mirroring my cranking. Just takes some getting used to.

Climbing steady at 150 knots and 1,700 feet per minute to the designated practice area—well away from any airways—I climbed through a hole in the thin overcast to bright sunshine on top. I leveled at 10,000 feet and found the step. She was very stable, an undesirable trait for a fighter. At 26 inches and 1,800 rpm the airspeed settled on 185 knots, or 212 mph. Remember, she was bred and born in the U.S. Navy. She trued at 220 knots, or 254 mph, and was burning 47 gallons per hour of green gas.

Fairly light on the controls, I gently pushed the stick forward and dropped the Cat's nose, and at 200 knots indicated gently pulled her nose up to just above the horizon and smoothly put the stick hard over left. As I watched the earth's horizon magically rotate 360-degrees to the right, she rolled perfectly to the left at a much slower roll rate than the P-51. I reversed the roll to the right and watch the horizon rotate gracefully to the left. I then dropped her nose and at indicated 220 knots, I gently came back and flew the little fighter straight up and over to the inverted and slammed the stick to the left in a perfect Immelmann, recovering back to straight and level flight. But not for long, as I reversed the roll to the right and stopped the roll in inverted flight with a little forward pressure on the stick. I was instantly hanging by all my weight on the harness and my feet tried to fall of the rudder pedals, but I had been there before, and I didn't let them. The Cat has an inverted fuel system so the Wright 1820 continued to run perfectly but I had to remember not to linger more than ten seconds as the oil system is gravity-fed and the engine would be starved of its lifeblood—oil.

I came back on the stick and pointed her nose vertically at the ground and held the Cat in a perfect power dive. I watched the brilliant white and flat cloud deck beginning to rush at me, still 3,000 feet below me. I watched as a perfectly round rainbow began to form, increasing in size as I perceived the effects of ground rush. Filling the center of the rainbow was the shadow of a nose on mid-wing—Wildcat growing in size by the second. I gently came left with the stick and the shadow imitated my movement by rotating inside the rainbow for a 360-degree continuous roll. As we merged, poof in, poof out, my windscreen was filled with Mother Earth once again, still 6,000 feet below me.

I glanced at my airspeed indicator and saw the needle pegged on 275 knots. She just simply would not go any faster. There is no red line speed 'cause the Cat will not reach her VNE (velocity never exceed) speed under any circumstances. Good ol' Grumman Iron Works. They really built a bulletproof fighter in the F4F Wildcat. I was amazed at how stiff the controls were at this speed and as I made a 5G pullout, I pushed hard on my stomach muscles and let out a loud holler to prevent high G blackout. I was slammed into my seat and my body weight increase to 1,000 pounds as I began to grey out, but I was young, and the scary effects went away as I eased out of the dive.

Still at 275 indicated, I eased the stick left and was shocked at how her roll rate had slowed down. Like flying in molasses. I realized why the Golden Rule is never get in a turning match with any Japanese fighters: you will get your butt shot out of the sky.

Turning final, gear down, flaps down, and trimmed nose high, I centered the runway and leveled out of the turn at 80 knots indicated. I always used the same indicated airspeed as I did in the SNJ-4. 100 downwind, 90 base, 80 final, and canopy opened on downwind. Over the threshold, back on the stick, and a feather-light full stall landing. I was in love again as I taxied in and shut down. I sat in the cockpit for a long time and soaked in the first flight in my new chariot, especially my three-dimensional encounter with the rainbow. A good omen, I thought, and one of those deeper-than-life experiences provided by the Spirit. The Cat truly was blessed, and was the most trouble-free aircraft I have ever been around. She even saved my butt one day by refusing to start, but that story comes later.

I retired to the watering trough with Keith and before long all of my pilot buddies' hands were performing loops and rolls until the wee hours of the morning.

Next day Jerry showed up and I was right. He was all smiles and repeated several times, "Yeah, I've always wanted to fly navy types." I figured I would have to handcuff him to the C-310 to keep my seat in the Wildcat.

The flight home to Sarasota went without a hitch. I had a call from Chuck and when I got him on the phone, he gave me the sad news that American League had called it quits. He asked me if I would fly co-pilot on DC-7B 813D to be delivered to Atlanta to a scrapper. "Of course I will. Man, that is really sad." "Yeah, it sure is," he returned. "How about you—what in hell are you going to do?" "No sweat. I got chief pilot position with Executive Airlines based in Boston." I should have known that Chuck would be all right. He wasn't one to whine or sit around.

We blasted off on Runway 22 at Sarasota and one-and-a-half hours later put 813D on the numbers at Atlanta for the beautiful DC-7B's last landing. We taxied over to the breakers yard and shut down. As we handed over the paperwork, I couldn't help but think of the gentleman receiving the paperwork as a cold-hearted killer and in my mind I already hated the sumbitch. That all changed as we finished a great steak lunch he bought for us, laughing the whole time thanks to his great sense of humor. Oh well, you really can't judge a book.

I noticed an F6F Hellcat tied down at the FBO and walked over to her. A tall, thin, middle-aged gentleman was working on the landing gear. After introductions, I found out he was a test pilot on the Lockheed Galaxy program and had just bought the Hellcat. He was excited to hear that I had just bought her baby sister, the Wildcat. He told me to bring the Cat up to Gainesville, Georgia, for a warbirds fly-in that would take place in three weeks.

"That sounds good to me," I said. My new friend said that he would love to fly the F4F and I said the same about the F6F—the deal was done. He then told me that he needed to get rid of a really good 12A that had belonged to an oil company in Oklahoma. "A 12A?" I asked. "Yeah, N99K, a Lockheed 12 with complete logs and low-time 985s." "Whadya want for it?" "Oh, I figure she's worth $12K." I tried not to choke on my words, "Les go have a look."

Later that same day, I ran into Chuck and he said, "I think I can get us a good price on a couple one-way tickets home." "Tell 'em they can shove their tickets. We are going to fly my new corporate L12A home." Chuck was all chuckles as he slammed me on the back and said, "Dave, yer too much."

Since I got my multi in a 12A, there was no need for a check out and after the paperwork and money wire transfer, Chuck and I strapped in and enjoyed the soft rumbling roar of her perfectly synced props. We split the wind at 185 mph and 43 gallons an hour with thoughts of Fred Noonan, Amelia Earhart, Paul Mantz, and how great the airplanes that came out of the 30s were. As we came down Victor 35 from cross city, I gave St. Pete approach a call. "Ah, St. Pete approach. This is Lockheed niner niner kilo, level 5,500 feet, 20 north V 35, squawking 1200 through the St. Pete area inbound Sarasota."

"Roger, niner niner kilo. Squawk 1100 and ident." "1100 here is the ident." "Roger, niner niner kilo radar contact 18 North Victor 35, maintain 5,500 feet to the VOR and then descend at your discretion." "Ah roger, niner kilo. Level 5,500, descend after St. Pete VOR." "Roger, niner kilo. What type Lockheed are you?"

Chuck looked at me with that wise guy grin that agreed with my next transmission 'cause he knew me.

"Ah roger, St. Pete, we are an Electra." Chuck broke into a wide smile and listened. "Ah, ah we got you at 165 knots, you got her slowed down for a reason?" We both knew that the controller thought we were the four-engine turbo prop Lockheed Electra Senior. Chuck looked at me, his eyes sparkling.

"Ah negative, St. Pete, we are running on two but there is no problem." Chuck broke up. A long pause and then as the controller keyed his mike we heard laughter in the background. "Yer one o' them 1938 Electra Juniors, aintcha?" "Affirmative." We all got a good laugh. Even today, I laugh about those great moments—free and friendly times we enjoyed that are all but nonexistent in these serious times we live in today. I miss those days deeply.

At that point I owned a 1931 Waco RNF, 1943 North American SNJ-4, 1942 Grumman FM2 fighter, and a 1938 Lockheed 12A, all bought at ridiculously low prices.

After landing, Chuck packed up and headed for Boston to begin his chief pilot job with Executive Airlines. I wished him the best of luck and felt genuinely happy for my best friend.

Back to the boredom of running an FBO but boredom and I don't get along well with each other and I vowed to continue my life of adventure regardless.

I can only think of two incidents that proved interesting during my stay at Dolphin Aviation.

One was when a student pilot on a long cross-country ran out of gas. Instead of deadsticking the 150 into a huge field that you could have landed a B747 in, she picked the river. Unhurt, but chagrinned, she said, "I thought it would be softer to land in the water!" The 150 was a total loss, but, what the hell, she didn't even get a scratch and we were all thankful for that.

The second incident was when one of our charter pilots, Bill, took our six-passenger Cessna 401 to Key West to pick up four people and bring them back to Sarasota. On climb out, one of the passengers stuck a pistol in Bill's face and hijacked the flight to Havana, Cuba. Bill said that when he landed and was told to shut down on the runway, he didn't know what to expect. They were quickly surrounded by machine gun-toting police and ordered out and to lay down on the hot asphalt of the runway until the police could figure out what was going on. When they figured out that the plane had been hijacked, bill and the three innocents were treated like royalty and given a nice air-conditioned office so that Bill could call Dolphin.

"Dave, you have a collect call from Bill and it's from Havana, Cuba," my secretary, Ellie, said with concern in her voice. "I know Bill can navigate better than that. Sumpin' must be up," I said, trying to inject a little humor into a serious situation. "Get Jerry in here," I added.

Bill gave us the scenario and I was given the direct phone number for the Minister of Aviation in Havana. I placed the call and a very pleasant voice answered. After the small talk, he put us all at ease, speaking to us with his perfect English with a slight Cuban accent. "Gentlemen, I think we have something here in Cuba you would like to have back." I was beginning to like this guy. "What is the procedure to get our aircraft back?" I inquired. "Oh, eet eez no problem. We require a landing fee, tie down, catering, and reimbursement for fuel." "Sounds okay for us, but we don't need catering or fuel." "My señores, eet eez a regulation. You must accept catering and fuel."

"Okay, how much will all this come to?" I asked. "Señores, we must charge you for catering for 100 passengers and 300 gallons of fuel and landing fee and tie-down based on the B727 because eet eez the smallest aircraft we have records for."

"You can see that this aircraft only seats six and only flew from Key West. It probably only burned 35 gallons at the most." "Oh, si, Señores, and my heart goes out for you but I can do nothing about eet eef you want your property to be returned."

I covered the mouthpiece with my hand and looked at Jerry. "We're getting hosed." Jerry shrugged his shoulders. "Okay, my amigo from Cuba. How much?" "Eet will be $2,500 American dollars and we can make the arrangements on the telephone. As soon as the money eez here, we weel release the aircraft and even geev eet a fighter escort to our defense zone."

"Sounds like a helluva deal, just one more question." "Go ahead, Señor." "You think President Castro would buy me a nice Cuban-cooked dinner someday?" I heard laughter on the other end. "Eet would be hees great pleasure, I assure you."

I thought, Well, if we are going to get hosed, it can't get any better than this. The Cubans were polite and friendly throughout the entire situation.

The hijacker was never heard from again.

Turning final on 22 at Gainesville, Georgia, canopy open, gear down, flaps down, I greased the Cat on and taxied up to the fly-in headquarters and shut down to a friendly welcome.

I had arrived at 10:00 a.m. and at about 2:00 p.m., Dub, the owner of the F6F Hellcat made arrangements for the two of us to give a close formation demonstration flight in our aircraft.

We took off and climbed to 6,000 feet in the practice area to test each other out. It soon became apparent that Dub was no beginner. I guess I passed test also and Dub radioed me and said, "76 Delta, form up. Let's give them a show." "Ah roger, you lead," I replied.

I closed up tight off his right wing in a perfect echelon right formation as we thundered across the threshold of No. 4 at 220 indicated and no more than 30-foot clearance between props and runway. I held formation and at the departure end, Dub pulled up and into a steep left climbing turn and I followed suit but loosened up by just a tad. I tightened up again for our second high-speed low pass. I thought, This has got to look really good.

We had agreed on the ground that we would make only two passes and then make an intrail formation landing so when Dub pulled up I counted three full seconds and began my pull up and it put me in perfect trail position behind Dub. "3, 2, 1, gear down," radioed Dub and I dropped my gear as he is dropping his also. We both slowed down at the same rate and held position perfectly on short final. "3, 2, 1, full flaps," and we both dropped full flaps at the same time. Pattern speeds for both aircraft were the same and our positions never changed. Dub touched down a little long, I touched down a tad short and taxied up to his right wing and we both taxied in in perfect formation and shut down in unison.

As the cockpit noise decreased to complete silence, I heard clapping and cheering from our small group of fellow aviators and their guests. Dub clasped my hand and threw his arm around me and asked, "Where in hell did you learn to fly formation like that?" I replied, "I had the best instructor in the world."

"Let's go and look over the Hellcat's flight manual and then go ahead and take her up." "I got the Wildcat's manual with me. You do the same." Shit hot, I thought. It was that way in those days, people were talented, honest, and rock solid in their word.

I gave Dub a cockpit check and then he took the Wildcat out and flew it like the expert he was. I had no worries about the outcome. The difference in cockpits were few, and as I strapped into the F6F's even roomier cockpit, I felt right at home. The galloping R-2800 was nowhere near the raucous gallop of the Wildcat's Wright 1820 and ground maneuvering was even better and much more positive. She also had hydraulic gear and flaps, easing pilot task loading dramatically. Runup complete, everything checked out and I lined up on two two and eased forward on the throttle. Her cockpit filled with the low rumbling roar of the P&W 2800 and she began to race down the runway at a faster pace than the wildcat and maintained perfect rudder control through liftoff.

Grumman Iron Works F6F Hellcat. I had an engine failure in this very plane my first time out.

I immediately understood why she replaced the Wildcat as a front line fighter as her climb rate was awesome and her flight control response was immediate. Climbing out at 170 knots she was maintaining close to 3,000 feet a minute. As I closed the canopy, I was surprised at how quiet she became and was at 9,000 feet in no time. I leveled off and went to cruise power, the airspeed indicator settled on 220 knots indicated and I came back on the power to long range cruise, settling on 185 knots indicated and the mule was drinking 83 gallons of green an hour. I ran the wheel and at 9,000 feet in low cruise, she was truing at 213 knots, or 236 mph.

I came back to high cruise and at 220 knots pulled the nose up and did a barrel roll to the left and was impressed by her P-51 fast roll rate. I started one to the right and as I got inverted I smelled smoke. I continued the roll, looked into my combat mirror and saw a long trail of white smoke. I instantly came back on the throttle to 11 inches manifold to take the pressure off of the engine. I distinctly heard Moe's voice as if he were sitting beside me. "Don't fuck it up, Davy." No kidding, I was in a big iron Grumman F6F WWII front line fighter for the first time and my reliable Pratt & Whitney R2800 2,000 hp engine just packed up and left town, leaving me out in the cold. At that point, I swear I heard wolves howling.

Out loud, I said, "Okay, focus. We gotta get this ostrich on the ground in one piece. Let's see, I am at 10,000-feet, field elevation 1,270 feet, figure 1,300, and that gives me 8,700 feet to go, and I am over the field. Best glide 100 knots indicated." I settled the aircraft on 100 knots and was pleasantly surprised to see she wasn't falling out of the sky but coming down at a steady 1,300 feet a minute. Of course, I was still throttled back to 11 inches and that helped a little.

Okay, 1,300 feet a minute down and I am coming to 9,500 feet. At 9,000 feet I will have six-and-a half minutes before I gotta flare. Think I will drop the gear now and go to 110 knots. It works. I got a little extra speed but my rate of sink still held at 1,300 feet a minute.

I thought, I will circle over the approach end of Runway 22 and make my last turn to final fairly close in and at 1,500 feet I can always slip her if need be. Spirit, don't let me hurt Dub's beautiful F6F. I made my final turn and rolled out right on final for 22 and 1,500 feet. "We're in a little close," I said as I fed in right rudder and left slight forward stick pressure and the Hellcat responded instantly, settling into a perfect forward slip, paying off altitude in a hurry.

"Not too much now," I said, and released pressure. "Gear down, canopy open, and no flaps," I reassured myself as I floated over the threshold and began my flare over the numbers for a great squeaker of a landing and just then the 2800 froze solid. Even wounded I loved the F6F Hellcat.

I watched a large group of people and cars racing towards me and surrounding the aircraft with the usual barrage of questions. We pulled the oil sump drain and, sure enough, the black oil in the bucket sparkled with cadmium silver flakes. "Main bearing," I said.

My little airshow impressed one person, as I was about to find out. She was young and attractive and completely out of her mind in the throes of lust, and she made no bones about it. I don't know whether it was the airplanes or our helmet and goggles but she was deep in her unreal world and, try as I might, I couldn't shake her. She kept appearing at different times of the evening's festivities and hinting with no shame and I was really getting sick of her.

I left early and as I was walking to my room, there she was. I was just about to tell her that I had other commitments elsewhere and my loyalties were with that commitment and wish her a good night. Just then, three men I had seen at the festivities came walking down the hall and didn't look very happy. I said nothing as one of the men took the woman by the arm, demanding that she go with him. One of the other guys looked at me accusingly and growled, "That's his wife." What in hell do you say? I know it looked bad, but, hey, buddy, I am innocent. "Good night, gentlemen," I said, and figured it would straighten itself out. I also thought that the guy ought to keep his wife on a leash. How to get your butt in trouble and just be an innocent bystander. Thanks, lady.

Next day I felt the frost coming from the husband and his little group and steered clear of them. Shit, I thought, I don't even know her name.

A rumor had started that I held the F6F inverted too long and starved the engine of oil, ruining the No. 14 main bearing. Hey, stupid, I did a barrel roll. There were no, I repeat no, negative Gs on the engine. I figured this whole dumb situation was getting out of hand and looked up Dub. I expressed my displeasure with the rumor-mongering and told him to find another R2800 and I would cover the price of it.

"Oh, no, Dave. I know it wasn't your fault," he said to me. "The offer still stands, Dub, and I am going to head south." It was two days before the end of the fly-in but I had a bad taste in my mouth for a few hard cases with big mouths, and made a promise to myself that I would never fly another man's airplane unless it had at least two seats and the owner came with me. I still feel that way today.

About two weeks later, Dub called me and said that he had located a good 2800 and asked me if my offer was still good. "Of course, Dub," I said. "I know that it was nothing to do with you and the bearing was ready to let go anyway but I need help buying this engine. They want $12,000. It is zero time and has complete logs. If you could cover me for half, I would be grateful." "I'll send you a check today." Dub signed off by telling me I was a man of my word.

A wet blanket was thrown, for my part, on the fly-in by this sleazy and embarrassing situation I had found myself in, but I had no guilt feelings about it. I have been embarrassed before and since and it was me that did it to me, but not that time. I guess nobody can get through life without stepping in it from time to time so to hell with them. The good news was that I got checked out in an F6F Hellcat.

I was sitting in the famous Hollywood stunt pilot's office of Frank Tallman and enjoying his engaging conversation with me about just anything and everything. He was such a personable guy that I felt we had been good friends for a long time even though I had just met him. Frank, tall and thin with one leg—he had lost the other pushing a go-cart for his young son—was the guy flying the twin Beech in the movie *It's a Mad, Mad, Mad, Mad World*. You might remember the scene where he flew it through a billboard. Of course, that is just one of many stunts that he and his partner, Paul Mantz—at the time recently killed flying a made-up contraption for the movie *Flight of the Phoenix*—had done for many major films in Hollywood.

I was at the Tallmantz Museum at Orange County Airport, California, to purchase N10564, a North American B-25 that was used in the movie *Catch 22* and called "Luscious Lucille." She was licensed and ready to go and I wrote a check to Paramount Studios—now don't start drooling again—for $4,500. That's right, four-thousand, five-hundred. You had a little cash in your pocket in those days, you could buy anything. Frank Appleby, a short, tough-looking guy with a personality to match, was chief pilot for Tallmantz, and was to be my instructor for the flight back to Sarasota. He knew his stuff when it came to about any aircraft built from 1903 to present, and that's no B.S. He test flew the 1903 Wright Flyer for Tallmantz for the Hollywood production about the Wright brothers. Of course, she was a perfect reproduction.

Now old Luscious Lucille was weather beaten and well used. She was the initial test ship that the US Forest Service used to prove the feasibility of using borate bombing to control wildfires. She was also used as a high altitude photo recon ship to supply spy photos of the sub bases at Vladivostok for the U.S. Army shortly after WWII. Because of her illustrious past, she now resides at the National Air and Space Museum at Silver Hill, Delaware.

The B-25 has always been one of my favorite medium bombers and I had always wanted to fly one. Well, now I owned one and was going to get type rated in this mean-looking beauty.

She looked pretty sad when I first saw her but her maintenance logs indicated that she was mechanically sound and pretty low times on engines anyway. I spent two days poring over her specs in her U.S. Army Air Corps flight training manual. She is known as a medium weight bomber at 19,976 pounds empty, with 980 gallons of fuel at 5,880 pounds, crew of two 360 pounds equaled 26,216 pounds and she could carry 9,831 pounds of bombs or extra fuel in a Tokyo tank to give her an all-up gross weight of 36,047 pounds. At economy cruise of 2,100 rpm and 30.5 inches of manifold pressure, she swallowed 150 gallons of green gas (100 octane) per hour and 220 mph or 190 knots for six hours and thirty minutes or 1,430 miles maximum. We always used economy cruise and, of course, never took her to max fuel range. Her Wright 2600-13 engines produced 3,400 horses at max takeoff power and since she was always flown light, she would become airborne at 110 mph indicated. It would have been a real problem if at max weight because V2 came 35 mph later at 145, but at the weights we flew her, no sweat. She would accelerate to 145 (V2) with no problem. She stood 15' 9" high, was 50 feet long, and had a wingspan of 67.7".

7-6: Luscious Lucille looked a little rough at first but we fixed that.

We entered Lucy from a little panel that would drop down just forward of the bombay doors with a built-in ladder for access. Stepping into her all-business, no frills cockpit, onto her lower top gunner's deck, and several steps later up a half-step was her cockpit flight deck. A tunnel to the left and before you stepped up to the flight deck led to the forward green house.

Strapping into the left pilot's seat in the fairly cramped cockpit, with Jim in the right seat, we began the pre-start checklist. The R2600 twin rows of cylinders need a lot of fuel from the electric primer, boost on high. Hearing the whine emanating from both boost pumps and primer pumps and looking back and under the cowl, I saw a stream of gas coming out from under the cowl. "You're wet!" hollered our ground personnel standing at ready with a wheeled fire extinguisher. "Turning No. 1 and clear!" I hollered back. "Clear!" came the reply. *Clunk* as the starter engaged the huge 1,700 horse R2600 and the three-bladed Ham Standard instantly began its slow rotation. I counted off ten blades and called, "Contact No. 1."

Jim went to the "Both" position on No. 1's magneto. *Chug chug* and the Ham Standard disappeared as a few cylinders came to life. Then, silence, except for a descending crescendo of whines as the big Wright gasped for breath, belching volumes of white smoke and then indistinguishable explosions as most of her 18 cylinders exploded into life. A ball of orange fire appeared, quickly blown away and followed by columns of streaming white smoke as the Ham Standard grabbed a handful of air, turning it instantly into a hurricane of wind behind her twirling blades and dissipating the smoke into a small cumulonimbus cloud behind the B-25's tail.

The 2600 settled into the typical, raucous Wright gallop, accentuated by the short stacks that increase the noise level substantially. It was music to my ears and I was in love with this eagle's voice.

Starting No. 2 produced the same show and symphony as her sister on the left side. We let both massive radial engines settle into their rhythms and warm up for ten minutes.

"Taxi check complete," said Jim. The B-25 has a non-steerable full castering nose wheel and very sensitive brakes that you must use tenderly to steer the bomber down the taxiway to try and keep this hoodlum in a straight line. Being new to the game, I would do what every new B-25 pilot does and tend to use too much braking left and right. As I hit one brake, she would dip her nose and her tail would bob up and down as she would jerk left and right. Everybody in the tower and on the ground were probably laughing their fool asses off as I was red-faced and desperately trying to take command of this wayward, mind-of-her-own, hippy flying contraption. My fears were confirmed as a voice from the Orange County tower crackled into my headset, "Ah what song are you dancing to, 564?" "Aw, shut up!" I replied and looked at Jim, who was grinning from ear to ear. Well, I showed 'em as I gave up positive control in favor of finesse and by the time we reached the runup pad I had the old buzzard reined in and under perfect control.

This was the first incident in a cross-country flight fraught with many more, and by the time I got my type rating, I was totally in love with this beautiful flying machine called a North American B-25.

I lined up on the runway and held position as I called for takeoff flaps, cowls open, fuel boost high, mixtures auto rich, bombay doors closed. I was also remembering that, like most radials, these Wrights did not have waste gates, so you must make sure to stop throttle advance right exactly at 44 inches of manifold pressure. Otherwise, especially at sea level, if you are not attentive you can overboost the manifold pressure limits and these 2600 don't have a sterling reputation to begin with.

"Ah, North American 564 you are cleared for takeoff. Wind 260 at 10 knots, make a left turn out after takeoff, speed and altitude permitting." "Roger, Orange County, 564 rolling. Left turn after takeoff."

There is always a moment of anticipation as you start forward on the throttles in a new and different cockpit, especially in a fire-breathing warrior like a B-25.

The cockpit noise went from the sharp staccato galloping of idle to a deep and increasingly louder roar as I slowly and evenly came up on the power. I nailed 44 inches and the roar became a deep-throated bellowing shriek as both Ham Standards hunted for max rpm of 2,600 giving the bellowing roar and added uneven pitch until both props evened out at max rpm.

Coming back on the yoke as instructed almost immediately and bringing the nose off the ground by just a few inches, the old eagle was alive and thundering down the runway at fighter-type acceleration. At 110 mph indicated, she left the ground as smoothly and cleanly as any aircraft I have ever flown.

"Gear up." "Coming up. Transition light is on." I looked back and under the No. 1 engine and watched the main wheel disappear into its well and the clamshell gear doors quickly close after the wheel disappeared, cleaning up the gaping hole that makes up the wheel well.

"Gear is up and locked, pressure is up 1,200 pounds," I heard Jim say over the intercom, our only source of communication as the cockpit noise level made it impossible to talk to each other in any other way.

I came back on the throttles to 42 inches and left the props up at 2,600 and established METO to ease the strain on our howling Wright 2600 engines as Lucy clawed the air and reached safe single engine speed of 145 mph or V2. I came further back to 38 inches and brought the props back to 2,400 rpm for climb power and settled on 150 indicated for climb.

"Cowls trail, flaps up, climb checklist." "Flaps coming up, cowls in trail," Jim repeated back. I felt her gently settle as takeoff flaps moved to full up position. I began our left turn and felt her controls not heavy, not light, but perfect for the finite control of this angel. I was also very impressed with her instant rudder control on takeoffs. Lucy was flirting with homesick angels as she settled on 1,800 feet a minute on the climb. What a sweet flyer she is. I watched thousands of specks and tiny straight lines—called houses and streets—going in varying directions and felt sorry for the poor slaves of gravity going about the job of apathy and boredom with no inkling of the powerful joy and freedom I was feeling as I looked down on their world slipping by beneath our powerful B-25 bomber.

"564, we are having an earthquake," I heard a startled voice in my headset from the tower. Apathy and boredom be damned, those folks are having a real natural adventure down there, I thought, as the Los Angeles Basin was rocked by a massive earthquake only minutes after we departed. Jim and I both stared at the ground but could see nothing out of the ordinary.

"Good luck, tower. Anything we can do?" I radioed. "Just pray for us and get the hell outta here. It's bad." I felt deeply for the people down below us and hoped for the best for all of them.

Our job was to fly Lucy to Tucson, but our minds would not let us stop thinking of the mayhem going on in L.A. Even though a wet blanket had been thrown on our flight, the scenery slipping below us was as usual awesome.

On the step and at low cruise of 30 inches and 2,100 rpm, the 25 was indicating 190 mph and truing at 207 mph and sipping 150 gallons an hour of green 100 octane fuel.

Turning final on 29 Right at Tucson International, gear down, full flaps, slowed to 125 indicated, trimmed nose high and crossing boundary at 110 indicated. I came gently back on the yoke and felt her all the way until 564 slid her feet onto the numbers 29R and I held her nose up for dynamic slowing. As the airspeed paid off, I used the last amount of it to gently squeak her nose wheel onto the pavement. Of course, I hit the brake too hard and Lucy began her burlesque-like bumps and grinds again. Oh well, there is always next time.

I got Jim packed up and on a flight back to L.A. with the promise he would call me as soon as he knew what was going on. "Don't worry about me, Jim, Tucson is an aviation town and all I care about is that everything is okay with everybody back home."

I checked into the motel on the field and later in the evening Jim called me and told me everything was a-okay with himself and everybody else, just a bit shook. We decided to continue in two days and planned for an early departure.

Strapped in and running the checklists, everything in the green, I pointed Lucy's nose down Runway 24L at Tucson International and came up on the power to 44 inches and 2,600 rpm. Lucy did her job and got everybody's attention as she thundered nose up slightly, down 24L, and gracefully lay waste to gravity in favor of weightless freedom.

"Gear up, METO power." "Gear is up and locked. Pressure 1,200 pounds." "Climb power, climb checklist." I listened and responded to each item on the climb check. We climbed out at 150 indicated and turning on course for our next stop at El Paso, 285 miles distant and one hour and twenty-five minutes flying time. We were making our flight across the country in short stages, not only for my training but to be able to visually check the old eagle out as she had been sitting in her nest for quite a while. Another reason for our short hops was for safety. We wanted to keep an eye out for any signs that would indicate trouble, such as loose oil line connections, hydraulic leaks, and for green fuel stains that should not be there.

We began a gentle right turn climbing off of Runway 24L and turning to 081 degrees for our course to the Cochise VOR on Victor 14 airway. I have always enjoyed flying over the desert and in the bright sunlight of this perfect day, this was no exception. I was enjoying the naked earth passing below us as I was immersed in my favorite melody—the deep and powerful roar of two massive and reliable Wright radial engines. Suddenly my earphones crackled to life as Jim said seriously, "Dave, we got massive amounts of white smoke pouring out of No. 2."

I looked over and Jim ain't kidding. White smoke poured out of the back end of the cowl and over and under the leading edge of the wing. "Fuckin' Wrights. Call Tucson and tell 'em we have a problem and are returning for No. 1 on Runway 24L." I retarded No. 2 to 11 inches manifold pressure to take the pressure off the engine. Deja vu—I think it's gotta be a main bearing again.

"Ah Tucson, 564 with a problem. We need priority for 24L." "564, we see it. You are cleared number one, any runway."

I made a 30 degree left banking turn to roll out on left downwind for Runway 24L, maintaining 145 on the airspeed. I told Jim to run the emergency checklist and that we will hold the gear until short final.

Turning final, Jim coached me to slow her to 120 indicated. This made sense. If we had to make a go-around, she would accelerate at our light weight to V2 or 145 mph with no problem. I saw no reason to shut down and feather No. 2 as it was still smoking but running smoothly. Now all I had to do was get the old vulture on the ground before she turned around and bit us.

"Gear down." "Gears coming down." I felt the gear *bump bump bump* as all three locked into the down position and the threshold was only about 300 yards in front of us. "Gear is down and locked. Three in the green."

At about 150 yards, I dropped full flaps and began to flare. I felt and heard the *erk erk* as the main wheel found the runway right on the big white painted number 24L. "Nice job, 564," called the tower. "Thanks, tower. That's enough excitement for one day. I guess we need to go to maintenance." "Ah, roger that, 564. Turn left next taxiway and there are several heavy maintenance shops to your right. Your choice."

We taxied up in front of an old WWII wooden hangar building that held several DC-4s sitting in front of it. Everybody was standing on the ramp enjoying the airshow we had just put on for them. As I got on the ground, I looked at the oil-streaked fuselage behind the right wing and at the sky where our flight path was still etched in the sky by a thin line of white smoke, painting an exact picture of our emergency approach against the deep blue Arizona sky.

A short, very thin gentleman approached us with his hand out and introduced himself as the owner of the maintenance shop. He invited us in for breakfast while his crew de-cowled Lucy and would give us an answer when we got back.

After breakfast, we returned to the maintenance hangar and were met by a short guy with black curly hair and the biggest nose I have ever seen on a human's face. "Howdy, name's Schnoz. I'm the AI." I could have guessed his name. Ol' Schnoz told me what I expected—that the No. 14 main bearing had let go, and as we were talking I noticed a black widow spider lowering itself out of the back end of the cowling. As it reached the ground, Schnoz put his foot up to crush the spider. "Hey, stop, Schnoz!" I told him. He gave me a puzzled look. I explained, "Any sumbitch that lives through that deserves to live, even if she is a freakin' spider." With a big grin on his gnarled face, Schnoz said, "Yeah, maybe yer right."

However, it was apparent that Spirit didn't agree as a drop of oil came out of the cowl and landed smack on top of the spider, killing it instantly. I kept the arachnid in a jar until years later it crumbled to dust.

"Well, what's next?" I asked Schnoz. "Take your pick. We got 16 zero-time 2600s, still in the can and papered." I paid $4,500 for Lucy. Dub's 2800 cost $12,000 and I was afraid to ask. "Oh, I figure $900 oughta be about good enough. We can have ya goin' in about two days." Trying not to reveal my joy at what I was hearing, I said, "Can I help?" He joked, "Yeah, you can bring us coffee when we ask." "I always wanted to be a gopher."

The next two days was prime time, what with Schnoz's great sense of humor and his happy crew. I didn't even get pissed when Schnoz and his jokesters coiled up a dead rattlesnake in the right seat of my rental car and then, with tears pouring out of their eyes from howling laughter, I made an emergency exit through the open window. I don't know whether Schnoz felt guilty about his joke but that night he and his crew took me to a local steak and beer joint and my money was no good. We ate steaks and drank beer and had a great time. I love this aviation business.

Lucy was all healed up and I paid the $1,550 bill and prepared for departure next morning. We figured we would make the next leg our test flight for our new No. 2 engine.

Leveling off at 7,500 feet and indicating 210 mph at a little higher power setting for the benefit of new valve seating in No. 2, I watched the naked beauty of the southwest desert slip by beneath the deep roar of our Wright cyclones turning at 2,400 rpm and pegged on 38 inches, giving us a true of 252 mph and gulping 185 gallons an hour. What the hell, gas was cheap in those days.

I looked off our left wing and to the north just visible was a long peak I recognized as Mount Taylor, New Mexico. The peak stands alone in a flat desert setting and rises up to 8,800 feet. Nevertheless, on a dark, moonless night in 1929, a Ford Trimotor slammed dead center into the small area of the uppermost portion of the peak, killing all eight people aboard. It was touted as the worst air disaster of its time. If the pilot had been 100 feet left or right of the peak, he would have come away with a fearful start, seeing the dark shadow of the peak passing eerily by his wing.

Our flight progressed with no other problems, and I felt comfortable with the healthy-sounding engines as we rounded the Black Range and lined up on final for El Paso International, Runway 22, a 12,000-foot runway that could accommodate anything you could throw at it.

Cleared to land, I crossed the boundary and greased 564 on the numbers. This time, ever so gently on the brakes, I brought the old girl to a gentle stop without demonstrating Lucy's dancing abilities. I was getting to know her and falling deeper in love. We taxied to Cutter and shut down.

Walking around my sweet flying chariot, Jim and I inspected her with a fine-toothed comb and found nothing amiss. As we were inspecting Lucy, a well-dressed man walked up and began talking to us. I figured he was a corporate pilot waiting for his people to show up. What the heck. We always gathered a crowd, wherever we were. He wanted to know where we came from, where we were going, what's in the bombay, and if we were IFR-equipped.

As we walked into the flight office, I thought his questions were kinda out of the ordinary and mentioned it to Jim. Jim smiled and said, "D.E.A." "Who in hell are they?" I asked, still being relatively innocent. "Drug Enforcement Agency. You watch, there will be a few more shortly. We will have a good time with them. Just keep your mouth shut."

Sure enough, two more well-dressed men showed up and the three of them hung around Lucy until we were ready to leave. They sure were obvious, I thought, nobody wears a suit and tie on a hot day like this. As we approached the 25, one of the D.E.A. guys walked up to us smiling and asked, "How long do you think it will take you guys to get to Lafayette?" trying to sound like just one of the guys. Jim put his hand on his chin and looked at the sky, deep in thought. Then he said, "Oh, I reckon two, maybe two-and-a-half hours." That seemed to satisfy them, and the guy said, "Well, you guys have a safe flight." "Yeah, okay, we'll see ya."

Climbing out of El Paso, temps in green, engines in sync and running strong, and all pressures where they should be, we leveled at 5,500 feet and took up a heading of 094 degrees. We got our airspeed settled on 190 indicated as we were going to make this leg at the economy cruise setting as part of the engine break-in procedure.

Me and my new love: Lucy

Forty-eight miles out of El Paso is a tiny town and navaid called Huspeth 115.0. It is in the middle of nowhere, so remote it's not even in the scope of radar coverage in those days. Jim said, "Let's do some air work and get you ready for your ride." "How about our new No. 2?" I asked. "We'll go easy on both engines and just simulate feathering at 12 inches manifold." "Sounds good to me."

We performed all of the procedures we would need to do with the FAA on board— single engine go-arounds, stalls, steep turns, demonstrate V1 to V2 acceleration on one engine, VMC on one engine, and manually extending and dropping the gear. You could pump the gear down with a long handle located on the floor behind the pilot's seat and one pilot had to get out of his seat and make sure to throw the locking pin device, also on the floor, just right or you couldn't lock the gear in place. You couldn't pump the gear up, only down. This wasn't real hard to do as the weight of the landing gears would help and the final lock position only took a little muscle.

The tough one was the manual flap control, located on the back bulkhead of the bombay and operated by one of the waist gunners. "Okay, waist gunner, I need full flaps," Jim said to me. Already a little winded from lowering the gear, I had to crawl over the bombay, drop down into the waist gunner's compartment and grab this big red painted crank handle and begin to rotate it until I could see the flaps fully extended. This was not easy to do and soon I was bathed in sweat.

After I got the flaps in the full down position, I crawled back over the bombay and flopped back into my pilot's seat, breathing hard and sweating. I looked at Jim, who was smiling. "If we had to land with that kind of a problem, I think we would make a no flap landing," he said to me. "Gee thanks, Jim," I said between breaths.

"Let's fly around out her for another 30 minutes," Jim said. I gave him a puzzled look and then broke into a wide grin as I realized what he was up to. "D.E.A.?" I questioned. He just smiled at me.

I watched the desert turn into fertile, green, flat land, and soon we were on final for Runway 22 Left at Lafayette. Turning off the active, we taxied to Noble Aircraft and shut down, leaving the bombay doors closed. We were one-and-a-half hours late on our arrival. Sure enough, there were three guys in suits and ties waiting for us and they were definitely not smiling. As we crawled down the crew ladder and stepped onto the tarmac the three men surrounded us.

"You guys are a little late," said one of them.

"Just a little," Jim said, nonchalantly.

"You mind if we look in the bombay?"

"Yeah, you got some ID?"

"Oh, no, we are just old airplane buffs and would like to see what it looks like," he lied.

"Oh," Jim said, "we are kinda busy. How about another time?"

They all pulled out their ID and badges at the same time, but Jim didn't stop. "You got probable cause?"

"You are one-and-a-half hours late. We could probably use that."

"Okay, okay, you got us." Jim crawled back up to the cockpit and as he opened the bombay doors, he hollered out, "Surprise!" The bombays opened fast and swirls of dust powdered the unsmiling, unfriendly agents in their crisp, clean suits.

They gave the bombay compartment the once over and then, without changing their expressions or saying anything, the three of them wheeled around and walked off in step with each other.

Jim said under his breath, "Sons o' bitches."

The drug trade was really just starting in those days and I suppose they were just doing their job and the B-25 was a prime dope hauler but we all still had a sense of real freedom and I suppose some of the anger was not only directed at the drug enforcement people but also at the low-life criminals that were giving us all a bad name.

Coming into Lafayette from Tucson, we flew over the southern Great Plains—an area that stretches from middle Texas to Louisiana and north to the Dakotas. It was the last area of the U.S. to be tamed. To the settlers from the east, it was a living hell with no trees and very little water. Inhabited by the fiercest tribe of warring Indians ever known in our history, the Comanche were not known for their humane treatment of the unlucky persons who, white or red, had the misfortune of being captured alive.

I experienced a blue norther—a swift-moving cold front—in the plains east of the

Rockies one winter, with winds of 90 to 100 mph and snow drifts 50 feet high, not to mention temperatures of 30 below zero. It was a totally unsurvivable situation without shelter. Little wonder the natural inhabitants were so tough, no wonder the settlers moving west were stopped cold in their tracks at the western edge of the east's lush forests for generations to come.

When I think about this area called the Great Plains, it makes me happy to be in the secure and cozy cockpit of an aircraft as I watch with fascination as this sparsely-populated area slips by beneath my wings. In this case, a B-25 Mitchell bomber in the southern portion, but nonetheless inhospitable, even today.

As we wing our way eastward to our next stop at Tallahassee, Florida, 485 miles at 190 knots and two-and-a-half hours on the flight plan. I watched as the Great Plains magically turned into verdant green, thick forest, almost on a straight line north and right at the 90th parallel, just west of New Orleans. I thought about our pioneers and what they must have thought when they first peered out through the forest at this endless and flat untreed grassland that stretched as far as they could see. I love these United States and feel privileged to have seen it all from the air. I thank the Spirit for throwing these adventures my way.

We dropped down to the Gulf Coast east of the old Mississippi and descended to 1,500 feet, really enjoying the scenery as we split the molecules at 220 mph on a heading for Tallahassee. Lucy, with her deep roaring voice, performed majestically in the smooth, clear morning air. We clicked off mile after mile of forest, rivers, towns, and white sand beaches, some with remnants of old Civil War forts still guarding the southern shores of the old South.

Erk erk the mains kissed the number 18 on the 6,076-foot north-south runway at Tallahassee, or, as we called it, "Tallahootchie." Later that afternoon, Jim took me out and completed my training for the type ride scheduled in St. Pete in two weeks. We even made a takeoff that the Doolittle Raiders had to perform to get the Mitchell off a carrier deck for the Tokyo raid. Lucy proved she could do it. Holding brakes and going to maximum power, I sucked the yoke into my belly and dropped full flaps. Straining to be set free, Lucy literally bolted out of the chute as I released the brakes and I had to come forward just a tad on the yoke to keep from banging the tail skid on the runway. Well below V.M.C., Lucy left the runway and after what seemed forever gained safe flying speed. You don't even think of engine problems during that critical time but Lucy broke ground in a record short roll of—I estimate—a mere 400 feet. Lucy was light and I can't even imagine doing that heavy as those hero aviators had to do off the pitching carrier deck on their way to give the Japs a heads up and a taste of their own medicine.

Jim signed me off for the ride and headed home that night. I checked into a motel for the night and called Jerry. I was signed off for the ride but could not act as PIC (pilot in command) so I needed a type-rated pilot to fly right seat and Jerry was the man.

"Hey, Jerry, how 'bout ridin' right seat on Lucy so as we can get her home?"
"Thought you'd never ask. I'll be there yesterday," was his response.

Getting ready to take Lucy home with Jerry Tyler

I always love Jerry's enthusiasm. He was not only an ace in P-51s but was in command of a B-25 squadron at the end of the war. He was a superb pilot in any kind of aircraft and I was chomping at the bit to gain some of his knowledge in the B-25.

As we walked toward Lucy, I noticed that an Air Force training squadron had showed up and the whole group was standing around Lucy, enjoying a real piece of history. We spent the next hour talking to these young heroes and it soon got around that Jerry was a bona fide P-51 fighter ace with eight confirmed kills and three probables. The admiration I saw in the eyes of these future Air Force pilots was awesome and Jerry was treated with hero status and deservedly so.

Pre-start check complete, we started Nos. 1 and 2. After start and according to the pre-taxi check, we closed the bombay doors. All of a sudden I saw a panicked group of Air Force guys waving their arms and jumping up and down, giving the cut signal. I immediately "stop cocked" both mixtures and shut down, thinking, Oh my god, we just killed somebody. A major standing under my window said, "You've got our commander in the bombay." I looked at Jerry's concerned face and hollered, "Clear the bombay," and opened the doors, fearing that half a body would drop out. But, as luck would have it, the Lt. Colonel just got the crap scared out of him and sheepishly clambered out of the bombay.

"Sorry, guys, I just wanted to see what was in the bombay and rode the doors up." "I bet you got a good look, eh, Colonel?" I didn't want to embarrass their leader in front of his men but I thought, You dumbbell, you coulda got killed.

So we restarted. No. 1 started her mechanical symphony with no problem. No. 2 moved about six inches and then the propeller just stopped. "Shit, what now?" I said in exasperation. "I think we just lost our starter motor," Jerry replied. "Guess we better de-cowl and have a look."

We pulled the accessory cowl and looked over the big starter motor, hoping it was just a solenoid but, on further inspection, it became obvious that the starter itself was fried. To make matters worse, there were four hidden bolts between 9 o'clock and 10 o'clock positions that were impossible to reach unless we loosened the engine from the mounts and pulled it forward about six inches so we could get a box end on them. At least, that is how it appeared.

"How in hell did we win the war with that kind of crap going on?" "Oh, they just pulled the engine, threw it away, and put in a new one, and were back in the air in no time," Jerry said nonchalantly.

"Wait here, I'll be back in a minute." "Where ya goin'?" "We are going to start her by hand." "What?" I asked in disbelief. "Just wait here."

I figured Jerry had a lot of expertise but I was thinking that maybe ol' Jer had been into the booze cabinet. I was thinking, How in hell could you ever hand prop a huge engine like this? Pretty soon Jerry came riding up in one of the line guys' pickups and jumps out with a long rope in his hands. "Here, wrap this end clockwise around the prop dome." So I climbed up the ladder and did as Jerry instructed.

"Now, crawl into the right seat and get No. 2 ready to start." I got ready and looked at Jerry, who had tied the other end to the bumper of the pickup. Hey, maybe this was going to work, I thought. Jerry gave the signal to the driver to pull forward. I watched as the big Ham Standard began to turn and I go "Both" on the mags. Instantly, the cockpit was reverberating with the sharp staccato of galloping explosions as No. 2 smoked her way into life.

Big smiles everywhere, and dozens of thumbs up all over the ramp as Jerry mounted the ladder and clambered into the cockpit. I relinquished the left seat to my learned and experienced friend Jerry Tyler and enjoyed watching him doing what he does best as he flew Lucy home to Sarasota.

After landing, I got the news from our chief lineman, Rick Fulwider, a young, good-looking guy with a bushel of unkempt red-brown hair sitting on top of his long, narrow face, that Executive Airlines had filed for bankruptcy. I immediately thought of my best friend, Chuck Meister, and felt real bad for him.

About two weeks later, I went into Jules' Pawn Shop, where I had been buying silver dollars and gold coins, not so much for a collection but because I figured gold and silver were going to do the same thing as old aircraft and that was to skyrocket in price, double bagger. I walked in and there was Chuck.

"Hey, Charlie-Q!" The minute he looked at me, I knew that things weren't right in the Garden of Eden. "Hey, Dave, I'm embarrassed that you ran into me here." "What's going on, Chuck?" Chuck, being brutally honest, replied, "I got laid off and I haven't been able to connect, so I'm broke." "What in hell have you got in your hand?"

Reluctantly, Chuck showed me his diamond wedding bands. "I got to, Dave. I got no money." "Like hell you do. You take those back to Martha 'cause you just connected. Yer workin' fer me starting right now."

Before his humble look turned to tears, I started right in. "I'm gettin' typed in a B-25 next week and as my chief pilot I need you to get typed along with me. I can't pay you a hell of a lot right now but, with luck, that will change. Here is a thousand bucks advance. Get your butt out to the field 'cause you got a lot of reading and flying to do."

The Spirit was at work that day and, as usual, threw another treasure right smack dab in the middle of my life's path. Chuck became my brother, much deeper than a best friend, and partner until his death in April of 2006.

Chuck and I showed up at the St. Pete G.A.D.O. for our check rides in Lucy to find the examiners almost in fisticuffs over who was going to give the ride in our B-25.

Lucy in all her glory

"What do you think, Chuck? You think we will have any problems with these guys?" "Could be we just smile nice." Yup, ol' Chuck was back to normal again as he conned the two flight examiners into believing that "the 2600 are fearfully dangerous engines and it would not be a very good thing to feather them on the actual ride." It worked. We both flew our rides without actually feathering either engine. Why beat hell out of your life support system if you don't have to. The FAA guys were not only excited but bent over backwards to accommodate us, very unusual for that agency.

We knew why we were getting the red carpet treatment: We had gotten a call from Col. Smith, co-commander of Patrick AFB, and he told us that General David Jones, the commander of Patrick, was retiring. Now General Jones was no ordinary general: he had been a young lieutenant in command of a B-25 on the Doolittle Raid on Tokyo, and this gave him status. Our conversation with the Colonel went like this.

"We understand that you have a B-25?"

"Yes, sir."

He then told us about the general's retirement. "Could you make a flyover the parade grounds on the 31st?"

"Absolutely, but the FAA guys are dragging their heels on our type ratings."

"Don't worry about a thing. You will be scheduled at 9:00 a.m. on Tuesday. Will that work?"

"We will be there with bells on."

That night I got a call from the head man at St. Pete G.A.D.O. "We have Dave Allyn and Chuck Meister scheduled for a type ride in a B-25 9:00 a.m. Tuesday." I couldn't resist, "You guys have a change of heart?" There was a pause and I could almost read his thoughts, Who the hell are these guys? "Just doing our job," came the reply.

Just doing their job, my ass, I thought, as we already knew that the headman at the FAA in Oklahoma City called our friend and didn't say, but ordered, "You make sure you take good care of Mr. Allyn and Mr. Meister. Is that clear?"

We didn't know it at the time, but we had the power of the U.S. Air Force behind us and our request for the type ride and we sure were not going to let the FAA know.

The ride went without a hitch and any future requests were met with "Yes, sir, whatever you need." Thanks, General Jones, your staff really went to town for you and our minor part in the retirement ceremonies of a great American hero. It was, and still is, a proud moment in both Chuck's and my lives. Glad to be of service.

"Patrick tower, this is North American B-25, November one zero five sixty-four circling left three-sixties. About one-half mile east of the restricted area. Standing by for instructions." "Roger five sixty-four. Radar contact one-half mile circling. Keep circling. We will call you for inbound pass over the parade grounds." "Five sixty-four standing by." "Roger, the general has no idea that you are coming." "Ah roger, we are honored to be here." "And five sixty-four, can you fudge it to 150 feet?" "No problem, we won't flat hat him. 150 is fine." "Roger five sixty-four. Understand, no flat-hatting."

We could hear laughter in the tower on that last transmission as we circled just east of the restricted line.

"Five sixty-four, roll out on a 090 degree heading and drop it on down to 150 feet. Cleared for the pass. Enter left downwind for Runway 21 Patrick. No other traffic cleared to land 21." "Ah roger Patrick. Cleared for the pass and left downwind 21, cleared to land." "Roger."

I called for climb power and started to roll out and nail 090 degrees. I started a gentle descent and leveled at 150 feet, airspeed indicating 230 mph. As we came up on the edge of the air base, I could see the parade ground and the stand where General Jones was standing in the center, flanked by his top brass. Box after box of his men were standing at attention on the parade ground.

Lucy scorched over them as I put the general dead center on the nose and Lucy whistled right over his head. Pulling up to 1,000 feet and turning left for the downwind, we slowed Lucy up and dropped the gear and flaps.

"Well done, five sixty-four. You wet our eyes." "Thank you, sir," I humbly responded. After landing, we were picked up by a follow-me jeep and he led us to a stop right in front of the reviewing stand. We shut down and crawled out and were immediately met with a firm handshake by the smiling General David Jones.

"Looks like a twin Beech entering the restricted area," said the general. (U.S.A.F.)

"Well I'll be a son-of-a-bitch!" (U.S.A.F.)

"Wow. You guys just don't know what a great moment you have given me today. Thank you from the bottom of my heart." Chuck and I felt a keenly happy sense of pride coursing through us as we spent the next 30 minutes listening to the general.

The Doolittle Raid on Tokyo has been one of my favorite subjects concerning WWII. I had read every book, seen the movie several times, and yes, even that stupid and untrue version in the latest movie. David Jones was mentioned several times in books and films and I couldn't believe I was standing in front of the same David Jones that I had read so much about. He related a story to us and through the fog of my memory I believe it was about him and his crew.

"We were walking down a road looking for the railroad line when a very old and thin Chinese gentleman approached us. One of our crew tried to make him understand what we were looking for by pantomime and his version of talk, using "choo choo, chop chop, woo woo" and all the time rotating his arms, trying to imitate the drive linkage on a train. The old Chinaman listened patiently, looked at our interpreter, and said in perfect Oxford English, "Oh, sir, I believe you are looking for the train."

General David Jones's retirement party just as he had completed his story. (U.S.A.F.)

We felt right at home. (U.S.A.F.)

Both Chuck and I enjoyed a marvelous lunch in honor of General Jones but because of some dull business I had to attend back at my anchor, Dolphin Aviation, we had to depart after we ate and couldn't stay the night when the real party commenced. I have always regretted having missed that part of the story about the great pilot and hero named General David Jones.

I was standing on a strut step with both hands on the wing strut 3,000 feet above the ground and outside of the Cessna 180. My jumpsuit was a blur in the 100 mph wind that was thrashing my body. I was waiting for the pat on my ass from jumpmaster Duffy Nathan that would indicate to me to kick my feet high and push away from the strut, spread my arms wide and thrust out my chest for my first parachute jump.

Ol' Duffy walked into my office. He was a stocky 5'10" man with a neck that blended right in with the widest part of his skull—as if he had no neck at all—and close-set blue eyes on either side of a good-sized nose. His mouth was friendly. He had a clear cut and cleft chin and a mop of dark brown hair falling on every point of the compass.

"Hey, Dave, hear ya wanna jump out of a perfectly good airplane. You fuckin' nuts?" "I doubt any crazier than you. The answer is yes." "Okay, I gotta give you ground school. Be down at the DZ (drop zone) Saturday morning and I'll get you going."

The DZ was a short grass strip located just outside of Venice, Florida, called Buchman Field and I arrived early that Saturday morning.

"How come ya wanna jump?" Duffy greeted me. "Has to do with the aircraft I'm flying but the real reason is that I have always wanted to." "That's as good a reason as any. Let's get to work. Yer gonna jump a T-10 and your reserve is a 24 Twil—a leg breakin' sumbitch if you have to use it."

We spent the next two hours practicing PLF (parachute landing falls), cut-aways, rules, parachute handling, and actual packing procedures. I wasn't really afraid because I really did want to know how to sky dive and use a parachute. My line chief, Rick Fulwider, an avid skydiver himself, set this all up for me.

I felt the slap and kicked out and away from the 180. I was suddenly alone in the air, the ground 3,000 feet below. I was amazed at the silence that had all of a sudden surrounded me. My body began to drop feet first as I felt the parachute start to lace off my back, activated by Duffy using a static line or "dope rope," as we used to call it. I watched as if by magic the ground rotate 90 degrees as my chute began to grab air and rotated me around to match its position according to my set of risers.

Bam! that quick I was dangling beneath a fully-opened canopy and looked at it, complying with the visual canopy check. All looked well. I began to relax and, supported by my seat harness, I was thrilled with the sight before my eyes and the silence I was experiencing. I looked between my feet at the ground, now 2,200 feet below. No camera can capture the three-dimensional effect of what it looks like from that perspective. I pulled first the left steering toggle then the right and the Erwin T-10 parachute responded immediately. You are basically coming straight down and at the mercy of the wind in that type of chute, with the rate of descent about 800 feet a minute. I was getting low now and was nowhere near the runway but over the trees south of the runway. Oh shit! But I somehow cleared the trees and did a perfect PLF (parachute landing fall) in the only open spot anywhere.

As I was gathering up my chute, several of the jumpers came bursting out of the brush. "Are ya okay?" "Hell, yes, man, that was more than cool," I said, excited.

Paul Polaro, a small, thin Italian guy from the Northeast coast with a wise guy face to match his wise guy personality and who was to become a close personal friend, said with a smile, "Aw shit, betcha pissed yer britches. I betcha ain't gonna do it again."

"Let's get packed and we will just see about that," I said. Paul slapped me on the back and said, "Good man." In short time I was standing on the step, my jumpsuit a blur while I waited for the slap and my second jump of the day.

I made five dope rope jumps and then Duffy took me up to 7,500 for a harness hold 30-second freefall to let me see the effects of a full terminal velocity freefall was like before I made my first 5-second delay unassisted.

We both went out the door of the 180, Duffy firmly grasping my shoulder harnesses. At first, we tumbled over each other and Duffy used superhuman strength to get me into the face-to-earth position as our rate of descent increased to 12,500 feet a minute. The wind screaming by my head was so loud that if I screamed at the top of my voice I would not be able to hear myself. I looked at the earth below me and had the impression that I was floating and not falling. I looked at Duffy's face distorted by the 125 mph wind blast. His cheeks gave me the impression of ocean waves marching up and down his face. Our jumpsuit sleeves were a blur as we roared earthward.

At 2,500 feet and 30 seconds in freefall, Duffy pushed me away and I put my left arm out in front of my head and came in with my right hand and grabbed the ripcord and pulled. A second later I was pulled upright, feet to the earth, as my T-10 strung out above me and then *bam*, I was stopped in midair 2,000 feet above the ground with a beautiful olive-green silk flower over my head. I enjoyed the peaceful quiet ride to the ground and landed in the middle of the grass runway.

Wow, was that a ride or what, as I raised my arms and hollered, "All right!" much to the joy of the other jumpers watching. I was hooked and I ordered my first chute: a gold P.C. (Para Commander) that was fully maneuverable and had a forward speed of 14mph. I had one of the first crossbow packs, a huge pack compared to the packs today, with a top-mounted reserve chute. The crossbow had an additional feature—a lead stop attached to the ripcord itself that would not allow you to lose the ripcord handle after you pulled. Great idea for us dummies that would let go of the handle after pulling.

Then somebody went in because of a horseshoe malfunction, always fatal. They found his pilot chute tangled on his ripcord. If the lead stop had not been there, the pilot chute would have carried the ripcord up harmlessly and the chute would have opened. Then it happened again and that's when I eliminated the lead stop from my crossbow system.

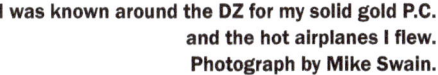

Hooking up with Gail at 11,000 feet over Zephyr Hills. Photograph by Mike Swain.

I was known around the DZ for my solid gold P.C. and the hot airplanes I flew. Photograph by Mike Swain.

Billy Revis was a crazy man but would have made an excellent test jumper for any parachute manufacturer. He would always show up at the DZ with some new type of design, sometimes he would be the first to jump it and lots of times the new-fangled chute would fail and Billy would have to go to his reserve. One day he showed up with what I believe was called a "Taradactyl," a triangular chute that had an astounding forward speed. To get this speed, there was also an astounding loss of stability. One day I watched Billy scudding through the air on a left downwind for his spot on the runway. He turned left base, and then final. As he leveled out on final at 200 feet his chute collapsed and Billy started to freefall. Oh shit, Billy has had it this time, I thought. At 50 feet, the chute reinflated and dumped Billy in a bramble bush on the side of the runway. We all ran over to him.

"You okay, Billy?" "Yeah, except for these bramble needles stuck in my ass." "What in hell happened?" I asked. "I dunno. That sumbitchen chute does that all the time." We had all see him at altitude doing what we thought was showing off by purposefully collapsing his chute and this was the first time we all realized that the damned chute was doing it on its own.

Billy also used to get close to the ground and undo his crotch straps and stand on his head, dropping to his feet at the last second before landing on his feet. He always got everybody's attention when he was in the air—a natural-born showoff. Billy told me one day he had always wanted to jump out of a real biplane, so we rolled out our 1942 Navy N3N-2, a beautiful WWII navy primary trainer.

Originally a seaplane, it had been converted to a conventional geared land trainer and was used as a naval primary trainer extensively. My N3N-2 had a 300 hp Lycoming radial that gave her a blistering 98 mph cruise, all the while gulping 15 gallons of 90 octane red gas per hour. Obviously, efficiency was not the name of the game in those days. But you haven't been to heaven yet if you haven't looped, rolled, done a Split S, or cavorted with fleecy Qs while flying an open cockpit biplane like the N3N. Well, Billy didn't really want to just jump out of the N3N, he wanted me to roll inverted and let him fall out of the front cockpit. There was plenty of clearance so I agreed to do that.

On jump run at 7,500 feet over the DZ, I pulled her nose up and rolled to inverted, popped the stick forward, and Billy departed the front cockpit. I kicked left rudder and sucked the stick back to the vertical and there off my right wingtip was Billy, both of us accelerating at the same rate and in perfect formation. Well, Billy wasn't going to lose the opportunity and reached out and grabbed the handhold on the wingtip and for about 3 seconds we were hooked up in freefall until I had to pull out of the dive and Billy went on to complete his 30-second delay. It was a hit on the ground and Billy and I did it several more times for the fun of it.

Mike Swain, skydiver extraordinaire and artist in the air with his camera, was another diver that I became close pals with. Mike had a speech problem in that he would stutter, not just a little but to the point of painful when asked a question. Being the extremely strong-willed guy that he still is, it never bothered him, and he would join in any conversation any time. Mike is a respected and well-liked guy wherever he goes.

One day a load was getting on board the jump plane. Mike was the last one to get on. There was an elderly couple standing there and the lady asked Mike what is was like to jump out of an airplane. Mike, being the gentleman he is, launched into this crescendo of "W-w-w-w-w-ell i-i-it's f-f-f-fu-fun." The lady, wide-eyed, put her hands up to her face as Mike got into the plane and said to her husband, "Oh honey, I hope that poor man doesn't have to count to three before he opens his parachute." Mike and I laughed a lot about that one.

Everybody on the DZ wanted to jump the N3N after I jumped Billy, and Mike was no exception. My only rule was that the jumper had to get out of the cockpit and walk to the trailing edge of the wing and exit from there.

Mike showed up with all his camera gear and loaded into the front cockpit. We climbed to 7,500 feet and he climbed out of the front cockpit and made his way back to my cockpit and, hanging on to my cockpit rim, he gave me signals using his free hand for number of degrees and his thumb to indicate left or right. Five left, two left, three right. I would correspond by kicking in left or right rudder to the degrees on the compass he wanted. When he pulled his finger across his throat, it meant cut the throttle and he would swan dive off the trailing edge of the wing. Mike gave me the cut signal and I cut the throttle. He grabbed my head with his hands, pulled me to his face, and kissed me right on the lips, then fell off backwards and snapped a picture of me just before I hollered, "You sumbitch!"

**Getting ready for Mike Swain's jump in the N3N.
Photograph by Mike Swain.**

**Mike in front, me in back.
Photograph by Mike Swain.**

Takeoff. Photograph by Mike Swain.

**Mike kisses me and snaps picture...
Photograph by Mike Swain.**

...and jumps. Photograph by Mike Swain.

One day Mike showed up at my office and excitedly worked his way through a conversation. It turned out that he had worked out a deal for us to fly to Grand Cayman Island and do the first sport skydiving and parachuting exhibition in the history of the Caribbean island.

"Who is coming?" I wanted to know. "Me, Duffy, our girlfriends, Rick, and you fly." "Fly my ass. I'll get Dale to fly the jump and I will do the flying there and back. But I wanna jump with you guys." "Shit hot," said Mike, grinning from ear to ear.

The day came and my skydiving crew showed up with all their gear, including 4 gallons of screwdrivers, and we load up on the Lockheed 12. I was almost afraid to do the weight and balance but we were right at the max for takeoff. The lovely old 12 bounded off the runway as if she were empty.

Getting ready to fly to Grand Cayman. Photograph by Mike Swain.

Over Cuba. Photograph by Mike Swain.

By the time we got to Key West, my skydivers had put a dent in the screwdrivers and were feeling no pain. "Ah Key West ground, this is Lockheed niner niner Kilo ready to taxi. DVFR flight plan to Grand Cayman Island via the Lejeune Corridor, Cuba." "Roger niner Kilo, Key West ground, we have no clearance over Cuba." "Okay, Key West, we will shut down and start making phone calls. Niner Kilo."

I called flight service and they told me that they filed it with Cuba and suggested I call their flight office and gave me the contact numbers. I could do one better—I still had the number for the director and head of Cuba's Aviation Administration.

I made the call and just as I got the director on the phone, Duffy hollered out, "Communist son of a bitch!" I shot Duffy, the teenage drunk, a look that should have knocked him down, but not Duffy. He just kept drinking as the others hustled him out of the room.

It was the same gentleman I had dealt with before and he was very accommodating, telling me, "Get started, and by the time you call the tower, your clearance eet weel be there." I thought, That was easy, almost too easy. Maybe he heard Duffy and they were going to shoot us out of the sky as soon as we entered Cuban airspace.

"C'mon, Duf, get your dumb ass in the airplane and let's get the flock outta here." We flew over Cuba via the specially set up Lejeune Corridor with no incidents and great control by Fidel's controllers. As we left the tropical shores of Cuba and took up a heading for the Grand Cayman Islands, I lost contact with Cuban ATC. "Niner niner Kilo, zees ees Luftflot 60. I weel be glad to rrrrelay forrr you," a deep Russian accent crackled in my headset.

"Luftflot, six zero that would be greatly appreciated." "Eez ourr plaesure, my frraynd." "Thanks again, have a great trip, Luftflot." "Und you alzo." That was a first. I would like to meet those fellow aviators from the other side of the Iron Curtain, I thought.

I dropped down to 1,500 feet, just the right altitude to skim through the very tops of the sea of scattered cotton ball Qs that stretched horizon to horizon and are always there in most tropical seas. We enjoyed the next 200 miles over the Caribbean Sea. The effect of skimming the tops of our little Q was a great speed show as we rushed at the top of our next cloud, it getting bigger and bigger with the effects of ground rush and then *whoosh*, we were in, and *whoosh*, we were out and set up for the next top, picking up speed and size, repeating the speed show over and over again as we progressed towards Georgetown at the Island of Grand Cayman.

At one point, one of the girls had to relieve herself so I picked up the relief tube in the cockpit and she unabashedly stuck her bare bottom between myself and Dale, another first, and proceeded to use it. When she was through, I took the relief tube and it was then that I found out that the exit end of the tube had come loose from its fitting and we had wee-wee all over the cockpit floor. Life's moments. Naturally, we spent our first hour at Georgetown washing and sanitizing the whole area that was affected.

Turning final at Georgetown and skimming in over the bright, crystal-clear, turquoise shallows at the approach end of the coral strip, we smoothly touched down and taxied to a waiting crowd, including the Governor General and his staff. "Don't worry about customs, gentlemen and ladies, we are all very excited that you are here. Come with us, if you please," said the Governor General himself. The people of Grand Cayman rolled out the red carpet for us and we couldn't do a thing. They took care of everything for us.

**Left base to final, Grand Cayman.
Photograph by Mike Swain.**

On the ground at Grand Cayman
(Rick Fulwider on right)
Photograph by Mike Swain..

Relaxing at Cayman.
Photograph by Mike Swain.

Molasses did this. Literally nothing
left of the ship.
Photograph by Mike Swain.

We spent the next day relaxing on the beach and later that afternoon we all made a great dive on the remains of a freighter that had been carrying molasses. Now if you don't think molasses is very explosive, you are wrong. As the story goes, sometime in the night a huge explosion shook the whole island and the freighter disappeared in a bright ball of fire and slipped beneath the calm clear waters of the Caribbean.

We donned our dive gear and dropped down to 60 feet and I was instantly taken aback by the carnage that lay before us. The pile of metal plates and twisted pipes resembled nothing you could even imagine as being a large freighter. It was literally a pile of junk that the initial explosion reduced this proud ship into in less than a second. No wonder nobody survived. It is now a habitat for myriad fish and coral and, in spite of her violent end, is now an intriguing underwater wonderland.

Next day, all suited up in our skydiving gear, the whole population crowded around us as we climbed aboard 99K, Dale Ziegler doing the flying, and took off for our first demo jump. I was elected to make a water landing in front of the spectators. As we climbed up to our jump altitude of 10,000 feet for a 60-second delay, everybody, as usual, had the pre-jump jitters and Mike Swain caught it all on film. Jump run, first Mike, who rolled over and snapped a spectacular shot of our red-suited sponsor, Bruce Harding, just after exit.

My turn. As I shoved away from the door and out, spreading my arms and beginning the fall feet down, I felt the air stiffen as I accelerated in the first 10 seconds to 12,500 feet a minute, or 125 mph. The wind was exploding around my body in a constant roar as I became stable and felt the euphoria of flight. The view below me was awesome, to say the least. The blue of the Caribbean and the turquoise of the shallows seemed six shades brighter in my adrenaline-heightened state.

I was screaming through tropical air when I heard a faint *tickety tickety tickety* on my helmet. Unbeknownst to me, it was my main ripcord that had become unhoused and was clicking against my helmet. I decided to pull high, at 2,500 feet, and that decision saved my life. A quick check of my wrist-mounted altimeter showed me passing through 3,000 feet and I brought my left arm over my head and my right hand in to grasp my ripcord. What the hell? There was no ripcord.

When you do extreme things like I have been known to do, your mind works in afterburner. I knew instantly that the ticking sound must be the ripcord handle floating over my right shoulder. No sweat. I pulled in my arms and bent slightly at the waist and *whoosh*, I was on my back, hoping that the ripcord would now be in front of me. Nope, no ripcord. I fooled around some more, trying to find the stealthy sumbitch, to no avail. At this point, I had lost track of time and when I looked at my altimeter, I was shocked to see the needle well in the red. Shit, I was low. I arched and *whoosh* I was face to the earth again, and what I saw was scary.

I was getting hefty ground rush on the ocean bottom that I could see easily through the clear water. I had no time to lose as I grasped the reserve handle and pulled. *Kabam!* I saw stars for a second or two. The reserve deployed but not before the skirt tangled the main ripcord handle and should have given me a fatal horseshoe malfunction but the Spirit is a skydiver too and ripped out two full panels of my reserve, releasing the main ripcord and also activating my main parachute. Now I had two parachutes over my head. I took a look at my altimeter and it said 500 feet. Phew, that was close. I had no time to lose. I would be splashing down in just a few seconds and I was way off target. I reached up and activated the right Capewell release and collapsed the main. Just as quickly, I activated my chest-mounted CO_2 life preserver. *Pop!* It hit me right in my face with a good wallop. The Spirit wasn't through with me yet and taught me a lesson I will never forget.

As soon as I got smacked in the face by my preserver, *splash*, I was underwater, but only for a few seconds before my reserve reinflated due to the wind. It jerked me to the surface, face-down. No matter what I tried, I could not get my face out of the water. Shit, I am going to drown. After all of that, I am going to drown. Close to panic as I couldn't hold my breath any longer, I heard a calm little voice telling me to pull either riser. With my last ounce of strength, I pulled the right riser and my chute rotated me 180 degrees. I had only once before tasted air that was so sweet. My chute pulled me into knee-deep water and I was able to collapse the reserve.

Just then, a native fishing boat came around the mangroves I had been drug up to and the two very concerned-looking natives broke into huge smiles and said, "Oh, mon, we taut you be daid." "Nope, I didn't make it this time. But I am shook." "Here, take a long trink dis rum. You be better." Well, I took a long, long "trink dis rum" and by the time we got back to the DZ at the dock, we were laughing and hugging like long lost brothers. A great cheer went up as everybody recognized me and my skydiving crew welcomed me back to life with a real shit-kicking party that lasted into the wee hours.

We left late the next day and landed at Key West to clear customs at 10:00 p.m. As the customs inspector was checking our baggage compartment and looking at our pile of reserve parachutes, he asked, "What's in these packs?" Well ol' Duffy, seven sheets to the wind as usual, replied, "Thash where we keep our pot." In unison, we exclaimed, "Oh, Duffy!"

After unpacking all the reserves and an intense inspection, we finally got out of there at 3:00 a.m. For several days I had an argument in my own mind and finally said, "Okay, Great Spirit, you are right. But I ain't gonna quit flying. Never."

First sport jump in history, Grand Cayman. Photograph by Mike Swain.

Lockheed 12, N99K, jump plane.
Photograph by Mike Swain.

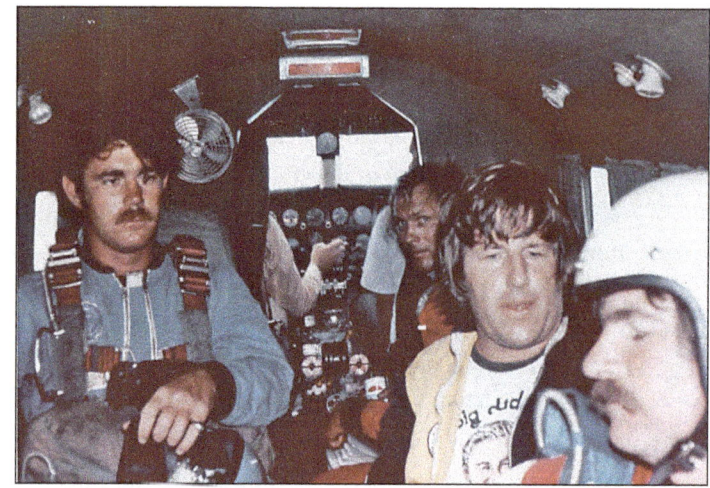

Pre-jump jitters, Duffy behind me, probably saying, "Don't worry, it's a good day to die."
Photograph by Mike Swain.

Second man out Bruce Harding, 10,000 feet, 60-second delay.

Back on the ground. Photograph by Mike Swain.

Shaken up, examining my ripped reserve. Photograph by Mike Swain.

8

Wings of Yesterday and Airshows, Barnstorming 1973 to 1982

Cockpit warmed by the bright sunshine, on auto-pilot, on course, all engine gauges and flight instruments steady and where they should be. The green plains drifting by below have started to thin out and show more tan than green as we leave West Texas and head over eastern New Mexico. You can almost see the border by the sudden change from green prairie to the different shades of tan as the desert takes command and lays naked the makings of Earth for all to see.

I love this kind of relaxed flying because it gives me time to do what I love best and that is to marvel at how Mother Earth has shaped herself through unimaginable force, pressuring up mountains, carving canyons, leaving towering mesas that are the remaining core of once mighty volcanic mountain ranges, now through incomprehensible time spans reduced to awesome, intriguing, vertical structures of basalt cores, scattered here and there all through the west. The arroyos and riverbeds snaking between these awesome cores give away nature's secret as to how she has, over time, used her primary tool—water—to shape the deceptively stable face of Earth as we see it today.

Looking through my cockpit window at this magnificent three-dimensional panorama, I can't think but how lucky I am to be where I am. The show, no matter where, always a fascinating one. You get to see the whole picture in detail at low altitude; medium, it is the actual layout of the land; and high, you see even more of the miracle and can take a VFR aeronautical chart and make total sense out of the different colored features laid down on a piece of paper.

I have never understood the uncomprehending mind of ground dwellers who say, "Oh, I don't like to fly in jets. They fly too high to see anything." Huh! Hey, people, you are looking at Mother Earth and she is talking to you, telling you her story. Oh well, I am glad she is talking to me. I am listening and deeply enjoying the show. My thoughts were rudely interrupted.

"Ah American League 816. Contact Albuquerque center on 127.6." "127.6. See ya," Chuck replied. "Ah Albuquerq, American League 816 is with you on 127.6. Level one one thousand, squawking 0414."

I had been wondering why we had been cleared, from the beginning, to an odd eastbound altitude of 11,000 feet rather than an even westbound altitude of either 10,000 or 12,000 feet. On rare occasions it had happened before and the Feds probably have their reasons. After all, the FAA has always operated in mysterious and strange ways.

"Ah 816, Albuquerque, climb to and maintain one four thousand, report level at one four thousand." "Roger, 816 out of one one thousand for one four thousand. Call you level."

"Shit, that's gonna give us a bit more headwind. Hell, we are above all the MEAs already," I said to Chuck. He agreed. "We will have to go to high blower climbing through 13,000," Chuck said.

The Wright 3350 turbo compound engine is equipped with a 2-stage blower system that will enable you to utilize sea level manifold pressures at high altitude and less dense air and will make the DC-7 perform at maximum peak performance with airspeeds reaching 360 mph and is the secret to making money flow in the high profit range for the airlines. Sounds great, but for one thing, we are not operating for max profit as we will still only use 62 percent power even in high blow and, secondly, shifting to high blow has been a source of potential problems for the mighty Wright 3350, so we always tried to stay out of high blow range. But the Feds were insisting.

Our procedure was simple. We would make a cruise power climb so as not to have to increase our rpms and at 13,000 feet we would pull back Nos. 1 and 4. Leaving Nos. 2 and 3 running at cruise would make the shift and return Nos. 1 and 4 to cruise, then pull back Nos. 2 and 3, make the shift to high blow and slowly return them to cruise. None of our passengers would ever know that we had done anything, much less know we had just climbed three thousand feet. Hey, we gotta win that game. No sense shaking up the mighty Chicago White Sox, right?

"Ah Albuquerq, 816 is level one four thousand." Sure enough, we now had a 22-knot headwind as we headed for the Salt Flats VOR in New Mexico. Over the past two hours and sixteen minutes, we had flown through Texas, New Mexico, and were now on Victor 202 heading for San Simon, Arizona, south and east of Tucson.

Our passengers, as usual, had been well fed with a five-star lunch catered on special flights by Dobbs House. We only carried stewards, no stewardesses, because of potential problems with the players. Billy Richer and Fred Ottenberg were our stewards on this flight. Billy, a tall, thin southerner with a family of eight kids, had a friendly attitude that everybody enjoyed being around. Fred, a short, wiry, dark-eyed guy with peppery dark hair, did a great job as steward but really excelled as an AI (aircraft inspector) mechanic who knew his maintenance procedures inside and out.

Ol' Fred used to just piss me off. He weighed 145 pounds, was in good shape, and could eat like a horse. Anything, anytime, day or night. On the other hand, I could walk by a bakery and breath hard and pick up five pounds. I hate people like Fred. Of course, ol' Fred would just taunt me with his shit-eating grin as he would launch into a triple-cheeseburger, washing it down with a super-size milkshake, while I was trying to enjoy a cup of black coffee. Sumbitch.

As we plowed the upper air molecules a little slower at now a groundspeed of 200 knots, I think about our dinner appointment at Mr. Autry's house and it wouldn't be long now. And, oh yeah, Fred, I am gonna eat and drink you under the table. That's a promise.

"Albuquerq center, 816 over Salt Flats VOR at :24, level one four thousand, squawking 0414, direct Deming at :03, San Simeon next." We had flown 1,600 miles and had been in the air for six hours and thirty minutes, and we still had 692 miles to go. That should put us on the approach to LAX in two hours and thirty-eight minutes. The flight would take us eight hours and fifty-five minutes and we would burn 4,200 gallons of purple high octane gas of our 5,800 gallon capacity, leaving us 1,600 gallons for reserve, or another three hours and fifty-two minutes of flying time if we needed it. Our DC-7 had only first class seating, so we could always fly with full fuel capacity any time we needed it because we were always light on the passenger loads.

"Eight sixteen Albuquerque center, you have traffic 12 o'clock five miles. A United DC-7B eastbound Victor 94 level at one three thousand." All three sets of eyes in our cockpit went on red alert as we focused intensely off our nose at the 12 o'clock position, looking for the other traffic closing on us at over 650 mph.

"Ah 816 negative contact looking." "I got him," I sang out as I saw just a dot that looked even with our altitude, although I knew he was 1,000 feet below us. "Contact Albuquerq, 816 has the United DC-7 in sight." "Roger, 816, maintain visual separation." I watched as the dot turned into a four-engine aircraft getting bigger by the second. As the DC-7 closed, the meaning and clarity of 650 mph became reality as the graceful four-engine airliner blistered by beneath our own DC-7 and I knew the United flight crew were probably seeing and thinking the same things we were.

1,000 feet just does not seem to be enough separation. It seemed too close at that speed. As jets began to dominate the air traffic system, the FAA increased separation altitudes to 2,000 feet and lately, because of so-called new technological advances, they have again lowered it back to 1,000 feet. At a closing rate in excess of 1,200 mph, I personally think the Feds are flirting with a major disaster.

Seeing the United DC-7 pass below us reminded me of a few years ago co-piloting the C-46 N355W across the Atlantic, listening to the conversation between a Sabena DC-7 and an Air Force 707 tanker.

Sabena: "How's the weather up there? We got pressurization problems and are slugging it out in the clouds."

USAF: "Oh, it's just beautiful and smooth, stars shining bright," really rubbing it in. "Oh, by the way, how's the turbulence down there?"

Sabena: "A little rough. And, oh, by the way, how is the pay up there?"

Dead silence.

I was grinning to myself as I pulled out my ballpoint pen and gave it four or five clicks.

I was standing in a field on a crop duster strip in Kennet, Missouri, on an overcast November day and looking at a big taildragger, high wing, eleven-seat, three-engine airliner from 1930, and a one of a kind. Chuck and I were looking at the only flying example of a Stinson S-6000 Model T Trimotor built as competition to the Ford 5-AT Trimotor and was used by lots of airlines throughout the 1930s.

The old buzzard was equipped with three Lycoming R680 300 hp radial engines that would pull her through the air at a mind-bending 98 mph in unheated comfort. She gulped 45 gallons of red 80 octane and had a four-and-a-half hour range.

This old girl first flew for Monarch Airlines, then Chicago and Southern, then American, and was then sold to a silver mining company that hauled supplies back and forth between their airstrip and the mine, carrying all sorts of equipment, including mules. On one trip, one of the mules freaked and almost kicked his way out of the side of ol' 153. The pilot had to make an emergency landing to save the old bird and the dumb mule. The silver mining company re-skinned 153 with aluminum and that's where she was when Chuck and I found her.

"Well, Joe, what do you think she's worth?" "Oh, I don't know, but I reckon, oh, I dunno, maybe, oh I jest don't know, I think, let me see here." Chuck and I watched as Joe started counting on his fingers, then put his chin between his forefinger and thumb and looked at the sky. Chuck and I exchanged glances. I broke the ice.

"Well, Joe, she is the only one left and no parts. I reckon you'll have a hell of a time finding anybody who will buy her. I'll give you $10,000 for her." "$15,000," Joe responded. "Split at $12,500," I countered. "Okay, done," Joe agreed.

I handed Joe a bundle of 100s and signed the paperwork. She was mine.

"How about a checkout?" I asked. "She only got a pilot seat. I ain't riding in that ol' bucket," Joe said with a gotcha grin, and then dove into his pickup and departed in a cloud of dust. "Damnit! I can handle her. She is just an airplane!" I hollered at the cloud of dust, and then looked at Chuck, who was about to collapse he was laughing so hard.

"Chuck, he thinks he has taken us." "Oh, no, Dave, believe me, we will get the last laugh," Chuck said to me with the confidence that I loved him for.

1931 Stinson "Model T"

Her cockpit with an instrument panel from a T-50

The Lycoming R680 300 hp engines gave her plenty of power

After strapping in and with no flight manual, Chuck and I, with all of our combined experience, had no problem figuring this ancient eagle out. The starter system was three foot-starter knobs like in 1930s period cars. I primed No. 2, the center engine, and depressed its floor-mounted starter knob with my foot. No. 2, being the only engine with a generator, started after a count of eight blades and No. 2 magneto snapped to both. A cloud of white smoke belched forth and I reveled in the galloping symphony only a Lyc 680 can play—a different tune than any other radial, but just as beautiful.

Chuck rode the unbelted right seat, actually a jury-rigged cushion seat top covering up the battery. I taxied her around the field and completed the runup and told Chuck, "Take the right front passenger seat and strap in so you can talk to me. You ready?" "Let her happen, cappen," he said with a smile.

I eased all three throttles forward and 153 stepped out smartly with absolutely no weirdness whatsoever. The cockpit filled with her deep-throated, throbbing voice and not really loud. We had no idea of what her V-speeds were so I held her on the ground until she felt solid, then gently came back on the large 360-degree wheel that is her yoke. The magic happened smoothly and gracefully as ol' 153 pooh-poohed gravity and lifted into the air. Since there is no overboost pressure on the 680, I held max power and settled on 85 mph for climb. As we climbed through 1,500 feet at an impressive 800 feet per minute climb, I pulled No. 1 (our left engine) throttle back to idle—you could not feather the prop—to see what would happen. Her climb rate slowed to 400 feet a minute and in perfect control she continued to climb.

"Chuck, mark down 85 indicated as V1 V2 (accelerate stop speed). I came back in with power on No. 1 and continued the climb to 3,000 feet. Her controls were fairly heavy but very positive. At 3,000 feet, I retarded No. 1 again and pulled the nose up until I had full right rudder and the nose began to start left. This came at 68 mph, so I said to Chuck, "Mark 68 indicated as VMC."

I pulled all three back and held the nose up. At 60 she shuddered and the gentle stall came at 56 mph indicated. "Stall 56 indicated." At cruise of 1,800 rpm and 21 inches and on the step the airspeed needle settled on 98 mph and her true, as ol' 153 split air at 104 mph and gulped 45 gph of red 80 octane gas.

I spotted Joe's pickup heading for Kennet, Missouri, and banked my ancient chariot hard over to the left and began a descending left turn to roll out and level at 50 feet and put his pickup bed between my legs as I dusted him off and pulled up in a 30 degree banking left turn. As I came around and put him on my left, I saw Joe standing beside his pickup, both hands clenched together over his head and a big smile on his face. "It's been a pleasure, Joe. Thanks for this great piece of history," I shouted out my open window, but I don't think he could hear me.

Completing my turn and climbing back to 3,000 feet, I turned to a heading for Memphis, Tennessee, where Chuck and I planned to do some takeoffs and landings before heading back to Sarasota.

"Ah Memphis approach, this is Stinson Trimotor 11153 two five north inbound international full stop." "Stinson 153, approach, make left turn 90 degrees for radar identification." We were equipped with only a communications radio, no nav and transponder. We didn't need it in those days. We made a left identification turn.

"153 radar contact. Turn right heading 125 degrees for vectors to the outer marker 18 Left." "Roger 153 to 125 on the heading, vectors to the outer marker 18 Left Memphis." "Ah roger 153, and did you say you are a Trimotor Stinson?" "That's affirmative. All three turnin' and burnin'." "Special request 153?" "Go ahead." "We got a Delta DC-7B that would like to take a look at you. The captain used to fly one. Would you mind if we had him do 360 turns one mile left of the marker so he and his passengers can watch that piece of history as you fly by?"

I was grinning from ear to ear and when I looked at Chuck, he was doing the same. "We are happy to do it, approach."

Sure enough, as we approached the marker, there was a DC-7B doing lazy 360s off our left wing. "And approach, 153 is at the marker and have the runway in sight." "Roger 153, contact Memphis tower on one one niner point three. And the captain of Delta says thanks, you made his day." "Same for us, approach. 153 is going to tower now."

We got that treatment almost everywhere we went. The ol' eagle was a great hit. We landed and taxied up to Memphis Aero, where we shut down and were handed another surprise. The line chief met us and told us that the boss wanted to see us. After introductions, he told us, "Welcome to Memphis. You guys have the whole airport in a delighted frenzy." "That's nice to hear," Chuck said with a quizzical look.

"What is your schedule?" "Well, we are planning to fuel and depart," I answered. "Would you guys mind spending the night, at our expense, and plan a departure at 9:00 a.m. tomorrow. The airport manager said that during our peak departure time in the morning they will make an announcement in the terminal and have some of the passengers on the observation deck to watch you take off. They are also going to have the departing airliners on the active taxiway lined up and have you taxi down the active for takeoff so the crews and passengers can watch."

I must have been standing there with my mouth hanging open in disbelief at what I was hearing. "Yessir, we can do that. I think the timing has to be right on so we don't delay anybody," I said. "Don't worry. We will take care of everything. Just call ground control at exactly 9:00 a.m. tomorrow, ready to taxi." "Okay."

They put us up at the Marriott, a first-class hotel, bought us dinner, and the airport manager and the head of the FBO joined us for a great evening of conversation and laughs. Before we hit the sack, I told Chuck, "You told me not to worry that we made a good deal and man, you are right again."

Next morning, we showed up early at 7:30 and pre-flighted and got everything ready for engine start at 8:45 to be ready to taxi at 9:00 a.m. sharp. The airport manager showed up and told us that all we had to do was call ground for taxi instructions and just follow them.

At 8:45 a.m. I called. "Memphis ground, this is Trimotor 11153 starting engines." "Good morning, 153, hold position and we will call you for taxi." "Trimotor 153, taxi to the approach end of 36 Left. We are going to have you taxi down the length of the runway and make a 180 on the numbers of 18 Right and do your runup in place. Call us when you are ready for takeoff."

As we taxied down the runway, I was amazed at the number of people all waving at us from the observation deck and even more amazing were the number of flag carriers nose-to-tail—almost all 737s—lined up on the taxiway with somebody waving to us from each cockpit.

We made our takeoff right on schedule and I held ol' 153 right on the deck until we were past everybody and then started a gentle climb out and a right downwind to pass everybody again while in the air.

"And 153, contact departure 124.65 and thanks for keeping our aviation history alive and well." "124.65 and thanks for the great southern hospitality." "Come back and see us, ya hear?"

I was deeply touched and for the first time felt we were doing something really worthwhile. I watched the pleasant green fields of Tennessee slowly slip by below as ol' 153 vibrated her way towards Thomasville, Georgia at a mind-bending speed of 104 mph. Trimming out the prop pitch on a Trimotor was a bit different. Coming back to 1,800 rpm on all three I first synchronized Nos. 1 and 3 and once they are synced, I brought back No. 2 to match 1 and 3 for a smooth roar that sounded so healthy to my ears.

We had no nav radio so we always flew 153 by dead reckoning and matching ground features to those on our sectional charts. I got real good at it. Flying and navigating in this manner is a real lesson in geography and one I am still proud of. After a few hours, we turned final to No. 4 at Thomasville, Georgia, and getting to know the old eagle better with each flight, I started greasing her on and that also puffs my immense ego. Hell, I was in love with an old lady.

Chuck and I decided to do our practice at Thomasville rather than the busy field at Memphis International. After a few T-and-Gs, Chuck, with his great flying skills and experience, found the bottom of the tires and the top of the runway and started greasing the old bird on as well.

We left Thomasville and flew the last leg home to Sarasota, where we put the old buzzard in her new nest amid much fanfare.

Oh, well, another great adventure and now back to the tedium the reality of running an FBO. Naturally, the office didn't see much of me as I had to tend to my flock of flying machines and, of course, my skydiving buddies answered the call of duty and just had to jump out of a Trimotor, not to mention the fact that she was a one-of-a-kind and the first group got into the record books as the first to jump out of a Stinson S-6000 Model T Trimotor in the world.

Of course, Chuck was right about us getting the last laugh. When the time came, we sold the Model T for $250,000 and I heard that she sold recently for a staggering $1.7M. I couldn't have had a better partner than good ol' Chuck.

Ellie came into my office in tears one morning.

"Ellie, what's wrong?" "It's Jerry." "What do you mean?" I asked, fearing the worst. Trying to regain control of herself, she answered, "He was in the doctor's office at Bethesda and had a massive heart attack. He survived but he is in intensive care."

I was devastated and felt my own heart beating wildly. Jerry survived the first big one but his flying days were over and he decided to retire and live out his last days with his good wife, Angela. Jerry was one of the best and an honest man and hot pilot. We stayed in touch until his death a few years later. His name is installed in the American Air Museum in England: Col. Gerald E. Tyler, 8 confirmed, 3 possibles. So long, hero fighter pilot. I am proud that you thought of me as your friend.

I went out to Wichita to bring home a brand new Cessna 414, a light pressurized twin, a good airplane that at altitude would give you an honest 250 mph cruise but was very short legged. She was tight on the fuel but was an excellent short-range fast transport, carrying up to six people. Even so, she was a light modern transport and though I enjoy any cockpit time in anything, she didn't have the heart and soul of the old fighters. Just before getting aboard the 414, I got tragic news that Doc Smith was found sitting in his chair with the TV tuned to the Flintstones. He had filed his final flight plan west while watching his favorite program on TV. The milk in his hand was not even spilled. Ol' doc stepped across the line painlessly—a good way for a good man to go. Another friend, and this time one of my best friends, had gone west.

Esther Smith, Doc's wife, told me that his North American A-36 divebomber was mine 'cause that's the way Doc wanted it to be. I thanked her from the bottom of my heart. I knew that Esther was left with only Doc's Social Security check for income, so told her that I couldn't accept it.

"I will do a business deal with you and give you $10,000 a year for ten years to buy the A-36." Esther remained my close friend for the rest of her life. Many years later, the value on the A-36 was in the seven-figure range.

I came down after a flight in Lucille to the news that my mother had had a major stroke while on vacation in Hawaii. She lingered for two years before going west. I always wonder if her mind was still okay but couldn't make her body work. I hope that is not the case as, being the good person she was, she certainly didn't deserve that.

During that year I lost three uncles, an aunt, and two young cousins. I refer to 1972 as the year of the reaper.

So far, I have had a life filled with glory and the Spirit was still there and wasn't through with me yet. This world, in spite of itself, is full of joy and adventure, but it will never bestow pure glory on any of us.

The airline industry was deregulated during this period and this opened the door for anybody to start an airline who wanted to. Bad move, as it also opened the door to many bankruptcies, including a number of major, long-time flag carriers—Eastern and Pan American, to name a couple.

My father owned an oil well survey company called Eastman Oil Well Survey Company. After my mother's death, he decided to sell and did so, splitting the profits between my sister and me. Thanks to his generosity, I could now do just about anything I wanted to.

Dad took his portion and, against my caution, bought out an airline that operated DC-3s and Fairchild F-27s in Georgia and Florida. Sure enough, there were some undeclared debts that cropped up after the deal was done. Even after the invaluable help from the Harris Trust Bank in Chicago, Dad fought the battle for five years but was unable to surmount the mountain of debt. Unfortunately, he joined the growing number of airlines in bankruptcy, taking his own fortune with it.

"Dad, let me refund the money from the survey company to you. I am going to sell out Dolphin and I will be okay." "I won't hear of it," he growled. "I still have Jungle Gardens and that will carry me through."

"Chuck, we got one hell of a collection of old aircraft. What say we go to the desert and put up an air museum to cover costs and sit tight on these old birds until they are worth a fortune and we can both clean up on them. You can be 49 percent partner with me." "Well, Dave, what about Dolphin?" "I just sold my shares and I am sitting pretty. How about it?" "You got a partner," Chuck said, pumping my hand and giving me his big smile.

For the next few months, Chuck and I haunted all the pawnshops in St. Pete, Tampa, and Sarasota and purchased a truckload of aviation memorabilia for next to nothing. One of the items, for which we paid $25.00, was a complete dining set, menu, and activity schedule that was on board the *Hindenburg*. That was just one of many priceless items we found. We also discovered three engineering and flying manuals from 1910, written and autographed by Wilbur and Orville Wright—price, five bucks each. The collector world was still in slumber in those days and we were wide-awake. Timing is everything.

Chuck and I put in long hours and hard work to make our move to Roswell, New Mexico, to store the aircraft and memorabilia until we could find a suitable place to build our museum—which turned out to be Santa Fe, New Mexico. Santa Fe was not my original choice as I had had conversations with an Ed Maloney who owned Planes of Fame in Chino, California. My ex loved Santa Fe and wouldn't hear of living in California at the time. She was one-hundred percent right about the crowded coast and the expensive living conditions in that part of the country, not to mention the idiotic leftist government who succeeded in turning the state of California from the land of milk and honey into the land of bankruptcy, serving sour milk and crystallized honey. I really don't know how it would have turned out had I gone in with Planes of Fame, but they are still going strong. So, Santa Fe was it.

The powers that be in Santa Fe were really great to us and welcomed us like brothers. Even though I was reluctant about Santa Fe, I have learned to love it here and find my neighboring locals to have a charm found nowhere else. Whatever the future held, I felt it would be okay in Santa Fe.

The day came to start moving aircraft with the first one being the Wildcat. I flipped fuel boost to high and listened to the high-pitched whine as the high pressure boost pump activated, pushing the primer switch up and feeding raw gas into the cylinders of the 1,250 horse Wright 1820.

"Clear, brakes, and contact," I hollered from the cockpit. "You're wet, clear!" hollered Chuck, standing fireguard. I felt the impact of the starter motor as it engaged and started counting prop blades as the big three-bladed Curtiss Electric propeller began to turn. At ten blades, I snapped the magneto switch to "both." The blades continued to go by my field of vision but no explosion of any cylinder and the prop continued to rotate. Sumpin' ain't right, as I let go of the starter switch.

"What the hell, Dave?" Chuck asked. "I dunno, Chuck. She won't start." "Hell, she was working great yesterday when you flew her." "Guess we better put our mechanics' hats on and try to figure out what's up with the old pterodactyl," I said.

We decowled ol' 2876 Delta and in a few minutes spotted a short stack that was missing, the hot gasses from the broken end were pouring directly on the titanium firewall and had burned a hole right in front of the high boost fuel pump.

"Holy shit, Chuck. If I had started her, I would have been a flamer right after takeoff." "Yeah, you sure would've, but that sure wouldn't have caused the engine to not start," Chuck answered with concern.

We repaired the damaged titanium firewall and replaced the exhaust stack and, as Chuck was saying, "Let's re-cowl and try again," I said, "What for? We still haven't figured why she won't start." "Okay, well, let's just give her a try, atmospherics or something." "Okay," I said reluctantly, "We will probably just have to de-cowl again."

I was convinced the problem had not been fixed yet as I crawled into 76 Delta's cockpit. I didn't even strap in or put my leather helmet and goggles on—I knew the problem was still there.

"You're wet." "Contact, brakes, and clear!" I shouted back.

Kathump! said the starter. *Row e row e row* said the prop, as she turned. I flipped the mags to both. *Cha chuk* said the engine, puking billows of white smoke and settling into a galloping symphony of a healthy 1820. I was astounded and as I looked at Chuck, he was too. I went ahead and shut her down and as it got quiet again, I said out loud, "Yer still there, aintcha Spirit?" "What's that?" asked Chuck. "Oh, nothin'. Let's call it a day and go drink a beer and think about this shit. I'll plan on an early morning takeoff," I replied, as I humbly uncoupled myself from my mighty chariot.

I flew the little fighter out to Roswell, New Mexico, and enjoyed every second of the flight. Everywhere I landed, I was received by the locals as an arriving hero and my oversized ego couldn't get enough. With my powerful, pretty eagle put to bed in our rented hangar at Roswell, I hopped a red-eye back to Sarasota for the next flight out.

The old Trimotor looked so beautiful in her new American Airlines period paint job of 1930. In the early morning sunshine she was sparkling like a jewel and looked to be raring to go. Chuck was flying with me and our flight was flawless right up to Hatch, just inside New Mexico, close to the Mexican border. I was violating all good sense and smoking this really delicious cigar. Chuck was checking our sectional chart as we soared slowly over the desert.

I was looking off and over our No. 1 engine at Mexico drifting by when I figured I would roll down my window and flip the cigar ash out and into the slipstream. As I did this, the ash came off the end of the cigar and went around the back of my head, sparks and all, and peppered Chuck's neck and head. Chuck reacted by throwing the chart up in the air and wildly beating the sparks off his head and neck. The chart, already opened, wrapped itself around my head and face, totally blinding me. I frantically pushed the chart off my face and it instantly departed out my open window and was gone in a flash, followed by my $5 cigar.

"Chuck, you okay? Shit, I am sorry. Man, you okay?" "Oh hell yeah, everybody oughta know what it's like to be on fire." Fortunately, he didn't really get burned and after we got control of ourselves from the waves of laughter, I vowed never to smoke again in any cockpit. Right up until Chuck went west, he and his great family and I would laugh ourselves silly over our adventures.

Next, Chuck flew the SNJ-4 N99DA and I took our lovely 1928 Stinson SM-8A out. I picked up N941W along the way as I collected antique aircraft. Eddie Stinson engineered and produced the SM8-A Detroiter in 1928 for use as an all-purpose aircraft.

That was an instant hit with the bush pilots in Alaska and South America. She was a rugged, big single-engine, four-place, highwing, fabric-covered aircraft, and was powered by one Lycoming R680 300 hp radial—the same engine that is on the Trimotor. The next page shows a picture of her in the left foreground, in our small museum building. She had heel brakes that took some getting used to. Light on the controls and indicating 98 mph and 15 gallons an hour, she is an honest good flying old eagle. The old bird will go into any field and haul a good load out with ease. The only fault I can think of is the fuel valve—either on or off—placed under and behind the lower end of the instrument panel. This configuration damn near cost me the aircraft one day.

The procedure when shutting down is to turn off the gas last thing, and I always did it that way. Taking off from Fort Meyers one day, fortunately with another experienced flyer in the right seat, I forgot to turn the gas valve to the "on" position. The engine would start even with the gas off because there was always some residual fuel left in the lines to not only start, but to taxi, runup, and get you 300 feet in the air, at which point an ear-shattering dead silence permeated the cockpit. The engine had quit cold from fuel starvation.

"Tom! Get under the panel and turn the fuckin' gas on!" I shouted as I headed for a crash landing in a very unfriendly-looking field. As I was beginning to flare and bracing for the worst, a wonderful roar shattered the silence as the R680 roared back to life at about 40 feet above the ground and pulled our dead asses out of the fire.

"Hey, Chuck, 941 Whiskey is grounded until that damn fuel valve is modified so it is visible in front of the panel," I told Chuck after we landed back in Sarasota. We modified it, and it is still in front and visible to this day. If I had been alone, I don't think I would have made it.

The flight out in 941W went without a hitch and so did Chuck's in the SNJ-4. Lucy was next and there was nothing I liked better than flying cross-country in a B-25. The engines are just behind your shoulder and you have this beautiful 180-degree panorama of scenery moving by below. When you crawl through the tunnel and into the forward greenhouse it is even better. I put a beanbag up there for any passengers to enjoy riding in the greenhouse when we were straight and level. I crawled up there and rode for a short time only once, as being PIC (pilot in command) I just didn't feel right being anywhere else than my duty station while the aircraft was in flight.

Our hangar at Wings of Yesterday, Santa Fe, New Mexico

The B-25 put in her nest, I headed for Santa Fe to check on the progress of our museum hangars being built. I also moved my family to a great house at the base of the Sangre de Cristo Mountains with a fabulous view to the west with Sandia Mountain to the south and the Jemez to the west, and a big valley in between. Things were coming together.

Things did come together. We got the hangars built, moved six truck loads of displays, flew all the airplanes from Roswell to Santa Fe, and had our grand opening in August of 1973. And what a party it was. We moved a full Coors truck into the hangar and all our new-found friends—basically the whole damn airport—and other friends from all over showed up. Before we opened the bar, we flew all the aircraft, making low passes, 360-degree overhead approach to landings, and Peter Gabriel, our museum staff jumper, made several jumps out of different aircraft. The airport was ours for the day and our pals in the tower had a field day. The day didn't go without a little excitement.

Bill Judd, chief pilot for the State of New Mexico, was there. He was a tall, thin, grey-haired gentleman who loved a good joke and had a great sense of humor to go along with it.

"Hey, Bill. You wanna fly co-pilot with me on Lucy for the opening pass?" "Shee-it yeah! Somebody's gotta do it!" he replied, almost tripping over himself with excitement. "Anybody wanna ride jump?" I hollered. "Shitch yeah!," hollered back a gravelly-voiced, medium height jokester named Frank Hoback, a banjo picker and pilot who loved old flying machines. We all strapped in and I guided Bill through the takeoff. We swung around and dusted off Runway 20 in front of the crowd at 250 mph indicated, then pulled up to 1,500 feet and got ready for a touch-and-go that Bill was going to make.

Perfect touch down, and Bill came in gently with the power and Lucy thundered back into the air again.

"Gear up, V2 145 indicated, and flaps up," I coached. Bill was doing an expert job of flying as I heard Frank's gravelly voice in my headset. "Hey, Dave, does No. 2 always smoke like that?" "Huh?" Bill and I looked out at our right engine and, sure enough, she was pouring out volumes of white smoke.

"Keep flying her, Bill. I am going to throttle back No. 2 back to 11 inches manifold," I said reassuringly, while saying to myself, "Shit! That's our good engine!"

"Bill, you're going to find out how to land a B-25 on only one engine." Bill, being the pro that he is, had no trouble and made a perfect landing. Deja vu all over again. It was our No. 14 bearing, just like the last time on our new replacement engine.

The excitement over, it just added more conversation to a great grand opening blast. About 2:30 a.m., the beer truck had to leave. "Everybody grab a bucket!" hollered Harry Oliver. Big and loveable Harry, with brown eyes that would double in size every time he would come up with some brilliant idea or be told a joke, belly hanging over his thin waist, and topped off with an unruly ball of reddish-brown hair, was first in line filling two buckets with beer from the tap as the driver courteously and slowly drove towards the gate. We managed to fill ten buckets before the truck got to the gate. When we emptied the ten buckets, our party was over. A great beginning to a great era in my life.

Pre-start checklist in Lucy, Bill Judd in right seat, me in left

People used to gather just to hear and watch those R2600s start up

Peter making a jump from the N3N before our grand opening crowd

Lucy on the takeoff roll for our grand opening

Inspection for Lucy, failed engine on the other side

We charged $3 each at the door, kids under twelve free. We flew flight demonstrations four times a day, using four different types of aircraft every day. We also did parachute jumps, usually out of the N3N bi-plane. We had a large display area with historical movies playing continuously and a static display of engines and propellers in both hangars.

Mike Swain came out and helped us put in a walk-around sound system and did a great job for us. Of course, ol' Mike couldn't leave without making a few demo jumps for the groups of people that were always there to watch our flying demos.

The nice things about our business was that we did not isolate ourselves from the crowd and would allow anyone to look—or even sit—in the cockpit and with the gyros still spinning down it would make quite an impression on the people. We also mingled and talked with everyone who came by.

One day I put Peter out of the N3N-2 and after he left the wing, I made a steep left turn and turned on the smoke to circle him as he descended in his parachute. As I came around to where I would usually see Peter a little below me, no Peter. I looked everywhere but still couldn't find him. My heart froze as I hesitantly looked at the ground, hoping not to see his crumpled body sprawled on the ground, probably right in front of the viewing stands. Relieved to see that was not the case, I looked up and there, about a thousand feet above me, was Peter spiraling away in a big, warm bubble of air called a thermal, climbing like a homesick angel.

I quickly turned on the smoke and pulled old 874's nose up and went to full power. As we went through 12,000 feet, I finally caught up with him. There was Peter hanging in his harness, doing a jig, and grinning from ear to ear. I gave him hand signals that I was going back to the land. Pulling the power but keeping the smoke on, I pulled old 874's nose up until she shuddered into a stall. Then, pulling the stick back into my belly and kicking full left rudder, the ol' eagle fell right into a spin.

In a spin, the aircraft is completely stalled and as long as you hold the stick all the way back the nose will stay pointed straight at the ground and the aircraft will spin around in vertical circles. From the pilot's standpoint, it doesn't seem like the aircraft is the one spinning but rather the surface of the earth you are looking at is what is spinning. The plane is literally falling out of the sky.

After a ten-turn spin and checking my altimeter to make sure my recovery was well above the traffic pattern, I released all pressure on the controls and the little bi-plane recovered instantly to straight down vertical flight. I held her nose pointed at the ground long enough to gain yellow-line airspeed to make her flying wires and cabane struts howl in the 140 mph blast of wind before gently pulling her nose back to level flight at pattern altitude right over the crowd in a 30-degree bank so they could look up and see the profile of our N3N and see me in the back cockpit and all the while hear the howling whistle of the wind through my flying wires supporting the top and bottom wings.

Leaving the power off so as not to interrupt the music of an ancient bi-plane in flight, I banked around in a 270 degree turn to line up on Runway 20 to grease a three-pointer on the runway right in front of the crowd. The people were waving and clapping as I taxied in and shut down, and after Peter landed, we all mingled with the crowd and let anybody sit in the cockpit, especially the kids. We usually spent up to two hours socializing after each flight and were rewarded by meeting lots of really great people and, on occasion, quite a few of our hero veterans who spent their youth fighting for their lives in these same cockpits. They pumped our hands, often with tears in their eyes, and launched into great flying stories.

A typical demo flight would go like this:

Chuck or I would be introduced to the spectators with a brief history of our flying careers, emphasizing our time flying American League ball teams around, then a history of the aircraft they were about to see fly. If I was flying, I would make a show of strapping into my parachute, adjusting my helmet and goggles, and doing the pre-flight. I would then climb into the cockpit and, with the help of the ground crew, strap in. I always had a cigar clamped in my jaws and the last thing I would do was to hand it to my helper and in a loud voice say, "Keep this going 'til I get back, will ya?" I always got a laugh out of the crowd with that one.

Start the engine and let her run at idle for a while to let her mechanical symphony please the crowd—and it always did—taxi out, and take off. No matter what the winds were, we always used Runway 20 so as to be in front of the people on takeoffs and landings. I really got good at crosswinds and downwind operations. I would then circle the field, building up airspeed and turn final at 1,200 feet and into a gentle dive to build my airspeed up to 250 mph indicated and make a very low high-speed pass down 20 and in front of the people watching. The old Cat would whistle by and as I passed by, they would be treated to the rumbling sound of a working Wright 1820. I would then pull up and make a climbing 180-degree turn to overfly the crowd at 1,200 feet and bend the old warbird over in a steep 360 overhead approach, cut the power. The crowd could see the Cat in profile against the sky as the landing gear was coming back down, then make a three-pointer on 20 in front of the crowd.

The end result was always the same after every flight and was the second-best part of the flight.

The Wright 1820s were a crowd pleaser

A 300 mph low pass in front of the crowd

Post-flight socializing was part of the show

After only a month of operations, it was clear that Wings of Yesterday was paying all of the bills and doing what we had hoped for. We weren't making money but were breaking even and summer was still coming.

We flew to airshows for gas and lodging and did a lot of this kind of work. We got a call from Delta asking if we would come to Atlanta, Georgia, with the Trimotor for their fiftieth anniversary. They also told us that American wanted us to make an appearance in Dallas as both airlines had owned 11153 in the 30s. The best part of the deal was that they were going to pay us, with a nice profit included.

David Ames, a tall, thin Virginian with thin blond hair, a smooth southern accent, and a face that resembled Glen Campbell, was sitting in the fathers' waiting room, waiting for his son Matthew to be born. I was there waiting for my daughter Heidi to be born. They were both born within minutes of each other—Heidi at 11:58 p.m. July 6 and Matthew at 12:10 a.m. July 7, 1965—under the eye of Hurricane Alma.

I think that hurricane gave Heidi the freedom to do what she wants in life. She has a happy and friendly demeanor and a sense of humor that has kept me laughing and giggling all her life. Gee, I wonder where she got that from? I think she gets a kick out of having a broad-minded old man that flies off-the-wall airplanes. I also encouraged her deep love for animals, and not just dogs and cats. She has a job training lions, tigers, panthers, wolves, and chimpanzees, and is presently working with a grizzly bear. All of the animals are rescues and Heidi is instrumental in giving these creatures a happy and full life while in captivity.

Heidi with her pussy cat (I call it a tiger)

Another of Heidi's friends

I like to think it all happened as I was taxiing DC-4 CF-UXB in from a trip to the Caribbean. When on the ground I heard Ron Bilib's voice charge into my headset," Ah UXB, ground, hold short on the taxiway for crossing tortoise." I looked at Buddy, "What 'n hell did he say?"

"I think he said hold short for crossing tortoise," Buddy replied. I looked out in front of our now stopped DC-4M and, sure enough, crossing *clumpety clump* in front of us was a huge 30-pound Florida gopher tortoise. Head out and totally focused on what his tiny brain was thinking, he crossed in excruciating tortoise slow motion. After our laughter subsided and ol' Tuffy was safely across, we taxied in and shut down.

I walked across the tarmac and out to the taxiway and gathered up Tuffy, loaded him in the car, and brought him home to my very delighted daughter Heidi. I looked out the living room window into our backyard and there was three-year-old

My favorite picture of Heidi

Heidi, dressed in her winter fur coat and a fuzzy bunny rabbit hat, with both her hands on Tuffy's back sides of his carapace, pushing and saying, "Go turtoo, go turtoo." Tuffy was having nothing to do with it. Both front claws dug in, head pulled in as far as it would go, and both of his hind elephant-type feet dug in at a 45 degree forward angle, making him totally immovable despite Heidi's efforts.

I like to think that was the spark to Heidi's insatiable love for all animals. In any case, it is one of many incidents that rest in the warmest part of my heart.

Life ain't all glory hole and Heidi survived my marriage break up in Santa Fe but was left with anger for her mother.

David Ames, with his friendly personality and great love of good jokes, became a member of my family of best friends. Although not a pilot, he has accompanied me on many of my flying adventures. At the time, I also had a seagoing 28-foot sloop sailboat. I taught Dave to sail and he was permanent crew on many sailing adventures also.

After we got contracted to fly 153 to Richmond, Virginia, and barnstorm rides for the show, I needed a ride hawker (selling seats for short rides) so I called Dave and asked if he would like to join us. In Dave fashion he replied, "Well, hell, yeah, Tiny. Ah don't care if'n they fire me. Ah'll be there, you betchyer sweet ass." Hey, this trip was looking up.

We damn near didn't make the trip. Fate played a role but I foxed the hunter and saved the day. The story goes like this:

Two days before we were to leave for Richmond three very portly ladies came into the museum and wanted a ride in the Stinson Trimotor. It was afternoon on a hot day, and I had my doubts. The old saying "When in doubt, don't" came into crystal clarity a little later. I just can't disappoint people, so I agreed to take them up.

All loaded aboard and full tanks for our Richmond trip, lined up in position. "Trimotor 153 cleared for takeoff. Make immediate right turn, speed and altitude permitting. I got one on final." "Ah roger. 153 is rolling," I confirmed.

I gently pushed all three throttles to the stops and nine-hundred ponies began their race down the runway. Ol' 153 showed no hesitancy and accelerated normally to lift off. I began a right turn at 100 feet and as I got through 90 degrees of heading change, I got the sick feeling that the old buzzard ain't doing what she should do. In fact, she was losing altitude at max power. Ya dumbshit. You shoulda picked up a little more altitude before starting that turn, I thought to myself. I was now in ground effect at about 30 feet and still pouring max power out of my now heating-up engines. I crossed an indentation bordering the field and dropped out of sight of those on the ground.

"One fifty-three, you having a problem?" came a very concerned voice from the tower. I didn't have time to talk, I had my hands full. "One fifty-three, you need the fire trucks?" Damnit, leave me alone, I thought, as I gently kicked in tiny stabs of rudder to make 153 do short increments of flat turns in hopes of eventually getting on heading for Runway 20. We were still in ground effect when I noticed a narrow three-story building looming up dead ahead. Unbeknownst to me, it belonged to the National Guard and was packed full of high explosives. I gotta make a decision: either hit the building or land just short of it in not good-looking terrain. Slam dunk—land.

Just as I was going to pull off the power, I felt lift and managed to nurse her up to 200 feet and clear the building. All three still at max power and my cylinder head temperature gauges were all in the red. I continued ruddering her around until I was on final for 20. I maintained max power to hold the altitude I had and didn't come off the power until the approach end of the runway slipped by. The second I came back on the power, ol' 153 was firmly, if not smoothly, on the ground. You lucky dumb bastard, I thought with relief flooding in. Oh shit, I bet I scared hell outta my three lady passengers. I'm gonna hear about this.

I followed the ladies out of the aircraft and as I got out, I was instantly drowning in female blubber as all three charmers were hugging me and squealing with joy, kissing and hugging me.

"Oh, thank you. Oh, thank you! Dave, you are a great pilot, the best in the world," they squealed as I stood there astounded. "I love old airplanes, golly, you fly so low you can just see everything!," squealed one of them as my jaw bounced off the ground. Chuck was standing there with hands on hips and his head cocked with his "Well you lucked out again" grin on his face.

I shrugged my shoulders with my hands up and said, "Shit, Chuck, luck had nothing to do with it. Ignorance was in full charge," which made us all laugh.

Briefing a small crowd just before flight. Very cold that day

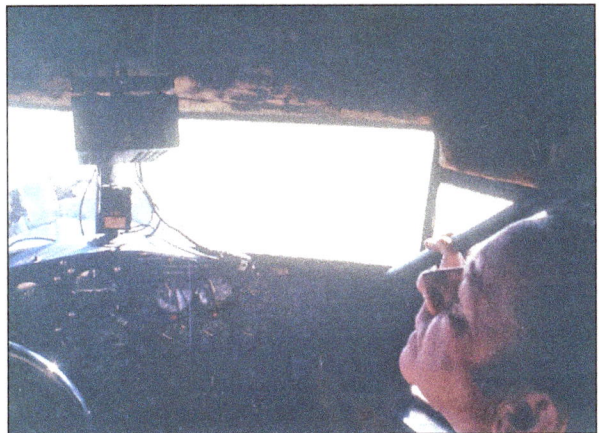

Chuck Meister in the right seat

Staying low at 98 mph indicated

A typical country field

Two days later Chuck and I strapped into Trimotor 11153 and made a predawn takeoff on the same runway I needed so desperately on the last flight. Temperature, very cool and density altitude at field level, the old eagle soared off the ground and climbed out like a homesick angel, well, maybe an angel with small wings, but still climbing comfortably.

I pointed her nose down the valley between the southern end of the Sangre de Cristo Mountains on my left and Rowe Mesa on my right. Leveling at 9,500 and putting the old girl on the step, I trimmed all three propellers to be in sync and the throbbing roar settled into a steady roar as all three propellers found an rpm that matched each other.

The airspeed indicator needle settled down on 98 mph indicated airspeed, giving us a true of 116 mph. these speeds still are not exactly accurate as the forecast winds for our altitude were 21 knots. Recalculating knots to mph, we actually had a 24 mph tailwind. That meant that the ancient magic carpet was blistering across the ground at a mind-numbing 140 mph and that put Sayer, Oklahoma, only 3.0 hours out, rather than the 3.6 hours we would have had if we didn't have the winds that the feds promised us.

Leaning out Nos. 1, 2, and 3 at night is always a pleasure because even though we used our tachometers to get to peak lean, you could fine tune by looking at the beautiful blue exhaust flames—not visible during the day—coming out of the exhaust orifice on each engine. When we leaned at night, our fuel consumption was steady at 43 gallons an hour, a full 2 gallons less than if we leaned during the daytime.

Our navigation was strictly IFR, or "I follow the roads" or, as it is correctly called, "seat-of-the-pants dead reckoning. We always stayed low so we could identify roads, railroads, rivers, towns, and sometimes the town's name would be in bold white letters with an arrow—painted on a roof or water tank—pointing to the airport. It was a hang over from early days, but they were still around here and there. This was the way everybody navigated in the 20s, 30s, and 40s and is all but lost today, what with all these newfangled computer TV screens everybody is diddling around with, putting their lives in the supposed perfection of a damned chip. Hope your chip doesn't crumble.

3.6 hours later, I turned the old goose on final for Runway 35, wind calm. So much for the magic of modern scientific computerized weather forecasting, what with all their dependence on chips and all. I seem to remember that 17/35 was a 5,000-foot dirt runway in those days. We taxied up to some old beat up fuel dispensers and shut down. A few yards away was a small wooden shed, painted white, with a locked door. Not another airplane in sight. The sign on the door read in bold hand lettering:

If you need me I'm in the bar across the street. Red

As we walked into the bar, the first guy we saw was a short fellow in Levis with a huge beer gut wrapped in a sleeveless T-shirt and a nest of red hair perched on top of his head.

"You must be Red?" I asked, smiling, impressed with my ability to catch on quickly. "Naw, a'm ol' curly. Raid's o'r yonder," as he threw a grimy thumb over his shoulder. "A'm Raid, what kin ah do fer you fellers?" asked the only guy in the bar that was completely bald. He did, however, have a gnarled, old, lined face that was red.

"Hey, Red, we need some fuel." "Shit balls o' fire. I nerry heard ya come in. C'mon boys." When old Red saw 153 sitting next to his ancient pumps he exclaimed, "Damn nation, fellers! Tha ol' sumbitch really fly?" Funny thing, I liked Red right off. "Hey, fellers, c'mon out, you jes gotta see thisun," Red hollered at the bar's open door.

Soon we had everybody from the bar, including the sheriff, the mayor, and the local newspaper photographer. We stood around and socialized for a while until we fueled up. It was like this just about everywhere we went. Old flying machines were catching on and I felt that we were in the right place at the right time.

After takeoff, I bent ol' 153 around and dusted off the runway, wagging our wings "au revoir" to our gaggle of new friends waving at us on the side of the runway as we roared past. "GSW tower, this is Trimotor 153 , outer marker, 13 Right, full stop." We had told approach that we had no nav and they told us, "No sweat, we will give you radar vectors to the outer marker 13 Right and hand you off to the tower."

GSW, or Greater South West, as it was called then, is Dallas-Fort Worth International now and looks nothing like it did in those days. GSW was American Airlines's new home base and they wanted us there for the dedication.

American absorbed—and don't hold me to this, I am going from memory— Monarch Airlines and along with it 153 in 1931. I believe 153 flew for American until sold to Chicago and Southern, which was bought by Delta, who was having their fiftieth anniversary, which was where we were headed to next in Atlanta, Georgia.

After landing we taxied over to the American Airlines facility and shut down in front of a large group of people, mostly in airline flight crew uniforms. As the engines came to a halt and silence invaded our cockpit, I said, loud enough for everybody to hear, "Hey, Chuck, this don't look like San Francisco to me!" This drew lots of smiles and laughs, and the stage was set for a great evening of eats and fun. Thanks, American.

We had a great dinner and met and talked with lots of pilots and American executives. Some of the younger pilots had never flown a reciprocating propeller-driven aircraft before, to my amazement. They were all ex-military and started out in jets and never flew anything else. Times were definitely changing.

153 on the American ramp

American Airlines personnel looking in awe at a piece of their history

Next morning, we bid our adieus to our new friends at American and steadied on course for Atlanta. Three-and-a-half hours later, we made soft contact on Runway 4 at Monroe, Louisiana. During refueling the old line chief was checking out a new line boy who couldn't have been over 16. The crafty ol cajun was just full of humor and had Chuck and I in stitches listening to him talk to his protégé. The kid was full of questions about his job and the Trimotor. The young lad asked, "She must be awful slow, ain't she?"

Before Chuck or I could answer, the old chief broke in, "Why, boy, they ain't nothin' slower." "They ain't?" "Sure ain't. One a 'em disappeared one night right over this here aeroport." "What happened?" the wide-eyed lad asked. "Well, sir, this ol' Trimotor were a buckin' some mighty strong headwinds and when it got right over here, they was a sudden turn around in the wind and it pushed the tail out in front of the nose and the ol' Trimotor flew right up its own ass and disappeared." "Ah, shoot, yur a joshin' me, aintcha?"

By this time, Chuck and I were wiping tears from our eyes. For the rest of the trip to Atlanta, Chuck and I would break into laughter thinking about the old cajun and his young helper. This world is full of great people and we met a lot of them.

Delta parked 153 nose-to-nose with a brand new Boeing 777 that was to make a trip over the Atlantic to London and inaugurate international service for Delta. Their fiftieth anniversary bash was a great success, due in part to an old Stinson Trimotor that was one of their first airliners in service so long ago.

Two days later, we growled our way to Richmond and landed on Runway 20 and taxied in to our assigned parking spot. Long, tall Dave Ames and his sons, Matt and Paul, were waiting for us. Dave, in Levis, blue shirt, and a cowboy hat, looked the part. He made a good barnstorming ride hawker, and I was happy to have him as part of the crew.

As we were happily greeting each other, I saw what I thought was a line crewman and hollered over to him. "Could we get a topoff here?" The lineman clenched his fists and stormed off in a fury. "What's up with that guy?" I asked. Dave, laughing, said, "Don't you recognize him?" "No." "That's the airshow's celebrity host. He is the star of a flying series on TV." "Oh, sorry about that. Har de har har."

Well, I guess I really insulted the brat movie star and he locked himself in his room and threatened to not show up for the show. I think the real life hero that he portrayed in the TV series would roll over in his grave if he knew of such goings-on. All is well that ends well and they finally coaxed the make-believe hero into doing his job. Hell, you don't even have to try anymore to get your butt in trouble.

We started barnstorming early next morning and for $15.00 a ride you could fly in a real 1930 Trimotor. We would takeoff, make a real wide closed pattern and land and do it again, all day, shutting down for the airshow and then starting again after the show until 10:00 p.m. Chuck and I would swap seats every five trips and by 10:00 p.m., we were both beat barnstorming pilots.

Dave was the perfect hawker and played the part like he had been doing it all his life. One morning, as we were about loaded and had one seat to go, Dave was trying to ease the fears of a reluctant middle-aged woman. "Why, it's as safe as sleeping in your own bed." "Well, the pilot was trained by Charles Lindbergh hisself." "Ya couldn't ask for a more well-built flyin' machine. She was built at the Armstrong Tank Company."

Sitting in the cockpit and grinning at Dave's salesmanship, I was about to call it to a halt when Dave, exasperated, said, "Gimme yo money and don't give me no mo' o' your lip, girl. Get on that airplane." To my surprise, she handed Dave the money and got on the bird. I think she had a great ride because she came back three more times. Later that night, three young black boys came up and couldn't speak, instead using hand signals to indicate that they were handicapped. They got it across to me that they wanted to ride. I made them understand that it was $15.00 each, and they looked up at me sadly and turned out their pockets to show me they had no money. My heart went out to them. What the hell, it's only $45.00.

"C'mon you guys, get on and strap in. I'll take ya." Going to full power for takeoff and at night to boot, the No. 3 engine puts on a real fireworks display. As I increased power, the exhaust port put out an ever-increasing blue flame that at max power brightens the whole cabin. Just after takeoff, I looked back and all I could see were six huge eyes focused intently on the exhaust flame coming out of No. 3. I came back on the power a little prematurely to lessen the flame and ease the tension. I made a wide pattern and came on in and landed. As silence returned once again in the cabin, I heard the boys scrambling to get out and one of them hollered, "Les get outta here. Dis thing am a fire dragon!" "Why you little shits!" I hollered after them. I got out and onto the ramp, where Dave and Chuck were in tears they were laughing so hard.

"Boy, did they ever con your ass!" said Dave between laughs. "That's alright, I got even with them," and then I started laughing too.

Big crowd at Richmond

A hard day in the office

Stinson S-6000 Trimotor 11153, one-of-a-kind

In three days, we hauled 1,153—not including the con artists—in one hundred twenty trips, for a gross of around $17,000. With Chuck and I relieving each other, we each flew five-and-a-half hours a day. Not bad if you could keep up the pace. Even at that, it was unbelievably tiring work.

It took us almost 18 hours of flying to get back to Santa Fe against headwinds all the way. At one point, we were doing only about 45 mph over the ground and watched an Allied Moving van overtake us and disappear over the horizon.

I never bothered about slow groundspeeds as I am always thrilled looking down on the surface of this beautiful world we live on. In this case, I enjoyed the verdant green valleys and forests, rivers, and towns drifting slowly beneath our ancient airliner as she steadily roared overhead. I watched the mighty Mississippi drift by below and the deep green surface slowly turn to the naked tan of the southwest, laying bare all the awesome features of nature's work to be seen by all. Man, I love flying.

The trip was a great success and we were to do more from time to time.

Sean Patrick Allyn was born Nov. 20, 1972. He was a happy baby, always quick with a smile. That never changed and is still with him today. One night when he was about three years old, I was saying goodnight to him. He had insisted on wearing my leather flight helmet to bed. Here was his little face inside this way-too-big leather helmet and goggles. He said, "Night, Dada." I remember his smile as I left the room. That, along with other memories of my son Sean, is stored in the warmest part of my heart with memories of all my children.

Sean was, and still is, a riot. Especially in his growing up years. Later, when he was twelve, he expressed an interest in diving and had accompanied me, my middle son Greg, and other diver buddies on numerous dive trips. He got certified when he was twelve and became my constant dive buddy on trips to dive in the North and South Pacific, Caribbean, Atlantic, and the Sea of Cortez. His sister Heidi is also a diver and accompanied us on many of our dives.

Sean Patrick Allyn ready to head for the glider port in the 195

Sean, a diver but not a pilot

Sean's first deep-sea dive at age 12, Palau Island in the Pacific

Seanito, as I call him, wanted to fly and of course I made it possible for him to do so, first in a glider and then to solo in a powered aircraft. One day Sean decided to circle his friend's house in a neighborhood just south of the city and dropped down to 200 feet to do it. The control tower's chief controller lived next door and was having a birthday party. Guess what his present was? You guessed it: a video camera. Caught red-handed, Seanito was grounded by the FAA for 90 days. They really didn't have to because I would have grounded him myself.

Sean must have thought he didn't want to disappoint me by telling me he really didn't have a deep interest in flying, but he finally broke down and told me. I think he was pleasantly surprised when I told him that I "would never force you into anything in this life against your will. That's a good way to get you killed. I just want you to do something that you want to do and be good at it." He decided he likes construction equipment and is happily struggling to make a living in that area.

He still loves boating, motorcycling, and has a real interest in gliding. He and his wife, Bianca, gave me a granddaughter, Charlee June, in April 2007. It don't get any better than that.

Being an Air Museum, we had a natural connection to the air show circuit. We connected with all the big names of the day: Hoover, Scholl, Fornoff, Beal, Poberesny, Hillard, Soucy, the Blue Angels, the Thunderbirds, and, of course, our local team "The Franklin Air Show."

Jimmy Franklin, his brother Stevie, and wingwalker Kyle put on, in my opinion, the most exciting air show on the circuit. So we planned a big air show for Father's Day 1978 Of course, Jimmy and his group were the main attraction, along with Corkey Farnoff and his little Bede Jet and others. There were also some local pilots, including me as the last act in the Wildcat performing a few maneuvers. On the last fast and low pass, I would blow up this building—supposedly with my machine guns—constructed specially for the stunt and for this I needed a dynamite expert.

Russ Deal, a good friend and neighbor, as well as owner/operator of Deal Excavating, was the perfect man for the job. There has never been, is now, nor will there ever be anybody like Russ. Medium height, thin, a steady stream of tobacco juice down the driver side of all his trucks, not to mention his perfectly aimed shots at any given moment spewing from his pursed lips. He loves the ladies, airplanes, and most anything that had to do with the air—the scarier the better, as he proved one day when we blew a panel off the side of our SNJ while doing a loop. The whole right side of the SNJ-4 tore loose at high speed, exposing Russ and me. He was riding in the rear cockpit and was now exposed to the elements, necessitating an emergency landing back at Santa Fe. As we got out of the aircraft, I was worried that I might have scared hell out of Russ, but he swept my fears away as he pursed his lips and let fly a big wad of tobacco juice, dead-centering a beetle plodding across the tarmac. Grinning, he said, "That was great. Best flight I ever been on."

I told Russ what I wanted and he said, "We will do it all. When you get down, people will be convinced you got real machine guns on the Wildcat." He was right. We planned on starting our airshow, the theme being the history of flight, with a group of local skydivers making a jump out of the Lockheed 12.

Shortly before the airshow, I was getting ready to load the 12 up with our skydivers to do a rehearsal jump exactly as they would do the day of the show. My ex, who was in nursing school at the time, had a friend who asked if her husband could come along and who had never been in an airplane before. I reluctantly agreed but figured that when I strapped a parachute on him and gave him ground training on how to use it, he would think better of going with us. He didn't.

I loaded the jumpers on board and our unsuspecting joy rider along with them. We taxied out and took off. It was an unusually moist day for Santa Fe, a condition that was very uncommon in the high desert. I climbed to 14,000 feet to give our jumpers a 35-second freefall and plenty of time to hook up in a four-man star using smoke. This oughta look great from the ground, I was thinking.

"Santa Fe tower, this is the Lockheed niner kilo on the initial for the jump." "Ah roger, niner kilo, give me a 360. I got one on final." I made the 360-degree turn and called again on the initial. "Niner kilo, you are cleared for the drop."

As we approached the target, I was getting relayed hand signals: five left, steady, two right, two more right, steady, steady, steady, and cut. I came gently back on the throttles to the stops holding the 12 steady on course and letting her slow down naturally, both engines at idle. I felt each jumper as they left the aircraft and knew when they were all out. I began to come back up with the throttles. What the hell? Neither engine was responding. I quickly changed tanks. Nothing. I tried priming mixtures rich. Nothing. Mixtures idle cutoff, full throttle. Nothing. I glanced at the O.A.T. (outside air temperature) gauge. "Oh, shit, the carbs are iced up," I said aloud.

Because of the dry air we were used to flying in, I stupidly got out of the habit of using carburetor heat when idling the engines. Besides, we never idle in flight. I just didn't think about it. I reached up and feathered both engines and dropped the gear. Being right over the top of the airport I wasn't worried about having to stretch the glide. I pegged the indicated airspeed on 100 mph and the old bird settled on 1,500 feet a minute down. Les see now, I am at 13,000 feet, the airport is at 6,300 feet, I got 6,700 feet to go to the ground and I am coming out of the sky at 1,500 feet per minutes. That gives me right at four minutes and thirty seconds of flight time left, my mind raced through the numbers. Shit, my passenger, I remembered.

"Get your ass strapped into a seat facing backward. I gotta make an emergency landing. Don't worry, we'll make it." I had no time for sweet talk. Hell, he wanted to come and I explained the risks. In a calm voice, I called the tower. "Ah Santa Fe, niner kilo. I am declaring an emergency." "Roger niner Kilo. What's the nature of the emergency?" "I am iced up and will attempt a deadstick landing at Santa Fe." "Roger niner Kilo, you are cleared any runway. We have the fire trucks on the way. Good luck, Dave," I heard my friend Bill say from the tower.

I heard Moe again, "This one is serious. Don't fuck it up, Davey." The old bird was coming down fast but flying perfectly. I was constantly judging height and distance and making minute adjustments with the controls. "Now." I turned short final and instantly know I have the runway made. Across the threshold a little fast but that's okay. I had lots of room, 8,400 feet in front of me. Touchdown, and I braked to a stop just past center field and enjoyed the great wave of relief flooding my mind right then.

"Phew, shit, we cheated death again," I said to my non-smiling, first time ever, white-faced passenger. Never saw him again. I heard the tower say, "We are breathing a lot easier now. Nice landing, Dave." "Yeah, me too. Thanks for the support." I would normally never tell this story, it's just too unbelievable but I got photographic evidence.

Turns out my good friend Ken Mock, a Vietnam hero with the DFC (distinguished flying cross) pinned on his chest, just happened to be standing opposite the approach end of 20 with camera in hand. Later that night ol' Ken showed up and presented me with this great picture of 99K just before touchdown.

Hey, those props are feathered. He is deadstick. Photograph by Ken Mock.

There were only three of us that put our airshow together. It seemed like we were working on it 24 hours a day, 7 days a week, and by the time the day of the show arrived, I was beat.

Committees belong in Russia and as far as I was concerned, are a menace to any possibility of making an airshow a success. Santa Fe put on quite a few airshows after our very successful one and lost money every time. They were all run by committee. We spent as much money on advertising as we did on acts and put 12,000 people on the field. Santa Fe airshow committee in all their combined knowledge spent little on advertising and were properly rewarded with little attendance.

So, with me as dictator, and Chuck as chief henchman, we did the airshow the way the dictator dictated and we were a success, but it certainly was not easy.

I was to participate in the opening skydiving act and then after Jimmy Franklin I was to fly the Wildcat on a very realistic strafing run. The plan was that I would miss on the first run and pulling up to a safe altitude, roll the Cat over on her back and pull through the "Split S" maneuver and come in low and fast on the second strafing run, this time hitting our little shack that would erupt in a fiery explosion. I would then make a victory roll and come on in and land. The crowd was going to love it.

Russ set up all the explosives and the machine gun trace with explosive charges that would kick individual dust clouds up about 12 feet and really looked like machine gun bullets hitting the ground and racing toward the building, not to mention the muffled explosions of each charge that sounded exactly like bullets hitting the ground. Russ was right. After the act, I had lots of people ask me, "How did you get permission to shoot real machine guns from your fighter plane?" Good job, Russ.

The day came for our airshow and the field literally filled up with a standing-room-only crowd. We were ready. We had security in place, several Coke and hot dog/hamburger stands, medical people, FAA paperwork done, air boss, static displays, C.A.P. cadets, and Zip Franklin and Bill Sweet to do the announcing.

The show started at 1:00 p.m. and lasted until 4:00 p.m. with continuous action the entire time. From beginning to end: locals making low passes in between the acts; the acts themselves going flawlessly, starting out with a few ancient biplanes doing impossibly slow loops and rolls to Jimmy Franklin and Stevie making impossibly low inverted ribbon pick ups with the vertical fin inches from the ground; Kyle riding Jimmy's top wing while Jimmy did a complete aerobatic act; Stevie flying the Super Cub with a ladder hanging down and coming in low picked up Kyle from a motorcycle; and, of course, the drunk act where Jimmy played the part of an obnoxious drunk in the midst of the crowd. He bragged about how he could "fly better than these beginners." I tried to stop him and then he hopped the fence, staggering out to the Cub after he pretended to knock me on my butt. He proceeded to thrill the crowd by doing the most impossible stunts imaginable in his overpowered Cub. The crowd stayed hyped for the whole three hours and were loving it.

After the drunk act, I was on for my WWII fighter act. I started the 1820 and belched lots of white, crowd-pleasing smoke. I overprimed so she would also belch balls of fire to get their attention. In the meantime, Zip and Bill were priming the crow over the speakers. "Ladies and Gentlemen, on a lonely Japanese-held atoll in the South Pacific, there is an ammo dump that must be destroyed to save lives." As the announcers were talking, I taxied out and made my takeoff. After takeoff, I made a steep climbing 180 and head a ways to get out of sight. Turning back to the show line, I carried METO power and built up airspeed at 800 feet to 225 knots indicated.

"Lt. Commander Ace Johnston has been separated from his squadron and is alone over Jap territory—a dangerous place to be." While Bill was talking, I was at 800 feet and heading right for the shack. "Ace Johnston spots the shack and begins to circle to confirm that this is the hidden ammo dump." Bill primed the awed crowd. At the same time, I bent the Cat over in a steep bank and circled the shack below me.

Wingwalker Kyle getting strapped in for the act

Jimmy just after the ribbon pick up, tail 6 feet off the ground

Coming back around for a look

Kyle, the wingwalker

"Ace Johnston confirms that it is the ammo dump and knows what he has to do to save lives of U.S. Marines pinned down on the beach." The crowd was now staring in anticipation of what was about to happen.

On the second circle, I leveled the Cat's wings and climbed to 1,500 feet and snapped her into a Split S. Pointing her nose straight at the ground and building up my airspeed, I leveled just above the ground and closed in on the target at 270 mph. Russ was right on, as I saw the ground in front of me erupt in two straight lines of dirt and dust, moving toward the shack and matching my airspeed. Hell, if I didn't know better, I would have thought I was actually shooting. The fast-moving line of bullets stopped just short of the building as I whistled low over the rooftop and began a pull-up to 1,500 feet again.

Stevie Franklin and Kyle

"Ace Johnston missed, but with plenty of ammo left I am sure he is going to try again." Of course, Bill Sweet was right as I snapped the little fighter onto her back and pointed her nose straight at the ground again. Leveling just above the ground at the precise moment the bullets started again, this time the target was reached. About twenty bright sparkles scattered all over the target and *kaboom!* a huge fireball laced in black rivulets of smoke explodes in a big ball in front of me. I flew right through it and the engine quite momentarily as it was starved of oxygen. I was only in the fireball for a fraction of a second before bursting out the other side. I never even felt the heat. In the clear, I gently pulled her nose up and into a slow victory roll. I heard later that at this point the crowd went wild, jumping up and down and yelling at the top of their lungs. The act was a total crowd pleaser and after landing, the reaction of the crowd waving and smiling was a sight to behold from my cockpit.

The Split S from the pilot's view

The other camera during the Split S

Kyle, wingwalker, Jimmy Franklin, Stevie Franklin

At an airshow several years later, I was announcing a pilot flying a Russian Sukhoi: "Straight up to vertical, he is coming to a complete stop and is inside his smoke and will appear in a moment for a hammerhead maneuver to continue his show." I expected to see him reappear out of the smoke tail first and do his hammerhead turn. Instead, he reappeared flat on his back and in a flat spin. I knew right then that he was in a world of hurt. He continued for two more turns and got the aircraft out of the flat spin and pointed at the ground. "You still got room," I said feebly, knowing he didn't have the room. Just then, he secondaried into a spin and I knew it was all over. He hit in a fiery explosion. I looked at my co-announcer friend, Ron, and said, "That's it, Ron. I don't give a shit if I ever see another airshow again. That's the fourth fatality I have seen. It ain't worth it."

Several years later Jimmy bought it at an airshow in Canada. Of all the airshow pilots I have known—and I have known a lot of them—there are only two left alive. It ain't worth it. And I still feel the same way today.

Our air museum was doing fine. We did not really make money but we made enough to pay the bills and keep our collection intact for the day we could sell out and make a small fortune. In the meantime, Chuck and I and several of our friends had a ball flying great airplanes to great fly-ins, meeting the personalities in aviation and enjoying life completely.

Four a.m. and my phone was ringing.
"Hello." "Mr. Allyn, this is the Santa Fe Fire Department. Your museum is on fire." "Shit, I'm on my way."

I got out to the field in record time to find the museum's center section that held our displays ablaze. I had put in 45-minute firewalls in both hangars and the fire had not made it into the hangars where our collection of aircraft was kept.

Against the fire chief's advice, Chuck and I went into the hangars and pushed all of our aircraft outside to safety with the help of Mike Montoya, our local employee. The fire never made it into the hangars but destroyed an invaluable collection of aviation memorabilia that was irreplaceable. For the first and only time in our friendship, I saw Chuck break down in tears at the realization that Wings of Yesterday was history. All of our many friends and people I didn't even know sympathized with us and stuck by us in friendship.

The final blow came when the insurance company accused us of starting the fire even though the police had the real culprits in custody. By the time we paid our lawyer bills after winning our case, we didn't have enough left to rebuild. So I gave Chuck enough money to pay off his house and we put our collection up for sale way before we were ready to.

The aircraft sold quickly and did exactly what I thought they would do and put money in the bank for both of us. Plus, we still had the hangars. We weren't dead yet.

One day a few years later, a young Air Force Lieutenant walked into our maintenance hangar and asked, "Do you remember me?" I looked at him questioningly. "I used to come out to the museum when I was a kid and you used to let me sit in the cockpits of your airplanes and let me play pilot." "Oh, yeah, I remember," I said.

He really did, and Chuck and I used to laugh a lot listening to this growling noise emanating out of the cockpit of usually the B-25, as our little friend was intent on a make-believe bombing mission.

"Well, you guys inspired me to become a pilot and I just got my fighter pilot's wings in the Air Force and have been assigned to an F4F Phantom wing in California. Just wanted to stop by and thank you a lot for what you did for me."

After he left, I looked at Chuck and said, "That just made this whole thing worthwhile." "You ain't just whistling Dixie," Chuck responded with pride written all over his friendly face.

9

Ferrying Old Airplanes and Our Good Friends, 1982 to present

"Ah Albuquerq, American League 816 over Deming at :03, level one four thousand, squawking 0414. San Simeon at :29, Gila Bend next," said Chuck to Albuquerque Center as I listened through my earphones. "Looks like we are holding 200 knots, still got a headwind, though it would be stronger at fourteen thou," I said to him. "I think it is going to ease up around Casa Grande between fronts," Chuck replied.

"Weather at LAX says we will probably have a minimum approach in drizzle and fog tops at niner around Palm Springs." "Probably give us 25 Left," Chuck guessed. I thought he was probably right as I gave my ballpoint pen another three or four snaps. Bill was focused on our analyzer. I didn't say anything and let him concentrate. I knew he would let us know if there was a problem. Bill, sitting sideways in his center-mounted engineer's seat which was located between Chuck and me, was concentrating on a little oscilloscope screen that showed many different patterns in thin jagged yellow-green luminous lines. Depending on the pattern, the lines told the engineer precisely what was going on in any one of the four engines at any time.

Bill finally spoke. "We got a minor problem with a cylinder in No. 4. I got an interrupted spark pattern in No. 18. Think it's loading up." "You want to manually lean past peak, Bill? Does sound like she's loading up on us," I said. "Yeah," Bill replied, looking at Chuck, who as captain had to give the approval. Chuck nodded in the affirmative and Bill, with his expert touch, began to very slowly retard the No. 4 mixture control. I watched the No. 4 EGT gauge and saw the needle move to the right, indicating hotter temps in the exhaust gasses pouring through our exhaust system and PRTs (power recovery turbines). The needle stopped and almost imperceptibly started back, and I said, "Peak temp." Bill minutely brought the mixture control forward so the needle went back to peak temperature and then he returned to his scope. About four minutes later, Bill squared himself in his seat and returned No. 4 mixture to the auto lean position.

"Yup, it's clear just loading up a little. Probably carbon build-up and it burned out at peak," Bill said with his smug "gotcha" smile. A good flight engineer can sure save your butt from a world of hurt just by doing his job. Too much build-up could cause a rough engine and a possible shutdown. But ol' Bill caught it in its infancy and cured it before it became a problem. Good going, Billy Boy, I thought to myself.

We crossed San Simeon VOR right on our ETA of :29 past the hour, still at 200 knots. Chuck gave the position report to Albuquerque and estimated Gila Bend, our next fix, 178 miles direct as per our clearance, at :22 past the next hour at 200 knots. This leg will prove Chuck a hero or a liar if his prediction of losing our headwind is true or false.

Ten minutes out of San Simeon, Chuck looked at me with his "I told ya so" smile as he pointed at the DME (distance measuring equipment) and, sure enough, our groundspeed indicator was up to 222 knots. "Yeah yeah, Chuck, we'll just see if it holds," I kidded him and clicked my ballpoint pen with the expected reaction from Bill.

"Albuquerq Center, American League 816 over Gila Bend at :47, level at one four thousand, squawking 0414, Blythe at :18, Palm Springs next." "Roger 816, Albuquerque Center, flight plan route contact Los Angeles Center on 128.15 over Blythe." "816 to Los Angeles Center 128.15 over Blythe."

Damnit, ol' Chuck is always right. Maybe someday I will get that kind of confidence. We picked up six minutes and were up to 220 knots, or 253 mph. I clicked my ballpoint just once this time and watched Bill's eyes focus on the cowl flap controls. I heard Bill mutter something under his breath about "damned cowl flap motors."

"What's up, Bill?" I asked. "Don't know. Gonna have to dig into our cowl flap motors when we get on the ground." "Phew, that's a hell of a job," I said, trying hard not to smile. "No shit, I am sure not looking forward to it."

Clint Fraser walked into our hangar one day and introduced himself to me. Clint had a happy demeanor and was always ready with a joke or a funny story. He attracted me like a magnet and we were to become great friends.

Clint served on the front lines as an army grunt in Vietnam and had taken to the air as a pilot when he got out of the army. Ol' Clint was not your average pilot 'cause he could fly anything—and I mean *anything*—with wings with above masterful skill. He would show up just to help us work on our aircraft, usually with his son, Brad, and daughter, Brook. I let the kids have the run of the place and they were always a pleasure to be around.

Clint was a pilot for the state and after a while I decided to check Clint out in our SNJ-4. I was not worried with any pilot I checked out in an aircraft like the SNJ, but was always cautious. We hadn't been in the air ten minutes when I realized that Clint was not a good pilot—he was a great pilot, an artist and master. You can tell by the silky smooth handling of the flight controls and the inner feeling that the pilot flying the bird was an integral part of her and flew her as if he or she were locked into the soul of each other. Only about 10 percent of the pilots in the world have this ability and Clint was definitely one.

I told Clint that he could fly the SNJ-4 anytime he wanted to. Clint wound up flying everything we had and became a trusted friend to boot.

We had a fly-in at Holloman AFB and they told us that they would buy the gas if we would bring the B-25 down. Clint was in the left seat and I in the right when we blasted off for Holloman. We were coming up on the Carrizozo turn in the Santa Fe Railroad tracks—a huge and long curve that put the northbound trains pointing straight at Albuquerque. Clint said I was napping at the time when he spied a long freight train rumbling its way about halfway through the turn. Clint figured he wouldn't wake me and gently put the nose down with the idea of dusting off the engineers in the front locomotive.

As soon as he started down, I woke up. Maybe it was the old sailor instinct in me, but Clint was looking at me with a smile like he had just gotten caught with his hand in the cookie jar. He nodded his head toward the train in front and below us. I said, "What in hell you waiting for, Clint?" You would have thought it was Christmas as Clint focused on his new and fun mission and started a shallow dive, bringing our indicated up to 240 mph. I watched from the right seat as this three-dimensional, very realistic movie played out. Clint maneuvered the Mitchell bomber so the cab of the first locomotive would pass directly below Lucy's cockpit. I watched the train locomotive grow in size as the ground racing by confirmed the reason why the locomotive was giving the illusion of growing like an inflating balloon—we were moving at it at great speed. Just before whistling over the cab, I saw one of the engineers with the upper half of his body out his window with both arms stretched out and thumbs pointing straight up.

Clint had a great smile of satisfaction on his face as we gently climbed back to our cruising altitude. As soon as we put the gear down on long final to Holloman AFB, a requirement on the checklist was to visually check the gear on each side. Me being the co-pilot, I secured my dark glasses with my hands and stuck my head out of my sliding cockpit window and looked at the gear leg and wheel. On the gear leg, facing me, there was a little painted square red patch that if positioned right confirms that the gear is down and locked. My head turned to look at this patch when a 140 mph blast of wind slammed into the back of my head and *tink*, there went the right lens of my dark glasses.

I pulled my head back in and looked over at Clint, who was just bringing his head back in from his own visual inspection. "Gear is down and locked, confirmed." Clint looked at me and instantly broke out into laughter. It was always like that with Clint. Everything was fun and funny. The only time it got serious was when there was some serious professionalism required in the cockpit, usually when things started to get dicey and that happened on a ferry trip in a DC-3.

Chuck and I picked up a ferry job to go to Florida and pick up two DC-3s that had been sitting for two years and bring them back to Santa Fe to get all the files up to date and relicense the two, then take them to Amarillo to go into the electronics trade in Mexico. I am sure some of you know about the electronics trade between the U.S. and Mexico. Legal out of the U.S., illegal into Mexico. There was lots of money involved with the smuggling of electronics into Mexico.

The freighter would take off legally from the U.S. and land on some desert road illegally in Mexico. The pilots would walk a half-mile away from the aircraft, all ready with an escape plan to walk out of Mexico should the federales show up. If caught, the sentence was 15 years in a Mexican jail, but for a certain amount of U.S. dollars paid to the judge, he would reduce the sentence to a few months. All of the pilots had the payoff money in the bank, just in case.

This was one of those many air freight industries that flirted with the insanity of making lots of money overnight and it could be done if you are willing to take the risk.

Chuck, myself, Clint, and Bill Judd saddled up to go to Florida and ferry the two old warhorses back to Santa Fe to prepare them to go to Amarillo to fly for this shady airline owned by a guy from India. The two birds were in sad shape but in airworthy and ferry-able condition after some minor labor by us. We pre-oiled the engines and they all started perfectly, even after sitting inactive for so long.

Ed Denham, partner in Dolphin Aviation and good friend

Chuck pre-flights DC-3 77B

Clear! Chuck Meister, Bill Judd in the right seat

&W 1830 belching smoke

P&W warming up

Approaching V2 98 mph on takeoff

Clint strapped into the co-pilot's seat and I was in the captain's seat. We started the pre-start checklist. N77B was an old war eagle that served as a C-47 transport in WWII for the U.S. Army Air Corps. She had seen better days but she was Douglas-strong and I had flown worse. The takeoff was normal and we made a climbing right turn to on course to fly over St. Pete. As I leveled off at 6,500 feet and felt for the step before retarding the throttles and props to cruise setting, I felt a slight shudder for just a second. Because of my time in DC-3s, I knew instantly that this shudder had no place in a healthy DC-3 and I went to red alert.

Indicating 148 and running smoothly, I retarded throttles and props to cruise setting when I felt the slight tremor again. Damn, that's coming from No. 1, I thought. I looked off the right wing and watched the Tampa Bay bridge drifting slowly by. Clint looked at me.

"You feel anything, Clint?" He shrugged his shoulders, communicating that he had not. Indicating 148, all engine instruments in the green, pressures were up, and all instrument needles were where they were supposed to be. For the moment, everything seemed to be okay. Maybe the shuddering tremors I felt were just a valve clearing some built-up carbon, I told myself, but I really didn't believe it. It was much more of a tremor for carbon clearing and I stayed on red alert. I was concerned enough to gently rest my right hand on the throttles just in case I had to move fast.

Kabam, kapow, kapow! as the whole aircraft shuddered under the impact of the explosions coming from No. 1 engine. I instantly focused on No. 1 and made sure it was not on fire. *Pow Pow!* I saw the whole engine trying to shake itself off its mounts. I didn't hesitate and went to idle cutoff on the No. 1 mixture, bringing the No. 1 prop pitch control all the way back, retarding the No. 1 throttle, and reached up and pushed the No. 1 feathering button all the way in and held it until the prop feathered into the wind and stopped.

"Clint, call Chuck. Tell him we just feathered No. 1 and are turning back to Sarasota." Clint was taken by complete surprise but got his shit together and performed his job like the professional he was.

"Feathering checklist, confirm V2 single engine speed at 98 indicated," Clint read. "Contact Sarasota tower 120.1. Tell 'em we just feathered No. 1 and are returning and need priority for number one at the airport," I told him. "Ah 77 Bravo, do you need the fire trucks?" Sarasota asked us. "Ah negative. But have them standing by. We are not declaring an emergency, yet." "Roger 77 Bravo. Trucks have been alerted. You are cleared number one. Any runway."

The old buzzard was flying fine on one engine and I decided to ease the cockpit tension. I looked at Clint, smiled, and said, "Welcome to the world of ferrying old aircraft, Clint." He smiled and wiped the make-believe sweat off his forehead. I said, "Now all we got to do is get this old pterodactyl safely tucked in her nest." I held the gear until short final. "Final checklist, gear down," I ordered.

As the gear was in place, a loud *beeeeeep* emanated from the gear horn, indicating that the right landing gear was not locked down. "Shit, let's carry 110 on the approach and continue and I will touch down, above V2, on the right gear first and prepare for a go-around." As we crossed the threshold of Runway 4, I eased in gentle cross control and gently touch the right landing gear and wheel on the surface. I felt a solid and not mushy impact, chopped the power on No. 2, and rolled to a stop. The gear horn was still sounding its warning. I shut everything down and thought, As far as I am concerned, the right gear can collapse. We are on the ground and stopped.

"Grab the gear pins and let's get outta this fire trap before it falls in on us," I said to Clint, who was already unstrapped and getting out of his seat. As I suspected, it was a corrosion problem in the gear horn circuitry, as the right gear was down and locked.

"It's true, isn't it?" I said to Clint. "What is true?" "This flying business is hours and hours of pure boredom interrupted by a few seconds of sheer terror, only it seems the opposite for me. Must be the type of aircraft I fly." Clint thought for a few seconds before replying, "Yeah, but I sure do love it." "A-men."

We pulled No. 1 off its mounts, crated it, and sent it to the Pratt & Whitney plant in New Jersey. Feeling a little depressed at the thought of how much this was going to cost, we all jumped on a red-eye back to Santa Fe.

About two weeks later I got a call from Pratt & Whitney and the rep on the other end said that the crankshaft retaining ring had been installed backwards at the factory and he was surprised that the engine had lasted as long as it had. "It should have shown up on the test stand run-in that we did here when the engine was first run. If you hadn't shut it down when you did, it would have unshipped the crankshaft and would have resulted in a catastrophic failure and destruction of the engine itself, resulting in an uncontrollable fire. Nice job on your part in getting the engine shut down so fast."

"Wow, I sure am happy it didn't go that far. I suppose the engine is junk. What's it going to cost to get a new one and send it down to Florida?" I asked, heart beating.

"Nothing." "Nothing?" "That's right. It was our fault and we stand behind our product. We are sending you a new 1830 and crew to install it at our expense." Pratt & Whitney dependable engines is also a dependable and trustworthy friend to the aviation world and I have worn their hat ever since.

We brought both DC-3s home with no further problems, brought them up to date, and completed our sale to the shady air freight company who promptly lost N28364 in a crash landing in Mexico on the first flight. I don't know what the fate was for N77B. I suppose she rotted away in some junkyard somewhere, an inglorious end to a glorious old warhorse that changed the history of the world.

Chuck in the DC-3

Why is flying so magical?

Sometimes ferrying an old ship can be lots of fun

Chuck with air traffic controller friend, Darryl

Short final to Santa Fe

Touch down, Santa Fe

No. 1 home safe

No. 2 home safe

Clint expressed a desire to learn how to scuba dive so he could join us in our diving adventures. I told him to get certified at the least as a rescue diver. All my dive buddies would—and still will—dive only with divers with a minimum of a rescue diver certificate and good ol' Clint did just that.

We spent many hundreds of dives and many hours of flying old aircraft together and became great friends. Clint went on to retire as a captain for America West, and then flew as a very experienced warbird pilot for the C.A.F. He got a job flying a C-130 on contract for the navy and air force practice flights for jumpers that were going on covert missions all over the world.

After landing his C-130 one night a year ago, Clint said he wasn't feeling good and was going to check in at the doctor's office. They found a lesion on his liver and gave him three months. Clint, always keeping to his flight plan, filed his final fight plan and three months later went west. Wherever that western field is, it is a hell of a lot better place now that my best friend has landed there. We all miss Clint a lot but are better people for knowing this guy with a permanent smile and always ready with a belly-laughing joke.

Extraordinary pilot, great dive buddy, and best friend: Clint Fraser, 1944–2010.

One day a medium height guy with a very handsome and rugged face, red wavy hair combed straight back, and jet-black friendly eyes that gave away his Spanish heritage wandered into my office. I wasn't going to make the same mistake I had made in Sayer, Oklahoma, and figured he was probably called "Curly."

"Hi. Name's Red. Red Roybal."

His sense of humor was very natural from the start and he loved a good joke. When you told a joke to Red and dropped the punchline, he would throw his arm over his opposite shoulder, snapping his finger and thumb. His face would break into sunshine as he laughed. I loved the guy from the start.

Red had an intriguing aviation career. He started with American Airlines flying DC-2s (that's right, people, DC-2s) and has since flown for airlines and ferried aircraft all over the world. Red and I were to become very close friends and ferried several airplanes together. It was always a special and great fun time to be with him.

"She is a doggy-looking old bitch," I said to Red as we were looking at this sad old DC-6 No. 2 we were about to ferry from Los Angeles to Denver. "Aw, she will fly fine, I think," Red said with a smile.

We strapped in and ran the checklist. The old P&W R2800s started with clouds of smoke that seemed to cast a blanket of fog over half the airport and filled the air with her galloping music as we let her warm up at idle.

The first DC-6s were basically DC-4s with R2800s and pressurized fuselages, and were also a little bit smaller than the production DC-6s. If you got type rated in a DC-7, you automatically got a type in a DC-6, they are that similar.

We taxied out and did our runup. "Douglas ferry N52242 cleared for takeoff, runway 30, runway heading," Burbank tower said. "Roger, runway heading, here we go," I repeated.

Red initiated the power through 25 inches manifold and then called for maximum power and the flight engineer took all four up to maximum takeoff power. I watched the flight instruments as co-pilot and called off transition speed of 50 knots indicated. Red tested the rudder and called, "Rudder control transitioning to flight controls." I called out, "V1 and V2." Red came back slightly on the yoke and we entered the magic world of flight in a heavy flying machine.

We climbed to and leveled at 9,500 and were roaring along at 200 knots indicated. All was well. "You see him, Red?" No answer. I repeated, "You see him, Red?" "Red, I got a high-wing Cessna 12 o'clock our level." Nothing. I watched as the Cessna closed at blinding speed and streaked just below our cockpit. Red looked at me and said with a smile, "Maybe he will think twice before he levels at the wrong altitude." "Red, you got a bit of the devil in ya," I said.

We dead-reckoned it all the way because none of our navigation radios were working. Just outside and north of Denver Stapleton we lost our only communications radio, so within sight of the airport we initiated a right triangle pattern with two-minute legs to indicate to ground radar that we had lost communications and to notify the tower. Sure enough, we got a steady green light from the tower and went in to land.

Red headed for Ohio to pick up a Lockheed Ventura to deliver to Puerto Rico and I headed back to Santa Fe. At 3:00 a.m. the next morning, the next leg ferry crew showed up and flew 242 out of Denver, headed for Miami. At 9:00 a.m. the real ferry crew showed up and wondered where 242 was that they were supposed to ferry to Miami. Somebody didn't do their job. You can't fly an airplane on a ferry permit at night. 242 had been stolen. It wasn't long before we found out why. Two weeks later, 242 was found on a mesa top in Arizona and from the seeds and residue it was obvious that she had been abandoned after a successful marijuana haul from South America.

She was flown off the mesa top and was lost in a crash on the landing. A bloody shame—she should be on display at the air and space museum today. Welcome to the world of ferrying old aircraft.

Red and I flew a lot together and it was always a great pleasure to be around him. I watched Red grow old and too weak to fly anymore and he finally filed his final flight plan in California with his sister nursing him in his final moments. Red left an old Cessna 180 on the field in Santa Fe and she is still there today, rotting into the ground. Every time I go out to the field, I go see her and think of the great times I have had with my cohort aviator, the pilot with the big smile and wavy red hair—Eloy "Red" Roybal.

5,000 hp 4360 on a Boeing Stratocruiser, Red's favorite type of airplane

One of my personal favorites: Lockheed 18 Lodestar

I have always had dogs and I think I like them more than some people. They always flew with me and were totally people-friendly. I landed at a major airport one day and snapped open the co-pilot side window so Apey (April) could stick her beagle head out the window, ears flapping in the wind. "Hey, who is your co-pilot?" the tower asked.

"She is getting checked out as captain next week," I replied. From then on, I was known as "Dog One" when I went into this airport.

Apey sound asleep between the rudder pedals of a 195 in flight

Best memories of two best friends

Suzy on watch

I had a prize-winning 1931 Waco RNF equipped with a Warner Scarab 145 hp radial engine. She would plow her way through the air at the awesome speed of 75 mph indicated and was a bear on takeoffs and landings, and don't even think of wheel landings. Only a damned fool would tempt her nasty side with a wheel landing with this devil in a princess disguise.

A prize winning 1931 Waco RNF

Taking first prize at Lakeland, Florida

1927 Curtiss Fledgling was just as much of a handful on takeoffs and landings as most old bi-planes

There was a homebuilder who was building a Pitts Special, another squirrely little ship. We made arrangements for me to check out and polish the flyer's techniques in a squirrelier than average aircraft and the RNF was perfect for the job.

The checkout went well and I told the student to give me a full stop landing. The flyer did just that as the student landed with the breaks locked. I became a passenger as I watched the nose go down and the bent propeller appear like magic as it made contact with the ground. The little bi-plane wound up standing vertically on its nose and stopped before ever-so-slowly going the rest of the way and *carumph* we were on our back.

"Are you okay?" "Yeah." "That's not what I meant by a full stop," I said, holding back my urge to kill. "I know." The flyer unbuckled the safety harness and I watched as he freefell out of the rear cockpit and imitated the landing we had just made.

I repeated, "You okay?" "Yeah." "That's not what I meant by let's get out of the airplane." "I know." I watched the student stand up and damn near knock himself out as he crashed his head into the cockpit structure. I just looked at him with a grin. "Jesus, you could screw up a two-car funeral."

Okay, okay, I figured the Spirit had punished him enough and I didn't want to discourage him any further. "Next time, stay off the brakes. Let's get this mess cleared up and let's go drink a beer."

The student went on to complete his Pitts and on the first landing wound up on his back again. Some people just ain't cut out for this kind a fun.

We rebuilt the top wing but never recovered it and left it uncovered and open so our museum guests could actually see how a wooden wing was constructed back in those days. It was a hit, producing many question-and-answer sessions. The other reason for not making her flyable was the altitude and high density days, Santa Fe being at 6,344 feet. The old Waco just didn't have the umph to make her a safe flyer at the Santa Fe Airport.

She eventually found a good home in Tennessee and the beautiful old goose is still gracing the skies today at a much safer altitude.

I get up in the morning and let my puppy dog best friends out the first time and I do my thing while their doing theirs before we go hiking. As I entered the bathroom and looked in the mirror, there was an old man looking back at me. One thing I noticed is that my eyes still sparkle a lot, but I sure don't feel inside the way I look outside. I am still young inside and still feel that thrill when I think of some of the hot airplanes I have flown or even the not-so-hot, like the wonderful 1917 Avro. 504, a First World War trainer that flew like a dream. I still feel keenly the adventure of a long-distance sail or the underwater universe I am so comfortable in. I thank the Spirit for the many great memories I have of the great adventurous life I have lived—memories that have pulled me through the tough times.

Most of all, I thank the Spirit for the marvelous characters I have had the pleasure of calling my friends, people like Andy Wells, USMC gunship pilot in Vietnam, and commander of the New Mexico Army national Guard. He is a peaceful, honorable guy who is always there when you or anybody else needs him. Dick Brown, head of Fish and Game, FAA flight inspector designee, and survivor of a terrible helicopter crash, has been a lifelong reliable friend who had great sympathy for me the day I landed an SNJ-4 with my head up and locked along with the landing gear. I did my job, though. After sliding to an embarrassing and grinding stop, I didn't forget to call the tower and cancel my touch-and-go clearance.

Clyde Hoyt, P-39 delivery pilot to the Russians during WWII, C-47 transport pilot USAAC, Branniff Airlines captain, and State of New Mexico senior pilot was a walking history and geological book of knowledge. He was fascinating to fly with, always keeping you on the edge of your seat as he talked about the geological makeup of the southwest no matter where you were. He also knew about the home grounds of the different Indian tribes as we flew over them. He would point out bombing ranges he used as a cadet that I had flown over and never noticed, ghost towns and their histories, mines, and his great failure in a uranium mine that he invested in. Shortly after that, uranium was synthesized and the uranium mining industry collapsed. But what the hell, he was, and always will be, a flyer. He flew with me to Alaska and I figured that finally we were someplace that ol' Clyde probably didn't know about. Wrong. He not only continued the geology lesson but said, "Hey, Dave, gimme 10 degrees to the right. Ya see that ridge coming off of that mountain to our right?" "Yeah." "It's called Nunapitchuck Ridge and just on the other side is where ol' Johnny Smith planted a P-38 one night. Here, let me have it."

As we flew over the ridge and Clyde banked our 500B Commander, sure enough there was an unrecognizable string of aluminum right where he said it would be. It was always a thrill flying with him. My good friend Clyde is gone now but I have a library of memories filed away in my mind.

Will Martin, a young guy just getting started, has the touch, in my opinion, and I consider him a friend. It was my pleasure to coach him for his tailwheel endorsement. I found him to be a very skillful young pilot. Keep it up, we will need good flyers like you to keep that fine touch going.

Ronnie Rippen's beautiful staggerwing, still flying today

A 1927 Ford Trimotor still graces the sky

To Clint, Chuck, Doug, and Dave, Doc, Iguana

An incurable romantic lost in time with the Spirit on my side. Wouldn't change a thing!

There are too many characters and friends who I have met through this marvelous world of flight to mention, but I will never forget any of them.

I have never fired a shot in anger or been shot at, although we went into some dicey areas in Central and South America. I have never dropped a bomb, lots of skydivers but never a bomb. I flew in a peaceful time and never having to fear for my life while flying these fire-breathing war birds has been pure pleasure and an honest blast, leaving me with joyful memories of all my flights. It just don't get any better.

There was danger in spite of the peaceful nature of most of our flights, like the time I was flying the F4F Wildcat at an airshow and through my own stupidity fell out of a maneuver and wound up pointing straight at the ground at 900 feet. I knew I was going to die. I even saw the exact spot I was going to hit and burn. I wasn't scared at the time, but I knew I had to do the most precise and delicate piloting of my career. I kept it together as I looked at the ground rush past the point of awesome. Throughout I used a surgeon's touch on the stick with gentle back pressure, blotting out of my mind what would happen if I didn't succeed. Slowly the nose came up and, according to witnesses, I leveled at less than 100 feet. I climbed out to 2,000 feet and sat back in the loud cockpit, just breathing in and out, thinking deeply about what had just happened, then dropping the gear and flaps and coming in to land.

When I got on the ground and taxied in to shut down, Chuck was standing there with a look on his face I will never forget. "That was too damn close, Dave." "No shit, I thought I was going to buy it, Chuck." "What were you thinking when you were looking straight at the ground?" "You remember one night when you told me if you know the spot where you are going to die, just don't go there? That's what I was thinking."

Chuck let out a feeble laugh. I was too exhausted to even smile. I stayed awake that night, running it over and over in my mind and thinking about what Chuck said to me later over a beer. He took a long pull on his beer, put it down, and looked me right in the eye. "Dave, quit this airshow shit." I looked him in the eye and said, "You got a deal, Chuck."

I never flew an airshow again.

Around this time, Greg Lill and I opened up a gliding operation named Diamond High Soaring in Edgewood, New Mexico.

Looking at my little round combat mirror situated on the upper right corner of the cockpit windscreen, I saw the vibrating blurred image of a Ventus sailplane squarely behind my tail and the tow rope attached to her nose and leading straight to my tail and hook. I was flying a Piper Pawnee and towing this graceful long-winged glider. I know she was an experienced glider pilot by the perfect positioning she has maintained behind me throughout the tow. We were at release altitude of 2,000 feet and I had put her directly into a booming thermal. I expect her to release and break right any second.

As I was thinking that, I felt the release as the Pawnee surged forward. I glanced at my mirror and saw the Ventus in a hard right climbing turn and the towrope imitating a coiling snake reacting to the release of the weight of the glider. I cranked the Pawnee into a steep descending left turn and chopped the power back to one-quarter throttle to begin my twirling ballet. I kicked in full right rudder and literally fell out of the sky to get on the ground as quickly as possible to pick up the next tow, thereby making money for my glider tow company, Diamond High Soaring, Inc. As I fell out of the sky, I thought that we had purchased a hell of a good tow plane by buying this Pawnee. She really does a good job.

I was hesitant at first but after a little arm-twisting and begging from my chief pilot, we loaded up in the 310 and split the molecules at 185 mph northbound for a little town just east of Denver.

Standing and looking at this old crop duster that showed her age and use, I thought she still looked a pretty old flyer and expertly designed for the job she was born to do. No doubt she had dumped tons of spray and towed beaucoup gliders aloft and lacked all the social graces that sleekness brings to fast flyers. She was definitely a workhorse and I loved her regardless.

Pouring over the paperwork and logbooks, I checked one item on her annual inspection to make sure it had been done. There was an FAA AD (air directive) note on the longerons that connect the motor and hopper to the cockpit firewall and they must be die-penetrant checked on each annual for corrosion—very important because if one or more longerons fail in flight, the engine and hopper will break away from the aircraft and cause catastrophic destruction of aircraft and pilot.

Satisfied after talking to the AI and checking his log book signature that this very important inspection had indeed been done, I purchased Pawnee N7030Z and we flew her back to our glider port in Edgewood, New Mexico, and commenced operations with 30 Zulu.

Continuing my steep cross-controlled descent, I timed it just right to roll out wings level on short final for our 5,000-foot long dirt strip at Edgewood. I kept 30 Zulu a bit high as I was still towing the rope and didn't want to snag it on our barb wire fence at the approach end of the runway. Hell, that could ruin your whole day. Little did I know then that no matter how careful I was, my day was about to be ruined anyway.

Over the fence and I noticed that we had a long line of gliders patiently waiting their tows. Money in the bank as I came back on the stick and planted 30 Zulu on all three halfway down the line of gliders. I made a quick jog left and then right to line up for the next takeoff and put the tow rope right in front of a yellow Schweitzer I-26 that I recognized as "Zinky" Zinkowsky's ship. Ol' Zinky, a short, athletic, friendly-faced guy of about 70, had been flying gliders since he was a kid and I was happy to have this real pro behind me on the next tow.

Our tow rope handler retrieved the hook end of the rope and attached it to Zinky's release latch, then ran back and grabbed Zinky's left wingtip and lifted it up. He then raised his arm and slowly waved his hand and arm back and forth, giving me the signal to slowly taxi forward and take up the slack in the rope. This done, the handler turned his head to look at Zinky's tail and Zinky moved his rudder pedal back and forth, causing his rudder to wag left and right, giving the signal to the handler to rotate his arm in a fast 360-degree circle and thus signaling that I should begin the tow.

I slowly came up to full throttle and was pleased with the healthy-sounding deep roar of the Lycoming 250 hp engine singing her throaty opera as she took the stage for another performance.

Ol' 30 Zulu staggered under the weight of the tow but quickly overcame the liability and began to step out. I looked in my mirror as the tail began to come up and saw Zinky already in the air and holding perfect position at the moment of lift off. I was beginning to put slight backpressure on the stick when my heart froze and I watched hopper and motor disappear from view. At the same moment, I was blinded by and buried in a thick cloud of dust, dirt, and noise as we crashed. Thinking quick at that moment, I released the tow rope, cut switches, and kicked in full right rudder to keep Zinky from inserting the nose of the I-26 up my butt. We ground looped to the right and came to a jarring stop, still enshrouded in a blinding cloud of dust. *Tink tink plink plunk* as bigger pieces of dirt clods ended their brief flights and landed on the fuselage and wings of our recently able flying machine that had been magically transformed into junk.

I needn't have worried about Zinky. When the old pro saw me disappear in a cloud of dust, he didn't hesitate and release the rope, kicked in left rudder, and flew around my left side. It was a real slick piece of teamwork and tightened the bonds of two brothers of the wind for life.

I unhitched and dove out of the cockpit and got clear of the old dragon, still fearing fire.

"Dave, Dave, you okay, you okay?" I heard as, still shaken up, I turned around and saw Zinky at full gallop towards me. "Yeah, but my knees are still shaking," I hollered back. Zinky grabbed me in a bear hug, slamming my back with both hands. "Hey, Zink, I sure am glad you were my tow. Nice job of flying." "I wonder if I could get a world record for shortest flight in history?" Zinky said as we both laughed in relief, the tension ebbing.

The next person to come running was Al Santely, an 80-year-old flight examiner and WWII hero born in Italy and a good friend of mine. Now ol' Al could talk you deaf but now all he could say was "Shit. Holy shit."

After we all calmed down a little, Al said, "Dave, come here. I want to show you something." He then asked me if the longeron AD had been signed off. I said, "Yup. It's in the logbook." "Well, look at this," Al said angrily.

Turns out three of the four longerons were corroded 75 percent through. Now I was pissed. "You don't suppose that friggin' Al in Denver is a goddamned liar, do you?" "Looks like it," Al said. Al wrote an article for the Italian National Glider Association and it was printed along with a picture of me pointing at the failed longerons. I began feeling sick inside as the realization of what had just happened sunk in. What if the longerons had failed just after my last release at 2,000 feet? All my friends would be standing on the rim of the smoking crater I would have made after my final one-point landing, raising a cold beer in memory of a brother gone west.

Screw that lying son-of-a-bitch Al from Denver. The FAA felt the same way and cancelled his aircraft inspector's license for life. My experience in the world of aviation tells me that 99.9 percent of the people in the air community are honest, decent people who will honor a handshake deal to the max. The other .01 percent sneak through the cracks and would, without regard for the safety of us all, lie about a serious condition and sell the un-airworthy aircraft rather than sink the time and money into the problem and make the old eagle airworthy and safe again.

Well, you aptly-named slimeball, you got caught and you are history, and the rest of us? We are real happy you are gone and I am still here.

Al went on to instruct and perform flight exams until his sudden departure in his late nineties. He flew until he died. So long, old eagle. See you out west.

Zinky moved out to Las Vegas and, the last I heard, still graces the thermals and plays with our thermalling feathered friends in his graceful long-winged flyer.

The Spirit was surely riding shotgun during that takeoff.

I saved my son, Gregory Thorsten Allyn, for last because he is the saddest part of my life.

Greg was born May 11, 1968, in Sarasota, Florida. He was a strong and healthy baby with light blond hair and deep blue eyes. He grew up in his first years around water and airplanes. When he was about four, he said that he wanted to fly in my airplane "that had no top." He meant the 1928 Crosley Moonbeam bi-plane. I strapped him into the front cockpit and took him up. We ticked through the edges of some puffy scattered Qs to give him the impression of speed. When we got down, he was asked "How fast did you go?" Greg thought for a minute and then started running in place as fast as his little legs would go. That memory, along with many others, is stored in the same warm spot as all of them are.

He showed a real interest in aviation even as a young boy. It made me very happy and proud.

I remember one day in a toy store little Greg was looking at a toy B-25 and this guy started telling Greg all about B-25s and it became apparent he didn't know what he was talking about. I just kept my mouth shut. Greg looked up at him and told him that he wasn't right and started reciting engine facts, speeds, and flying characteristics while this guy just stood there with the expression I had seen before: "Who the hell is this kid?" I was amazed at how much my little Greg had retained from what I had told him about B-25s. I came home one night from the field and saw Greg with my souvenir Nazi helmet on and a stick over his shoulder, playing soldier by himself. I made up my mind that a retirement community is no place to raise a child and moved to Santa Fe. It was a good move and within just a few weeks, Greg and Heidi both had a batch of new friends.

Greg's interest in aviation continued to grow and I continued to open doors for him at every opportunity. When he was almost 14, we started flying gliders together and on his fourteenth birthday Greg soloed. I was so proud of him.

We spent all of our weekends flying gliders and I remember Greg telling me he "couldn't imagine a life without flying." I was convinced that this was a lifelong relationship and felt secure and happy.

Greg wanted to try scuba diving and I opened the door for that as well. We went diving together many times a year for many years and he was a good dive buddy.

When it came time to graduate from gliders to power, I made the Cessna 195 available and Chuck instructed him for his private pilot's license. I don't think anybody his age got their private in a complicated C-195, a huge step up on the aviation ladder. He had the use of any of our aircraft and eventually I even got him type rated in a Lockheed L-18 Lodestar and this was to open the door to a good aviation career for him. He took advantage of it, flying as a bush pilot in Alaska, then getting on with ATI (Air Transport International) as a freighter co-pilot on international flights, and then finally getting on with a major U.S. carrier. I was so proud of him and so happy for him.

Gregory T. Allyn, first solo, 14th birthday

Greg's solo in the C-195 on his 16th birthday

Greg was a good dive buddy but it really wasn't his cup of tea.

Greg got married and had two daughters, Victoria and Bailee—two sweet girls who, when I would come to visit, would play their little games with me, which was a delight. Since then Greg and I have taken different paths, and I wish my son all the best.

Victoria Allyn

Bailee Allyn

Charlee June Allyn

It was also at this time that my fortunes took a huge hit and I watched my savings evaporate. Of course, nobody would hire a 65-year-old pilot, as it is a young guys' game. So that was out. The good news is that the Spirit is still there and put school bus No. 34 right smack dab in the middle of my life's path.

From the cockpit of hot airplanes to the cockpit of the tortoise-like school bus, oh my aching back, but a man's gotta do what he has to do. I wasn't worried about driving this lug but I was terrified of how I was going to handle kids ages six to eleven and a bus full of the little cannibals to boot. The Spirit must have had a big grin because it didn't take long before I was head-over-heels in love with the little monsters. There were times when I wanted to take the whole bunch out and hang the lot of them, but they would always counter with drawings or some paper artistry they had spent all day working on to give me with sparkling eyes and a hug and tell me they loved me and that I was the best bus driver in the whole world.

Now, Spirit, that just plain ain't fair, I say. I gave them doughnut parties, brought my picture albums of diving and flying, and that always resulted in question-and-answer sessions. I have had eight of them up in an airplane on the Young Eagles program and have two that are seriously thinking about being pilots. Some of my kids call me Grandpa and it is truly like having 60 grandkids around me twice a day. The Spirit is always right, if you give it a chance. The best part was yet to come.

My first year of driving, I met Cassandra and Fabian Rivera, two of the most charming and delightfully funny kids I have ever met. The attraction was immediate and I feel that it was meant to be. After Christmas break that first year, I asked the two, both being from Mexico, "How was your Christmas?" Cassandra looked at me with tear-filled big brown eyes and said, "My dad, he got no money. We didn't have nothing." I actually felt my heart break. So the next day I went downtown and bought presents and a freezer full of food for their mom and dad. I loaded it all on the bus and all the way home—they were the last kids to be dropped off on the route—little Cassandra could not stop questioning me.

"What dot Dived, what dot?" "Oh, I don't know." "Come on, Dived, you must tell me." "It's top secret. I can't tell you." "Please, Dived, you mus tell me or I tell my mom and she get real mod to you." "Too bad. I can't tell you. It's a secret." "No it not, you big liar." "Too bad." "Dived you mean," as she folded her arms across her chest and put her angriest look on. "I am the meanest guy you can ever meet." "Please Dived?"

This went on until I got to their beat up old trailer and both Cassandra and Fabian stood next to me with the most heart-wrenching sad looks. Cassandra said sadly, "Dat ees all, Dived?" "Well, no. You need to take your presents and food and go have a great Christmas!"

The screams of delight were deafening. One thing led to another and I was adopted by this Mexican family. I now have four Mexican grandchildren (besides my own three who I never see anymore)—Cassandra, Fabian, Angel the son of Araseli who is Cassandra's sister, and Guadalupe (Lupé), who is the daughter of Cassandra and Fabian's cousin.

Cassandra and Fabian Rivera, my home rings with their laughter

Lupita and Angel

The Rivera family lived in a beat up old trailer in a sleazy part of town and Mom and Dad worked hard and didn't come home until after 6:00 p.m. I delivered the children at 4:00 p.m. so instead of leaving them alone for two hours, I made arrangements for them to come home with me and I would help them with homework and cook dinner for them, then take them home. Soon I was joined by Lupé and Angel, and it became a weekend event, filling my house with laughter, and in the summer I bought a cheap inflatable swimming pool and they were here almost every day. I taught Fabbie how to shoot and took them flying. We hiked, picnicked in the mountains, and went boating. It could only be better if my own grandchildren were also here to join in the fun.

Milly, Lupita's mom, bought her a little dog who promptly got run over right in front of four-year-old Lupita. Lupé was traumatized and couldn't stop talking and crying about it. She wanted to tell Jesus how to feed her dog but didn't know how, so I loaded her in the 170 and flew over to a mountain top that I knew had a cross.

"Look, Lupé, now you can tell Jesus what you need to tell him." So she told Jesus how to feed her dog and when we got down, her tears had stopped and the trauma vanished. That was one hell of a great flight and I logged it as such.

Anger is the path to self-destruction. It permeates the souls of your own family like slow molasses and can eventually destroy them also. It turns meaningful friendships away and will leave you in a lonely world—a world that has so much joy to offer if only you open your heart to it. The key to this joy is forgiveness.

10

ILS to LAX 25 Left

"Los Angeles Center, American League 816 over Blythe at :18, level one four thousand, squawking 0414. Palm Springs at :41, Paradise next." "Roger, American League 816, Los Angeles Center radar contact, after leaving Palm Springs descend to and maintain niner thousand at Bands intersection. Report Bands intersection, report leaving one four thousand, report level niner thousand, expect radar vectors to the 25 Left outer marker at Los Angeles International. No delays expected, weather 200 feet, one-quarter mile in fog and rain."

Chuck repeated the clearance and pulled out the approach plate for 25L and gave me one that I clipped on to my approach pad attached to my yoke. It was right in front of me so all I had to do on approach was just look at it for reference.

"Looks like a minimums approach at LAX. Let's review the missed approach procedures." Chuck, Bill, and I studied the procedures and store it in the back of our minds. With a minimums approach there is always the possibility of the weather to go to below minimums while you are on the approach. This necessitates a missed approach and go-around. If you are minimum fuel, you will immediately go to your alternate. In our case, since we still have plenty of fuel, we would go to a certain fix and hold until the weather lifted enough for us to make the approach.

I could see the layer of clouds on the horizon and the tops appeared to be at about 9,000 feet, right where we should be leveling. While I was studying my approach chart, I inadvertently started clicking my ballpoint pen and all of a sudden I felt my wrist in the firm grip of Bill's hand as he pulled it up and pointed at my pen, saying, "Ah ha! It's you!"

Chuck cracked up laughing, and I looked at Bill with a surprised look. "Me?" "Yea, you sumbuck. You been doin' that since Florida." "Bill, you don't think I'd do anything like that to you, now do you?" "I owe you one, Allyn. You'll get yours." "Hey, Bill, look at it this way. Now you don't have to tear into those cowl flap motors." "Yeah, you just wait. You got one coming."

We all got a good laugh out of that and then returned to the business of flying the DC-7B. We hit Palm Springs on schedule and at :46 were at Bands intersection.

"Ah L.A. Center, 816 is at Bands :46, leaving one four thousand for niner thousand now." "Roger 816. Report level at niner and slow to 180 knots." "Roger, report level at niner and slowing to 180 knots." "Gimme 115 BMEPs across the board and trim. Seatbelt light on." "In range check list," I commanded again.

"Ah L.A. 816 is level at niner thousand." "Roger 816. Turn right heading 258 degrees for vectors to the outer marker 25 Left at LAX." "right to 258 degrees for vectors."

We were skimming through the tops—flash in, flash out. I loved these moments when you are just in and out of the tops. It's always a speed show.

"816, L.A. Center. Contact Los Angeles approach 128.5." "Los Angeles approach, American League 816 with you on 128.5, level niner, squawking 0414, heading 258 degrees." "Roger, 816. Radar contact five past Paradise descend to and maintain two thousand, turn left heading 250 degrees for vectors 25L, outer marker, report level two thousand feet." "Roger out of niner for two, report level, 250 degrees on the heading, 816."

We were headed right for the outer marker and were picking up the ADF signal for the marker and also the ILS signal. "Ah 816, L.A. approach, slow to 165 knots." "Speed brake out trim at 115 BMEPs." Bill set the power and Chuck dropped the main landing gear to help slow us down. The airspeed settled on 160 knots. "118 BMEPs across the board."

Just a touch of power and the airspeed sticks on 165. "In range flaps." "L.A. 816 is level two thousand." "Roger 816. You are two miles from the outer marker. You are cleared for the approach. Contact tower 133.9 at the marker." "133.9 at the marker, 816 roger." "Final checklist, gear down." "Los Angeles tower, American League 816 at the outer marker inbound." "Roger 816. Cleared to land 25 Left." "2,500 on the rpm, gimme 24 inches across the board."

I watched the airspeed settle to 125 and the localizer needle centered and glide slope bar in a perfect crosshair. Now all I had to do was keep it that way. We were really in the soup with straight line rivulets of water streaming across the windscreen as we descended down the glideslope at 125 indicated in zero visibility. Just grey.

"Approach flaps, 26 inches across the board." "500 feet to go, airspeed 125," Chuck backed me up. "24 inches," and I watched our airspeed slow to 120 knots. "Coming to minimums, 50 feet to go to missed," and then "Break out, I got the runway," Chuck says in a soft low tone.

I looked up and saw the approach lights racing me to the threshold. "20 inches, full flaps." I felt the old 7 hump up and slow with the effects of full flaps. I rolled the trim back until I had forward pressure on the yoke with my hands. As the threshold drifts by under us I released the pressure and her nose rose just slightly and I help a little with back pressure. We literally grease on and the only way we know that we are on the ground is by the rumble of the wheels on pavement.

"I got the power and chop all throttles." "I'm ready for reverse," as Bill pulled the gate bar back and sets the prop pitch to reverse. "Four brown lights, ready for reverse." "Just gimme 18 inches in reverse. We got plenty of runway."

"Nice landing, Dave," Chuck said. "Yeah, nice job," Bill echoed. "Thanks, guys. Guess I got lucky. It's probably my last in a 7, my next one will be in a 4 Northstar. Thanks for giving me the leg, Chuck."

We made the dinner party at Mr. Autry's home and it was great. We ate, drank lots of beer, and talked flying most of the night. It was late and we were sitting and not saying much when our movie star host looked at me and said, "You know, Dave, this flying business is nothing but an addiction." I sat a moment and then looked at Gene and replied, "Yeah, but it's the best damned addiction you can possibly get."

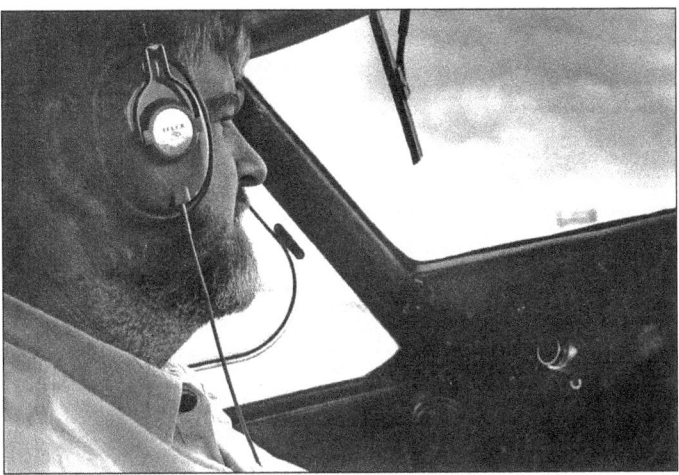

Thank you, Great Spirit. It's been a helluva great ride!

Appendix A

Aircraft I Have Flown

Straight and Level only:
   Short Sandringham B.P.

As Pilot in Command:

1914 Avro 504K Lehrone 90
985 Stearman PW985
Aero Com Shrike IO-520
Aero Commander 500B
Aero Commander 680
Aeronca L-16 C85
Beech 99 PT-6
Beech Bonanza C0470
Beech D-18 PW985
Beech D35 C-185
Beech Duke Lyc 540
Beech F35 C-225
Beech Kingair 100 PT6
Beech Q65L IGSO-480
Beech Q80 L IGSO-520
Beech Q88 L IGSO-520
Beech Staggerwing PW985
Beech Super Baron L540
Boeing B-17 WR1820
Boeing PT-17 C-R220
Brunner-Winkle Bird
Bushmaster 3 PW R985
Canadair DC-4M RR Merlin
Cessna 120 C-85
Cessna 140 C-85
Cessna 150 L-180
Cessna 172 C145
Cessna 177 CGO160
Cessna 180 C0470
Cessna 182 C0470
Cessna 185 C550
Cessna 195 Jake R275
Cessna 206 CJO-520
Cessna 210 C 520
Cessna 210P C520
Cessna 310 CIO-470

Cessna 337 IO-470
Cessna 337P C510 520
Cessna 401
Cessna 414 C520
Cessna 421 CGSIO-520
Cessna 421C IGSO 540
Cessna Aerobat C110
Cessna Conquest PT6
Cessna L-19 C-0470
Cessna Skylane IO-470
Cessna UC78 275 Jake
Citabria L180
Colonial Skimmer L 0360
Crosley Moonbeam Menasco 125
Curtiss C-46 PW2800
Curtiss Fledgling Challenger
DeHavilland DHC-2 PW985
Dessault Falcon
Diamond D-40
Douglas DC-3 PW1830
Douglas DC-3 W 1820
Douglas DC-4 R2000
Douglas DC-4M RR Merlin
Douglas DC-6 PW R2800
Douglas DC-7B WR3350TC
Fairchild PT26 I200
Forney Aircoupe C-85
Globe Swift GC-1A Lyc 200
Grumman American L180
Grumman F6F PW R2800
Grumman Wildcat WR1820
Howard 250 WR1820
Howard 350 PW R2800
Howard 500 PW R2800
Jet Commander
Lockheed 12A PW985

Lockheed 749 Connie WR 3350
Lockheed L-18 WR1820
Lockheed T-33 Viper
Luscombe 8A C-100
Maurane MS 762 Turbo Meca
Merlin Allison TJ
Mooney Mite C85
MU2 Turbo Jet
N.A. T28 WR1820
N.A. TF51D RR Merlin
N.A.B. 25J WR2600
Navy N3N-2 Lyc R680
North American AT6 PW1340
North American SNJ PW R1340
Northrop Gamma W-R1820
Piper 250 Commanche
Piper Apache Lyc 150
Piper Aztec L520
Piper Cherokee L180
Piper colt L-150
Piper Commanche L180
Piper Geronimo L 180
Piper J3 Cub C-65
Piper PA-34 Seneca
Piper Pawnee Lyc 540
Piper Super Cub L 180
Piper Tomahawk L-100 hp
Piper Tripacer Lyc 180
Piper Vagabond C-85
Pitts Special LO 360
Riley 310 C520
Ryan PT22 Kinner Radial
Savoia Marchetti L-540
Spartan Executive PW985
Stearman C3R WR J65
Stinson S-6000T Lyc R680
Stinson SM8A Lyc. R680
Stinson SR9 LR680
Taylorcraft C-85
Turbo Commander T.P.
Vultee BT-13 R985
Waco QDC Warner 145
Waco RNF Warner 145
Waco UPF-7 C R220

Simulators:
DC-6
DC-7
F-15
F4F
737
777
Link Sweat Box

Helicopters:
Bell 47 Takeoff, land, hover

Gliders:
Blanik L-13
Grob 103
Grob Astir
Grob Two Place
Schweitzer 2-33
Schweitzer 1-26
Pilatus B-4 30,000'

Motor Gliders:
Grobe G109A

Parachutes:
Cheapo
32' Para Commander
T-10
28' Tri-Conical Low Porosity

Hot Air Baloons:
Simco Butane

Appendix B

Characters and Friends

Author's Note: I know I have missed a few, but in my book you all count.

Bill "Buck" Buckingham	Corporate Pilot
Ed Casey*	P-38 WWII and Flight Instructor
Bones*	C-47 WWII and Flight Instructor
Silvia Roth	Flight Instructor, 99 Race Pilot
Harpo Wilde	Corporate Pilot
Bill Stevens*	AI Mechanic, Flight Engineer
Captain Dusty Burk*	B-52 Command Pilot, Air Transport Captain
Bevo Howard*	Air Show Pilot
Bob Hoover	Air Force Test Pilot, Airshow Pilot
George Priester*	FBO Operator, Pilot
George Priester, Jr.	FBO Operator, Pilot
Gene Soucy	Airshow Pilot
Paul "Poopdeck" Poberesny	EAA Founder, Airshow Pilot
Tom Poberesny	EAA President, Airshow Pilot
Bill Fornoff*	Airshow Pilot, Naval Aviator
Corkey Fornoff	Airshow Pilot
Captain Jim Hendrickson	E.A.L. Captain
Captain Lou Translou	E.A.L. Captain
Capt "Herman the German" Wilhelmy*	E.A.L. Captain
Sid "Doc" Smith*	Flight Surgeon, Army Surgeon, WWII Pilot
Ed Denham*	FBO Operator, Pilot
Duffy Nathan*	Skydiver
Gail Davis	Skydiver, Homebuilder, Pilot
Gene Autry*	Pilot, Owner L.A. Angels, Movie Star
Smoky Burgess*	Major League Ball Player
Willy Mays	Major League Ball Player
Al Lopez*	Major League Chief Coach
Tex Mitchell*	WWI Fighter Pilot, WWII Transport Pilot
Michael Spradling	Air Ambulance Pilot
Floyd Barlow*	Glen Curtiss Demo Pilot, ret. 1925
Frank Hoback	NM State Pilot, Borate Bomber Pilot
Bill Judd	NM State Pilot
John Maldonado	NM State Pilot
Clyde Hoyt*	P-38 Delivery Pilot; Captain, Braniff; NM State Pilot
Kip*	Chief Pilot, NM State
Mike Warren	New Mexico State Pilot

Frank Tallman*	Movie Stunt Pilot, P-40 Pilot WWII
Frank Pine*	Movie Stunt Pilot
Red Roybal*	Airline Captain
Jimmy Carlin*	Captain. Anything that would fly, specialty Corrosion Corner
Ball Brothers*	Specialist on anything that flies, Miami
Bill Tanner*	Captain out of Corrosion Corner
Captain Dick Sylvas	E.A.L.
Captain Jim Peavy	E.A.L., Cropduster, Corporate Pilot
Geoff Venaklausen	FAA Inspector, Corporate Pilot
Pete Ward	Major League Ball Player
Bill Veeck*	Major League Owner
Ed Russell*	E.A.L.
Paul Polaro	Skydiver
Danny	Skydiver
Rick Fulwider	Skydiver, Fire Chief
Captain Alonzo Edwards*	Airline Captain
Fred Ottenburg*	Steward, A&I Mechanic
Captain Wolfgang Boden	Captain, Condor
Captain Joachim Illenberger	FW190 Fighter Pilot; Captain, Lufthansa
Captain Ivan Joachim*	Captain, Aeroflot
Jim Applebee	Movie Pilot, Borate Bomber Pilot
Charlie Hillard*	Airshow Pilot
Jim Steel	Navy Fighter Pilot
Captain Bill Harris	Airline Captain
Jim Beck	Skydiver
Ron Bilib	FAA Tower Controller
Dick Brown	Chief Pilot, NM Game and Fish
Bernie Armstrong	NM State Pilot P-51 Fighter Pilot WWII
Russ Colton	Body Builder Instructor
Grif Hodson	Duster Pilot, C-82 Hump Pilot WWII
Mel Chrystler*	Duster Pilot, C-82 Hump Pilot WWII
Chuck Grace*	B-24 Bomber Pilot WWII, Airline Pilot
Chris Lavick	Pilot, Long-lost nephew
Ray Meenan*	Deepsea Diver, Photographer
Bill McKinney	Friend, Private Pilot
Larry Salganic	Aercoup Banner Tow Pilot, Jet Fighter Instructor
Dave Row	Experimental Aircraft Builder, Pilot
Bernard Romero	Pilot, Construction Company Owner
Jim Valencia*	FAA Inspector
G. C. Johnston	FAA Inspector
Chester Smith	Commercial Pilot Instructor
Peaches	Deepsea Diver, Instructor
Sef Perea	Mechanic
Mike Montoya*	Mechanic
Bob Taylor	Antique Aircraft Association Founder

Art Kimberly*	Sea Captain
Dave Kruger	Pilot, Sea Captain
Troy	FBO President, Pilot
Randy Harmon	Corporate Pilot
Jim Arender	World Champion Skydiver
Captain Larry Banstetler	Air Freighter Pilot
Andrew*	State Police Helicopter Pilot
Chris	A&I Mechanic
Turk Anderson*	A&P Mechanic
Kenny Line	Chief
Bernard Romero	Excavator, Pilot
John Wayne Haynes	Cowboy, Long-range horse rider
Casper	Expert Cowboy Singer and Guitarist
Zinky Zinkowsky	Glider Pilot
Rick Shores	Airline Captain
Dr. Martha MacDonald*	Psychiatrist
Julio de Diego*	Artist

*Gone West as of time of publication.

Glossary

Abort: Stop the takeoff roll or landing segment
ADF: Automatic Direction Finder, a navigational instrument
Aileron: A flap on the outer wing that banks the aircraft left or right
Airspeed Indicator: An instrument that indicates apparent speed
Altimeter: An instrument that measures height above sea level
Atmosphere: A gas envelope around Earth that enables aircraft to fly
Attitude Indicator: An instrument that tells the pilot attitude—high, low, left, right

Bail Out: To leave a crippled aircraft in favor of using a parachute
Belly: Bottom of an aircraft's fuselage
BMEP: Brake Mean Effective Pressure; a means of determining percent of power
Bomb Bay, or Bombay: A compartment that houses the bombs on bombers
Borate: Slurry; substance used to drop on and retard forest fires
Breakout: Sudden clearing of clouds as an aircraft is flying through

Cargo Bay: Compartment behind pilots where freight is stored
Cavitation: When prop tips break the sound barrier and produce a cracking sound
Corrosion: A white powder produced by the breakdown of aluminum
Cowl: The housing that surrounds an engine
Cowl Flaps: Small flaps that open or close to regulate engine cooling

Depression: Weather condition produced by a low pressure system
Descend: To reduce altitude
Ding: A dent in wing, tail, or fuselage

Elevator: A flap attached to a horizontal stabilizer to make the aircraft go up or down
Emergency: Any condition that threatens safe flight
Endurance: Fuel range measured in hours of flight
Engine Types: Recip (reciprocating); Radial; Opposed; Inverted; V; X; Rotary; Inline; Turbine; Jet; Rocket

FAA: Federal Aviation Administration, a regulatory and enforcement agency
FAR: Federal Aviation Regulations
Fix: A point on a navigational chart
Forced Landing: An unexpected landing caused by an inflight emergency
Front: An approaching weather system

GADO: General Aviation District Office, an FAA field office
Gear: Landing wheels and associated parts that protrude from under aircraft

Gear Lights: Small green, red, and amber lights to indicate position of landing gear
G-force: Positive G-force is heavy and can lead to pilot blackout; negative G-force is light and can lead to pilot redout. A 200 lb. pilot weighs one "G" on the ground.
Go Around: Abort the landing and go around for another try
G.U.M.P.: A universal final check of gas, undercarriage, mixture, prop

Hammerhead Stall: An aerobatic maneuver to reverse direction while in straight up (vertical) flight
High Speed Stall: Aircraft will stall when G-forces exceed lift capability
High Wing: An aircraft with the wing above the fuselage
Homing In: A navigation term meaning to focus in on a radio beam
Horizon: Earth's horizon as viewed from the cockpit
Hot Shot Pilot: A pilot with more nerve than good sense
Hot Start: When the temperature suddenly goes out of control when starting a jet engine

Ice: Rime ice or clear ice forms on leading edges
Ice Boots: Inflatable rubber boots on leading edges that break away ice
IFF: Indicate Friend or Foe, transponder peacetime term
IFR: Instrument Flight Rules, used when in clouds and flying blind
ILS: Instrument Landing System
Indicated: Speed according to instrument, always lower than true airspeed
Intake Cowls: Small air intake to cool certain parts of accessory section
Inverted: Upside-down flight, an aerobatic maneuver

JATO: Jet Assisted Takeoff, performed by using small rocket bottles which are activated on takeoff
Jerk: A pilot who has had too much to drink
Jet Stream: Strong winds in the troposphere
Jettison: Dumping fuel to diminish weight
Jettisoning Vents: Vents under the wing that can be opened by the pilot to dump fuel in flight

Kill Lift: Pulling out spoilers on a glider which diminishes lift on the wings
Kiss the Numbers: Make a smooth landing
Kollsman Window: Small window on the altimeter that reads barometric pressure

Latitude: Horizontal lines on a map that determine degrees north or south of the equator
Lazy Eight: Practice maneuver to teach coordination in flight
L/D (L over D) Ratio: The amount of lift created divided by the amount of drag it creates by moving through the air
L.F.: Low frequency navigation radio aid
Lift: The force that directly opposes the weight of an airplane and holds the airplane in the air
Link Trainer: A small training device to teach pilots to fly blind; also known as the "sweat box"
Longeron: Adds strength to aircraft structure

Longitude: Vertical lines on a map that determine distance from the International Date Line (IDL), measured in degrees

Mach 1: The speed of sound
Magneto: Delivers spark to cylinder plug (aircraft engines have two magnetos in case one fails)
Manifold Pressure: Measured in inches of mercury at the manifold
Max Gross: Maximum all-up weight of the aircraft
MEA: Minimum En route Altitude for radio reception and ground and obstacle clearance
METO: Maximum Except Takeoff; first power setting below max power setting
Mixture: Determines amount of oxygen in fuel from carburetor to engine

NACA: National Advisory Committee for Aeronautics (became part of NASA in 1958)
NDB: Non-Directional Beacon, navigation on the ground
N-Number: N = North America for aircraft identification
Nose: The very front of an aircraft
Nose Trim: A small wheel next to the pilot for trimming out heavy control feel of pitch. A small tab on the elevator is the trim tab.
Nose Wheel: Strut and wheel under the nose of an aircraft, used for steering
N Strut: Three struts forming the letter "N" connected to upper and lower wings on a bi-plane to add strength

OBS: Omni Bearing Selector, fixes the course to or from the station
Oleo: Strut filled with oil to soften the impact of landing
Omni: Navigation instrument that works off of a VOR
On Top: Above a solid layer of clouds
Outer Marker: NDB fix that determines beginning of the ILS approach to the runway
Over the Top: Highest portion of a loop, just as you start down

PBM: Patrol Bomber (Navy)
P-Factor: Describes propeller effect
Pirouette: A combat maneuver used in WWI to gain gunnery advantage
Pitot Tube: Invented by French pilot Pitot, converts air wind pressure to an instrument that reads in miles per hour
Power Dive: Going straight down using maximum power
PRT: Power Recovery Turbine, uses exhaust pressure to increase horsepower
PT: Primary Trainer, USAAC
Pull Out: Recovery procedure to get out of a dive
Pusher: An engine and prop facing at the tail

Qs: Puffy, little clouds that can develop into major thunderclouds

Ratty: Aircraft in need of repair
Reciprocal: 180 degrees from the course being followed on the compass
Red Nav Light: Left wingtip light

Reverse Pitch: A change in propeller pitch resulting in reverse air flow
Ripcord: Activating device for a parachute
RNAV: Area navigation
"Roger": Radio acknowledgement in the affirmative
"Rolling": Confirming takeoff instructions
Rotating Beacon: Red rotating light on top of vertical fin and/or belly
Round Robin: A flight plan that leaves Airport A and returns to Airport A
RPM: Revolutions per minute, internal engine speed
RVR: Runway Visual Range, how far down the runway you can see

Separation: Altitude separation between aircraft in flight
Severe Turbulence: Violent wind drafts that can potentially destroy an aircraft
Slipstream: Air wake turbulence behind an aircraft in flight
Sloughing Off Ice: Propeller slings ice off of blades
Snap Roll: A high-speed stall produced by rapid back movement of the control stick causing the aircraft to spin horizontally
Spacing: Distance between aircraft under positive control
Spin: All surfaces are stalled and aircraft rotates around the nose, going down vertically
Spoilers: Small flaps on wings to spoil lift, mostly used on gliders
Stall: Wing loses lift and can no longer maintain flight
Stall Buffet: Shaking caused by wind burble just prior to the stall
Stall Warning: A device in the cockpit that sounds a buzzer 10 knots before the actual stall
Straight In: An approach to landing with no maneuvering involved
Swoop: Sky diver term for fast dive and recovery under canopy in flight

TACAN: Tactical Air Navigation Aid, navigational radio
Tally Ho: Visual contact between two aircraft in flight
Taxi: An aircraft moving on the ground under its own power
T-Bird: Lockheed T-33 jet trainer
Tetrahedron: Triangular structure on the ground used as a wind direction indicator
Thunder Bumper: Pilot term for operating inside a thunderstorm
Top Off: Fill the fuel tanks
Tops: Tops of clouds or on top of a layer of clouds
Torque: Turns the opposite way from how the engine turns
Tower: Control tower controls air traffic in five-mile radius
Trail: Aircraft in trail one behind the other
T-Tail: Horizontal stabilizer attached to the top of vertical stabilizer

UHF: Ultra High Frequency radio
Undercast: Bottom of a cloud layer

V1: Accelerate stop distance; the speed at which you can abort the takeoff and still stop on remaining runway
V2: Safe engine out flight speed used on multi-engine aircraft
Vertical Flight: Either straight up or straight down

Vertical Stabilizer: A fin on the back that sticks up vertically and stabilizes yaw

VFR: Visual Flight Rules, clear weather flight

VHF: Very High Frequency radio communications and nav

VMC: Velocity Minimum Control/ speed at which you can no longer control the yaw of the aircraft with an engine out

VNE: Velocity Never Exceed (Red Line), damage or destruction could occur

VOR: Visual Omni Range, navigational ground station

VSI: Vertical Speed Indicator, indicates the rate of climb or descent

Wind Sock: Cone-shaped cloth sack that indicates wind direction and speed

Wing: Horizontal plane that gives ability to fly

Wrung Out: End of a series of aerobatic maneuvers

Wx: Weather information

X-Engine: A reciprocating engine with four banks of cylinders forming an "X" when looking straight on

Yaw: Aircraft moves left or right on a level plane controlled by rudder

Z-Marker: Used to be known as the middle marker on the ILS; no longer in use

Zodiacal Light: The light on the horizon that remains after sunset or before sunrise

Zoom: An old term for low flight

www.ingramcontent.com/pod-product-compliance
Lightning Source LLC
Chambersburg PA
CBHW081113160426
42814CB00035B/299